A Moral Truth

A Moral Truth

150 years of investigative
journalism in New Zealand

Edited by *James Hollings*

MASSEY UNIVERSITY PRESS

First published in 2017 by Massey University Press
Private Bag 102904, North Shore Mail Centre, Auckland 0745, New Zealand
www.masseypress.ac.nz

Text copyright © individual contributors, 2017

Design by Gideon Keith. Typesetting by Carla Sy

A catalogue record for this book is available from the
National Library of New Zealand

Printed and bound in China by Everbest Ltd.

ISBN: 978-0-9941415-8-3

CONTENTS

CONTENTS

The earliest visitors to New Zealand were struck by the long white cloud that floated above the land, and named it Aotearoa, land of the long white cloud. The name carries something of the optimism that inspired emigrants to risk a long voyage in search of something better. Those clouds signalled landfall — as well as rain, that bearer of life. But a cloud can have another purpose; it can shield, or hide.

Many times, when telling people that I was gathering material for this book, I had a response along the lines of 'That will be a short book — there isn't much of that in New Zealand.' For some reason, the belief is common that there is little or no investigative journalism done here. Weigh this book in your hand and judge for yourself how true that statement is — and this collection is probably less than a tenth of all the stories I could have included. There is in fact a long and rich tradition here of journalism that holds power to account, that goes beyond allegation and denial to reveal hidden truths.

Some of the stories in this book will be well known to New Zealanders; many will not. Some, I hope, will still shock and disturb you. All, I hope, will make you proud of the craft, cunning, persistence, compassion and sometimes brilliance of those journalists who unveiled them. And, of course, of the courage of those men, women and children whose stories are told here.

What exactly is investigative journalism? And how does it differ, if at all, from other types of journalism? It is sometimes argued that all journalism is investigative, in that it seeks to tell a truth. Many journalists, including some whom you will meet in these pages, believe that all journalists should investigate, in some way or another. Nevertheless, most books on investigative journalism agree that there are some things that set it apart from the journalism we see in our daily newspapers or on our favourite news sites, and watch and hear on television and radio. The great Australian journalist John Pilger, whose anthology of world investigative journalism was the inspiration for this book, suggests that good investigative journalism holds power to account, and acts as a check on power. For him, it is not just about 'detective work', but must also be journalism that 'bears witness and investigates ideas' (Pilger, 2004, p. xiv).

Journalism has also been called the 'first draft of legislation', because it often exposes problems so compelling that governments need to pass laws to fix them (Burgh, 2000). Many of the stories in this collection did just that; the investigation into the disaster at the Pike River Mine is just one example. Another useful definition is that, unlike daily journalism, investigative journalism seeks to go beyond allegation and denial to get to the truth of an issue. Investigative journalists have also been called 'custodians of conscience' because their work attempts to build shared moral values (Ettema & Glasser, 1998, p. 200).

Others argue that investigative journalism must do all those things *and* must also unearth some systemic fault. If you have seen the film *Spotlight*, in which investigative journalists were determined to uncover not just cases of child abuse but also why the system allowed the abuse to continue, you will agree that this is important.

In the US, emphasis is placed on thoroughness and impartiality and on the accretion of empirical detail, perhaps in the hope that some objective truth can be unearthed that will make a solution unarguable. Its great triumphs, such as the Watergate stories, have helped make investigative journalism a respectable part of mainstream American journalism culture. The Anglo-European tradition, by contrast, is usually quicker to resort to polemic, more likely to be politicised and much less respectful of authority structures. The New Zealand tradition, at least as far as I can tell after reading hundreds of pieces for this collection, is mostly closer to the British experience, although, as this collection shows, it embodies both.

In choosing pieces for this book, I have generally applied most of the above definitions at one time or another. Not all these stories necessarily try to hold some form of power to account; some just set out to bring something to public attention, something the public needs to know. Hilda Rollett's exploration of domestic service, for example, does not name any fiendish matrons or question the social and economic conditions that created a class of domestic servants.

What I have tried to collect are stories that reveal some hidden truth that is in the public interest, not merely *of* public interest, and a truth that wouldn't have come out otherwise. A few — quite a surprising number, as it turned out — were the first draft of legislation, or did result in some kind of government action. Pat Booth and Jim Sprott's epic campaign to expose police planting of evidence meets the highest standard of investigative journalism, by any definition. So does Philip Kitchin's exposé of a sleazy sex ring of police officers.

But some stories were chosen simply because they seemed to speak a truth — perhaps one that had little impact at the time, but one that has been borne out by history. Robin Hyde's inquiry into the plight of Bastion Point Māori in the 1930s was decades ahead of its time, as was Jim Tucker's into the pollution of waterways in Taranaki in the 1970s. One of the most exciting finds was the quality of reporting in *Te Hokioi*, the independent Māori newspaper of the

1860s. *Te Hokioi,* the voice of the King movement, has been disparaged as a propaganda sheet by contemporary critics, and even recent historians, when some of its journalism was anything but.

Another important criterion that emerged was that the best stories have something undeniably original, or new, about them. They often raised an issue that nobody had really realised was an issue. Nicky Hager's revelations about the National Party's smear tactics prior to the 2014 election is one example. There are many other good investigations that explore an issue already developed by others — in these cases I have tended just to choose the first.

One trend that comes through strongly is the fearlessness of our early journalists and the editors who published them. When they saw injustice, they attacked it head on, with all the rhetorical skill they could command. *Truth's* attack on a rampant and incompetent security service, in wartime, was extraordinary; a classic of brave, independent journalism.

Another theme is the quality of the writing; I defy anyone to read Jack Young's account of the hanging of Albert Black without revulsion. While not a true investigation, perhaps, in that it took no more than a day's attendance at prison, it undoubtedly reveals a hidden truth, on an issue of undeniably public interest.

What conclusions can we draw from this collection of investigative journalism in New Zealand?

First, one is struck by how it is often a distant echo of overseas trends. So, for example, we have the emergence of an indigenous press, following the example of Haiti, in the 1860s. As the 'yellow' (or populist) press reached its zenith in the early years of the twentieth century in Europe and the US, so we had the beginnings of one here, with the formation of *Truth.* The bile-flecked columns of this publication matched US publisher William Randolph Hearst's and UK publisher Alfred Harmsworth's yellow papers for populist appeal, and quite often it wielded its rhetoric in good cause. *Truth's* campaign against the execution of Tahi Kaka was courageous, at a time when the death penalty was widely accepted. Where the US had Nellie Bly, the pioneer of stunt journalism, New Zealand's (admittedly rather staid) counterpart was Hilda Rollett (writing under her maiden name of Keane).

That special creature of the 1930s, the left-leaning literary correspondent, giant of both fiction and non-fiction (think George Orwell or John Steinbeck), had its counterpart in Robin Hyde, whose poetic gifts enriched her journalism.

Later, the widespread mainstreaming of investigative journalism in the 1960s and '70s had its parallel here in the social issues campaigns that came to characterise *Truth,* and later *The Auckland Star* and *The Dominion Post.* Locally, this mainstreaming reached its peak in 2006, when state-owned Television One and the private newspaper chain Fairfax combined to publish Philip Kitchin's stories about a police sex-abuse ring. This investigation demonstrated the power of the mainstream media at its best. A thorough inquiry by an experienced journalist, well supported by courageous editors and publishers, was expertly packaged and presented for maximum impact to an enormous combined audience. No government could ignore its findings. It demonstrates, too, one upside of the takeover of small independent newspapers in New Zealand by a couple of large corporates in recent decades. It is highly unlikely that the Louise Nicholas story could have been pulled off by the *Rotorua Daily Post* or *Bay of Plenty Times*. In fact, one of the complainants in that story, Donna Johnson, did try to interest her local paper in her story — without success.

Another trend worth noting is the ebb and flow of investigative journalism in New Zealand. At times it is the preserve of the lone independent; at other times, the mainstream media, for a mixture of commercial and other reasons, takes an interest. A glance through the contents page of this book will show you that certain publications have had golden eras of investigative journalism before the torch is passed to the next.

This trend was noted by the US journalism scholar Mark Feldstein, who suggested that it required a coincidence of supply and demand. The supply of investigative journalism, he argued, seemed to depend on there being a demand for it, through the emergence of a social crisis, with a consequent public hunger for answers; and on a supply of it, through the availability of some new form of technology to distribute it. This explained, he argued, the surge of investigative journalism in the early 1900s in the US, when unrestrained capitalism, mass immigration and urbanisation were creating intense social pressures and a penny press had emerged to explain it. Likewise, in the 1960s and '70s, the social upheaval brought by student politics, the Vietnam War and the sexual revolution found its voice in the new medium of television (Feldstein, 2006).

This 'muckraking model', as Feldstein called it, does throw some light on the New Zealand experience. It explains neatly, for example, the emergence of an independent Māori-language press in the Waikato in the tense years of the early 1860s, when the arrival of a press suddenly gave printed voice to simmering tensions. But it does not explain the relative lack of investigative journalism at other crucial times, such as during the Depression of the 1930s, when there was also a new technology available — radio. Nor does it really explain the lacing of themes that thread through this collection: the unease over capital punishment in the 1950s, race tension in the 1970s, and the general theme of concern about the unaccountability of police and security organs and the unrestrained power of the state that runs through many investigations from the 1940s onwards.

A more useful way of understanding what kind of investigative journalism will make an impact comes from British sociologist John Thompson, in his work on public scandals. He argues that the public is only really moved when a scandal touches on some central moral value that we all share. This theory has been used convincingly by journalism scholar Michael Schudson to explain why the various 'gate' scandals since Watergate (Irangate, Nanny-gate, Whitewater-gate, Monica-gate) had so little impact. The answer is that none of them really mattered to the American public, because none transgressed a central moral value. In other words, most Americans agreed that a President breaking US law by trying to obstruct justice was wrong, but far fewer cared whether their President had an affair (Schudson, 2004; Thompson, 2000).

How do these arguments apply to New Zealand? What are the central moral values that emerge?

Several writers have noted the strongly utopian theme that runs through New Zealand's history (Smith, 2011). From the signing of the Treaty of Waitangi, to mass immigration, the social welfare reforms of the 1900s and 1930s, the anti-nuclear stand and, more recently, the free-market reforms, New Zealand has not been afraid of half-measures; it has reached for a vision. Behind much of the journalism here can be discerned the outlines of this utopianism: many seem to derive their moral outrage from a sense of utopianism gone wrong, where confidence in the soundness of institutions has proved misplaced. Think Pike River, the Crewe murder inquiry, among others.

In another sense, much of this journalism appeals, optimistically perhaps, to a sense of fairness it seems to assume in its readers that may not actually be there. *Truth* on the killing of Kaka, or the crucifixion of conscientious objectors, or capital punishment; Hyde on the plight of Ōrākei Māori — these stories and many others seem more about asserting a new or different moral structure than suggesting that a commonly accepted one has not been followed. Many of these stories seem ahead of their time, or look forward to a time when values may have changed.

This leads on to a second underlying value: consensus. New Zealanders, it has often been noted, value this highly. Many of the stories in this collection are about, in one form or another, abuses of our utopian belief in consensus. They are a challenge to a collective silence about crimes or injustices that are being hidden in plain sight; well known within a community, but not spoken of. They are about challenging what German scholar Elisabeth Noelle-Neumann called the 'spiral of silence' (Noelle-Neumann, 1964). This is when an idea is wrongly believed to be widely held because those who believe the opposite, even though in the majority, all believe that they are in the minority and are afraid to speak up about it (Noelle-Neumann, 1964). The Louise Nicholas story is perhaps one such; it seemed that the sex-abuse culture was widely known of in the police well before this story came out. This suggests that if there is a cultural explanation for the constraints on investigative journalism in New Zealand, it is the collective unwillingness to speak out, to be the lone voice in the village, particularly when that voice may be threatening some utopian image of ourselves that we are all supposed to share. To be an investigative journalist in this country thus requires a journalist to sometimes go beyond the usual restraints of objective reporting and risk becoming painted a campaigner; to risk being seen as a whinger, a complainer, in a country that values doing-it-yourself and a positive attitude. While journalists may be happy to take this risk, getting their work published depends on having not just journalists who will campaign but editors, too.

Campaigning is a role that has never sat easily with newspaper editors, or indeed with many journalists in New Zealand; many, I would argue, see pushing investigations as uncomfortably close to campaigning and somehow mutually exclusive with fair, balanced journalism. This is a shame; and a fallacy, I believe. Anyone who has seen the role the editor of *The Boston Globe* played in pushing the *Spotlight* investigation will understand the crucial importance to investigative journalism of having an editor who is not timid. Moreover, it misunderstands what the audience wants. Underpinning all good investigative journalism, scholars have found, is what Natalia Roudakova calls 'integrity of social judgment', or a moral purpose (Roudakova, 2009). This, as she and others have rightly pointed out, is ultimately far more important in the public eye than a ritualised balance or neutrality. An attempt to consider both sides of the story is important, but it is a means to an end — the end being integrity of social judgement, or fairness — rather than an end in itself.

To put it another way, it is not fair to ignore or minimise valid concerns just because you cannot get a response or 'balance'. Some of the journalists in this book were driven by a quite unobjective passion and had to work hard to fortify their zeal with verifiable detail; others began their enquiries with professional detachment and found that they had to learn to manage an increasing emotional attachment to the story. I learned, reading these stories, that investigative journalists come in all forms, whether zealots or clinicians; but what they all share is the persistence to pursue a story as far as it takes, and a determination to get it right.

This brings us closer to the real reason for the sporadic nature of investigative journalism in New Zealand. Bold, brave editors who are prepared to risk community and official opprobrium, and know how to manage the legal risks of publishing challenging stories, are not common. But when they are in place, good reporters gravitate to them and legends are made. This is closer to an explanation for the trend noted earlier: that in New Zealand, publications have golden eras, and those eras coincide with editors, as much if not more than with reporters. Thus we have *Truth*, from 1940–1970 under James Dunn, *The Auckland Star* in the 1970s and early '80s under Pat Booth, *The Dominion* in the 1980s under Geoffrey Bayliss, *Metro* in the late 1980s to mid '90s under Warwick Roger, *The Dominion Post* in the early 2000s under Tim Pankhurst, and more recently *The New Zealand Herald* under Shayne Currie, and Potton & Burton (Nicky Hager's publisher) under Robbie Burton. This suggests that it is editorial quality, rather than a shortage of journalistic talent or some kind of boardroom conspiracy, that defines investigative journalism here.

One other factor is important here. The bravest editors have often had a good lawyer behind them, one who knew not only the rules of defamation but also how and when they applied, and who believed in a free, responsible news media just as much as the journalists. James Dunn's experience in defamation cases gave him the confidence to make *Truth*'s editors so bold; Robert Stewart and Peter McKnight have done the same for Fairfax, as has Steven Price in more recent times for Nicky Hager. A good lawyer is normally part of the team on big overseas papers; journalism in this country would be stronger if there was a similarly close partnership here.

Another factor affecting investigative journalism in New Zealand is our culture of censorship. As I point out in the introduction to Chapter 29, there is almost a code of official omertà about significant parts of New Zealand society. Many New Zealanders, fed the official line that we rank highly in international measures of transparency, would be surprised to find that journalists in some comparable democracies have much greater access to official information. This culture of censorship is, I would argue, one of the great blind spots in the New Zealand discourse, and has had a chilling effect on journalists' ability to fulfil their watchdog role.

Another theme that comes through clearly in this book is that for journalism to last, it needs a human face. Though years may have passed, in the best of these stories we can still feel the pain of Tahi Kaka, Albert Black, Arthur Allan Thomas and David Dougherty. The best stories show, not just tell. The planted cartridge case, the hangman's sunglasses, the schoolhouse with the walls of a fort — these images tell more than words can. The best reads are unafraid to take a stand. They do not waste space or the reader's time with specious denials. Where a denial is relevant, or useful, it can add to the narrative, but formulaic balance looks especially irrelevant with the passage of time.

A further theme that emerges is the relevance of journalism in the New Zealand democratic system. It is at times an essential lubricant when the wheels of justice have frozen. By not only revealing wrong but also exposing the inaction of the bodies whose job it was to prevent it, it helps build a case in the forum of public opinion that politicians can no longer ignore. Booth's relentless work on the Arthur Allan Thomas case (Chapter 11) was a disturbing reminder of the concentration of power in New Zealand. Only when Booth gained a personal interview with the Prime Minister, and persuaded him that there was a case to answer, was a Commission of Inquiry held, an independent Australian judge brought in and the distortions of the case against Thomas revealed. But after Nicky Hager's revelations in *Dirty Politics* (Chapter 30) about the apparent abuse of power by the Prime Minister's Office, where was the New Zealand equivalent of the US Senate's inquiry into the Watergate break-in? Why did Parliament not use its own investigatory powers? Likewise, the weakness of official watchdogs such as the Office of the Ombudsman should be of concern to all New Zealanders.

As many reading this book will realise, a lot of very good investigative journalism has had to be left out. I would like to have included many of the good investigative journalists now working, such as Simon Collins, David Fisher, Eugene Bingham, Paula Penfold and others. Sometimes this was because the work simply did not read as well in hindsight as it did at the time, or because it touched on a theme that was already covered by another story, and sometimes it was simply for lack of space. Likewise, this collection does not acknowledge the investigative work done by television and radio journalists over the years. Again, this collection does not seek to be definitive, but to show some of the main themes of investigative journalism in this country.

While nearly all these stories carry one or two bylines, they are all in some sense a team effort. Good investigations require the backing of a courageous editor. It takes one kind of courage to write a story attacking the security services in the middle of a war. It takes another kind altogether to start a printing press when a representative of the government is on the phone threatening to put you in jail, as the editor of *Truth*, Brian Connolly, found out in 1942. It is the editors who have to face the legal bills and worry about the jobs of the rest of their staff.

Above all, these stories reveal the resilience and enduring power of New Zealand journalism. Many of the stories had a real and measurable impact at the time of publication or shortly afterwards. Sprinkled as they were throughout the daily and weekly output, their true significance was not always seen at the time. But they give the lie to suggestions that New Zealand journalists are unwilling to investigate. With the right cause, and the right editor behind them, they can tell us what lies behind the cloud. They show us, above all, that on the right story, with the right effort, journalism can convey a moral truth.

Burgh, D. (2000). *Investigative journalism: Context and practice.* London: Routledge.

Ettema, J., & Glasser, T. (1998). *Custodians of conscience: Investigative journalism and public virtue.* New York: Columbia University Press.

Feldstein, M. (2006). A muckraking model: Investigative reporting cycles in American history. *Harvard International Journal of Press/Politics, 11*(2), 105–120.

Noelle-Neumann, E. (1964). *The spiral of silence: Public opinion, our social skin.* Chicago: University of Chicago Press.

Pilger, J. (2004). *Tell me no lies: Investigative journalism and its triumphs.* London: Jonathan Cape.

Roudakova, N. (2009). Journalism as 'prostitution': Understanding Russia's reactions to Anna Politkovskaya's murder. *Political Communication, 24*(4), 412–429.

Schudson, M. (2004). Notes on scandal and the Watergate legacy. *American Behavioral Scientist, 47*(9), 1231–1238.

Smith, P. M. (2011). *A concise history of New Zealand.* Melbourne: Cambridge University Press.

Thompson, J. (2000). *Political scandal.* Cambridge, UK: Polity.

Editor's note

Not all the texts in the book are reproduced in their full original form; the use of an ellipsis indicates where text has been removed because of space constraints. The pieces included in the book are not intended to be facsimiles, and the original layout of some made them difficult to read easily in book form. Therefore some changes to their layout on the page have been made. Wherever possible the orginal usage of language, which today may seem idiosyncratic or archaic, has been retained.

CHAPTER ONE

The first shots

1863: New Zealand's first independent Māori newspaper exposes secret government military preparations for the invasion of the Waikato.

Te Hokioi (E rere atu-na) (The soaring war bird) was New Zealand's first truly independent Māori newspaper. It published only nine issues, mostly in late 1862 and early 1863, but had an influence beyond its size. In the months leading up to the bloodiest phase of the New Zealand wars, *Te Hokioi*'s reporting of the colonial government's war preparations and Māori opposition to them helped mobilise the Māori independence movement.

After a few years of relatively peaceful co-existence, by the early 1860s European settlers were agitating to open up the rich interior of the North Island to land sales. The larger Māori tribes in the area decided that they needed to unite to resist European pressure. In 1858 they had crowned a King, Pōtatau Te Wherowhero, who presided over a conclave of leading rangatira, or chiefs. This King movement, as it became known, argued that the Treaty of Waitangi guaranteed them sovereignty over their own lands. In 1862, Pōtatau's successor, Tāwhiao, drew a line south of Auckland, along the Mangatāwhiri Stream, which European troops could not cross without it being taken as a declaration of war.

The colonial government, under Governor George Grey, was alarmed at the growing strength of the King movement and was determined to enforce British sovereignty. Grey began preparations for crossing the so-called Mangatāwhiri Line, while still talking of peace. By late 1862, tensions were wire-tight.

As in many wars, the first shots were not from guns but from printing presses. At first, the colonial government had an advantage. It had its own Māori-language newspaper, *Te Karere*, and also enjoyed sympathetic treatment from the many English-language settler newspapers.

But the King movement had a surprise up its sleeve. Three years earlier, two young Waikato Māori, Wiremu Toetoe and Hemara Te Rerehau, had travelled to Vienna as guests of the Emperor of Austria. They had been trained as printers, and given a printing press. When they returned home, the press was set up in Kingite territory, at Ngāruawāhia. Taking its name from the fabled, extinct giant native eagle, *Te Hokioi* set about countering the torrent of anti-Kingite rhetoric from European papers (Oliver, 2013).

Te Hokioi's editor was Wiremu Patara Te Tuhi. His Māori name was Te Taieti, but he had taken a Māori version of the name William Butler when educated by Christian missionaries. As well as editing *Te Hokioi*, it appears he did most of the writing. Intelligent and well-educated, Te Tuhi was a close relative of Tāwhiao, and so had a good grasp of current issues. Although some of *Te Hokioi*'s content was plainly designed to persuade, what is striking about much of the reporting is how factual and topical it was. Like any good investigative journalist, Te Tuhi set about putting facts in front of his readers — facts that the colonial government would rather they did not know.

He reported Kingite views about how the Treaty of Waitangi should be interpreted, and wrote favourable reports about the indigenous government recently installed in Haiti. He reported, dispassionately, on a major hui in 1862 on whether to oppose Grey's plan for a road into the Waikato. Although it included arguments both for and against the road, Te Tuhi's report made it plain that there was widespread concern that the road would be used to bring in troops and big guns. Capturing the powerful oratory of the Ngati Porou leader Eparaima, it said: 'If the entrails were taken out of a man he would die; and therefore if the road is open through this Island, it will die; now let it be closed.'

Te Tuhi also reported a crucial meeting between Grey and Waikato emissaries at Auckland, on 6 February 1863, at which Grey expressed concern about a letter he had received from Waikato tribes threatening to destroy the main European cities. *Te Hokioi* reported that the emissaries had explained to Grey how this threat had been made in response to what they saw as a threat to invade Waikato, evidenced by the return of the main colonial army to Auckland and the beginning of the construction of a road towards Waikato. They also explained to Grey that another worrying act for Waikato tribes was the symbolic pulling up of a post marking the Mangatāwhiri Line, by John Gorst, a colonial official, in early 1863. When put to Grey, he said that Gorst had been wrong to do this. Again, this was reported in *Te Hokioi*. Its readers thus had a remarkably balanced report of both Waikato concerns and Grey's response (Unknown, 1863a).

Just before war started, Te Tuhi had perhaps his greatest scoop. In March 1863, he revealed that a large new 'school' being built on the border of Kingite lands looked suspiciously like a military barracks. The building was being constructed at Te Kohekohe, on the west bank of the Waikato, by carpenters sent from Auckland, with the permission of Wiremu Te Wheoro. Te Wheoro was chief assessor for the area, a title that combined the roles of magistrate and police chief. He was opposed to the King movement and was a government supporter. The building's location was provocative; it was well south of the nearest government redoubt, at Te Ia, and clearly inside King territory.

King movement supporters were suspicious — they were aware that Grey was building up troops in Auckland, and of rumours that an invasion of their lands was imminent. They had already told Grey not to send armoured gunboats up the river, although they were willing to allow trading boats. Any new building, especially a government one, was likely to be viewed with concern.

A group of Kingites, led by Wiremu Kumete Te Whitiora and accompanied by Te Tuhi, went to confront Te Wheoro and find out the true purpose of this building. When, after heated discussion, Te Wheoro refused to stop work on the building, the Kingites seized all the timber and rafted it back down-river to Te Ia. They then held a hui with the Governor's official, John Gorst, where he tried to justify the building. Gorst had already incensed the Kingites by, on Grey's orders, setting up a rival Māori-language newspaper to *Te Hokioi*, called *Te Pihoihoi Mokemoke i Runga i te Tuanui* (*A Sparrow Alone on the House Top*), two months previously. Gorst then wrote a loaded version of the incident in *Te Pihoihoi Mokemoke*. Fed up, a Kingite armed party seized the paper and expelled Gorst from Kingite territory. *Te Hokioi* carried two accounts of the incident. The first, in its March 1863 edition, is a brief 'newsflash'. It is reproduced below.

The second account below was published in the April edition of *Te Hokioi*, and, according to historian Lachlan Paterson, was no doubt intended to justify the expulsion of Gorst, as well as the ejection of the timber (Paterson, 2004). It is almost certainly written by Te Tuhi. He later acknowledged that it was his idea to throw the timber into the river, though he had not realised it would lead to violence. Te Tuhi's account is good, convincing journalism: a factual, eyewitness account giving verifiable details, including names, places and times. It not only reveals the true purpose of the building — that it was a preparation for war — but it also establishes that it was done with the direct knowledge of the Governor. Like any good journalism, it does this by close questioning of Gorst. In the spirit of investigative journalism, it reveals details that were being hidden, and holds power to account. If any Kingite supporters had any doubt that Grey intended to invade in the near future, this report would have helped remove them.

The propaganda battle did not last long. In those tense months of early 1863, events were moving quickly towards war. In July, Grey's invasion of the Waikato began. Te Tuhi put down his pen and took up arms for the King movement.

Respected for his wit, good nature and intelligence, Te Tuhi was also a noted carver. Near the end of his life, his face became widely known when he sat for the famous portraitist C. F. Goldie (Oliver, 2013).

In the short term, perhaps one of *Te Hokioi*'s main achievements was to prove to many Waikato Māori that Grey's real agenda was to crush the King movement, at least as a military force. Gorst confirms this in his book *The Maori King*, saying that when *Te Hokioi* published a letter from Grey reprimanding the King for leading an armed force in support of Tauranga Māori, this confirmed for many Māori that Grey was deeply opposed to the movement and that it would have to fight for its independence (Gorst, 1864 &

2011). *Te Hokioi* published a detailed justification from Tāwhiao, in which he pointed out that at no point had Europeans been threatened. In fact, Tāwhiao was fundamentally a pacifist, and was assisting, as the King, Tauranga Kingites in the defence of Tauranga (Mahuta, 2013). Always, on the eve of every major conflict he sent emissaries to plea-bargain peace (Roa, 2014).

But *Te Hokioi's* influence went beyond this. Translations of its reports were carried by the main colonial newspapers. These reports have often been dismissed as Kingite propaganda, but a closer reading suggests that this is a simplistic interpretation. The reports — such as the size of the hui that the King movement could summon — demonstrated to colonists the growing (albeit still limited) power of the King movement. Moreover, the sophisticated philosophical and intellectual ideas that underpinned its argument for a different interpretation of the Treaty of Waitangi, one that allowed for a partnership of sovereignty between the Crown and Māori, while unpalatable to many colonists at the time, now seem remarkable for their moderation.

I am indebted to Tom Roa, of Waikato-Maniapoto, senior lecturer at the School of Māori and Pacific Development, University of Waikato, whose tūpuna include Te Tuhi, Toetoe and Te Rerehau, for advice on this commentary, and especially for the translation that follows the excerpts. The translation is adapted from that of the *Daily Southern Cross* (Unknown, 1863b), but there are significant differences. For example, the *Cross's* translation describes Gorst as Mr (Te) Gorst, but this translation argues that the tone used in the original Māori is more ironic; hence he is referred to here simply as 'Gorst'. The original text often did not use capital letters at the beginning of sentences. The orginal style has been preserved.

Gorst, J. E. (1864 & 2011). *The Maori King*. New York: Cambridge University Press.

Mahuta, R. (2013). *Tawhiao, Tukaroto Matutaera Potatau Te Wherowhero*. Retrieved 2014, July 20 from Te Ara — the Encyclopedia of New Zealand. http://www.TeAra.govt.nz/en/biographies/2t14/tawhiao-tukaroto-matutaera-potatau-te-wherowhero

Oliver, S. (2013). *Te Tuhi, Wiremu Patara*. Retrieved 2014, July 21 from Te Ara — the Encyclopedia of New Zealand. http://www.TeAra.govt.nz/en/biographies/1t78/te-tuhi-wiremu-patara

Paterson, L. (2004). Nga Reo o nga Niupepa: Maori languages 1855–1863 (Doctoral dissertation). Otago University, Dunedin, New Zealand. Retrieved from https://otago.ourarchive.ac.nz/handle/10523/5144

Roa, T. (2014). [Email to editor].

Unknown. (1863a, March 24). The beginning of a dialogue about the house at Te Kohekohe. *Te Hokioi*.

Unknown. (1863b, June 13). The *Hokioi*, in *Daily Southern Cross*, p. 3. Retrieved from http://paperspast.natlib.govt.nz/cgi-bin/paperspast?a=d&d=DSC18630613.2.13

Ngaruawahia, 24 Maehe 1863

Te Hokioi, 24 March 1863

He rongo no te Whare a Wiremu i te Kohekohe.

No te 8 o nga ra, o Maehe 8, 1863. I puta oho rere mai ai kia maua i Rangiriri, i te po o te wiki, ka tae mai etahi tangata no Pokeno, he korero kia rongo ai nga tagata katoa i te ti kanga o taua whare; e kia ana e 10 nga ritenga, he Whare Whakawa, e 5 nga Ruma, he ku ra, e 2 nga Ruma, 2 hoki nga ruma moenga, 1 ruma mo te tahu kai, ko nga tikanga ia o roto o taua Whare nui atu, ko te hanga o taua whare he mea karapoti i nga taha, ko waenga, i tu whera. "ka rongo maua kua ara te whare i te kohehe, katu mo te wahi tonu, I te atu ka hoe te Ope, me nga tangata korero kia te Wheoro, tika atu kei te tono kia whakahokia nga papa ki te IA, tu ai, ki te pihi I a te kuini, kihai tera i ngawari. ka tahi te Ope ka mau ki nga papa ka toia ki te wai, ka kite tera ka toia kiuta, a hoki mai ana te Ope. no te 16 o Maehe ka hoe ano te ope, he mahara ake tenei tera ranei e pai e aha rane kei te Atua te whakaaro.

News about Wiremu's house at Kohekohe.

8th of March 1863. This news came to us suddenly at Rangiriri. On Sunday night people came from Pokeno with word for everyone to hear about the purposes for that building, saying that there were understood to be 10 pre-arrangements: a Court House, with 5 rooms, a school with two rooms, and 2 bedrooms. 1 room for food preparation. There were other arrangements for the building. It was to be surrounded [by walls] with an opening in the middle [of one wall]. We heard that the house at te kohehe had been erected for that [purpose and place]. In the morning the group set off with other spokespeople to Te Wheoro to demand that the timber be taken back to Te Ia to the Queen's piece [of land]. That wasn't kindly received. So they took hold of the timber and hauled it to the water. With that the group left and came home. On the 16th of March they carried on [in their journey] realising that whether good or bad was to come was up to God.

Ngaruawahia, 26 Aperira 1863

Te Hokioi, 26 April 1863

Ko te timatanga o te korero mo te whare ki te kohekohe, i korerotia ki Maramarua, maehe 23 1863.

"Ko te kupu tuatahi, kia kaua e tu taua whare ki te kohekohe, no te taenga o Waikato ki reira, ka mea a wiremu, ki a waiho ki a tu ana, kia kotahi, ma koutou, kia kotahi taha ma matou, mutu whakauaua te iwi;

ko te ahua o taua whare, i karangatia ai i mua hei whare karakia. Ki te
kohekohe Hei whare whakawa ki reira hei whare kura, pirihimana hoki i te wa i
whakaiapopototia ai nga papa, ka tino matau matou, kua rereke te ahua o taua
whare. Kua tua karapoti nei, koia ano, he ahua no te timatanga o te pa Hoia ki
te Ruato. No te 8 Maehe 1863 ka korerotia mai etahi o matou e haere tonu nei, ki
te Ia, I o etahi o nga papa, no te Ia, kei te mahia e nga kamura, Ia maranga taua
whare. I rokohanga mai ano maua e noho huihui ana, he rapu tikanga mo te iwi,
i Rangiriri i e noho ana. ko te meatanga ake a te runanga, e te iwi me haere katoa
tatou kia whakaritea he ritenga mo taua whare, kia pera ano te ahua me to mua.

ko nga mea tenei i whakaritea i taua haerenga, ko nga papa o te Ia, me
whakahoki atu ki reira tu ai, ko nga papa o konei me waiho i konei hei whare
whakawa, hei whare ranei mo maua ki te kohekohe. ka pakeke te korero
a Wiremu ratou ko ana hoa ara, ko te kupu tenei, ekore matou e pui kua
whakahokia atu nga papa. katahi karere atu nga taitamariki, toia ana e tahi o
nga papa ki te wai, karere mai a Wiremu ratou ko ana hoa, kei te whiu atu i nga
papa ki uta, ka tau kumekume noa iho, a ka mutu. ko te meatanga a Wiremu, me
kati ra e te iwi me waiho ki ta koutou. ka mea te iwi me ata whiriwhiri marire
he ritenga mo aua papa. I te aonga ake o te ra, i te ata ka mea atu te iwi e W.,
kua tukua paitia ranei nga papa nei kia matou? ka mea a Wiremu e kore ahau
e pai, me waiho aku rakau ki a hanga, hei whare kura ki ko nei. ka tahi ano ka
tino pouri matou katoa, tapahia ana te aroha ki a ia, ka haere ki tenei kupu me
haere atu koe, me nga papa o konei o te Ia, haere katoa atu ki to te Kuini wahi,
kei noho koe. Hoki ana matou, ka hua e whakangawari iho i tana whakaaro, Hei
whakapakeke tonu i ta ratou whakaaro ki nga kai korero, ki te iwi hoki.

Maehe 19 1863

"ka noho te tahi pito o taua huihui, rapu tikanga ki Rangiriri, ka turia ano te
korero he pei atu mo taua whare ki te Ia. I te mea ano e korero ana te iwi, ka
puta mai a te kohi, raua ko te waiti. ka mea a wiremu kumete, e te kohi na
wai te tikanga„ ote whare kite kohekohe? ko te kohi, na wiremu-Te wheoro.
ko w. kumete, nana anake ranei?—ko te kohi naku te tahi wahi, na kawana i
whakapumau.—ko wiremu, he aha te tikanga o taua whare?—ko te kohi, he
whare kura pirihimana. —ko Wiremu e kore koe e pai kia hoki ki te wakamutu
i te mahi a nga kamura? ko te kohi, ekore au e hoki, engari kei a kawana te
tikanga ko Wiremu e hoa, me hoki tahi tatou, e haere ana hoki matou ki reira,
ki te whakahoki i nga Papa ki te Ia ko te kohi kahore he tikanga i au, keia
Kawana te tikanga. ko wiremu e hoa. me hoki tahi tatou, e haere ana hoki
matou ki reira, ki te whakahoki i nga Papa ki te Ia ko te kohi kahore he tikanga
i au, keia Kawana te tikanga. ko Wiremu ki te hoki koe, ki te whakamutu i te
mahi a nga kamura, ka tatari ano matou kia Kawana, ka korero koe e hoki, kua
riro nga Papa ia matou ki te Ia, me nga kamura hoki. ko te Waiti e hoa ma kei
pa o koutou ringaringa ki nga papa. ko Wiremu mehemea ka hoki korua ki te
whakahoki nga papa ki te Ia, ekore o matou ringaringa epa. I te 20 o Maehe,

ka haere te Ope tae atu ki te Kohekohe, e ruke ana i nga papa ki te wai, he mea kahupapa, I te 21 o Maehe, ka rupeke nga papa te kahupapa, I te 22 o Maehe, ko te Ratapu moe tonu iho. I te 23 o Maehe, ka hoea nga papa, a tae tonu atu ki te Ia ko nga kai hoe 235, ko nga mea i noho i te Riparoa 35. I to maua taenga atu ki te Ia, ka rohea ki te taura te tahi pito, te tahi pito, kotahi tekau o nga Pirihimana, me nga Rangatira toko 5. ko te take i peratia ai, mo te tangata o te Ope kei puta atu ki waho, mo te pakeha kei tapoko mai ki roto, kei whara i te rakau. I te mea ano e taruke ana te iwi ki te whiu i nga Papa, ko te haerenga mai o etahi pakeha, kahore i ata mohiotia, engari kua kite i te rohe taura. no te whiunga ake o nga papa, mei kore tika iho ana te taunga ki runga ki te tumuaki o taua Pakeha ka kitea mai e tetahi maori, ka hopukia i nga pokihiwi, whakaarahia ake, ka tau iho te katerina ki te aroaro. mei tika ki te upoko kua tino mate rawa. I te hokinga mai. ka moe ki te Riparoa, ko te tokomaha o taua ope nei e, 470. I taua po, ka whakaarohia nga heote kohi. ko tana unuhanga i te pou a Neri, i Mangatawhiri. ko taua whakatete kia te Hokioi, ara, i ana kupu pokanoa ki te whakahe ki te kingi.

"ko tana tohe ki te whakatu i te whare hei whakatari kino ki te kohekohe, ki te iwi hoki. ko taua, kore e rongo ki te whakahoki i nga Papa ki te Ia, me nga kamura: koia i mea ai te runanga na tatou anake i whakahoki pai atu nga papa ki te ia, ehara nei i a te Kohi tenei me pera anohoki ia, me nga papa me whakahoki tahi atu e tatou, ratou ko ana papa ki te ia, noho ai, ko ta matou i pai ai, aia, ko ta te Runanga me nga Rangatira katoa o Waikato, me taiapo atu ia te kohi ratou ko ana mea katoa. me whakahoki atu ki te ia. kei turi, kei pake, kei whakatete. ka huri

Na te Runanga, me nga Rangatira katoa o waikato enei korero.

The beginning of a dialogue about the house at Te Kohekohe, discussed at Maramarua, March 23rd, 1863.

As soon as the Waikatos arrived, their first statement was that the building should not be erected at Te Kohekohe. Wiremu [Te Wheoro] said, "Let the building stand there, one part for you [the Kingites], the other for us." Discussion ended badly, without a clear conclusion.

The building at Te Kohekohe was supposed to be a church, a court house, and a police school. When the timber was milled we [the Kingites] knew for a certainty the building had another purpose, and when the surrounds were set it was clearly the same as the soldiers' fort at Te Ia. On the 8th of March some of the people having travelled on to Te Ia informed us that the carpenters had prepared the timber which was from Te Ia, and so the intention was clear for the building to be erected. They met with us in council as we debated our course of action with the people who lived at Rangiriri. The council instructed the people to go and to all agree a course of action for the building, which should be as earlier arranged.

This is what was decided: the timber from Te Ia should be taken back there; the timber from here should be left here for the purpose of building a court house or another structure for our own use at Te Kohekohe. Wiremu [Te

Wheoro] and his followers stubbornly did not agree and said they would not let the timber be returned to Te Ia. Then some of our young men rushed over and hauled some of the timber into the water. Wiremu [Te Wheoro] and his friends rushed down and dragged the boards to shore again. They argued, but soon gave up. He then told the people that it was up to them. The people said that they should consider peacefully what was to be done with the timber. Next morning the people asked Wiremu [Te Wheoro] if he had given them the timber. He said, no, that the timber should stay to build a school there. Then we all became angry, and ceased to have any kind regard for him. Our word to him was for him to go away from there with the timber, to go to the Queen's place at Te Ia, and stay there. We would go home, with the wish that he might relent. Their stubborn attitude to our speakers and to the people continued.

March 19 1863

A section of that council stayed to consider a course of action for Rangiriri. It was again proposed that the building should be taken away, to Te Ia. Because the people were debating this, Gorst and Te Waiti [a government supporter] came out. Wiremu Kumete asked Gorst by whose authority the building was being erected at Te Kohekohe. Gorst replied "Te Wheoro's". Wi Kumete again asked whether anyone else was involved. Gorst replied, "Yes, I played a part, and the Governor agreed." Wiremu [Kumete] asked what the building was intended for. Gorst said it was to be a police school. Wiremu [Kumete] then asked Gorst to tell the carpenters to stop working. Gorst replied, "I will not, it's up to the Governor." Wiremu [Kumete] then said, "My friend, let's all go back together. It is our wish that we take the timber back to Te Ia." Gorst said, "It's not up to me, it's entirely up to the Governor." Wiremu [Kumete] then said, "If you go and stop the carpenters, we will wait till the Governor comes. You can then tell them that we took the timber and the carpenters to Te Ia." Te Waiti said, "Friends, do not lay one finger on that timber." Wiremu [Kumete] then said, "If you two go and take the timber back to Te Ia we will not lay a finger on it." On the 20th of March the [Māori] Group went to Te Kohekohe and threw the timber into the river beginning to make a kind of raft.

On the 21st of March the timber raft was completed. The 22nd of March was a Sunday, so we slept in. On the 23rd of March the timber raft was paddled to Te Ia. There were 235 paddlers. Thirty-five stayed at Te Riparoa. When we arrived at Te Ia, two parts were roped off, one section with 10 policemen, the other with five chiefs. The reason was so that the Māori Group would stay inside their section, and that the Pākehā wouldn't get hit by the timbers. The people were totally absorbed in throwing the timbers ashore. Some unknown Pākehā came along, saw the roped-off section, but when the timbers were thrown ashore, they could well have hit the leader of that Pākehā group. A Māori saw this, caught him by the shoulders, and pushed him up just as a piece of scantling flew in front of him. If it had struck his head he would have been killed. When we went back we slept at Te

Riparoa, our group numbering 470 men. That night we were unhappy with Gorst's wrongdoing. He pulled up Neri's marker post, at Mangatāwhiri, he insulted the *Hokioi* and was disrespectful to and abusive of the King.

His arguing for the building at Te Kohekohe would have brought more trouble to Te Kohekohe and to the people, along with his refusing to take the carpenters and timber back to Te Ia. That is why the council decided we alone would take the timber back safely to Te Ia. Gorst had nothing to do with it, and we decided to send him back with his timber to Te Ia. It was our wish, that is, the council and the chiefs of Waikato, to banish Gorst and all his property, and return them to Te Ia. He is deaf, inflexible, and lacks respect. That is all.

This statement is from the Council and all the Chiefs of Waikato.

CHAPTER TWO

The first clash

1894: *The Evening Post* reveals that the head of the defence force is to resign over interference in defence contracts by Premier Richard Seddon.

In 1894, the man who was to become perhaps New Zealand's most charismatic leader was just one year into his reign. Richard Seddon, the boisterous publican from the West Coast goldfields, had slipped into power the year before after the death of the reforming Liberal John Ballance. A big man, with a ferocious appetite for food, drink and work, he is credited with transforming the position of Premier from a mere chairman of the board to something approaching a presidency; hence his nickname, King Dick (Hamer, 2014).

But his dominating, and at times uncouth, style made enemies. One of these was Colonel Fox, a gentleman officer who had been appointed to oversee the colony's defences. Fox had made numerous recommendations for improvements, but Seddon, newly appointed Minister of Defence, had his own ideas. Relations became increasingly strained, until Fox tendered a letter of resignation.

It might have remained an internal bureaucratic dispute were it not for the intervention of Edward Gillon, the editor of the capital's main newspaper, *The Evening Post*. Leslie Verry, in his history of Independent Newspapers Ltd, argues that Gillon was a pioneer of professional journalism in New Zealand, through his willingness to risk jail rather than compromise his journalistic principles (Verry, 1985).

Born in England, Gillon's family immigrated to New Zealand in 1851, when he was nine. By the time he came to edit the *Post*, in 1884, he had spent all his working life in newspapers, including reporting for Parliament and editing the main press agency of the time. A Freemason, he was also passionate about journalistic ethics and was a founder of the New Zealand Institute of Journalists. Verry says Gillon was determined that the Institute should not be a trade union but instead a body concerned with 'maintaining a high standard of honour among its members'; in particular by obliging journalists to take all risks necessary to protect their sources (Verry, 1985).

Gillon was soon tested on this, when he was subpoenaed in a court case and asked to reveal a witness. Told that he could be fined or jailed for contempt of court, he refused; the judge did not press the point. Verry argues that the case was ground-breaking, as it set a precedent of press freedom. The principle was soon tested again, when the *Post* got hold of Fox's resignation letter and printed it. The story was a sensation; the government was forced to set up a Royal Commission of Inquiry. Gillon was subpoenaed; he refused to attend. The Commission, aware of Gillon's previous stand, likewise did not press the point. Seddon tried to take his own revenge; he banished *The Evening Post* from government buildings, although the ban did not last long (Verry, 1985).

Two articles are published here: details about the original letter, as published in *The Evening Post*, and an editorial by Gillon outlining the impact of the revelations. The language seems overblown now, but was not uncommon for the times. Gillon, in particular, was known for his Shakespearean rhetoric. Although the story seems unremarkable by today's standards, it represents the first known clash between the fourth estate and the state in which the principles of journalistic freedom were tested. Like any good investigative journalism, it revealed facts in the public interest, which would not have been otherwise revealed, and it called power to account.

Hamer, D. (2014). *Seddon, Richard John*. Retrieved 2014, July 24 from Te Ara — the Encyclopedia of New Zealand: http://www.TeAra.govt.nz/en/biographies/2s11/seddon-richard-john

Verry, L. (1985). *Seven days a week: The story of Independent Newspapers Ltd*. Wellington: INL Print Ltd.

COLONEL FOX AND THE GOVERNMENT
Evening Post, 4 April 1894

The communication forwarded by Colonel Fox to the Premier at Auckland, and which we recently referred to, reached Ministers to-day, having been forwarded by the Premier. It consists of two letters. In one, Colonel Fox expresses his desire to be released from his contract with the Government conditionally upon his being granted a sum of £1000, as reasonable compensation for the loss he has sustained in coming out here and the termination of his engagement. A further condition is, passages back to England for himself and his military servant. In the event of these terms being accepted, a formal resignation is attached, and reasons why the conclusion of the engagement is desirable are given.

The reasons are very numerous, but the chief are that the Premier, as Minister for Defence, controls the whole of the Defences and Defence Force, in consequence of which the Force has deteriorated; that he has retained the services of useless officers and non-commissioned officers, and of corps recommended to be disbanded, this presumably for political reasons, as the Premier knew money was urgently needed for the chief ports; that the Premier has refused to allow him (Colonel Fox) to take up the duties of Commandant, and he is therefore Commandant only in name; that he (Colonel Fox) required a staff officer, and recommended the appointment of one, and his recommendation was ignored; that the Premier sent an officer of his Department to make extracts from his (Colonel Fox's) letter-book behind his back; that the Premier laid the Volunteer report on the table of the House of Representatives in such a manner as to prejudice him and it; that the Premier sent that report to various persons asking their opinions upon it, but only published that of Sir William Jervois, which differed in some respects from the report, and did not publish that of the Colonial Defence Committee, which was in favour of it; that he (Colonel Fox) was detained in Wellington for a month doing nothing, on the ground that he was to be consulted *re* an ammunition contract, which, however, had not yet been put before him; that the Premier asked his opinion as to the Martini-Henry rifle contract, and then sent his memo. of advice to the contractors; that on receipt of Sir William Jervois' letter the Premier suspended the arrangements which he (Colonel Fox) had made for sending six big guns to England to be chase-hooped; that the Defence plans were transferred to the Public Works Department against his recommendation; that without reference to him the Premier consulted a subordinate officer as to what stores which he (Colonel Fox) had said were required should be dispensed with.

Colonel Fox further states, that as it was apparent that his advice was either unsought or disregarded, he was Commandant only in name, and therefore the Government must approve of his action in resigning.

THE COMMANDANT AND THE GOVERNMENT

Evening Post, Friday, 6 April 1894

The publication of the contents of Colonel Fox's letter to the Premier asking to be relieved of his engagement, has fallen like a bombshell into the Ministerial camp. It is perhaps the most scathing exposure that has ever overtaken any Ministry. So terribly damaging are Colonel Fox's accusations, so indisputable the facts on which those accusations are based and by which they are supported, that we have not the slightest doubt Ministers would have used all the means in their power to suppress the indictment, and to induce Colonel Fox to withdraw his letter and retain his office on almost any terms, had not the disclosure we have been enabled to make rendered suppression or concealment impossible.

Ministers cannot deny the accuracy of the summary we have given of the contents of the Commandant's letter, the full text of which they must now perforce sooner or later publish. They must also plead to the charges on which Colonel Fox has arraigned them, and it is difficult to see what plea they can advance save that of Guilty. They cannot even add to this the further plea of extenuating circumstances. They must answer at the bar of public opinion for what they have done, even if a Party majority should save them from sentence in Parliament.

We write advisedly of the Ministry as a whole having been guilty in this matter, although it will be remembered that when in a former article on the treatment experienced by Colonel Fox the words used admitted of general application to all the Ministers, although we did not distinctly so apply them, and indeed to some extent particularised Mr. SEDDON, the Commandant wrote to us to correct the impression which what we had said might convey, that the Ministry "generally" had treated him with animosity and hostility.

It was honourable and generous of Colonel Fox to endeavour to protect from censure those members of the Ministry who had not personally treated him in an unworthy manner, but the public has nothing whatever to do with Colonel Fox's private or personal relations with individual Ministers. To the public every member of the Ministry is equally responsible for the attitude and action taken by the Premier, as representing the Government, in dealing with Colonel Fox. What that attitude and action have been, Colonel Fox has set out in his letter asking to be relieved of his engagement, and the summary of that letter published by us shows what the damning facts are.

From a public point of view the Commandant's letter to the Premier more than bears out every word which we have written on the subject, even to the censure on the Ministry "generally." We were, of course, glad to receive and publish Colonel Fox's single correction to our previous article, because by his taking exception to a single statement, which was rather implied than directly made, he practically endorsed everything else that we had said. This indirect testimony was especially valuable at the time, as it was then doubtful when, if ever, the contents of the letter to the Premier would see the light.

Now that the nature of its contents is known, everyone can form his own opinion of the shameless manner in which Colonel Fox has been evilly entreated by the SEDDON Government and its chief. We think that opinion will throughout the colony assume the form of general indignation that an officer and a gentleman like Colonel Fox should have been subjected to the coarse insults, and contemptuous as well as contemptible treatment, of the man who is unfortunately New Zealand's Defence Minister and Premier at the present moment. Happily the Premier and Defence Minister does not in this matter represent the feeling of the people of the colony, or even of that section of it enrolled in the Volunteer Force.

The general public has been quick to recognise the high personal qualities of Colonel Fox, the fearless independence with which he has acted, and the sound sense by which his recommendations have been distinguished. These characteristics have been apparent even to civilians. The Volunteers generally have further been equally ready to recognise in the Commandant the highest soldierly qualities, thorough technical knowledge, a sincere devotion to duty, and an impartial sense of justice. All classes recognise the great benefit which the colony might have derived from the services of such a man had not the Government for some inscrutable reason, in pursuit of its tortuous policy, refused to avail itself of his advice, and used all means in its power to thwart, harrass, and undermine him. History repeats itself. The first British Resident in New Zealand was shrewdly described by the Maoris as "a man-of-war without guns." The epigram exactly describes the condition of impotency to which it has been the aim of the Government to reduce the officer specially chosen and detached by the Imperial Government to assist the colony to put itself into a condition of efficient defence.

After the experience Colonel Fox has had, we are never likely to be able to secure the services of another Imperial officer for any purpose whatever. The Imperial authorities will not willingly expose any of their servants to a repetition of such indignities as Colonel Fox has been subjected to. It is enough to make every true colonist blush with shame to peruse the record of the treatment by the head of the Government of a man who was recently described by one of England's greatest generals, speaking to a well-known New Zealander, as "one of the smartest officers in the British Army." Colonel Fox is an officer and a gentleman. The Premier of New Zealand is — Mr. SEDDON.

CHAPTER THREE

Slums and servants

1903 and 1904, *The New Zealand Herald*: Hilda Rollett investigates Auckland's slums, and the privations of household help in Auckland's wealthy Remuera.

Hilda Rollett (née Keane) is one of New Zealand's great pioneering woman journalists. Hard-working, adventurous, level-headed and courageous, she is reminiscent of her famous American contemporary, Nellie Bly. Like Bly, Rollett had a gift for finding stories that would light the public imagination, and she was willing to try unorthodox methods, such as going undercover, to get them. Like Bly, she was basically a fair-minded writer, who tried to see both sides of an issue but was not afraid to call out injustice when she saw it. She, too, was one of a new breed of woman journalists making their mark in the new, powerful popular press. Both put their careers first, both married late, and both maintained a strong interest in journalism throughout their lives.

Born Emma Hilda Keane, on 18 May 1873, in Auckland, she was the eldest of six children of a hotel-keeper. The family moved to Christchurch, but Keane eventually returned to Auckland to attend Auckland University College. She got a taste for journalism in 1899, when she started freelancing for *The New Zealand Herald*, and joined the *New Zealand Illustrated Magazine* in 1902. When, also in 1902, she married the journalist Frederick Carr Rollett, she kept writing under her maiden name.

The two series published here generated widespread interest; the slum series, in particular, generated a flurry of letters to the editor as well as action by Auckland City Council. It says a good deal for Rollett's business acumen that she got them published in *The New Zealand Herald*, by then the city's biggest paper. Although commercially innovative — being the first to introduce a rotary press, and classified advertising organised by subject — the paper was known for its conservative stance. Neither article carried a byline, probably because Rollett was employed at the time as assistant editor at the *New Zealand Illustrated Magazine* — but it is well accepted that she was the author.

There are echoes here of the contemporary trends in US journalism — the use of undercover reporting, and the fascination with social trends, such as rapid urbanisation, city slums and domestic labour. Both show the hallmarks of the professional investigator — the use of several examples, the search for corroboration for unusual claims, the reliance on verifiable empirical detail and, above all, the use of first-hand observation.

Like the muck-rakers in the US, Rollett's writing also reflects the contemporary passion for amateur sociology — the 'objective' descriptive style and the attempts to draw conclusions. She went on to investigate women in prisons and schools. But there was a more personal interest. According to her biographer, Janet McCallum, Rollett wrote the article on domestic service for *The New Zealand Herald* in part because she was herself interested in what a woman's role was. She believed that home duties came first, but that women should be good managers (McCallum, 1996).

In 1916 and 1917 — well into her forties — she and Fred had two children. Rollett continued her successful freelance career, and when Fred died, in 1931, she supported the family on the interest from their savings plus her freelance income of £250 a year — a remarkable sum in New Zealand for those times. She contributed to several US and UK journals — she was the first New Zealand correspondent for the *New York Sun* — and also wrote fiction. McCallum says that a highlight was winning a top place in the first overseas competition organised by the Lyceum Club in London, in 1905 (McCallum, 1996).

Rollett was active in public service, on the board of the National Council of Women and involved in the Plunket Society's 'Save the Babies' campaign in the 1920s. She was a founder and later president of the League of New Zealand Penwomen. Her skill as an artist — she was taught by C. F. Goldie — enabled her to work as an art critic for several papers. She remained active in journalism, living in Auckland until she died at the age of 96, in 1970.

McCallum, J. (1996). *Rollett, Hilda*. Retrieved from Te Ara — the Encyclopedia of New Zealand: http://www.teara.govt.nz/en/biographies/3r26/rollett-hilda

THE SLUMS OF AUCKLAND. A SURVEY OF THE CITY BACKWATERS

New Zealand Herald, 7 August 1903

"Hovels worse than in East London." No. I

"That there has been neglect in the past is evident from the large number of ruinous dwellings — hovels — which would not be permitted in the East

London slums." These words are applied to Auckland, and they appear in the last report of Dr. Makgill, the district health officer. The report is a year old, and yet, judging from a tour made by a representative of the HERALD, specially detailed for the task, Dr. Makgill's description, so far from being overdrawn, is but a very mild observation on the existence of a state of things which is really most deplorable in so young and so progressive a city as Auckland.

Not only is there no change for the better in the character of these dwellings, but there are, unfortunately, no signs of any improvement for the future. The purposes for which these inquiries were made — an undertaking more interesting than savoury — were to ascertain whether the class of dwellings referred to by Dr. Makgill were indeed "slums," in the ordinary sense of the word, and, if so, what were the rents paid by the tenants; and, finally, who were the landlords?

In regard to the landlords . . . it should be stated at the outset that, although the names are in the possession of the writer, curiously disposed persons may, if they think it worthwhile, learn the particulars for themselves from the same sources of information as were open to him; i.e., the Public Health Department, the City Council's published records, and the tenants themselves. So far as identification of slums and their owners is concerned, all that will be done in the case of the one is to indicate in a general way the locality, and in the case of the other, to draw composite portraits, including characteristics and a little life history attached to names, which for reasons sufficiently obvious to newspaper readers, will be fictitious — the only element of fiction in a very sordid story.

Take, as an example, a little patch of slum property, located near Ponsonby Road, a very fine open thoroughfare of its kind. Down in a damp gully is situated a terrace of five tiny houses, in which diseases of a febrile character have never been absent for a year at a time since the places were built. These houses are let at 7s 6d a week, and they consist of a tiny front room, into which the street door opens; with a lean-to at the back; upstairs, and perilously steep stairs, too, are two box-like rooms. In one of them the rotten wallpaper is hanging down in strips like the bark of a blue-gum tree. In the other room the paper is stained with those curious impressionist pictures, in monochrome — the natural products of a leaky roof.

. . .

"And who is the owner of the houses?" one of the ladies was asked.

"Oh, Mr. Glibb. Don't you know Mr. Glibb? He owns most of the property round here."

"Does he ever do up the place for you?"

"I have never asked him. There is a woman next door. She's out now, but she told me that if you ask for anything to be done he raises the rent. We are going as soon as we can get another place."

They all say that; and they all dread to apply for any change or improvement for the better; only in one instance of a great number of places visited — and there is not room in any daily paper to refer to anything like half of them — did the tenants of typical slum property have a good word to say for their landlord.

. . .

The reason the woman above referred to was leaving the house after having been in it only three months, was that she had fled there from another slum landlord, but found her lot made worse. "It was out of the frying pan into the fire," she added, "and Glibb wants to charge us 6d a week extra for using the passage between the houses for our wood. We won't pay it, we can't pay it, so he says we must go."

The passage was a little space of 18in [45cm] wide, between two and three of the houses, which were built as one, and it was evident that it was left for the convenience of the tenants. How the landlord had the effrontery to demand 6d a week extra for the use of ordinary access to the backs — or fronts — of the houses, is a question that only he can answer.

Three of the houses are empty. "They went at four in the morning," said the woman, with a smile full of meaning.

. . .

But let us take another little lot of desirable property for investment. This is located in the North Ward. There are three two-roomed cottages, all having one common yard, one common water tap, one common drain, and one common arrangement of a sanitary sort. The cottages had never been painted, there was no guttering round the roof, permitting the rain water to drip, drip, drip, for years, until the blocks on which the cottages rested had sank, buckling up the floor, and casting two of the houses on one side. In the case of one of them there were no steps up from the sidewalk, which was here too narrow to permit it, consequently the door was barred-up. The rent of these places was 6s a week. Opposite was a four-roomed house inhabited by two families with a yard of about 10ft [3 metres] square. It is in a fair state of repair, but nothing had been done to it for some years; the paper on the walls, where not covered up with the pictorial pages of newspapers, was black with grease below, and a rich dark grey above, where woolly dust and cobwebs clung between the ceiling and the walls. Here was uttered the same cry, "We are afraid to ask for anything to be done for the rent will go up. The landlord has told us that he intends making the rent 12s because we are two families."

One woman living in a dirty little cottage of three rooms in the same district, for which she paid 8s a week, said she had been there four years, and had paid 7s 6d until a new stove was put into the "kitchen," as an extension of the back door was called, when an additional 6d a week was put on to the rent for the stove. This was three years ago, and the tenant had not inquired whether the stove had not been paid for by this time, fearing the inevitable result of additional rent. These properties also belong to Mr. Glibb.

Another landlord is, let us say, Mr. Michael Hourigan. One little block of his, of six houses, six months ago were let at 9s a week; to-day 10s is collected from each of the six houses save one, which was let a fortnight ago for 11s. There are five compartments in the houses dignified by the name of rooms, but the divisions in the cases of four of the rooms are mere bulkheads; the fifth room is partly underground, the back of it penetrating the side of a clayey hill.

From the backs these tenements resemble those tower-like houses that one may see going up any day on the fringes of Brussels and Antwerp; but, oh, how unlike, how utterly different to the neat, clean, well-built, and comfortable Belgian houses, are those in this little block of six. To them there is no yard, but a fenceless area of sticky clayey ground, common to all the tenants, the water taps and sanitary arrangements to match, and also two sinks, one of which was stopped up, and had been in that condition for the past month. There was an old well on the premises which was only partially filled in, while in a corner of the common ground was a rubbish hole.

. . .

In some of these particular houses two families are living together, and as the ground at the back in wet weather is coated with miry clay beyond the conception of even the Psalmist, and as it is the natural playground of the tenants' children and their numerous little friends, it follows that a woman must have the heart of a lioness to attempt to keep her place clean. Women with spirits of this sort, if not unknown to slumdom, are not plentiful in it. And how can they ever be? "You can't keep the house clean at all," observed one lady. "Why, look at my wood heap out there in the rain. There's no shed for it, and Hourigan says he don't see why he should put one up. If he did everybody else would want a shed, and he'd have to charge another 2s a week at least."

Leaving the backs of these places and looking over the fence at another similar block, which faces it, notwithstanding that a street approach to the houses is invisible, one may see a row of six four-roomed cottages. In this terrace of six human habitations there is a rental of £2 14s a week, out of which has to be paid 6s 6d a week in rates to the Municipal Council and the Government. . . . The rooms in two of the houses visited were close and stuffy, swelling of rotten wood, and particularly of the soakage from [a] stable — now, happily in the course of rectification. The front rooms opened on to the alley, the doors being flush to the sidewalk. The little back rooms were half-filled up by the stairs to the two top rooms. In these upper rooms there were no fireplaces, the windows were nailed up, and it was not possible to ventilate the rooms when the doors were closed. No repairs had ever been made to the places within the memory of a lady who had lived there for 14 years, and had raised a family of eight children, three of whom had been born in this house. The sanitary arrangements were at the end of the alley, a cul-de-sac, and provision was made for six houses that was just sufficient for two. [One house] was occupied by a widowed dressmaker with four children, and the rent was 5s a week; there were two rooms, but no provision for the storage of wood or coal, while the only water tap was outside in the alley.

No. II

New Zealand Herald, 11 August 1903

The risk from fire in some of the houses which the present writer visited in the course of his investigations into slumdom in Auckland is very great. One house was occupied by four families. It contained 16 rooms, let off in two suites of five and two of three rooms; the rents amounted in the one case to 10s 6d, and in the other to 6s 6d a week, so that the house yielded to the owner, who lived off the premises, £1 14s, less rates, which, so far as could be ascertained, were levied on the basis of a house let at 14s a week. . . . The risk of fire in such a place is fourfold, as there are four separate establishments all under one roof, and four individual responsibilities.

. . .

A little farther down the street in which this tenement house is situated is a row of small three-roomed cottages, let at from 7s 6d to 8s 6d a week. The 8s 6d cottages have an extended porch at the back, which is also, euphemistically, termed a room, hence the extra shilling. The houses, like hundreds of their kind in the city, hang on to the side of a hill. There are two rooms on the first floor, one opening directly into the street, the other, the back, having the stairs leading to the third room beneath it. Where the family of nine, ranging in ages from three years to 40, stow themselves away at night is somewhat of a mystery, until three or four loose planks in the back of the lower room are pointed out, and then it will be seen that a very tiny room, dark, and somewhat damp, has been built up of rough planks and old sheet iron underneath. As this is the work of the tenant, the credit of its construction cannot be attributed to the owner, who might also collect another 1s a week for it.

. . .

It must not be imagined that all the people who live amid the wretched surroundings of some of Auckland's slums are either poor or shiftless. It frequently happened during the tour of the writer that some of the most miserable of the places were inhabited by their owners, or that the landlord or landlady lived in the same block. This was the case with a little quadrangle formed of some 13 two and three-roomed cottages. The houses were let at 5s 6d a week for two rooms, and 7s 6d a week for four rooms, it being always understood that a subdivision of any sort counts as a room. There was one water tap for the whole of these houses, one common drain, and the sanitary arrangements, sufficient for three houses only, had to do duty for 13. Several of the tenants complained of leaky roofs, others again expressed themselves perfectly satisfied with the conditions of the houses, but all were agreed that the owner, who lived on the premises, made it perfectly clear that the rent was due, and must be paid on every Monday morning.

. . .

The square of 13 cottages was duplicated by another little lot of property in the South Ward, consisting of four wretched places, two rooms in each; water and sanitation sufficient for two houses. The owners do not live on the premises, but close by. They are two very old ladies, and seemingly very poor, notwithstanding their property. Their years and infirmities have robbed them of the energy of the typical slum landlord and landlady, consequently the payment of the rent is left to the honour of the tenants, who as a general thing do not pay, or if they do pay anything at all, it is "now a shilling or two, and then another shilling or two." Damp, close, and dark was the house in which these old ladies lived, and rank grew the grass and weeds in front of it. "We shan't need a house long," said one of them, and brightening up she exclaimed, "No, we shan't be here long, we're waiting for the angels to carry us away."

. . .

A few doors off was another cottage, belonging to a lady who has much property of this kind in various parts of Auckland. This house is hidden away behind a cluster of three tumbledown little "shacks." It is let at 7s a week, contains four rooms. No repairs have been done inside the house during the seven years the present tenant has lived in it. He has himself, at his own expense, papered one room, but as he feared the raising of the rent if he went on with the work, the owner intimating as much, he says, he discontinued.

. . .

There had been fever in this house, and then the Sanitary Department stepped in and insisted on a thorough overhauling of the drains, and the removal of adjacent stable, but nothing else has been done to the property for at least seven years, said the occupier, but the rent was raised last year.

Then there are unregistered lodginghouses contributing very largely to the extension of slumdom, of which there are several in the city. Letting beds by the night constitutes a lodginghouse, whereas a bed let by the week comes under another heading, nevertheless there was one house visited the owner of which made no secret of letting beds by the night. The charge was 9d a night or 4s a week. There were six rooms in the house, divided by a series of partitions into 12 apartments. In eight rooms there were two single beds in each, in two rooms there was a double bed in each, and in the kitchen three beds were made up, while an absolutely dark recess contained a bed also. When full of bed-occupying tenants, the house must hold something like 30 people, not counting the guests who during holiday times are accommodated with a shake-down on the floor.

Such houses as these must necessarily be conducive to the growth of a slum population, because the people who gravitate to them, either from choice or necessity, become accustomed to the conditions of the place, and invariably perpetuate them when they leave it; while the neighbourhood in which it is situated rapidly becomes like it if it be not so already.

Another similar property, all owned by one man, consists of two houses, a cottage, and five little huts no bigger than fowlhouses, in the big garden at the back. Men only are received at this establishment, but the owner admitted that he could put up 60 guests, while at Christmas time he was always full; what full meant it was impossible to say with certainty, but it would work but at something like £10 a week from the rentals, against which, of course, must be set losses sustained by defaulting tenants, but judging by the manifest astuteness of the owner the losses must be comparatively few.

The next and final article will deal with some types of slum landlords, the effect of their properties on the sanitation and morals of the city, and the suggestion of some possible remedies.

No. III

New Zealand Herald, 14 August 1903

Landlords of slum property are pretty much the same all the world over. In Auckland the type has its well-known characteristics, though here, as yet, it is only represented by a few. Of course, there are landlords and landlords, but the slum landlord is too often only concerned with getting as high a rent as he can for his property, irrespective of all considerations affecting the comfort, health, and convenience of his tenants. Then there is the absentee landlord. All the tough work is left to his agent, whose business it is to collect the rents, and to remit the same, shuffling the responsibility for repairs and maintenance on to the landlord, reminding tenants of their option to go or to remain. And then there are the owners, too, who do not appear at all. They always blame their agents when they do appear, and the agents always blame the owners. "I told her about the rain coming in," said the tenant of a three-roomed cottage, let at 7s 6d, in the South Ward, in referring to the landlady, and landladies are generally more difficult to deal with than landlords. "And what did she say?" "She blamed me for not telling the agent, and I told her that he put all the blame upon her, and between 'em I get nothing done."

It is always so where the agent's responsibility to the owner is restricted to the collection of the rents, and this was proved to be correct by a statement made to the writer by the head of one of the leading house agents in Auckland, a firm of more than local celebrity.

"If we look after our tenants," said this gentleman, "we find they co-operate with us. If we do anything to improve the house and maintain its habitability, we retain our tenants; it pays us to keep them at a trifle below the ruling rents for such properties. Of course, there are 'bad marks,' but we have had very little experience of them. I think I am right in attributing their disqualifications as tenants of decent cottages to the treatment of owners of the places in which they have been accustomed to dwell."

An obstacle to sanitary progress

The Health Department, the City Council's officers, the doctors, the police, the Salvation Army's social officials, the ministers of all denominations, whose work is not confined to ministering to the intellects of their flocks, know full well how slum property stands in the way of sanitary progress, and not only checks all honest, sane, and rational reform, but actually thwarts the efforts put forth for the maintenance of public health at its normal level. Dr. Makgill holds that "the majority of the ratepayers (of Auckland) think that the whole duty of the civic representatives is to keep down the rates, and they regard dirt and disease as necessary evils," and dirt and disease are conspicuous features in the slums of Auckland, as indeed they must be, constructed and conducted as so much of this property is at present. Infectious and contagious diseases finding a lodgment in favourable localities, and a mere cursory examination of some of the slum centres in Auckland carries with it confirmation of the statement of a prominent medical man here, that Auckland has in it all the conditions necessary for a most virulent outbreak of smallpox. "There are places so bad," said one doctor in an interview accorded to the HERALD recently, "that in the interest of my patients as a whole I positively refuse to visit them." . . . In the absence of expert knowledge one is compelled to assent to the statements of men who know what they are talking about, whose words are taken down in evidence against them, to be used as the occasion requires, hence no excuse is necessary for concluding this paragraph with the following words of Dr. Makgill's report on Auckland: — "There are a large number of old ruinous buildings totally unfit for habitation, in which the poorer classes are compelled to take refuge. Whole blocks of these exist here and there. . . . The landlords of these unwholesome spots have by their neglect forfeited all right to consideration."

. . .

For three years or more the Municipal Council has had before it a new set of by-laws. When they will be completed no one as yet seems to know, but as they stand at present they will place in the hands of the civic authorities power of which they have long felt the need. These by-laws have been framed largely to deal with the slum evil, which, if the laws are faithfully and diligently enforced, will bring Auckland up into line with cities of equal size and importance. So far for one remedy; but a useless one unless the present staff of sanitary inspectors is increased. At present the Government provides a district health officer and an assistant, who are expected to cover a territory extending over 360 miles in one direction and 200 in another, including, of course, Auckland city. The City Council has a chief inspector and one assistant, who are responsible for 9000 houses, any one of which may require two and three inspections in a week. As a matter of fact, it occupies an inspector between eight and nine weeks to inspect every house. . . .

. . .

Dr. Makgill suggests flats as a way out of the slum problem, but flats cannot be regarded as aids to desirable reform. They would be, however, more than palliatives, and if properly constructed at the outset, conveniently situated, and economically built, would do a very great work in emptying the slums. As an investment they would not return so much to the Council, if it built them, or to private individuals, or philanthropic bodies, as the existing hovels do, but they could be trusted to yield at least six per cent on the capital, "provided always" that they are built on economical lines, and let at prices well within the compass of the people upon whom some of the slum landlords wax fat.

   . . . As our friend, the house agent, stated, backed by many years of valuable experience of Auckland, "After all the best thing for the work people is to own their own houses, as many of them do, although, I fear, some may find they have paid too much for them. The great difficulty, of course, is the raising of sufficient capital to make a start. It is not the State that should grapple with the housing problem, but the people themselves, and yet the state of affairs is very acute in Auckland just now. We know of no decent places to let under 25s a week; 10s to 14s houses, none; 15s to 18s houses can be obtained, but are few. We know of no places vacant for people who can pay no more than 5s 6d to 8s 6d a week. Personally our firm declines properties of this sort, preferring the landlords to collect the rents, and themselves deal with the tenants. To reputable house agents this class of business is both unprofitable and uncongenial."

. . .

Much that has been written here has, no doubt, proved unpalatable to persons having the best interests of Auckland in their jealous keeping, but the truth has been told, and a realisation of the condition of affairs is the primary step towards progressive action. Shortly, it has been shown that people in the majority of cases are compelled to live in squalid surroundings in Auckland, that they pay as much in rent as they can possibly afford, that the owners of these slum properties are concerned with no other business than the collection of as much rent as they can wring from the tenants, and that the City Council, according to its lights, if slow, is surely doing something, if not all it might do, towards remedying a recognised evil feature of the city.

   Those persons who are not prepared to accept the descriptions of the slums as they have been here recorded are at liberty to do, as an ex-city councillor did recently, go round the places personally, and perhaps they would confess with him their previous ignorance of the existence of a very serious state of things. As St. Jerome has laid down, "If an offence come out of the truth, better is it that the offence come than that the truth be concealed."

A MASQUERADE. HOW I SAW DOMESTIC SERVICE No. I

New Zealand Herald, 12 March 1904

One hears so much now of the Domestic Service Problem that I bethought me that the best way of finding out the real state of affairs was to investigate for myself. I therefore decided, taking advantage of my husband's absence, to close my house and seek employment as a domestic. I have never kept a servant, and have, I consider, a very good knowledge of housekeeping. If ever I do keep help my investigations in some homes of this city will, I hope, guide me as an employer. Remembering always that the names given are fictitious, and that the localities are hopelessly mixed, the reader may gain some insight as to how many Auckland homes are managed.

I looked carefully down the "Wanted" columns for something to suit me; but the advertisers were either people whom I knew or who knew me or they required references. The former case was impossible, the latter hopeless without forgery or the divulgement of my plan. I had recourse then to the registry office. I sat for some hours in the outer room of one of these establishments. I was not alone. There were other women there, mostly of the resigned class. One of them became friendly. She was no longer young. She told me that she had been out of a place for months, that people now wanted young girls, "smart-like, like yeself." I acknowledged the compliment, and asked what kind of work she liked. "I was cook," she said, "to Capt'in Smith for ten years." Then followed such a string of the captain's "ways" that I saw some reason for her non-employment. . . . I was called in then to the office.

"Emma Jones!" the stout lady repeated my name after me. She looked me up and down and all over, and much as I had prided myself upon being neatly but plainly dressed I felt my confidence oozing out, and was inclined to repent of my rash seeking for adventure. However, the scrutiny was done at last, and the lady asked questions.

"How long had I been in my last place?" Then I replied in what may mildly be termed borrowed language. I said that I had been four years. I had, indeed, for I had kept my own house all that time. She asked where, and feeling quite safe I gave her what was my real name. After a fair amount of questions — and explanation on my part — the stout lady perused her list.

"How would you like to go where there's a large family?"

"Very much," I replied. She looked astonished, and said:

"Oh! you don't look as if you would like it. You would get on better in a smarter place. Now, let me see, here's Mrs. Gosson. She's not long married — no children. Ever wear caps?"

"No; but I don't mind."

"Well; she insists upon black afternoon dress, white muslin apron, and caps. She wants a smart girl, young" — here she looked at me again; but fortunately I looked five years younger than my real age. . . .

"What wages?" I asked.

"Oh! wages? Yes! Oh, yes! Seven shillings! You see there are only two of them, not like as if there were children."

Under the circumstances I personally did not care a rap what were the wages, but I had to act my part. So I promised to see Mrs. Gosson that night, and left, feeling quite elated at my success.

That night I took the Remuera 'bus, and right out, nearly as far as one could get, I, after many times going to the wrong door, found Mrs. Gosson. She was young, and "style" was written all over her. She asked me to sit down in the hall, and tried to elicit information. She was somewhat exacting, I found, but she evidently liked my appearance. She hinted that seven shillings a week was good wages for a comfortable home and only two people. I thought it prudent not to look too satisfied. She asked about my "young man," and looked relieved when I denied his existence. Finally, she gave me to understand that if she engaged me she would let me have one night a week, a monthly half-holiday, and every other Sunday out. Other matters, of attire and work being alluded to, she promised to "ring up" the registry office next day.

In two days' time I had begun my new life at Mrs. Gosson's. I confess to a tinge of disappointment when I saw my bedroom. It was so ridiculously tiny. I measured it one day. It was eight by five feet. It held a stretcher, a vile blue quilt covering the same, and my trunk, which was my washstand and dressing-table. . . . All things considered I did not enjoy my first night in the cupboard off the kitchen.

On Wednesday morning my alarm went off at six o'clock. I had a great deal to do before breakfast. My own room had to be tidied, the dining-room swept and dusted, an early cup of tea taken to the mistress' door, the bath filled, shaving water heated for the master, the table set for breakfast and the meal itself prepared. . . . At eight I rang the gong and — though I ought to have known better from my own experience — carried in breakfast.

They came at last — Mrs. Gosson in a pretty morning wrapper with lace dangling about the wrists. I caught the words, "I am going to begin as I mean to go on" — and then the bell tinkled.

"Emma!" in quiet, dignified tones, "Mr. Gosson's porridge is cold."

I took the plate, and returned with some oatmeal that I had wisely kept in the saucepan. They looked at each other and I fancied he smiled. However, the rest of the breakfast passed off well enough.

. . .

After breakfast I cleared the dishes, put the silver away — and what an accumulation she liked on the table! . . . This took me until quite half-past nine. Mrs. Gosson was busy with the paper. She sat on the verandah. Then there was the bedroom to tidy and my kitchen to scrub. It was dirty enough, too. I thought I should never get that range polished. Anyway, I got through it and washed out an accumulation of dish towels, swept and dusted the hall, and then Mrs.

Gosson came to me. "Emma!" she said, still in dignified, keep-your-place tones. "You forgot your cap this morning."

I felt for it, and found that she was right.

"Some people do not care about dress in the mornings," here she brushed an invisible crumb from her dainty muslin wrapper; "but I am particular on that point."

. . .

"See if we have enough potatoes. And can you make any puddings?"

"What kind, madame?" I fancied she frowned at the persistence of my courtesy.

"Oh! some kind of boiled pudding, with a nice butter sauce; You know?"

. . .

I prepared lunch at twelve o'clock and had the house to myself by half-past one. It took me a long time to turn out that drawing-room. . . . [My] mistress arrived home at five o'clock, followed fairly closely by two friends. Her husband brought with him a gentleman.

I was rather proud of that little dinner, and tremendously hungry. . . . But I heard things. Curious how people regard a servant as an automaton without any feeling.

"Seems a nice girl, Mrs. Gosson." This just as I was out of the room.

"Ye-es; pretty fair."

"Did she cook the dinner?"

"Well, partly."

When I came in with the pudding the ladies were discussing things seriously.

"Yes; and she actually boxed my Kathleen's ears. I wasn't going to stand that."

"I should think not. You dismissed her, of course?"

. . .

The visitors went at eleven, and after I had brought in hot water I was told I might go to bed. It was half-past eleven.

Next day I had an accumulation of three weeks' washing and the consequent ironing at night. . . . I pleaded trouble at home, hinted at sickness there, and went, feeling very mean. But there was another girl to come.

No II.
MY SECOND EXPERIMENT AT DOMESTIC SERVICE

New Zealand Herald, 19 March 1904

My second was what may vulgarly be styled as a "terror." She had money enough, too much, indeed; gave me, without question, 15s a week, and in the first week, of my stay presented me with a brummagen brooch, a good silver watch, a whole piece of dress material, and loads of promises. [I] was somewhat embarrassed; but supposing that most girls in the position (we scorn situations in these days) would gladly accept the gifts, I felt that I must do the same. Fortunately for me I have only the brooch left. How, I will tell you later. When I went to Mrs. McPhey's there were three girls there, of ages from 17 to eight. All were adopted. I was told that in confidence by Mrs. McPhey when I had been in the house three hours. She seemed to take a great liking to me. "You may take it easy to-day," she observed, as she showed me to my room. It was really a palatial affair for a servant, much larger than any room in my own home, carpeted, and well furnished. I discovered afterwards that it was the guest room.

"I don't say I'll always let you sleep in here," she said, with a peculiar twist of her mouth and chin. "But we'll see. Here's the wardrobe for your clothes, and you may use that chest."

. . .

"Now, come downstairs, Emma, and see what you think of my new drawingroom and—"

I interrupted meekly with the suggestion of changing my dress.

"Yes, yes, of course. You change. Would you like a wrapper? It must be a tiring journey all the way here. Oh, well! If you won't, you won't. Well, you just change, and I'll put the kettle on for some tea. Katie!" screaming this at a most unnecessary pitch over the banisters. "Katie! Put the kettle on, and get out some cake." Katie did not answer, and Mrs. McPhey flew down the stairs, and I had another revelation when I heard her rating poor little Katie most unmercifully. I began to wonder if Mrs. McPhey had not mistaken me for some expected guest.

But she had not, for, in a short while, a scream came up the stairs.

"Emma! Emma!" I finished my waist-belt on the way down, and flew. I found my way to the kitchen. Katie, a child of eight, was sitting on a chair crying, and Mrs. McPhey . . . began to tell me, at the top of her voice, the many failings of the poor child. I asked what she had done.

"Done? Didn't you hear me call her? And when I came down, she was outside playing."

"Perhaps she did not hear you?"

"That's just it. She ought to have heard me. That child's always trying to escape doing things."

I determined to act on the hint, and to obey promptly so long as I stayed with Mrs. McPhey.

I looked round and found the teapot, and was again looking for the caddy, when Mrs. McPhey snatched the pot from my hands.

"She's going to do it. Get up, you lazy little thing, and make the tea!" I think Katie was grateful for any order definitely given.

. . .

Next day I was awakened at five o'clock. Mrs. McPhey came in to me, in her robe de nuit, to inform me that she and I were going to "turn out the rooms."

Breakfast in the kitchen of porridge, bread, and some jam . . . did not last long. The master went to the city early, and the children were sent off to school. One room had been finished before breakfast, and in some marvellous way, which since I have never been able to understand, the mistress and I cleaned thoroughly seven good-sized rooms. Certainly we did not stop for lunch. Mrs. McPhey would not hear of it. She grew cross towards mid-day, and by five o'clock was a hurricane. I became frightened. Nellie appeared from school, and put her bag of books on a chair in the kitchen. Mrs. McPhey darted at them, threw them out of the window, and caught Nellie a sounding box in the ears.

She saw my horrified look and turned on me.

"You? You lazy lump! What are you standing there for? Do you think I pay you 15s a week to gape? I have had to do all the work this day."

I was so tired and hungry with a day's hunger that I nearly cried. The other poor little girls came home and received a frightful scolding for not having come with Nellie. Then the three of them were sent to walk a good two miles to the store for some butter. They had another reception on their return for taking a long time. Dinner that night was a farce. I was commanded to stay out in the kitchen.

"What does a servant want dining with me?" demanded Mrs. McPhey.

"I don't know; I mean I don't mind," I replied, very meekly.

And if that bell went once, it went a dozen times during a meal which consisted of tea, bread and butter. First the milk was almost thrown at me. It was condensed milk, and I had mixed it wrongly. Then the tea was too weak. Then they must have some more bread cut. . . . Then I hadn't fed the parrot. I felt rather inclined to kill the poor wretch. Then I was sent upstairs for a handkerchief. Then Grace was expelled, sent to have tea in the kitchen — and I know not what other trivialities. . . . She was a perfect fiend that night. Her husband went to bed at last, and she came again to me, and after another storm, suddenly burst into tears and asked me to forgive her. I must not think of leaving her. It was then that she presented me with the brooch from her own dress.

So things quietened at last, and we slept the next morning until eight o'clock. Mrs. McPhey was very gracious, kept the girls from school, and took us all for a drive.

. . .

After some shopping in Queen street, which resulted in the dress-length for me, a silver watch for Katie — it was taken away from her that night and given to me — and as many chocolates as the girls wanted, we stopped at a butcher's and the poor man had to send for the second time that day his carrier to the house. But we had cakes and pastry and the provisions, and, having had two meals in town, were anything but hungry. Mrs. McPhey, however, would have a joint of meat cooked. Dinner was ready at a quarter-past seven, and not even Mr. McPhey seemed to want it. It struck me that he was wise enough always to dine well in town. If he had not done so, he would have suffered most of the time from a diet of tinned stuff, seasoned with his wife's capricious temper.

I stayed at this house for ten days in fair comfort. Then Mrs. McPhey could hold in no longer. She made such a scene one night that the eldest girl ran away from home early next morning. And of all persons in the world I was accused of abetting her. My watch and my new dress material were taken away — how I longed to throw them at her! — and I was given such a morning, Mrs. McPhey was out in the afternoon — and such a night as I never want again. At two of the next morning — after I had slept one hour in peace — she came to me, ordered me out of bed, and made me — I was afraid not to do it — made me take a solemn oath that I did not know where Grace was.

I did what she ordered, and I did something else — I packed my trunk, left on the dressing-table my current week's wages, and I waited till the poor master was out of the house. Then I went. I believe the carter whom I sent for my box found it out by the roadside! Poor Mrs. McPhey!

No. III
A DOMESTIC SERVANT'S WORRIES
New Zealand Herald, 26 March 1904

Poor helpless Mrs. Dayhew! I stayed three weeks longer than I had intended, in pity for the woful hopeless helplessness of my mistress. From sheer incapacity to do anything else Mr. Dayhew had certainly been a benefactor to the State. She had nine children, and she was only 30 years old. Her husband was 20 years ahead of her in age, and when she went out with him, one never wondered why he married her. The little featherhead was not pretty. It was only when she began to chat and laugh — she had the merriest, most infectious laugh imaginable — that one realised how attractive she was. . . . Sometimes, and, indeed, more than half of her life, she had "blues." But the other part, into which an unexpected guest, an outing, or a gift would easily transform her, quite made up for the blue part, and like everything else, I, too, used to laugh with her and love her.

When I first came to her home in Ponsonby, she was out. I rang the bell. No one answered. Yet I was punctual to the minute. I sat down to wait. After a very long time a ten-year-old girl came in at the gate wheeling a perambulator with two babies, and in her wake two small children. She was a pretty girl, and, in spite of her untidiness had nice manners.

"Mother's out!" she said, when she saw me. "But if you will come in I will make you some tea." The other children stared mildly at me.

"I'm the new servant," I explained.

"Oh? Mother must have forgotten. Please come in and I will show you your room. Rupert, don't suck your thumb!"

Then, reassuming the quaint little grown-up manner, "Mother did not tell me your name," said Miss Eileen, leading the way upstairs.

"Emma."

"I don't know where mother meant you to sleep, but Louie used to look after Rupert and Muriel. They sleep in here."

"Here" was a big, untidy room, with two small cots and a single bed. None of them had been made that day, and there were toys and clothes and biscuits on the floor. The children's voices rose from below.

"I'm afraid Rupert's hitting the babies," said Miss Eileen, and she left me. She seemed to have some authority over the little ones, for she soon had them quiet, and was calling up the stairs to me. . . . It was now four o'clock, and I should have liked to tidy that bedroom. But I thought I had better find out about dinner.

"I've put the kettle on the gas," said Miss Eileen. "And I think the babies want more milk, don't you?" I looked at the bottles and agreed. And Rupert rubbed a dirty fist into his eye and said, "Want a biscuit," and began to cry. Muriel, the other toddler, looked gravely at him a moment, and cried also. . . . I saw some means of getting a dinner ready, and attended to the babies.

I got things under [way] by five o'clock. Miss Eileen had a book, and was reading. The babies were asleep, at the wrong time, of course, and the other two were playing upstairs somewhere. I was just going to investigate there when the bell rang violently.

"Oh! I'd forgotten all about you!" It was Mrs. Dayhew returned. "Dear me! That is funny! And you look as if you'd been here all the time! Hullo! my darlings!" This to the toddlers who were making way downstairs. "No, don't touch Muvver's frock! Oh well, just one kiss!" And she seemed really fond of them.

"I suppose you found your room, Louie? Oh, I forget! It's Mary, is it not?" My correction was lost in her prattle, and I was Louie all the time I stayed in the house. . . . Nothing seemed to matter when she was in this mood. I began to explain about the dinner. She scarcely listened.

"Oh, just get what you like. Louie! Send one of the children to the shop!"

. . .

"I'm going to do all the cooking to-day," my mistress observed one afternoon. "You take out the children, Louie."

So I took those who were to be found. There were five with me.

"Stay out till six, Louie!" I heard from the window. I stayed. And when we came back, Mrs. Dayhew was in the blues. She had made a cake, in which she forgot the sugar; she had burnt the meat pie intended for dinner, and she had left a pile of washing up — you know what a cook's dishes are — that made me cross. She was lying down. She had "a vile headache." The little ones were cross and hungry. They had no bath that night. I really had no time, and I felt in as big a muddle as the lady. Nita wouldn't stir, and Eileen was out. Dinner got ready somehow, very badly, at about seven o'clock. I was ashamed of it. The little boys came home tired, from a party, and Mr. Dayhew seemed to lose his temper with his wife.

. . .

51

Considering the lack of attention they got, . . . those babies were angels. The little boys were always dirty, always mischievous. One of their favourite feats was to walk on top of the piano and jump. No discipline of any kind. Their mother was out most afternoons, often entertained, and never bothered her head about the children. They thrived well enough, somehow. . . .

Mrs. Dayhew implored me not to leave. But, hypocrite that I felt, I almost told her that I was only masquerading. And I am going soon to see her, if only to see how the mother of nine is faring. Like everyone else, I'm foolishly fond of the little incapable. But she'll come out all right. Those people always do. And I know that her present servant is a good faithful soul. I hunted her up myself.

No. IV
DOMESTICS IN CLOVER
New Zealand Herald, 2 April 1904

"You're a conceited prig, Emma! You think because you have only upstairs work to do that you may put on airs in the kitchen."

"What's wrong now?" I asked. But I knew. The baker's boy had asked Cook Mary where the new girl was to-day. . . .

I appeased her finally by offering to do her hair. This always took. My fellow-servants did not disguise their admiration of my handiwork. At last I got her away, and I settled down to the darning. There was a rattle at the lift. I answered it.

"Are you there, Emma?" called one of the boys of the house.

"Yes."

"That's all."

He was not a bad boy as boys go. But when I had got up for the third time to answer that knocking I took no notice on the fourth. Then — doesn't it always happen so? — it was Miss Ina. She was cross, and did not mind showing it.

"Emma! The fire is low. Come and put some coal on." . . . She could have done it quite easily. But she was a young lady who would not take a shovelful of coal from the scuttle a few inches away, not as long as there was a servant in the house. Perhaps she was right.

When I got down again Mrs. Rickard's bell rang.

"Fill my hot-water bottle. Tell Miss Ina I want her."

"What for?" asked Miss Ina. "Why didn't you ask her? Go and see what she wants." Of course Mrs. Rickard wouldn't tell me, and I had to carry another message.

"Oh! dash it! You are an idiot, Emma." And she rushed past me. I waited upstairs awhile, but thought it time to go when altercation became very audible. I re-commenced darning.

. . .

[Mrs. Rickard] lifted the bucket and put on more coal. She had not cooked for many years, and had forgotten the ways of ranges. Her pastry was quite ready, and the stove was not. However, she "bested" poor old Mary by telling her to bake the pastry for tea; that it would do no harm by standing awhile. I think the last straw came when Maud came in after tea and ate a tart. Of course Mary never looked at them after putting what returned to the kitchen on the dresser. Maud did not know that the mistress had been cooking.

"My goodness, Mary!" she exclaimed, "that's lovely light pastry! I'll have another," which she did. Then Mary, who had been a slumbering volcano, burnt into tears, and it took a long time to pacify her.

I left out of friends with Mary. She attacked me one day, and, to show her displeasure, did not set my place at the table. I didn't care. Maud sulked. She was very loyal to Mary. This gave me my opportunity. I gave notice the next day; said I couldn't get on with Mary.

"Ah! I'm sorry. You've done your work pretty well. But I can't dismiss Mary for a new girl."

So that's how I got out of a good place.

No. V
THE GOOD MISTRESS
New Zealand Herald, 9 April 1904

She was the kindest woman in the world, and she treated her servants not as servants, but as human creatures. . . . She was very particular, would not leave a particle of dust, would not have an inch of food wasted; but she helped like a Briton. Old Dick [who worked in the garden] told me that the last girl had been delicate and had a delicate sister. Mrs. Bagehot asked the latter to come for a visit to her sister and made her stay for six months, nursing her [to] health and finally sending her home quite strong and well.

"To-morrow we'll turn out the drawing-room, Emma." That "we" does make a difference. And we turned it out in so thorough a manner that I was ashamed of my own housekeeping. Walls were dusted from ceiling to floor, curtains taken down and shaken, the door washed with all the woodwork. To me it had all looked perfectly clean. Nor was this a spring-cleaning. It was only the usual round. We went through the rooms, cleaning and polishing, every fortnight, besides the usual daily sweeping and dusting.

My mistress gave me wrinkles in cooking, too. She was the most economical housekeeper I have ever known. She could make delicious cakes with dripping, and the most tasty dishes out of a cold joint.

"You're looking pale to-day," she said to me. "I think you had better run into town this afternoon. Walk in and take the car back. You can do some shopping for me. And when you are dressed come to the sittingroom."

I did, and the kindly soul insisted on my drinking a glass of wine.

"There's your car fare, and don't walk too quickly in."

Then another day, when we had cleaned out a large room, she said to me at dinnertime — we dined at mid-day — "When you've finished the dishes, Emma, lie down for an hour. There's not much to get ready for tea and I do not expect visitors. If anyone comes, I'll open the door."

Of course, one could have lain down anyway, but it made all the difference to receive the consideration which thought of it. It obviated the necessity of jumping up suddenly when steps came near, and of feeling ashamed to be caught idling.

Each morning we discussed the dinner. . . . And Mrs. Bagehot gave me the most detailed instructions, how many potatoes, just how much meat, which jam, even which dish.

"You don't have many visitors, Emma!" she remarked.

I stammered out something. I was ashamed of deceiving her. She was so large-hearted and unsuspicious.

"You may, you know. And if you would like a friend to stay for a while I do not mind. Of course she must help you with your room and the washing and those things, so that you have no more to do."

I almost confessed the deception, but I said that my friends were mostly married.

. . . Over her pastry or cakes, which she usually made herself, except those she let me make — for she said I ought to know how to do everything — she used to discuss the news of the day, ask my opinion about things and generally treat me as an intelligent being. . . . Do not think there was no work to do? There was. She entertained simply, but quite often. She seldom had her spare room untenanted. Often she had more than one guest. But there was a regular round of work to do in the morning, with an hour or two off in the afternoon. There were orders, which were given pleasantly but which were intended to be obeyed. And the house was the cleanest I have ever seen. Every cupboard had its regular cleaning, and the mistress seemed to know every board in her house.

I stayed here till Maggie came back, quite well again. Then when I was leaving, I confessed. Said I really wanted to see what domestic service was like. Mrs. Bagehot was interested.

"It's not really deception," she said, "because you have worked — at least while you've been here, I know. And I suppose there's no harm in trying to find out, if it is not merely idle curiosity. It may do you good in your own home, too, because there is something to learn from everyone. I always think that the average servant girl has the chance of becoming a very good housekeeper, because, if only she is interested, she can pick up so many hints from different mistresses."

"Even from incapable mistresses?" I asked.

"Most certainly; for if only she's honourable, she has the opportunity of taking the responsibility of managing. That's a very useful experience, but girls do not often value it. They presume on it. It is so difficult to get a girl who is in sympathy with her mistress. . . . girls are too apt to take advantage of a weak mistress, that they study their own comfort, and abuse their chances. There are, I know, mistresses who do not give any consideration at all to their servants. Well, of course, they do not deserve good girls; but, in the average household, the girl may be quite happy if she will let herself be so. But — here's my experience — if you want a good servant, give her certain defined duties, give her certain defined time of leisure, and draw the line, not socially of course, but so that she may recognise that in the house you are mistress and she must do the work that you appoint to be done. Don't leave things to her discretion. Tell her what you want done. Then see that she does it. Never get into the habit of letting her choose her work. That's fatal. Let her respect you, and respect her yourself.". . .

But again; I see nothing demeaning in working for another woman. As to the effect on the constitution, which, by the way, includes the temper, the domestic life far and away outshines that in factories and offices, where masters are often many. Of course there are bad mistresses; but then there are bad servants; and the number of good, kind women is larger than we sometimes think.

CHAPTER FOUR

A hanging and a hangman

1911: *NZ Truth* campaigns against the hanging of a Māori teenager for a murder, and exposes the identity of the hangman.

The early 1900s were times of optimism in New Zealand. After the civil wars of the 1860s and the economic depression of the 1880s and '90s, things were at last looking up. The economy was surging, buoyed by wool and meat exports to Britain. Immigrants were pouring in, lured by the promise of plentiful jobs, good food and land for all. Even the 'native question' seemed to be solved, or at least quieted. Premier Richard 'King Dick' Seddon's claim that New Zealand was 'God's own' country seemed to have some truth.

But in 1905, a man stepped off the boat from Sydney with a less benign view. John Norton, a hard-drinking, foul-mouthed newspaper proprietor, had a plan to show New Zealand a kind of journalism it had never seen before. Norton was the owner of *Truth*, a Sydney paper that relished raking muck and scandal, and crusading against the rich and powerful. He was a master of what historian Redmer Yska has called the 'pungent populism' then making fortunes for William Randolph Hearst in the US and Alfred Harmsworth in Britain, as mass education and urbanisation created a ready market for their mass, cheap newspapers (Yska, 2010).

Norton's *NZ Truth* printed its first copies in June 1905. Aimed squarely at the working class, and with a crew of Sydney-trained reporters, it began a series of crusades on social issues, mixed with lewd coverage of trials and city gossip (Yska, 2010). Within three years, what Yska calls its 'carefully balanced blend of parochialism, sensationalism and anti-establishment crusading' had it crowing that it was the top-selling paper in the Dominion (Yska, 2010).

Like many papers at the time, it was viciously racist, especially against

Chinese and African people. Māori, though, after the upheavals of the Land Wars, seemed to have earned special status as 'brown Europeans'. With Māori armed resistance crushed, and the Treaty of Waitangi mouldering away in a government basement, Māori culture was now safe for commercial consumption; there was a popular interest in depictions of Māori culture, such as the portraits of C. F. Goldie. *Truth*, in its usual exaggerated way, was soon to exemplify this trend, with a campaign that for once justified all the formidable resources of maudlin sensationalism it could bring to bear.

Tahi Kaka was 17 years old when he was arrested and charged with the killing of a gumdigger, John Freeman. He confessed, was found guilty of murder and was sentenced to hang. *Truth* took up the story, and worked hard to cast doubt on the safety of the conviction. Its campaign ran over three weeks in the winter of 1911. Much was made by commentators unsympathetic to Kaka of his supposedly callous, unremorseful demeanour at his trial. As *Truth* found out, that was most likely because his English was so poor he could barely understand what was going on. It also attacked the verdict of murder, when the evidence clearly suggested, due to a lack of intent, that the charge should have been manslaughter. It was undoubtedly echoing wider public concern, as the Bishop of Auckland had raised similar disquiet (*NZ Truth*, 1911).

Truth's campaign barely had time to get going before the law took its course, and Kaka was dead. The paper then turned its attention to the state's executioner, and set out the careless, undignified manner in which the state had recruited him, much as it would have advertised a rubbish contract. *Truth*'s relentless pursuit of this man, and its destruction of his alibi, may not have saved Kaka's life, but it did make it harder for the hangman to do his next job. Such was the odium these stories helped create that eventually the state's killers were forced into the grotesque ritual of wearing sunglasses and raincoats on the scaffold to try to keep their identities secret. With the help of a later, equally outraged *Truth* (see Chapter 8 on Albert Black), Tahi Kaka's last wish eventually came true.

The excerpts printed here include *Truth*'s attempt to show the real reasons for Kaka's demeanour at the trial, an examination of the flaws in the Crown case, an account of Kaka's last hours, and part of the account of the search for the hangman.

NZ Truth. (1911, June 11). Shall Kaka Die? Mercy for a misguided Maori murderer [Editorial]. *NZ Truth*.

Yska, R. (2010). *The rise and fall of the people's paper*. Nelson: Craig Potton.

TAHI KAKA'S CASE
What Lawyer Hackett Says

NZ *Truth*, 17 June 1911

"Truth's" Auckland correspondent writes:—

On Tuesday the condemned boy was visited by Lawyer Hackett, who defended him at the Supreme Court. To a "Truth" representative, subsequently, Mr Hackett gave a very dismal picture of the condemned cell, which was in pitch darkness, only relieved by a guttering candle. The hapless youth was lying on a rude couch, utterly dejected: "He looked haggard and very ill," said Mr Hackett, "and my personal feelings were so keenly touched that I simply could not stay any length of time in that awful cell of misery. The boy spoke with difficulty, and a sob was in his voice. He was suffering terribly. His brother, who has been ill in the hospital, yesterday paid Tahi Kaka a brief visit, and the meeting was a very painful one."

Mr Hackett went on to say that from his opportunities of close observation both before and after the trial, he was quite positive most unfair statements were being circulated as to the boy's callousness. Since the sentence of the court was imposed upon him, the condemned prisoner had changed very much in appearance, said his counsel, his face bearing every trace of acute mental suffering, while the prison records show he scarcely gets any sleep, and takes very little food. In conclusion Mr Hackett said, "I felt strongly tempted to tell the boy of the movement in favour of a reprieve, but it seemed to me that it would be cruel to buoy his hopes until some tangible result came in view. But no man who could have seen Kaka as I saw him could doubt for a moment that he is in the very depth of despair, suffering most terribly, and far from callous as to the fate before him."

Jack Kaka has given a short sketch of his unfortunate brother's career. He says Tahi lived with his father in a bush settlement at Tauhoro for the first 13 years of his life, working in the bush with his father. His father believed in the Bible, but did not like the churches, and he never sent his children to school. When he left home, Tahi could not even speak English. He went to a shop-keeper at Kawa Kawa, who sheltered him for some days, but told him he would be no use about the shop till he could speak English. Then he went to the Hukerenui Hotel, and worked there for some time. He afterwards worked in the bush, and for farmers in the Whakapara district. Tahi, said Jack Kaka, had never been to school, and he picked up what English he knew after leaving home. He could not write English, and could not write even good Maori.

No doubt Kaka's stoical attitude throughout his trial was the outcome of a mind that could only partly grasp the nature of the proceedings, and should not have been so readily ascribed to callousness and indifference, and it is doubtless now equally true that the gallows have for the young Maori boy just as indescribable horror as it has to other mortals.

THE KILLING OF KAKA

NZ Truth, 24 June 1911

"Poor, reckless, rude, low-born, untaught;
    Bewildered and alone."
These two lines would make a fitting epitaph to inscribe over the
dishonoured and nameless grave of [Tahi] Kaka, the hapless Maori lad, who
was on Wednesday last strangled to death by order of the Executive Council.
Surely this was a despicable way for New Zealanders to signalise their LOYALTY
TO A CHRISTIAN KING on the very eve of his Coronation. Tahi Kaka expiated
his crime on the gallows, but will human-hearted New Zealanders condone
the act of the members of their Executive Council in disregarding the strong
recommendation to mercy of the "twelve good men and true" by whom the
untutored and semi-savage Maori boy was tried, and also the thousands in all
parts of the Dominion who appealed in vain for a reprieve? "Truth" thinks not.

Be it remembered at the outset that this Tahi Kaka would never have been
in custody, he would never have been tried for the murder of John Freeman, and
he would never have been found guilty of the crime for which he has received
capital punishment, but for his own voluntary admissions. His defence at the
trial was that an eccentric man had, as the result of an altercation, thrown a
[gum]-digger's spear at him, and then violently attacked him and threw him to
the ground, where a desperate struggle ensued. This, the boy frankly admitted in
the witness-box, so frightened him that he became excited, and, freeing himself,
assailed his adversary with a broom-stick in self-defence.

When he saw that his heavy blows had killed Freeman, Kaka said, "I first
cried for my dead mate and I then got afraid. I wanted to run away, but didn't
know where to go. I had no money. I then thought of Freeman's money and
took it from his pocket." When asked by his lawyer why he did not go and tell
someone what had happened, the boy replied, quite innocently "Because I was
frightened, THEY WOULD NOT BELIEVE ME." This practically was the sum
total of Tahi Kaka's defence, and it is a remarkable and incontrovertible fact
that the evidence of the prosecution did not contain a single line to disprove
this, except by introducing conjectures of various witnesses. There can be no
shadow of doubt in the mind of any unbiased man or woman who carefully
read the evidence that there remained a reasonable doubt in favour of Kaka's
sworn statement that he killed John Freeman in self-defence. The Maori boy was
entitled by every canon of English justice and British fair play to the benefit of
that doubt.

It is indeed hard to conceive what influenced the Executive Council to
over-ride the jury's strong recommendation to mercy, and confirm the death
sentence. We learn from the most trustworthy source that the Executive
Council received an official report which actually decided the fate of young
Kaka. That report is stated to have emphasised the fact that when Freeman's
body was discovered, the skull WAS DETACHED FROM THE TRUNK and lay

several feet away. The suggestion was actually made to the Executive that the head was slashed off with the spade Freeman was carrying. It was further suggested that the hole at the back of the murdered man's skull was the result of a blow with the back of an axe. The implements were sent to Wellington so as to explain the feasibility of this theory. It is not, of course, difficult to conceive that if this terrible theory once became fixed in the mind of anyone — even an enlightened member of the Executive Council — it would prejudice him coming to a decision. "Truth" has every reason to believe that this theory was so forcibly advanced that it sealed Tahi Kaka's fate.

The appalling injustice of the Executive Council admitting such a suggestion to sway them is revolting to anyone with a sense of justice, because, be it understood, even if the theory could have been substantiated even by circumstantial evidence, it should never have been introduced. The Executive Council is not empowered to re-hear, re-try, and re-sentence any man. Its duty in this case was to have simply considered the jury's recommendation to mercy on the depositions taken at the trial. Anything beyond that in the way of evidence or suggestion should never for a moment have been allowed to enter into consideration. At the trial it was not suggested by the Crown that Freeman's head was decapitated by force; in fact, the inference was that in the course of decomposition, which was very far advanced, THE HEAD HAD BECOME DISCONNECTED and rolled down the steep slope. The evidence of the post mortem examination, which was very exhaustive, never suggested, for a moment, that any force had been used to sever the head from the trunk. If it had been slashed off with a spade there would have been unmistakeable indications. Therefore, this theory, which was spread about broadcast while the petition for the reprieve was being signed, was absolutely without a foundation in fact.

. . .

One wonders, if the order had been reversed, and the murderer had been a white boy instead of a friendless Maori lad, what would have been the result? Would the recommendation from the jury have been ignored? Would the Auckland daily press have maintained such a cowardly silence in their editorial columns? No. It was time to make an example of someone, and KAKA WAS THE MOST CONVENIENT SUBJECT.

A lot of silly talk has gone round about the alleged racial feeling and colour prejudice in New Zealand. The exponents of this new doctrine point to South Africa, where the commutation of death sentences on blacks for brutal assaults on white women and children has led to grave scandals. The cases are not parallel. In South Africa Kaffirs and half-breeds out-number the whites. Most of them are brutal, debased, and a ruffianly lot. Maoris are not. In fact, the white population of this Dominion includes far more men who could reasonably be classed with the South African Kaffirs than could be found amongst the Maoris. Maori custom, in regard to sexual relationship, is lax and illegal when compared with European standards, but one does not hear of unprovoked attacks by Maoris upon the wives or daughters of European settlers in the back blocks, who have often to live with Maoris as their only neighbours. Nearly all the human beasts who are dragged into our courts for offences of this kind are whites. The argument that it is necessary to hang Kaka as an object lesson to his fellows, warning them that they must keep in their place, and thus avert a serious menace to the lives of settlers in lonely districts, is ridiculous nonsense. The plea is as weak as most of the others advanced by those whose morbid and inhuman wishes would no doubt be gratified when the bolt would be drawn at Mount Eden on Wednesday morning and Tahi Kaka was launched into eternity, where, at least, he cannot receive less mercy than he did from the enlightened Executive Council.

. . .

On Tuesday night Kaka was visited by Bishop Crossly and two chaplains, and after they left he sobbed for some time. Shortly before one o'clock in the morning he fell into a restless sleep and did not awake until just on six o'clock. He refused breakfast or any stimulants, and again spent some time with his spiritual advisers (Rev Hawkins, the Maori Missioner, and Rev Budd, the prison chaplain).

. . .

A few minutes before eight the big bell of the gaol started to toll, and the sheriff, gaol officials, chaplains, and newspaper representatives stood in the corridor outside the condemned cell, while Hangman Sharp entered. Kaka's arms were quickly pinioned to his side by straps, and while this was being done, the hapless boy turned to the warders and remarked in a steady voice: "Good-bye, I'm pukaru now." Just on the tick of eight o'clock the cell door opened, and the party formed a grim procession to the place of execution, some twenty paces away. The gallows were erected in the court yard, and stood 15ft from the ground with 83 steps, and the rope, ready noosed, hung in position over the trap-door. Sheriff Thomas and Gaoler Pointon led the way, then came Surgeon Murray, then the Revs. Budd and Hawkins in clerical robes. Next came Tahi Kaka, walking firmly and without assistance from the warders. The hangman, who followed in the rear of the condemned boy, wore white trousers and blue cotton shirt open at the throat. Kaka created a truly imposing figure as he walked slowly, but unflinchingly, to his doom.

. . .

On reaching the platform Kaka immediately stepped on to the fatal trap-door and glanced up at the gruesome noose to see if he was in a straight line.

The Rev. Hawkins then concluded the burial service in Maori, while the condemned boy glanced down at the prayer book he held in his hand, opened at an illustration of the Crucifixion. This finished, the hangman stooped to pinion the prisoner's ankles, and while this was being done the boy glanced down and remarked, in quite a casual tone, "You pretty smart at your work." Then the chaplain started to read the Lord's Prayer in Maori, and Kaka joined in repeating the words softly, but quite distinctly.

When this was ended, Sheriff Thomas asked: "Is there anything you wish to say?" The boy, without a sign of emotion, looked up and said, in a firm and unquivering tone, "Yes; I hope I will be the last man hung, that is all."

The hangman then stepped forward to pull the white death mask over the boy's head, and while this was being done Kaka was noticed to straighten himself up and stand like a rock ready to meet his terrible doom. Just as the mask was being adjusted the boy was heard to murmur, "Haere Ra," the Maori phrase for farewell — not an exultant "Hooray," as reported by the daily press. Another moment and the lever was pulled, and Tahi Kaka swung to eternity.

. . .

After the execution the chaplains spoke feelingly of the magnificent behaviour of Kaka during the whole time he lay in prison awaiting his awful sentence. They protested most vigorously against the suggestion that the boy was callous and unfeeling.

The body after hanging for an hour was cut down, and an inquest held. The gaol surgeon declared the cause of death was dislocation of the vertebrae, and that death was instantaneous.

A verdict was returned accordingly.

Editor's note

Truth spent the next two weeks trying to find out who the hangman was. On 1 July it published an interview with a Wellington bricklayer, Steven Smart, who denied being the hangman. After getting testimony from a shopkeeper who said Smart had bragged of his work, *Truth* went back again to Smart's cottage in Thorndon.

THE NEW HANGMAN
NZ Truth, 8 July 1911

Further inquiries in municipal circles made since [the] last issue of our Northern edition, have elicited the fact that Steven John Smart, while in the Wellington Corporation's employ as a bricklayer, applied for two or three days' leave of absence to visit a sick uncle at New Plymouth, and such leave was granted. Ten days elapsed before he returned, such absence covering the date on which Kaka was executed in Auckland. Meantime it was freely rumoured that Smart had gone to Auckland to carry out the execution, and had actually done so. Some of his fellow employees state that he had made no secret of his intention, and a pretty general feeling of resentment was aroused. On his return, in view of what was current, Smart was dismissed from the Corporation's employ in consequence of his having overstayed his leave without reasonable excuse.

The matter cropped incidentally before a committee of the City Council, when one councillor twitted the City Engineer with having a hangman in his employ, but that official said he had not; "Well, you had," PURSUED THE PERSISTENT COUNCILLOR, to which the City Engineer replied that he was no longer in the Corporation's employ. Smart's name was not actually mentioned during this colloquy, but there is no doubt to whom the allusion was made, and it instanced the general feeling about the matter.

Smart's statement to our representative that he was not dismissed, but left of his own accord in consequence of unpleasantness, is, we are authorised to state, absolutely untrue. Had he remained in the Corporation's employ, the discontent would probably have resulted in serious trouble, and his unauthorised absence furnished a valid reason for his dismissal.

Our representative called upon Mr C.B. Jordan, acting Under-Secretary for Justice, and asked if he would disclose the name of Kaka's executioner, but that gentleman said that beyond issuing instructions that a suitable man be engaged, he really had not interested himself in the man's identity. Mr Jordan said he personally did not know the man's name, and could not say whether his name was Sharp or Smart or otherwise.

. . .

Consequent upon the disclosure of the above information, our representative again sallied forth, to No. 10 St. Mary-street [in Thorndon, Wellington], and this time was successful in seeing Smart. Our representative was ushered into a back room. . . . Confronted with the information in the possession of "Truth," Smart admitted that his first statement to our representative was correct "barring going to New Plymouth."

"Didn't you go there at all?" queried the pressman.

"No, I didn't," was the immediate reply.

"Then, wasn't the letter of June 13 genuine? Was it only a blind?"

"Yes, it was genuine, but I never received it. After my application of June 12, I went straight to Auckland, without waiting for a reply. The answer was received and opened by my brother-in-law."

"Then how did you get this job? Did you see the sheriff?" — "No."

"You surely must have seen someone. Surely you called upon the sheriff, didn't you?"

"Yes, I did see the sheriff."

"And secured the job?"

"Yes. I will leave it at that. I GOT THE JOB. I prefer to say no more. I have a wife and four children to keep, and I have to consider them."

Our representative saw a dear little chubby-faced child of four or five on the premises, and she seemed anxious to display her "new frock" to our representative, to whom Smart explained that she was his eldest hopeful.

Stephen John Smart justifies his position by the old Mosaic law: "Thine eye shall not pity, but life shall go for life, eye for eye, tooth for tooth, hand for hand, foot for foot." — Deut. xix., 21.

"Truth" understands there were thirteen applications for the job, so it will be seen Steve Smart was lucky to get it.

Smart openly states that should another opportunity offer he will not hesitate to apply for the hangman's job.

CHAPTER FIVE

Field Punishment No. 1

1918: *NZ Truth* queries the brutal treatment of New Zealand soldiers by crucifixion.

The First World War remains New Zealand's greatest man-made disaster. One in ten New Zealanders (100,000) went to the war; of those, a horrifying 18,500 were killed — a toll believed to be the highest per capita loss of any combat nation. Many simply disappeared, their bodies blown to mist by high explosive or lost in the bottomless mud of the Western Front.

As the war dragged on, and casualty lists mounted, it became harder to get volunteers. In 1916, Labour Party leaders were jailed for sedition for opposing the introduction of conscription. By 1917, writes *Truth* historian Redmer Yska, there were 200 conscientious objectors detained, many at Wanganui, and rumours were circulating about beatings and forced marches (Yska, 2010). Worse, 14 objectors were sent to the front and subjected to the barbaric 'Field Punishment No. 1': strapped into a crucifixion position for long periods on a gun carriage, sometimes within range of enemy shellfire.

One of these was Archibald Baxter, who was later to become famous as the author of the anti-war tract *We Will Not Cease* (A. Baxter, 1968). It was hard for newspapers to get serious criticism of the conduct of the war past wartime censorship, but *Truth* began a low-level campaign. It managed to get some general articles, which questioned crucifixion as a punishment, past the censor. Then it took up the case of Baxter and others. In the context of the all-pervading censorship then in place, the publication of these letters, and the account of the heated exchange that Baxter's supporters had with the Minister of Defence, Sir James Allen, shows a determination to prise back the veil of official secrecy about treatment of the conscientious objectors that is worthy of the term investigative journalism. Yska argues that Baxter's case helped to create a wave of sympathy for the 'Conchies' that led to much more sympathetic treatment in the next war (Yska, 2010). One reader, Millicent Brown (the daughter of the University of Canterbury's distinguished founding professor Macmillan Brown), was so moved after reading Baxter's letter that she eventually married him (M. Baxter, 1981). The couple settled on a farm near Dunedin, and remained active in the peace movement. *We Will Not Cease* was written during a trip to London to address a war resisters' conference.

Baxter's quiet influence can be seen in the trajectory of his sons. The elder, Terence, followed his father's lead and was jailed for conscientious objection in the Second World War. Their younger son, James Keir, was to become arguably New Zealand's best-known poet. Archibald Baxter's biographer, David Grant, quotes James K. Baxter's poem 'To My Father' to illustrate the character of the man who became a model for conscientious objectors worldwide:

> . . . *I have loved*
> *You more than my own good, because you stand*
> *For country pride and gentleness, engraved*
> *In forehead lines, veins swollen on the hand;*
> *Also, behind slow speech and quiet eye*
> *The rock of passionate integrity. (Grant, 1996).*

Baxter, A. (1968). *We will not cease*. Christchurch: Caxton.

Baxter, M. (1981). *The memoirs of Millicent Baxter*. Whatamongo Bay: Cape Catley.

Grant, D. (1996). *Baxter, Archibald McColl Learmond*, from the Dictionary of New Zealand Biography. Retrieved from Te Ara — the Encyclopedia of New Zealand. http://www.teara.govt.nz/en/biographies/3b19/baxter-archibald-mccoll-learmond

Yska, R. (2010). *The rise and fall of the people's paper*. Nelson: Craig Potton.

BAXTER'S BREAKDOWN
Neural Condition Causing Anxiety
NZ Truth, 29 June 1918

Dear "Truth," — I sincerely hope that you will be able to print this letter and enclosed communications. The subject is that of Archibald Baxter, listed by the authorities as a religious objector. Sent away with reinforcements in July last, along with 13 others; and treated continually since then simply as a disobedient soldier, because our policy with regard to conscientious objectors does not recognise the claims of conscience except in the case of Quakers, Christadelphians and Seventh Day Adventists. In consequence, Archibald Baxter has been punished so often for refusing to do what his conscience forbade him to do, that he has broken down in brain as well as body. His last letter to his parents, and the subsequent communication from Base Records office here, copies of which I enclose, will put the whole thing before your readers far better than any further words of mine — Yours, etc., B. E. BAUGHAN. Sumner, Christchurch.

Copy of Archibald Baxter's letter:

Somewhere in France, March 5, 1918.

My Dear Father and Mother, — I have just time to send you this brief note. I am being sent up to the lines to-morrow. I have not heard where Jack and Sandy (his brothers) are. As far as military service goes, I am in the same mind as ever. It is impossible for me to serve in the Army. I would a thousand times rather be put to death, and I am sure you all believe that the stand I take is right. I have never told you since I left N.Z. of the things I have passed through, for I knew now it would hurt you. I only tell you now so that if anything happens to me you will know. I have suffered to the limit of my endurance, but I will never in my sane senses surrender to the evil power that has fixed its roots like a cancer on the world. I have been treated as a soldier who disobeys (Number 1 Field Punishment). That is hard enough at this time of the year, but what made it worse for me was that I was bound to refuse to do military work even as a prisoner. It is not possible for me to tell in words what I have suffered, but you will be glad to know that I have met a great many men who have shown me the greatest kindness. I know that your prayers for me are not in vain. I will pray for you all to the last. It is all I can do for you now. If you hear that I have served in the Army, or that I have taken my own life, do not believe that I did it in my sound mind, no matter what anyone says. I never will. We are all standing together, although we are not far apart. I have not much more time, but I will write again as soon as I can. — Your loving son, ARCHIE BAXTER. (Passed by Censor.)

Copy.

Base Records Branch N.Z. Military Forces.

Wellington, May 14, 18.

Mr. John Baxter, Brighton, Dunedin.

Dear Sir, — Re 47814 Pte. Archibald MoL. Baxter, I have to advise that a cablegram has been received from overseas, stating that the above-named soldier was admitted to Hospital [in the] United Kingdom on May 5, and his mental condition was causing anxiety. I sincerely trust that with care, rest and attention, Private Baxter will soon be restored to his normal health. — Yours faithfully, B. A. MORRIS. Chief Clerk.

Inquiries of the Defence Department show that Archibald [McColl] Learmond Baxter is one of the 14 men embarked last July. He is not "listed by the authorities as a religious objector." He appealed on religious grounds, but, though notified of the hearing, did not take the trouble to attend and place his case before the Board. His appeal was consequently dismissed, and he was sent into camp, where he refused to obey orders. This man cannot be classed as a "conscientious objector" who has failed to satisfy the Board that he is a "religious objector" within the statute, because he did not attempt to satisfy the Board; nothing remains for him but to obey the law. He is, as a matter of fact, listed by the authorities as a "defiant objector."

In view of an exaggerated impression as to the severity of No. 1 Field Punishment we understand that the Defence Department intends to issue an official statement on the subject claiming that the punishment cannot be classed as brutal.

The Minister Interviewed Allegations Concerning "Crucifixion." (From "Truth's" Dunedin Rep.)

NZ *Truth*, 6 July 1918

While at Dunedin Sir James Allen, Minister of Defence, received two deputations concerning the treatment of the conscientious objectors.

Mr. C. E. Statham, M.P., introduced the first deputation to the Minister, which consisted of Mr. P. C. Triggs (president) and Messrs. J. D. Smith and M. Silverstone (vice-presidents), and Mr. L. F. Evans (secretary) — all of the Otago Labour Council. The deputation demanded (1) that an open inquiry be held concerning the treatment of conscientious objectors imprisoned at Wanganui; (2) that the men concerned shall have the right to be represented by counsel; and (3) that no restrictions shall be placed in the way of the men calling witnesses.

Mr. Triggs said that the inquiry should be as open as possible to the public in every way. They considered that under no circumstances whatever should men be subjected to the very BARBAROUS TREATMENT ALLEGED. The mind of the public had become very unsettled on the matter, and they looked for an open inquiry — not a secret one.

. . .

Women's International League

On Friday evening last a deputation from the above body (Dunedin branch) was introduced to Sir James Allen by Mr. Sidey, M.P. The speakers were Miss McCarthy (president of the League), Mrs. Harland, Mrs. Baxter, Mrs. Hiett, and Mrs. Randall. Mrs. Hiett spoke on behalf of the parents, and Mrs. Randall regarding the deported fourteen.

. . .

Mrs. Hiett said she represented the parents — two of whom were present — of conscientious objectors. These men had all been honourable and dutiful citizens, and the deputation wished the men to be returned to New Zealand, and an inquiry held into the cruelty that had been inflicted on them; if not, that the parents should have communication with them. Mrs. Harland, one of the parents, had interviewed you six months ago, and asked for information about her son, and what he was doing. You promised, but so far nothing has been done, and she has had no information about him.

Mrs. Randall read a letter from a soldier describing what he saw the conscientious objectors suffer, and detailing the methods of "crucifixion." Archie Baxter had been tortured. Would the Minister do everything in his power to get the wrongs righted and see that such atrocities would not occur again? The deputation would like to know if other men had been deported recently?

The Minister: No.

Mrs. Randall, continuing, said that the "crucifixion" atrocity was too cruel for the Hun to adopt.

The Minister: The problem of the conscientious objector is a very serious and difficult one. He had to administer the law as made by the representatives of the people, and that he had tried to do so to the best of his ability. The deputation said that Mrs. Harland had not heard from her son. As promised, he had some time ago communicated with the authorities in the United Kingdom, and asked for a report about every one of the conscientious objectors who were deported, and the report, which was published in the papers, gave an account of what was known of each of the men.

. . . "I am glad to hear that there was no such thing as 'crucifixion' now in the New Zealand Army," said Sir James, "and I would like the public to know it, because it has been circulated by those opposed to the Military Service Act that 'crucifixion' is still going on. I want the public to understand that this word 'crucifixion' is a misnomer."

Miss McCarthy: You should request the authorities at Home to abolish that form of punishment. It drives men insane. Archie Baxter was crucified.

A Lady: If that's not punishment, what is it?

The Minister: No; it is the tying up of a man to a gun wheel.

A Lady: How shockingly cruel and un-British.

The Minister: It is cruel to send a man to the trenches.

A Lady: And it is unjust to inflict cruelty, and an injustice to suffer it.

The Minister said that if men were religious objectors they had an opportunity to escape service altogether, while if they were conscientious objectors they had the right to object to combatant work and to do non-combatant work. He knew very well what some of the conscientious objectors were, "I have seen them individually, and ASKED THEM ABOUT THEIR CONSCIENCE, and I have come to the conclusion that 60 or 70 per cent of them are defiant shirkers trying to escape service under the plea of conscience. I asked one man on what [he] built up his conscience and if he believed in the Bible. 'No,' he said. Do you believe in anything? 'No,' he said, 'nothing in particular.' What have you read to make your conscience what it is? and his answer was: 'I've read what I thought suited me.' I said on what basis is your conscience built up? and he had nothing to say."

What have you to say to that? asked the Minister.

A Lady: That is not Archie Baxter's case. The man you so addressed may not have been gifted enough to express himself suitably. Archie Baxter was a religious objector, and how did you treat him?

Another Lady: Deportation, crucifixion, then the lunatic asylum.

The Minister: I have sent a cablegram to London to inquire about Baxter's case, and I hope to have a reply in two or three days. Statements have been made as to what happened [to] Baxter in England and France, but it was hard to prove them. I advise the deputation to await the reply to my cablegram. Many men who went to the front suffered mentally afterwards.

The Minister then had a private interview with Mrs. Baxter, who, it is understood, brought under the Minister's notice the letters concerning Baxter, copies of which were published in "Truth's" last issue.

CHAPTER SIX

Rainbow visions

1937, *The New Zealand Observer*: Robin Hyde investigates the rights of Ngāti Whātua to Bastion Point.

Visitors arriving at Auckland by sea, who motor up the Rangitoto Channel and then turn to head towards the city's business district, pass, on their left, a series of imposing bluffs. One of the most prominent is named Bastion Point or, to give it its original name, Takaparawhau. For centuries, it guarded the gateway to Auckland for the native Māori inhabitants, Ngāti Whātua Ōrākei.

It has been a bastion in other ways, too. For it was here, for 507 days in 1977 and 1978, that Ngāti Whātua made a final stand to stop the last of their land being taken. Starting as a sit-in protest at a government plan to sell their ancestral seat to property developers, it became a bitter, and at times violent, protest at the alienation of all Māori from their land. It ended, at dawn on 25 May 1978, when 800 police and army personnel began pulling down tents and dragging protesters to waiting vans, in full view of television cameras from around the world. The scenes were disturbing to many New Zealanders. Many have described it as a watershed moment. Within a few years, a process was begun of addressing Māori claims to their land, fisheries and other property; the Bastion Point claim was the first to be heard under this process.

Some of the seeds of this process were sown 40 years earlier. In 1937, a young woman reporter began the first serious journalistic investigation into the Māori claims to Bastion Point. Robin Hyde would not be the last reporter to set foot on the point, but she was one of the most original, effective and determined. Her stories helped galvanise supporters of Ngāti Whātua, and were a direct forerunner of the 1977–78 protest.

Hyde's real name was Iris Wilkinson. Born in South Africa, to an English father and an Australian mother, she'd grown up in Wellington in a house of committed socialists. Always ready to argue a point, with a flair for writing, burning energy and a passion for the underdog, she soon found her way to journalism. She started, still in her teens, at *The Dominion* newspaper, then worked her way around many others. As Gillian Boddy and Jacqueline Matthews note in their superb introduction to their collection of her journalism, Hyde was a natural journalist, her incredible energy turning out copy on political reporting, book reviews, domestic advice and colourful undercover forays (Boddy & Matthews, 1991). One, exposing charlatans such as the growing fashion for the occult, was headlined 'Wicked witches weave wily spells'. By the age of 24 she had given birth to two sons out of wedlock, the first of whom had died (she later retrieved his name, Robin Hyde, for use as her pen-name); the second was fostered out. By 1930 she was in Auckland, an editor at the weekly pictorial *The New Zealand Observer*, working feverishly to report on the plight of the poor as the Great Depression deepened. By 1933, aged just 27, Hyde was exhausted. She became a voluntary patient at Auckland Mental Hospital. Over the next four years she began to recover, finding time to write four novels, and two outstanding collections of poetry that cemented her reputation as one of the country's foremost poets. But she had not forgotten journalism, and it was while a patient that she heard about the plight of a small Māori village at Bastion Point, in the suburb of Ōrākei (Boddy & Matthews, 1991).

The village was nestled above the pretty beach at Okahu Bay, on the point's western edge. Hyde heard that the Auckland City Council planned to demolish the Māori settlement there. The village (papakāinga in Māori) was perched on a few acres, all that remained after the rest of the point had been taken by the government for a military base during the Russian invasion scare of the 1880s. The base had never been built, and the government had given the land to the city council, for a park. However, city fathers, egged on by do-gooder public health officials, claimed that the village, lacking proper sewerage and water, was a health hazard, and wanted to sell it to developers for prime waterfront housing. Hyde, with her well-honed ear for cant, knew that something was up and took up the cause.

Instead of simply interviewing officials, she went and saw for herself, and interviewed the inhabitants. Digging through documents, she found an unpublished report of a Native Land Court hearing, by Judge F. O. V. Acheson, that showed the government had promised Ngāti Whātua that the land would be returned to them when it was no longer needed for defence. Her reporting was unusual for the time; it saw past the stereotypes of the poor uneducated native, and gave the inhabitants a dignity that did much to broaden their support. It incited supporters to petition the country's new socialist Prime Minister, Michael Joseph Savage. He eventually stopped the development (and is buried in a memorial tomb at Takaparawha).

Hyde's Ōrākei stories were the culmination of, and a fitting tribute to, her journalistic career in New Zealand. She left soon after for Europe, travelling via China to report on the Japanese invasion. She made her way to the front line, where despite almost losing an eye in a beating given to her by Japanese soldiers, she sent back reports that helped spur the New Zealand government to send £10,000 worth of medical supplies. From China, Hyde travelled to London, reaching there in late 1938. Just three weeks before the outbreak of war, she was living alone, depressed and in ill-health. Friends in the New Zealand government arranged to bring her home, but the day an embassy official arrived with her documents she was found dead, apparently from an overdose of the amphetamine Benzedrine. Almost a contemporary of that other great female New Zealand writer of the period, Katherine Mansfield, Hyde is remembered today almost entirely for her fiction.

Hyde's reporting on Ōrākei provided a stay of execution for the village, but only a stay. During the Second World War, more of the point was taken by the government for defence, crowding Ngāti Whātua onto a tiny strip of land. Even this was eyed by developers, and in 1951 Auckland City Council evicted the remaining Māori and burnt their houses. In 1977, the government decided that it no longer needed the land it had taken for defence, and proposed a high-income housing development. Two days before bulldozers were due to start work, Ngāti Whātua and supporters occupied the land. International supporters arrived to join the occupation, including US country singer John Denver. Although the protesters were evicted, the development was stopped. Ten years later, a new Labour government began a national conciliation process aimed at restoring rights guaranteed to Māori under the Treaty of Waitangi, signed in 1840. The first claim to be heard by the Waitangi Tribunal under this process was that pertaining to Bastion Point. The tribunal recognised Ngāti Whātua's claim and returned most of the Point to it, along with other land and compensation. In its report, the tribunal quoted extensively from Hyde's newspaper articles, including her phrase 'Rainbow visions' (Boddy & Matthews, 1991).

Boddy, G., & Matthews, J. (1991). *Disputed ground: Robin Hyde, journalist.* Wellington: Victoria University Press.

Who Says the Orakei Maoris Must Go?
Some facts about the 'Mass Kidnapping' – Echo of Native Court Proceedings
New Zealand Observer, 8 July 1937

"Nobody wishes to deal harshly with these people" [a] conclusion reached, and expressed in the dulcet tones of Sir Ernest Davis, after it was announced at the last meeting of the Auckland City Council that the Acting-Minister for Native Affairs, Mr. Langstone, had arrived at his decision — the "73 native adults and 48 children, including 13 Rarotongans," now resident at the native village of Orakei, must go.

"This is my home. Here will I rest forever, for I have desired it." You mayn't recognise the quotation, but it is from the Bible, and to be seen on the grave of an old Maori at Orakei. He may, or may not, have relied upon an appropriate pakeha text. According to the New Zealand Herald, "The owners of two small areas of an acre and an acre and a half respectively declined to sell, and are still in possession. The church and cemetery site of a quarter of an acre was also not alienated. The price paid by the Crown for the 40 acres was about £10,000. As no immediate use was to be made of the property, the natives were allowed to go on living there." Now, though apparently in the interests of a garden suburb and a view, the white residents of Orakei are perfectly willing to hunt the living natives from lands which have been their ancestral right and property for so many years, surely the Maori dead will be allowed to lie in peace. Or will tombstones also clash with the rainbow visions and the town-planning schemes?

If you take a 'bus and go to Orakei (a blue clear curve before Mission Bay and St. Helier's, with hills above and the garden suburb mincing like Agag on those hills), you won't see anything very picturesque. As the reports obtained by Sir Ernest remark, "of 17 dwellings, 13 were shacks and only three really suitable for habitation." On one hand is a clay path through a paddock to the little graveyard, on the other a small, not very ornamental meeting-house, which is kept clean, and does harbour an elderly piano — Orakei's home grown fun, if the young people wish to hold concerts or dances. There is a church, small-size, and behind the paddock (where on the day of my first visit one melancholy Jersey was tethered and lowed her sorrow), the first group of dwellings.

Maoris sit on the verandahs of their wooden houses, which are certainly not going to give any American tourist the thrill Zane Grey got out of his first New Zealand mako.

. . . By risking your shins and your stockings scrambling up a steep hillside, you will come on other Maori houses, much the same, except that some of them are tents instead of shacks, poorly furnished, and with an occasional plot of kumaras or other vegetables. Most of what is said against the Maori dwelling places, as at present constituted, is true enough — except that they are the dwelling places of very decent people, who, given a chance, would probably keep their premises as creditably as anyone could expect, and who have hung on to their long-threatened shacks at Orakei with the courage of despair.

Nia Hira, one of the Orakei leaders, expressed himself with quiet dignity in saying that one could not expect the Maori people to put much heart into their homes, until they knew that these shacks *were* their homes. One comes across minor anomalies. A smiling Maori offers a string of wet schnapper for sale . . . one of the biggest fish businesses in Auckland gives the Orakei Maoris sacks of fish-heads, and these, boiled up, serve as a staple article of diet.

The incidence of notifiable infectious diseases, "including tuberculosis, dysentery and enteric fever" is nearly twice as high at Orakei as anywhere else in Auckland city. On the other hand, the Maoris have said it is impossible for them (their titles to land or dwellings having been under dispute for years), to obtain facilities for proper sanitation, drainage or lighting. They also point out that the old Maori system of drainage wasn't bad of its kind. But every winter, loose metal washed down from the motor-road above their flat blocks up their drainage, such as it is, with results that can be imagined. It is awkward, but the road is not their road, and the motor cars most certainly are not their motor cars.

. . . My knowledge of the Orakei people is very cursory, but nobody who visits them once or twice can come away with the impression that they are so much human driftwood. In the lightless and ill-sanitated shacks are young Maori men and women of excellent education, whose knowledge of English would probably put our knowledge of Maori to shame. Many are probably in very poor circumstances but others have fought to qualify themselves for a civilised way of living. One Maori resident is a qualified nurse, for instance: another, as quiet and pretty an eighteen-year-old girl as you could wish to meet, fully qualified herself at an Auckland college for work as a shorthand typist. Given a little security, and a chance to exercise the racial pride and self-respect which is never dead in the Maori, there is no reason to suppose that the rest of Orakei's young people and children can't do as well.

. . .

The model pa scheme . . . fell through. "The deadlock between the Lands Department and the former native owners prevented anything from being done," says the New Zealand Herald; which does not, however, give particulars of the deadlock.

. . . This proposal of bulk transportation of a community of people, numbering over a hundred, without regard to their will, is the most dictatorial suggestion, and would be the most dangerous precedent, any Government could adopt.

> *The people responsible for the bright idea (it is hard to think that the Hon. F. Langstone thought of it lone-handed), should come out into the open, and say where the Maori must go, why they must go, and at whose bidding they must go.*

This is only the moral aspect of the case — a moral aspect which gives the Orakei Maoris the right to remain, under improved conditions, at Orakei. The legal aspect is an extremely complicated one. The facts can only be given piecemeal. . . .

Last week, the Orakei people held a big korero over their problems. All is silent, so far, about the steps they may take. Of course, the 2½ or 2¼ acres are still the property of individuals among them: but equally, of course, these cannot support a tribe or tribal remnant, and then again, if rates in the garden suburb happened to go up, as is not beyond imagination, how could the Maoris pay them? This is clearly a case for the white man in general, and the Aucklander in particular (Auckland comes into it even more than the Government, for each city knows and should carry its own responsibilities) to do either a really generous or a really contemptible thing. Half-measures would leave a bad taste in the civic mouth — if it has any palate at all. And the geraniums would never grow in that garden suburb. As one Maori woman puts it, "the roots of Orakei go deep."

No More Dancing at Orakei

New Zealand Observer, 19 August 1937

In the Observer, a few weeks back, you may have read the salient points of the Acheson Court Report, 1930, which had never been published before. Still more documents important to the Orakei case are allegedly in the files of the Government departments. Will the last ever be produced? The fate of Orakei may perhaps rest on this.

. . .

But getting back to Orakei — the first little meeting was held up in a Queen Street office, about a week before August 10. . . . Very few Maori people were present at the meeting, for at the earlier gathering it had been said, "Let iron clash only with iron. Let the pakeha settle this with the pakeha." But a living link with Orakei, and representative of one of the leading hapus, Mrs M. Babbington, spoke in thanks. The Rev. Wiremu Panapa mentioned that although people speak of the Orakei Maoris as having received £70,000 for land sales, of this amount £33,000 went to pakeha lessees, and £7,000 to white Government lawyers, leaving roughly £30,000. Remember that Orakei at the time the landsales began was about 690 acres in area. Only 40 acres are now under dispute. Yet when, the other day, I said to a member of the Government, "The trouble is that the Maoris are sitting on £35,000 worth of land," his instant reply was "£100,000 worth." Neither the Crown nor present-day owners can complain.

. . .

For the past several months, Orakei has given up holding any dances. It has its own hall, a piano and young people who loved dancing, but as soon as its lights went on, an undesirable element in the form of white visitors with the usual flasks arrived. Rather than risk any suggestion of rowdyism Orakei dances no more.

What the Orakei Maoris themselves say, according to people, pakeha and Maori, who have worked among them and known them for many years, is simple enough. No other forty acres would be the same as the papakainga at Orakei. Orakei is not only a village, but is dignified as a marae. Their heart is with their land, and they believe that if the Prime Minister and his Government know all the facts, it will be proved the 40 acres was reserved for them.

At least one of these promised reservations is recorded, in deed form, and should be in Government possession, according to Judge Acheson's Court report. Judge Acheson stated that he could himself remember having seen the deed, years ago, but at such a distance of time could not recall its exact terms. The Maori concerned was a notable man of Orakei, Wiremu Watene: two early settlers who remember Wiremu Watene very well say that to the end of his days, Watene protested he had never sold the six acres on the flat. The subject used to excite the old man to passionate oratory, but Watene is gone, his title never confirmed. Another person, very deeply versed in the affairs of Orakei Maoris, told me that what happened was this.

Watene was given definite assurance that the six acres were his for ever, even though he argued with the Crown's purchasing officer that he might be signing away his whole land interests. Some time afterwards, he applied for concreting work to be done on the six acres, and was then informed that by a regrettable misunderstanding, he had sold his whole possessions, after all. He was given a chance to buy back this reservation, but by then he had no money to do so. Such irregularities, or suspicion of irregularities, are not very healthy matters for consideration of a tribe rendered landless against provision of the Native Lands Act. Even what Chief Judge R.N. Jones has to say in his report, given in 1932 after the fiasco of the Native Land Court enquiry presided over by Judge Acheson, is not reassuring:

"As for the promises said to have been made about the papakainga portion, the Court finds that it is unable to report adequately upon them, and it refers to other matters, including suspected irregularities in connection with the part of the officers of the Crown, in connection with such purchase, but it must be remembered that the Judge (Judge Acheson) had only one side before him." (This, after the Crown representative, Mr. Meredith, had withdrawn from Court under instructions from Wellington, taking with him both his documents and his associates, and failing to produce for inspection the files the Native Land Court applied for, seems an odd comment.) "Doubtless, if a wrong had been proved, the Crown would endeavour to rectify it, although its title could not be assailed for that reason."

Put in language less polite, if it could be proved to the satisfaction of a white Appeal Court that any of the purchasing agents for the Crown had talked the Orakei Maoris into a belief that they could sell their other land interests and keep their papakainga, the Crown would apologise and do its best — but the Crown would still be the title-holder. It is interesting to remember that while these landsales were going on at Orakei (the Crown purchasing officer buying on the spot, cheque-book in pocket), Maori petitions from Orakei, asking for investigation of the actual ownership of the land, were lying on the table at Parliament.

. . . Auckland's Mayor, Sir Ernest Davis, "stumped" Orakei before the last municipal elections, and his sympathy drew a solid Maori vote. It was Sir Ernest who communicated the Hon. F. Langstone's decision, "The Maori must go," to the City Council, and though he may have had a tear in his eye, he then saw the removal as a necessary measure.

There are important reasons, however, why the present Government should not receive too much immediate criticism. It is true that their Acting-Minister for Lands made the actual pronouncement, true also that their new garden suburb looks down from Orakei hills, and threatens the papakainga area in the interests of a park and playing-field for white children who will live in the new Orakei houses . . .

But a plan, showing a lovely stretch of green where today the cluster of shacks and the meeting-house occupy the land, was drawn up long before there was a Labour Government — even before Labour carried the slightest weight in Parliamentary opposition. It is lodged at the City Council offices today. I'm not quite sure of its year, but think it was 1912.

Again, the Labour Government was not in power when the land was auctioned off by the Crown; nor yet in 1930, when the Native Land Court of Enquiry with Judge Acheson on the Bench, produced his report. Another Government then held the reins . . .

So much can be said against any argument that the Government is the chief or only villain of the Orakei place. The Government, none the less, is situated right in the middle of a quicksand of ugly rumours about Orakei . . . Firstly, it has been very widely suggested that at the auction of Orakei land sections, three sections at least, were never open to public purchase.

The story (which may be either a misconception or a downright misrepresentation, but which has travelled quite far enough to need contradiction, assuming its untruth), is that private persons, acquiring these sections, disposed of the options to a syndicate of prominent Auckland business men, who have under consideration the building of a large block of residential flats, but who do not intend to exercise their options unless the Maori village, which "spoils the view," is cleared away. Secondly, it has been said as often, and from as many quarters, that a further intention is to procure a licence for this building, if erected, and also to licence a hotel at St. Helier's Bay.

. . .

Since Mr. Savage's return, and the growth of public feeling over Orakei, the attitude not only of the Prime Minister himself, but of other Ministers and Members, has been very open-minded, and there is every reason to hope that the round table conference or confirmation in title of their 40 acres asked for by the Maoris, may be granted. . . .

But a settlement of native houses, restricted to proper numbers and conditions, and owned by Maoris who pay rent, mustn't be held to spoil the view. It would be infinitely worse if what had been Maori land, historic, and bound by the strongest ties to its own people, suddenly grew one of those enormous yellow warts which sprout up here and there in Auckland: and if out of the wart arose a geyser of beer.

CHAPTER 7

To catch a spy

1942: *NZ Truth* defies wartime censorship to expose the fake spy, Sidney Ross, and how he fooled security police into embarking on a hunt for Nazi saboteurs.

The months of early 1942 were a dark time in New Zealand. The war was going badly; the German army had swallowed most of Europe and seemed on the verge of sweeping British forces from the Mediterranean. Then, after the loss of most of its naval assets in Asia to the seemingly invincible Japanese navy, Britain had informed the New Zealand government by secret cable that it could no longer defend New Zealand. Japanese planes were about to bomb Australia, and it seemed only a matter of time before they arrived in Wellington. When invasion is imminent, everyone becomes suspect. So when the Minister of Works, Bob Semple, received a phone call early in 1942 from a man claiming to have knowledge of a Nazi spy ring, it was not surprising that he listened carefully and then alerted the Prime Minister.

The story of how the convicted con-artist Sidney Ross sent the newly formed Security Intelligence Bureau on a wild goose chase has been told many times. Ross was a small-time fraudster who had just finished a sentence at Waikeria Reformatory, in the centre of the North Island. Upon his release, on 28 March 1942, he was given a ticket to Auckland. In his lively account of the hoax, *The Plot to Subvert Wartime New Zealand*, Hugh Price says that Ross scribbled over 'Auckland' on his ticket, and wrote 'Wellington' instead (Price, 2006). It was the first thread in an elaborate web of deceit. Arriving in Wellington, Ross booked into a suite at the plush Hotel Waterloo under a false name, had a bath, then telephoned Semple and spun his yarn.

His timing was superb. By an extraordinary coincidence, the government had just that morning learned that a real Nazi spy ring had been rounded up in Australia. Semple got Ross to retell his story to the Prime Minister, Peter Fraser, who instructed the head of the Security Intelligence Bureau, Major Kenneth Folkes, to follow up. Folkes was an English solicitor sent to New Zealand the year before to set up the new security service. He seemed to swallow the story whole; he gave Ross a fake identity as Captain Calder, and lavished cars, money and expensive hotels on him while he toured the North Island collecting 'information' on saboteurs. Ross was uncovered only when a local policeman noticed the resemblance between 'Captain Calder' and a photo of the con-man Ross in a police bulletin.

If the story had been kept quiet, Folkes might have survived. But *Truth*, with its excellent police sources, got in first. On 29 July 1942, it began printing the story below. When the government's powerful Director of Publicity, J. T. Paul, heard about it, he immediately rang *Truth* editor Brian Connolly. He told Connolly that the article was subversive (and therefore the editor could be fined and jailed), and demanded that printing be stopped and all issues recalled. On the advice of *Truth*'s lawyer, Connolly refused, unless the order was in writing. 'He said he'd get back to me, and I heard no more from him.'

The story was a sensation; Price argues that it provided much-needed comic relief at a dark time. But underneath the laughs at the Keystone Cops incompetence of the Bureau were serious concerns about its secret police-style spying on ordinary citizens. Many in the press also hated Paul, who was prone to use his powers to suppress anything that might embarrass the government, regardless of whether it was a security risk or not. The story can't be said to have led to Folkes' demise directly; Fraser called him a 'misfit' and wanted him out. But with the facts in the public domain, it made it inevitable. Folkes was sent back to England, his organisation was disbanded and its work given to the police. *Truth*'s determination to challenge censorship had a ripple effect: the editor of *The Manawatu Times*, Robert Billens, fined for comparing Paul's media gagging to Nazi Germany, won the case on appeal (Price, 2006).

Price, H. (2006). *The plot to subvert wartime New Zealand.* Wellington: Victoria University Press.

Security Police Badly Hoaxed by Impudent Gaolbird "Capt. Calder" Exposed

NZ Truth, 29 July 1942

THE OUTSPOKEN people of Australia were recently roused to angry comment on the Public Relations Department (an intelligence organisation) whose activities earned an unprecedented public rebuke from no less eminent a judicial authority than Dr. H. V. Evatt, the Attorney-General.

But just what the people of New Zealand are going to think about the Security Intelligence Department, a special body of individuals entrusted with the internal security of the Dominion when they are confronted with the gigantic hoax perpetrated by an ex-gaolbird in recent weeks, should be somebody's business.

Peddling a fantastic story of his discovery of an alleged plot to assassinate two Cabinet Ministers, while an unwilling guest of His Majesty at Waikeria, this ex-convict gained the confidence of the security police and was sent off to Rotorua to live a life of luxury in the thermal regions.

Not until hundreds of pounds of public money had been spent at the instigation of this arch-imposter, was the fantastic official masquerade terminated. Then as the result of the observations of an alert young constable who had committed the rogues' gallery to memory, the civil police, as on other occasions, took a hand and blew wide open the smartest piece of confidence work ever attempted in the Dominion.

Apart from the comic aspects of this monstrous bluff, it has a very serious side. First, the manner in which the security department was so blatantly hoodwinked strongly suggests that it is high time its personnel was subjected to a rigorous overhaul.

Secondly, while such an organisation may be required for the protection of State and Government in wartime, the public are also entitled to protection from the accusations and suggestions made by any dangerous rascal who may succeed in foisting his services upon this department.

Thirdly, the authorities should see that any secret dossier or reports compiled as a result of the Rotorua exploits of this rascally imposter, and which may reflect on or mention the names of innocent people, are instantly destroyed under police supervision.

For some weeks past, the people of Rotorua and district have been seething with the story of the mysterious comings and goings of security intelligence officials. Now that there has been a showdown, they are indignant about the whole thing.

Released from prison at the end of March, this impudent crook was interviewing a Cabinet Minister in Wellington the following day, according to "Truth's" information. As a result of the interview, he was referred to another Minister, whom he told that while he was in prison, German agents had communicated with him and enlisted his services.

Then, obviously, to create greater confidence, the ex-gaolbird told the second Minister of a plot to assassinate him and a colleague. Quite certain that he could be of use to the State if he acted as under-coverman, while working with the phantom enemy agents, he was placing himself at the disposal of the authorities.

The Minister arranged for the ex-convict to be referred to an officer of the security organisation, who swallowed the bait, hook, line and sinker, with the result that the crook became a member of the secret service, vested with all the far-reaching powers that go with membership, notwithstanding the fact that he frankly admitted he had a criminal record.

Given a generous expense allowance, a powerful American car and authority to draw almost unlimited supplies of petrol, the new member of the security organisation installed himself in the Grand Hotel, Rotorua, under the pseudonym of "Captain Calder."

Fortunately for the honour of the Army, this dirty crook was not given a military uniform, or at least did not dare to wear one while bathing under the public gaze.

From time to time, "Captain Calder" was away from Rotorua for considerable periods, and almost as regularly, sent his chief a series of colourful and sensational reports of alleged developments. He reported localities, plans and personages supposedly involved in a complex sabotage and invasion project, and gave highly circumstantial accounts of interviews and talks he had had with several people.

Sucking the bait with avidity, the security organisation were in high feather at the Hollywoodenish activities of their new super-sleuth.

A security police big-wig is reported to have actually flown to Rotorua by special plane on several occasions to discuss progress and plans with the priceless "Captain Calder," who must have been bursting his sides with the way the security big boys were swallowing his "disclosures."

It is even stated that this cool card persuaded his August superiors to take aerial photographs of certain spots. For all the use they were, they might just as well have photographed whaka from the air or tried to photograph the odours that arise from geyserland!

Always a few jumps ahead of his superior, "Captain Calder" lived a life of luxury for over three months, when a young constable unmasked him and promptly reported the matter to his superior.

Inquiries then revealed that the dashing "Captain" who had carved a niche for himself in the secret service of the Dominion, was just a cheap crook.

Finally, the position became so bad that the matter found its way into the hands of the Police Department. Some of the best detective officers in the Dominion, comprising Senior-Detectives A. M. Harding, P. J. Nalder and P. Doyle (Wellington) and Senior-Detective J. Walsh (Auckland), directed by the ablest criminal investigator the N.Z. police force has produced in the last quarter century, Superintendent James Cummings, went to Rotorua to unravel the gigantic plot discovered by "Captain Calder."

Two days later, they returned to their respective stations, having proved conclusively that the arch-plotter was "Captain Calder" himself, and that his "startling discoveries" were just the product of a fertile mind bent on making some easy cash without working for it.

Needless to say, "Captain Calder" has been relieved of his appointment after having a wonderful time at the expense of the Dominion's war effort, and two houses costing a pretty penny, which were established as a part of the scheme of things in "Calder's" head, were closed down.

It is conceivable that the two hard-headed Ministers were in no frame of mind to toy with "Calder's" disclosure of plans for their assassination, and handed him over to someone else in order to ascertain whether he was a lunatic, liar or genuine.

Had he just been released from an internment camp where the inmates are openly hostile, he *might* have learned something of a wild-cat scheme to shoot persons representing authority that *might* have been worth investigating.

Even if "Captain Calder" succeeded in hoodwinking the security officials with highly circumstantial tales of plans for assassinations he would have been quickly run to earth had those most intimately concerned had a little more faith in responsible police officers who have spent a lifetime rounding up and sorting out crooks of "Calder's" ilk; and who (amongst the real top-notchers at any rate) will, in "Truth's" opinion, hold their own with the best in the Empire, in spite of a cumbersome system and poor facilities and equipment.

This incident emphasises the apparent need for an investigation and overhaul, where necessary, of the security organisation before there is a repetition of these blunders and the attendant orgy of jitterbug spending.

But apart from all this, there is a serious danger that innocent people (as they turned out to be in this case) may suffer appalling damage and be the victims of a grave miscarriage of justice, when the security organisation, fooled up to the hilt by a crook, employs him on work which should be done by a man of the highest personal integrity.

It will be iniquitous if any secret dossiers compiled from the information supplied by "Calder" are not destroyed forthwith, because the merest suggestion that a person has been under the surveillance of the security police may damn him in the eyes of his fellow citizens.

After this latest display of melodramatic fatuity, if the authorities still feel that it is necessary to maintain a security organisation separate from the Police Department, which has earned the respect of the community over a long period of years, it is to be hoped that greater use will be made of men with sound experience in these matters. What are required are New Zealanders with solid commonsense and alert minds, who will not fall for the fantastic humbug of the first glib-tongued imposter who comes along with a story that even a Hollywood scenario writer would turn his nose up at.

CHAPTER EIGHT

The last bastion of Victorian cruelty

1955: *NZ Truth* covers the hanging of Albert Black and encourages the abolition of the death penalty.

Truth, that bastard child of a back-alley printshop in turn-of-the-century Wellington, had grown up. No longer an urchin troublemaker scrounging the fringes of the establishment press for a few crumbs of news to feed its rag-tag readership of misfits and outcasts, by the middle of the twentieth century it had grown into a confident and commanding presence. Its strident, read-me tone hadn't gone, but behind it now was a serious punch — readership. By the mid-1950s, *NZ Truth* was selling over 350,000 copies a week — far more than anything else — and was probably read by three times that number. Its influence, range and vigour were unrivalled. No politician could ignore it; even Holyoake, the National Party's unflappable genius of the common touch, kept it on-side.

Along with its new-found power, *Truth's* editors and proprietors of the period seemed to feel a sense of responsibility to take a lead on social issues. It sent its reporters on increasingly bold forays into the darker corners of New Zealand society, poking at taboos that no other paper had dared touch.

The first signs of this came in 1951, when anti-Communist paranoia was peaking. The country was paralysed by a strike by waterside workers that had virtually stopped all exports and imports. The government, fearing economic disaster, passed draconian emergency regulations that gave it the power to arrest without trial, censor newspapers and search homes for 'subversive' people or pamphlets. *Truth* took a stand, publishing an account of a search on a harmless boarding hostel in Island Bay, Wellington. There is nothing remarkable about the reporting, but what is remarkable is that it was published, in a time when most newspapers did not dare defy the emergency regulations. *Truth* showed the absurdity of the logic behind the police search: 'I told [the detective] I was a Labour Party supporter. He replied it was obvious I had Communistic tendencies.' (*NZ Truth*, 1951). The story showed the quixotic tendencies of *Truth;* usually keen to bait Communists, it had a finely tuned ear for official cant.

Next, in 1953, came one of its biggest scoops. It showed that Commissioner of Police Eric Compton — the country's highest-ranking police officer, with direct access to the Prime Minister — had tapped phones, particularly of bookmakers. The story led to a Commission of Inquiry, and eventually Compton's resignation. Although a good piece of investigative reporting by the paper's police reporter, it was not a complete win for *Truth*. The inquiry did not support many of the paper's other claims, such as that Compton was blackmailing bookies (Yska, 2010).

By the mid-1950s, no longer just content with stories that appealed to its bread-and-butter readership, *Truth* was increasingly prepared to wield its ink on behalf of truly outcast groups: the mentally ill, unmarried mothers, discrimination against Māori, and even victims of brutal school canings. A surprising sense of moral conscience seemed to be taking over *Truth*. Together with all that power conferred by its towering circulation seems to have come, almost by the back door, a sense of social responsibility not driven by anti-establishment resentment.

It seems almost fate, then, that it fell to *Truth* to take up perhaps the most important cause of all. In the mid-1950s, *Truth* was to turn its formidable arsenal of moral outrage on one of the last bastions of Victorian cruelty — hanging. Capital punishment had been banned by the former Labour government, in 1935. But it had returned under the hard-line anti-Communist law-and-order policies of National in 1951. *Truth* had been keen to support many of National's policies — Redmer Yska writes that it was behind some of the attacks on left-wing members of the Peace Council (Yska, 2010, p. 114). But it differed sharply on the issue of the death penalty.

When, in 1955, 20-year-old Albert Black was sentenced to hang for the murder of a man in a milk bar, *Truth* saw its chance. Its editor, Ted Webber, asked Jack Young to cover the execution. Webber encouraged Young to 'tell it like it is'. Young did so, brilliantly. Printed here, in full, his account still drips with horror. Young believes that the article had a lot of influence in the decision to end capital punishment (for all but treason) in 1961. He says that everyone was feeling upset about the hangings, and Webber saw it as a chance to show people what really went on.

'It was graphic stuff, one of the turning points . . . you were basically able to know what was going on. Most people really didn't have any idea at all. But when you read *Truth*, as most people did in those days, you got the revolting details. I think it had a lot of influence' (Yska, 2010, p. 115).

Other social issues were soon in *Truth*'s sights. In the late 1950s, *Truth* challenged the hidden horrors of the country's network of mental asylums. These gulags, often hidden in the countryside, were brimming with victims of one of the most tragic social experiments of the time: the idea that locking up mostly harmless mentally ill people against their will, and sometimes subjecting them to compulsory and barbarous treatments, would somehow help their condition. It wasn't until the 1990s that these camps, home to thousands, would eventually start to empty.

Other campaigns followed. One explored the plight of unmarried mothers who did not qualify for a state benefit. Another took schools to task for brutal canings of students. In an era when corporal punishment was considered normal, it was a brave step for *Truth* to question the practice.

NZ Truth. (1951, July 4). Victim of "Terrible Enemy": Detectives Search Home. *NZ Truth*.

Yska, R. (2010). *The rise and fall of the people's paper*. Nelson: Craig Potton.

THE MACABRE DRILL OF A N.Z. EXECUTION
NZ Truth, 14 December 1955

"Truth" agrees with the official dictum that executions should not be sensationalised. This is not a sensational report, but a sensitive, firsthand impression of a New Zealand execution — the most recent of them. In this newspaper's view, if hanging is to be a deterrent to murder, the publication of these details, rather than their glossing over, serves that purpose.

By contrast with the dignity and majesty of the law as it is personified in the black-capped judges who read sentences of death to murderers convicted in our courts, the execution of the sentence is an incongruous and makeshift business.

Admittedly, the technique of hanging persons by the neck until they are dead, as it is practised in this country, is getting smoother all the time.

For instance, the trapdoor in the scaffold at Mount Eden Gaol, which once fell with a noise like a boiler cover and slammed clanging echoes through the prison corridors, has been muted so that now it drops with a thud dully audible not far beyond the confines of the execution yard.

In the light of their experience those who manage the procedure have been able to introduce other small modifications as they went along, so that the hanging technique could be made "more streamlined," as one official put it.

. . .

Not of much interest to the man on the gallows, the innovations have been designed to make some contribution to the peace of mind of the people who have to watch him die. There is room for more.

The burden of hanging murderers is unloaded on to the shoulders of subordinate civil servants. The man directly responsible for the conduct of the hangings in New Zealand is an officer in the Department of Justice at Auckland. He is not the first officer; nor even the second officer.

In law the person responsible for the conduct of executions is the sheriff of the district in which the condemned man was tried. But because Auckland is the only place with facilities for dispatching the condemned, the duty devolves upon the Sheriff of Auckland.

In fact he does not preside, because he had a nervous breakdown after officiating at two hangings. A deputy was appointed in his place.

. . .

It is this civil servant who is charged with deciding the moment when the death penalty — pronounced after grave deliberation by a learned judge of the Supreme Court, debated and confirmed by Ministers of the Crown and authorised by the Queen's representative, his Excellency the Governor-General — is exacted. The trap is sprung when he raises his hand.

As he did about seven o'clock on the night last week when a young Irishman, Albert Lawrence Black, 20, was hanged for the murder in Ye Olde Barn Cafe, in Queen Street, Auckland, of Alan Keith Jacques, 19.

Two minutes and seven seconds before, Black had left the condemned cell in Mount Eden Gaol, shepherded by the four warders of the "death watch." He did not walk bravely, or imperturbably or any other way, to the scaffold. As they all do, he shuffled.

He shuffled because the movement of his body was harnessed. His arms, at the elbow, were shackled to his body with broad leather straps, his crossed hands were strapped in front of him, and his legs were pinioned above the knee.

Careful planning goes into preparing a man who is to be hanged. The idea is that he should be as near a rigid log of wood as possible when he is dropped.

For this reason he is dressed in a stiff canvas coat, and steps out of his own shoes into a pair of heavy boots.

The purpose of hanging is to cause death by dislocation of the neck or nervous shock. To achieve that purpose, a careful formula is adhered to, so that the length of the drop, which varies according to the weight of the condemned man, will effect the desired result.

The movements of each person who takes part are worked out like a macabre drill. Mistakes here can bring unpleasant consequences. (At an execution, not held in this country, a warder plunged through the trap with the condemned man and lay with both legs shattered in company with the swinging corpse.)

Knowledge of these things engenders in the minds of those who witness an execution the crawling and ever-present fear that something may go wrong.

. . .

One of the things that may go wrong is the prisoner. No matter what his demeanour may be at the hour of execution he must be taken and hanged — even if he has to be dragged up the 17 steps to the scaffold platform. To guard against that possibility the prisoner is given what a medical man would call "sedation" — what the layman would call a shot of dope.

Understandably, conversation between members of the party waiting in the superintendent's office a quarter-hour before Black was executed was a little stilted.

At five minutes to seven the party, warned to walk quietly, went in single file through a long stone corridor, keeping to a strip of coconut matting laid in the centre of the glossily polished floor.

On each side, the corridor was lined with boots placed outside the cell doors. The "judas holes" in the cell doors were closed.

Down a short flight of stairs guarded with a steel rail the party went on past three cells a short walk away from the execution yard. In the middle cell Black waited.

The execution yard at Mount Eden is in fact a courtyard surrounded by high stone walls in the centre of the prison. It is covered with wire netting. Over the wire netting canvas is laid.

The party assembled along one wall facing the scaffold. The canvas overhead, not very secure, lifted and thumped and banged like a ship's sail in a gale of wind blowing outside. The wind blew down into the yard.

The scaffold is a high steel structure. The platform, to which the condemned climb, is 17 steps away from the ground. Canvas is lashed around the supports so that the space beneath the platform is concealed.

. . .

The scaffold is lighted from overhead with a powerful electric bulb. The light shines on the white rope coiled beneath the metal gallows and on the noose hanging over the trap. Black came into the yard. Witnesses had not seen him pinioned. This was another improvement on past procedure.

At a prior execution witnesses waited outside the condemned cell while the sheriff called upon the superintendent to surrender "the body of the prisoner."

They waited while a gibbering human jelly was led forth and supported on his sagging legs as warders fumbled with shaking hands at the straps about his body.

Black came into the courtyard. He appeared, fortunately, to be composed. His guards led him up the steps.

As he climbed slowly there was time for thought. What sort of scene would be enacted on those steps if the death watch had to handle a recalcitrant prisoner — someone like the American negro who fought for 20 minutes in front of the electric chair? What if it were a woman?

When the Government decided in favour of execution why did it not build a proper execution chamber with a trapdoor in the floor dropping to a cellar beneath?

Death comes to men in many forms. Black met death at the top of the stairs in the shape of a chunky figure dressed as if for a fishing expedition on a stormy day.

This was the hangman. He wore a felt hat pulled down low over his eyes. To hide his eyes he wore sunglasses. His chin was sunk in the collar of a long topcoat buttoned all the way up the front.

. . .

This garish figure waiting at the back of the platform looked ludicrously out of touch, like an actor in some fifth-rate melodrama.

He was properly clothed. So long as he is disguised, the hangman may wear what he chooses. There is no formal dress for the occasion. One New Zealand hangman favoured a skin-tight Superman-style black costume.

Black turned from the hangman to face the sheriff and witnesses. He was asked if he had anything to say before the sentence was executed.

Black looked down; wished everybody a happy Christmas and a prosperous New Year. The warders closed around him.

They pinioned his ankles, drew the noose down over his neck and placed a white hood over his head.

Witnesses could not see this. They were shielded by the warders. This was yet another improvement.

At a previous execution the warders did not stand in front of the condemned man. This was the time witnesses shuddered to see the white bag tucked, ever so gently, under the noose around the condemned man's neck.

The warders moved away from Black. He stood alone. For a moment. The sheriff raised his hand carrying the warrant of execution.

. . .

Death in dark glasses performed his office. Black was no longer there. The white rope was taut. The watchers winced from the thud of the trap as from a shot. The rope oscillated like a leisurely pendulum.

The wind in the courtyard clutched at the canvas covering the bottom of the scaffold. In one corner it lifted. Nobody looked down twice. Had that been a boot-heel in view?

Two priests of the Catholic faith, which Black had embraced in the last few weeks of his life, prayed for him.

The superintendent went to the back of the scaffold; stayed there a short quarter-minute. It was finished. Nothing had gone wrong.

The witnesses walked out of the execution yard. On their way they passed a pair of empty shoes outside the door of the condemned cell.

An hour had to elapse before Black's body could be taken down. It was waited out in the prison office. Taut nerves unravelled; tongues loosened.

It was agreed Black had "died game." So he had, and in doing so had done everybody a signal favour.

There remained the inquest to attend. It was brief and formal. So was the verdict.

The witnesses left the prison. They were few in number. Very few people are entitled to attend a hanging. Any justice of the peace can go; the Justice Department cannot refuse his application.

There was a justice of the peace at Black's execution. An elderly grey-haired man, he is a familiar figure at hangings. He says he is interested in "the psychology" of hanging. Which covers a wide field.

The Government says hanging is a deterrent. In that case one would not expect the Government to be unduly reticent about the fact when an execution is to take place.

In fact those who have to attend are warned as late in the day as possible so that they will not be able to spread the word around.

Press reporters who have to attend as representatives of the public have been warned that they are expected to be "restrained" in what they write, and that if they "sensationalise" reports of executions they may lose the "privilege" of attending.

Prison officials are not allowed to say what a condemned man does, says or reads, or how he behaves, or whether he repents, while he is waiting for the end. Far from anybody being ready to describe the condemned man as a horrible example of the fate that awaits murderers, nobody is supposed to know anything.

The Government, it is understood, knew very little about the mechanics of capital punishment when it introduced it. It is doubtful whether its members have much more first-hand knowledge now.

For the technique of execution the Government applied to the British Home Office. It has made some adjustment. The black flag is not hoisted over the prison here as it is in Britain, nor is a notice of the execution posted at the prison doors. The Government's attitude appears to be that, deterrent or not, the less people know about hanging the better.

Criticism of the method is not an argument against capital punishment. Murderers may deserve to die. It may be that the prospect of death does deter would-be murderers.

What happened to them may not matter; what can happen to the people who have to hang them does.

CHAPTER NINE

A colour bar

1961: *NZ Truth* exposes racism in Pukekohe.

Among *Truth*'s many campaigns one story, although quite short, stood out to me. 'Sorry, mate, but we don't cut hair for Maoris' exposes the casual racism of provincial Waikato. Again, it is not the kind of story that present-day marketers, conducting a focus group of its mainly white readership, would have flagged as part of the paper's brand. Nor, without names or details, is it verifiable reporting. But it is so obviously against the grain of contemporary attitudes that it has a moral authority that somehow stands out.

It is not clear why *Truth* suddenly developed a strong social conscience. Perhaps it was the rebellious spirit of the 1960s, which *Truth*, always quick to sense the national pulse, had picked up on. It was probably also the influence of new blood. In 1961, Rod Barrett arrived from Johannesburg's *The Star* to take over the editor's chair. A former literary editor, he appointed J. F. Clark, also from *The Star*, news editor. *Truth* historian Redmer Yska writes that Barrett commissioned 'thoughtful hard-hitting articles on social issues', as well as the 'Girl of the week' in 1962 (Yska, 2010). Although Barrett did not last long, the papers he helped craft were unusual for their commitment to true investigative reporting on social issues that were genuinely in the public interest.

None of these stories seems particularly surprising by today's standards; but by the standards of the time, *Truth* was setting a benchmark in moral courage, a mark that makes it the outstanding investigative newspaper of the mid-twentieth century in New Zealand. It was a mantle the paper was to hold until the spirit moved to *The Auckland Star* in the mid-1970s.

Yska, R. (2010). *The rise and fall of the people's paper*. Nelson: Craig Potton.

Sorry, mate, but we don't cut hair for Maoris

NZ Truth, 3 October 1961

Pukekohe is a town with a colour bar. And Pukekohe, prosperous centre of a big market-gardening area 32 miles south of Auckland, has a big number of Maoris in its 5700-odd population.

It also has a considerable number of Indians and Chinese, most of whom work the gardens of the slopes of the fertile Pukekohe Hill. But the colour bar applies only to the Maoris.

If you are a Maori in Pukekohe — and almost one resident in seven is:

- You cannot sit upstairs at one of the local picture theatres.
- You can go to only two of the town's half-dozen barbers with the certainty that you won't be subject to the humiliation of being refused service because you are a Maori.

Even some beauty salons have refused Maori women admission.

According to a Maori social worker, Pukekohe is the most segregation-minded town he has ever been in.

Most Europeans in Pukekohe ignore the problem. A few grudgingly acknowledge it exists, but "don't think it's very bad."

One young Maori truckdriver from nearby Waiuku told me that he went to the pictures in Pukekohe with two pakeha mates.

His two mates were told they could go upstairs but that he would have to sit downstairs. . . . Today no Maoris sit upstairs.

. . .

Indian and Chinese children attend the white primary schools. Maori children attend the Maori primary school on the outskirts of town.

There is now no compulsion about which school a Maori child attends. All schools are open to Maori and white alike.

But only a handful of Maori children attend the other primary schools in Pukekohe. Most Maori parents prefer their children to attend the Maori school.

Drinking, too, till recently was a sore point with the Maoris of Pukekohe.

Till only a few years ago Maori men were barred from one of the local hotel's two bars. Maori women could drink only in the section next to the hotel — if their husbands brought them out their drinks.

Today — and this is the only bright spot — there is no hint of discrimination at the hotel. Maori men can drink in whichever bar they choose. Maori women can drink in the lounge bar and have exclusive use of it from 3pm on Fridays and Saturdays.

Several of the barmen and probably the majority of the customers are now Maoris.

Pukekohe's Maori leaders have done their best to fight the colour bar that rends their town. But the fight seems hopeless. The Maoris have pocketed their pride and resignedly accepted the discrimination.

They shrug their shoulders if the barber will not cut their hair. It's a bit tough but there's another bloke along the road and he will.

It's tough that one theatre will not allow you upstairs, but there's another one just started up and Maoris are allowed upstairs there.

Most local Maoris have accepted the colour bar and learned to live with it.

But imagine the shock and humiliation of an out-of-town Maori passing through Pukekohe who stops for a hair cut. He walks into a barber shop, sits down, picks up a magazine to wait his turn. Then someone taps him on the shoulder and tells him: "They don't cut Maoris' hair here, mate . . ."

One well-spoken young Maori summed it up. He was leaving his job in Pukekohe and heading back to his home near Thames.

"Being a Maori in Thames isn't like being a Maori in Pukekohe," he explained.

CHAPTER TEN

Dishonourable discharges

1972, *Taranaki Herald*: Jim Tucker pioneers environmental journalism in New Zealand, investigating dirty dairying and polluted rivers in Taranaki.

It's taken a long time for New Zealanders to wake up to the slow poisoning of their beautiful country.

The environmental movement started back in the 1920s, with the formation of the Forest and Bird Protection Society, but widespread protests against destruction of the environment did not get under way until the 1960s. The construction of enormous hydro-electric dams at Lake Manapouri, in the South Island, made people aware that development had a cost: the destruction of irreplaceable forests and the life they sustained. The Save Manapouri movement is often credited as the true beginning of environmental consciousness in New Zealand. It was to gain victory in 1972, when the incoming Labour government agreed to conservation measures to protect habitat threatened by the Manapouri project.

In that same year, a young reporter at the *Taranaki Herald*, Jim Tucker, began his own environmental campaign. In one of the most pro-farming provinces in the country, a bastion of the dairy industry, he undertook an exhaustive investigation of the hidden cost of unrestricted farming (Tucker, 1972). His 11-part series stands out for its thoroughness, its fairness and the quality of the writing.

Tucker says that the decision by his editor, Rash Avery, to run the series, was courageous.

> *After a couple of the articles appeared he was threatened with*
> *some sort of retaliation (he never disclosed what) by the dairy*
> *industry. That did mean we included an extra part to the story*

covering what the dairy industry claimed it was doing about
pollution, but nothing else was changed. (Tucker, 2013).

The series won Tucker a Dulux Award for Feature Writing, as well as an award from the Conservation Society of New Zealand.

Although his series was not widely reported outside Taranaki, it had an impact there. When Tucker retired in 2012, he returned to this story, updating it and expanding it into a book. As part of his research, he found from reading the minutes of the Taranaki Catchment Commission that every case of pollution reported in the series was eventually investigated, although not all were resolved for many years.

But he also found that although the visible outfall cases have long since been sorted, the province's rivers, like most in New Zealand, suffer the effects of algal growth fed by the indirect run-off of nitrogen from farm paddocks (Tucker, 2013).

It is perhaps significant that Tucker's series began with Waitara. Something from these articles must have lodged in the public mind, because 15 years after he wrote them, the threatened destruction of Waitara's last remaining shellfish beds by a proposal to build another sewage outfall ignited a claim to the Waitangi Tribunal. The tribunal was at that time almost unheard of, but its decision — that the planned outfall breached Māori rights to their fisheries guaranteed by the Treaty of Waitangi — led to the major constitutional shift in favour of Treaty obligations that took place in the late 1980s.

Tucker went on to win more awards as a writer at *The Auckland Star*, and through a succession of high-profile journalism roles, before becoming a leader in journalism training.

Tucker, J. (1972, April 1). 'Pollution and water don't mix'. *Taranaki Herald*.

Tucker, J. (2013). [Email to author].

The Dirt Around Us

Taranaki Herald, from 1 April 1972

The tide is full. The river is wide and brooding, poised for the next move in a monotonous routine of ebb and flow.

An old woman and a youth fish for herring from the wharf. Thin, nut-brown fingers tug at lines. Rod and reel flick lazily. Plump fish wriggle in buckets. They are oblivious to the sight below. Down there, the surface of the river is thickly congealed with fat and foamy wastes. Around the wharf piles the water boils as herrings feed in a frenzy, bobbing and biting at the clots of effluent whirling by.

The water for yards downstream is concealed by clouds of fatty matter which spread out from the bank and form themselves into patterns of cumulus-nimbus and stratus.

To the uninitiated the spectacle is fascinating . . . and horrible. To the people of Waitara it is part of life.

"Not for me, dear. The cats, for the cats. I wouldn't eat anything out of here," says the old woman. "You need a bath after a day down here. I suppose they'll do something about it one day." She flicks the ringlets of fat from line and is intent on her fishing.

The biochemist lowers the tray of trout fingerlings into a river and stands back to watch. It takes them exactly seven minutes to die, he notes in his file.

. . .

The bulldozer driver stops his machine and walks over. "We're healthy round here; well fed," he says. "Put a couple of bits of bread together in the air and you've got a sandwich any time."

The odour is overpowering. On the opposite bank of the Waiwakaiho River a pipe discharges red and yellow liquid. It tumbles down 30ft before spreading its stain on the river.

The colours are astonishing. They change from brilliant red to dull crimson, to mustard, ochre and back to red — all with the variety and frequency of a coin-operated fountain.

Downstream people net for whitebait and swim.

"It would be the last place I would swim," the harbour-master says with a smile. "It's one vast toilet. You can see the toilet paper floating between the wharves. It's been like it for years."

. . .

The street is empty, quiet. A door to a factory opens and a man pops his head out and scans the footpath. He disappears and moments later a thick orange liquid runs along an open drain from the factory and spills into the Mangaotuku Stream. The colour is soon absorbed by the turbid stream as it flows away into the tunnel under central New Plymouth.

The rod bends sharply as the trout snaps up the lure and races away upstream. The angler wins the fight to land the fish — but something is wrong. The trout is an albino. The fisherman presses a finger into the creature, and the indent remains. The smell is nauseating as white discharge oozes from the fish's mouth.

"City water . . . nothing comes out of there but city water," the dairy factory manager maintains. Three-quarters of a mile away seagulls gather over a white liquid which pours from a pipe and runs down the beach.

. . .

There may be anything from 3000 to 4000 instances of man-induced water pollution in Taranaki. One estimate puts the figure closer to 5000.

The majority are milking shed and pig sty discharges; the worst are towns and industries that empty their untreated wastes into the nearest watercourse.

. . .

The result is that millions of gallons of effluent are being discharged into Taranaki's rivers and coastal waters each day. The effect is that our environment is being constantly changed. In some cases it is being damaged.

There is nothing new about this situation. Taranaki has grown up with pollution. With its dairying economy and unique physical make-up — a mountain surrounded by a roughly circular plain crossed by 365 rivers and streams — the province has traditionally used its waterways to dispose of wastes.

These practices have, until recent times, been relatively small-scale and acceptable. Today most are not.

. . .

The months of preparation involved in compiling this series of illustrated articles revealed that while industry and local authorities in Taranaki have generally accepted that better disposal methods are inevitable, many have yet to do something about it.

. . .

An interesting finding was that industrial firms are not alone in the field. Three of the seven local authorities in the surveyed area are putting questionable discharges into waterways, and at least half the farmers do so. In New Plymouth itself the biggest source of pollutants seems to be private individuals, who use the city's streams to get rid of everything from waste oil to crayfish carcasses.

. . .

Some examples of pollution cited at the beginning of this article are still occurring at this moment. Some are under action; some are not. They may indicate that pollution has reached alarming proportions in Northern Taranaki, but the actual situation — including abatement work planned or being done — must be considered before judgments are made.

. . .

Waitara is a pleasant town.

It nestles around the bulk of its one big industry, the freezing works, and spreads over both banks of a wide, brown river. More than half of the 5000 or so people who live there rely on the works for a living. They put up with the smell; they harden to the daily spectacle of fat and waste going into the river.

The fact that the lower reaches of their river are a vast drain for raw sewage from their toilets, discharges from the works and effluent from the wool scouring plant, has largely been accepted. Life has been that way for as long as anyone can remember.

My investigations showed that the average person is not unduly concerned at the condition of the Waitara River. He continues to fish in it, drive boats on its surface and even swim there. Or he ignores it altogether.

Not everyone in Waitara is like that, of course, and in patches the tolerance appears to be wearing thin. A series of public outcries over the state of the river during the late 1960s may be having some result.

Although sewage, fat and various washings still go into the river from borough and works, the first moves to stop it are afoot. Shortly a $165,000 saveall will begin work to remove much of the fat from the waste water that comes from the freezing works. A year ago settling tanks were built to clarify wash water from the works stock yards. The Waitara Borough Council decided at a recent meeting that sewage treatment must take first priority in future works.

The wool scouring company gives assurances that plans are under way to either recirculate wash water or come into the town sewerage system once treatment is installed.

The wheels are undeniably beginning to turn. But the few residents who have voiced concern over the river in the past, claim that action has not come quickly enough, that there is still a great deal to be done to clean up the river and that the only motivation behind the current action (or promise of it) is the threat that pollution control is going to get tough in the next couple of years.

One such resident is Waitara medical practitioner, Dr Peter van Praagh. He feels the lower reaches of the river are "definitely a health hazard." Anyone swimming there or taking shellfish could contract typhoid, hepatitis, salmonella or gastro enteritis. He claims that the increase in hepatitis cases in the area recently may be connected with the polluted waterway.

"It's a nice place," he emphasised. "I like living here. But the river and the smell from the works are bad. People don't like it, but they don't complain enough. If they did, I'm sure something would have been done long ago."

. . .

He said pollution must come before pavements. It was admirable to have nice footpaths for mothers to wheel their prams along, but the town should get its priorities right.

The crux of the matter appears to lie in the Waitara Borough Council and the freezing works company, Thomas Borthwick & Sons A'asia Ltd, coming to some agreement over how the town's massive disposal problems will be met — and who will pay. So far the company has been reluctant to talk about the problem and although the council is pressing for further meetings with company representatives, the situation appears to be in limbo.

. . .

No test results are available to show exactly how far the river has deteriorated, the true effects of tides or even if the river's condition is at all constant. Comment must be based on visual observations of what is going in and any obvious physical signs of deterioration.

One thing is known. The river is already polluted when it gets to Waitara. Hill country run-off and erosion, farm disposal and dairy factory wastes all contribute to the water's condition before it makes its last mile-long plod to the sea.

The Health Department's supervising inspector of health, Mr G. R. Oliver, says that no coliform counts have been taken in the river, although they would "undoubtedly run into thousands."

He is not particularly concerned over the river's condition, he told me, and in comparison with similar problems elsewhere the situation was not worrying. The river was constantly flushed out by the tides and this did a great deal to offset the effects of discharges.

> "If the river was not tidal at this point, we would have something to worry about. In the meantime any urgency about the river must follow local public opinion."

He did warn that it was not safe to swim in the river between the bridge and the sea.

While the works has taken the brunt of public protest over discharges into the river, informed opinion considers the borough's discharge of raw sewage into the river to be potentially more dangerous.

Although the sewerage system itself has an anticipated life of 15 years, the method of disposing of the end product is primitive. In 1946 five large septic tanks were built on the banks of the river and all domestic sewage finds its way to these.

With subsequent population growth — Waitara has become a dormitory town for New Plymouth and the Bell Block industrial area — some of the tanks have become inadequate to the extent that raw sewage is passing straight through them into the river without even primary treatment.

The Mayor of Waitara, Mr A. D. Wilson, said the borough council was adamant that sewage treatment was the number one priority. He said the river was not satisfactory in its present state and with river classification coming up it was essential for Waitara to put its house in order. He said that although the new saveall at the freezing works would prevent much of the fat going into the river, he understood that effluent from the works fellmongery would still enter the water.

With the freezing works easily the largest generator of sewage in the town, any decision on the town's sewage treatment would have to take the works' requirements into account, he said.

At present the borough had no sewage treatment plan drawn up, although the possibilities had been looked at. The most promising appeared to be some form of primary treatment and then discharge through an outfall into the sea. Whatever proposal was adopted it was likely to cost half a million to a million dollars and the ratepayer would carry the burden. Returns would come, of course, from charges to the freezing works for use of the new system.

What of the freezing works?

. . .

District manager Mr Ian Smith said the company's policy could not be revealed at this stage. Personally, he felt the suggestion of a seaward outfall was the best to date.

He did supply some statistics. At peak killing the works was discharging up to 400,000 gallons of liquid an hour. Half of this was cooling water which was taken from the river and returned with no change in condition.

The rest was service water which was used for a variety of purposes in the works. When it went into the river it contained washings, spillages, fat globules, effluent from the fellmongery and some diluted blood washings from floors.

No offal was put into the river. In fact, the economics which governed the operation of a freezing works demanded that nothing was wasted. If possible every part of the animal should bring some return.

Mr Smith agreed that the human factor occasionally entered into the problem. Wastes from the fellmongery would not be treated by the new save all. He said the company was fully aware of the impending enforcement of regulations governing discharges into waterways and the problem was being studied.

. . .

The manager of the wool scouring works in Waitara, Mr J. R. Wilson, says the company has a problem with effluent disposal. Every hour 3000 gallons of waste water containing strained washings and detergent goes down a drain into the Waitara River a quarter of a mile away; every 14 hours a larger discharge of about 10,000 gallons is released.

"We've got a problem and we're working on it," he told me. "We expect to go on to softer detergents soon and we're looking at methods of recirculating our water. Failing that, we'll discharge into the Waitara sewerage system when treatment is introduced."

The net result: a river that is always opaque, occasionally coated with congealed fat and other wastes, sometimes smelly — and rarely pleasant to look at or float on. And yet, somehow, a lot of people find it acceptable.

. . .

Of the several thousand known cases of water pollution in Taranaki, more than 80 per cent involve the province's farmers. At least half of the farmers in Taranaki are discharging effluent into our waterways, if the statistics taken from one county are an indication.

In its survey for the Taranaki Catchment Commission, the Taranaki County Council found that 399 of the county's 801 farmers were causing "gross pollution" of rivers and streams. Another 165 were responsible for minor pollution. Catchment Commission officials feel that these figures are a reasonable reflection of Taranaki's overall situation.

. . .

It has been estimated that between half a million and a million tons of animal wastes are being put into waterways by Taranaki's farmers every year. With more intensive stocking and farming methods, the amount continues to rise.

The effect is that almost without exception every one of the 365 streams that come off Mt Egmont is partially polluted by the time it gets to the sea.

Almost every water supply in the province, if it comes from a stream, is affected by farm discharges. In some cases rivers are steadily polluted as they flow through farm after farm to the extent that farmers well downstream cannot even use them for watering stock. Only those farmers at the top of most streams would dare use them for household water supplies, although this depends on the number of farms which are polluting a particular stream and how badly.

One might ask: how has this seemingly monstrous situation arisen, and why?

. . .

The answer is relatively simple. In the early days of Taranaki agriculture the use of streams for getting rid of the limited amounts of stock waste was acceptable. Stocking was light compared with today (an area which once carried 5000 cows might have as many as 10 times this today) and the flow in the streams in summer was greater.

In other words, there was far less going in and more to dilute and carry it away. Consequently nearly every cowshed was built on the banks of a stream.

But farming has developed enormously in the last 25 years and greater numbers of animals are confined on less land. Greater numbers of cows are being milked per cowshed, more pigs raised per sty and more chickens per poultry house. In the past dairy farmers needed to cope with only five per cent or less of the total manure discharge, while today, with the use of wintering sheds, silos and other intensive feeding systems, they must dispose of greater proportions.

. . .

The drainage of wastes from pig farms has increased many times as well, but for different reasons. Units of 2000 to 3000 pigs have become common because of the need for dairy factories to dispose of large quantities of whey.

As one pig produces the daily waste equivalent of two adult people some idea is gained of the disposal problems faced by a farmer with 3000 pigs. He needs a sewage treatment system for a town the size of Waitara.

All these factors have combined to produce the present situation in which streams are being overloaded with animal wastes and water quality is deteriorating. Why have they been allowed to get away with it?

That's easy to answer. The local authorities, Health Department and acclimatisation societies who up to now have been responsible for trying to keep the rivers clean have had quite enough to do in dealing with the serious cases of discharge, such as those from dairy companies, without worrying about individual farmers.

. . .

The wastes produced by one farm do not, in themselves, represent much of a threat to a waterway, but if every farm along the length of a river is polluting it, the effects are serious.

To their credit, many of our farmers have seen the light and are doing something about their waste discharges. It is estimated that at least half, however, have adopted the attitude that they will do nothing until they are made to or until their neighbours upstream stop their discharges into the river.

This attitude was encountered all too often during the course of this investigation. With acclimatisation rangers we inspected a number of "problem" farms in the survey area and the response to our inquiries was monotonously similar:

- "Yeah, it's bad . . . but Joe B. up the river is putting stuff in, too. You want to have a look at his set-up."
- "Oh well, I suppose I'll get around to doing something one day . . ."
- "I'm not really interested in doing anything until I'm made to."

. . .

On one farm we visited, the cowshed wastes were allowed to run out and down a concrete track to a bridge across a river. There they had accumulated a foot or so deep, with the excess spilling over into the water or running down into a huge pool of liquid cow manure in a nearby paddock. This, too, was seeping into the river.

When I called with Mr T. N. S. Watt, an acclimatisation ranger, the farmer was in his shed while his wife told us he was over the back of the farm. When Mr Watt explained that he had the right, as a ranger, to inspect the stream for pollution, the farmer suddenly appeared to confront us.

He said that he was trying to do something about the problem and was setting up a pipeline to the rear of his farm. Mr Watt told me later that the acclimatisation society had been at this man for the past seven years to take action . . . so far he had done nothing.

Not every farmer is like that, of course, and some we visited were happy to show us what they had done to abate pollution. One particular case was Mr Ken Donald of Warea Rd, who has installed a sump, automatic pump and spray irrigation system at a cost of $600. Mr Donald sprays the manure from his cowshed on to his pastures and so far is pleased with the performance of his system.

. . .

Cow manure from milking sheds and the wastes generated by a pig farm have serious effects on a stream. They lower the level of oxygen in the water to a point where aquatic life is killed and encourage the growth of undesirable sewage fungus and algae. They also discolour a stream badly, especially in the mornings and evenings after milking time. These effects make it important that farmers dispose of their animal wastes correctly and efficiently.

. . .

In conclusion, the investigation showed that so far the Taranaki farmer has been generally overlooked in the drive to clean up the rivers. But with the action against pollution beginning to harden, our farmers must prepare for more than a passing frown for failing to cope properly with a problem that faces us all.

CHAPTER ELEVEN

The Crewe murders

1972–1979, *The Auckland Star*: Pat Booth campaigns to free Arthur Allan Thomas from prison.

The Crewe murders have exercised an extraordinary and enduring grip on the New Zealand psyche. As well as a lengthy police investigation, they have generated two murder trials, a judicial inquiry, a Court of Appeal hearing, a Privy Council hearing, a Royal Commission of Inquiry and a Royal Pardon. Apart from the media coverage of each of these judicial steps, the saga has generated no less than five books from various investigators, a feature film and, currently, two dedicated websites — and still the mystery of who killed the Crewes remains.

Incredibly, although the murders occurred more than 40 years ago, as late as 2014 there was yet another police investigation under way. No other crime comes remotely near to matching the drama of its macabre and inexplicable events, or the length and bitterness of its aftermath. In many ways, the house at Pukekawa where the murders took place is to New Zealand what Dallas's grassy knoll is to the US. But it is quite likely that this saga would have ended much earlier, and wrongly, if it had not been for the almost random intervention of Pat Booth.

Some people set out to become investigative reporters. Others, it seems, have it thrust upon them, by coming upon something so wrong that they simply cannot let it go. Pat Booth was one of the latter. His moment came on the evening of 16 April 1973. It was near the end of the second trial of a young farmer, Arthur Allan Thomas, for the murders of Jeannette and Harvey Crewe. Booth was driving home from his job as deputy editor of *The Auckland Star*. He had been following the trial, as he thought it would make good copy if an interview with Thomas could be secured. As he drove past the court, he made a sudden decision. If there was a park, he would call in. As he puts it in his memoir: 'At that moment, a car pulled out to leave a vacancy directly outside the court. Destiny had made a special space for me' (Booth, 1997). He stayed to watch the jury return on the night of the second trial. It was the beginning of what became a seven-year investigation that eventually exposed the fabricated evidence used to frame Thomas, and led to his pardon.

If it had not been for that moment, Booth would have seemed an unlikely candidate to become a crusading investigative journalist. He was a reporter of the old school — he'd worked his way up through the ranks, first as a cadet at the *Hawera Star*, then later at *The Auckland Star*. He was a good newshound, getting, among other scoops, the first interview printed by a New Zealand newspaper with Sir Edmund Hillary after his conquest of Everest, the inside scoop on the victims of the Tangiwai disaster in 1953, and breaking the news of the National government's military intervention in Malaya in the 1950s. By the 1970s he was married, deputy editor at the *Star* and assured of a smooth glide up the managerial ranks and eventually to a gold-plated retirement.

All that changed that night in April 1973. Booth began, often in his own time, an investigation, one that led to truly sensational revelations that galvanised the country. Meetings to campaign for Thomas packed more than 2000 people into the Auckland Town Hall. The investigation concluded seven years later, in 1980, when a Royal Commission of Inquiry vindicated Booth's findings. The government pardoned Thomas and paid him $1 million in compensation, but refused to take action against the police officers it said had fabricated evidence. Finally, in 2014, a three-year police inquiry finally agreed with the conclusion reached by Booth and the Commission many years earlier: the shell case used to convict Thomas could not have fired one of the bullets that killed the Crewes (Lovelock, 2014). An independent review of that inquiry by QC David Jones went further, saying that the shell case was almost certainly planted by police officers (Jones, 2014).

It's probably hard for people today to understand just how important the case was. It pitted a bewildered young farmer, whose only allies were (apart from a strong family) a determined journalist and a lone scientist, against the full might of the police and the courts. In some ways, especially as a loss of public innocence, it was New Zealand's Watergate. Like Watergate, it built slowly. It had its share of dirty tricks: phone tappings, fabricated evidence, burglaries, anonymous tip-offs, and cover-ups. Like Watergate, it asked the public to decide whether something was rotten in one of our most important institutions — the police force. Like Watergate, it took a combination of journalism and an official inquiry with all the power of the state behind it to finally flush out the truth and set Thomas free.

Several things stand out as remarkable about the Thomas investigation. First, its length. From the moment Booth, on instinct, pulled into that car park, until the end, when he accompanied Thomas home from prison, the investigation took seven years.

Second, Booth's method. He is a good example of Carl Bernstein's description of his and Bob Woodward's methods when investigating Watergate: 'There was nothing particularly remarkable about our methods. What was remarkable was what was yielded by our methods' (Behrens, 1977). Booth did what any good reporter, or detective, does. He read the previous material and checked it — by talking to every witness he could, by finding witnesses that the police had not bothered to talk to or had conveniently ignored, by checking records that the police had not checked, and by wading through piles of manufacturers' records of shell and bullet production to become an expert in that area. He, and his collaborator, Dr Jim Sprott, took nothing for granted.

Booth proved that a blood-stained watch, which police claimed Thomas had wrenched from Harvey Crewe's wrist, belonged to another man. He proved that a police claim that Thomas had met Harvey Crewe on the Crewe farm while working for a top-dressing company was false. Booth also found witnesses who discredited the police claims that Thomas had been motivated by jealousy because Jeannette had rejected his advances years earlier. But the slam dunk that sealed the fate of the police campaign against Thomas was the extraordinary saga of the cartridge case. That story is told here, in an excerpt from his memoir *Deadline* (Booth, 1997).

The word crusade has strongly pejorative connotations in most New Zealand newsrooms, with those that pride themselves on at least an attempt at objectivity and impartiality. If you understand the often violent, and turbulent, history of New Zealand, the strong divisions of class and race that still exist, and how close the country has come on occasion to tearing itself apart, the danger of irresponsible rhetoric to our fragile consensus is high. But the tragedy of New Zealand journalism is that this understandable distaste for polemic has at times engendered a blandness that can tar even the most impartial of investigations by labelling it a crusade. For most, the kind of engagement that Booth had with the Thomas campaign entailed crossing a line between journalist and lobbyist that many feared to cross — even though by a more reasonable standard he was simply pursuing the truth. I suspect that by crossing that line, in the eyes of some at least, Booth wrote himself out of a higher career in newspaper management. He told me that he was asked by his bosses to tone down the coverage on the Thomas inquiry, but refused to do so (Booth, 2009).

Unlike some journalists, for whom the thrill of the chase or the process of investigation is their main motivation, Booth's main driving force was simply to right injustice. It is to his enormous and lasting credit that he was prepared to risk, and ultimately sacrifice, a job he loved for doing what he believed was right. For Booth, the human connection has always been more important than pleasing the right people. It gives him his warmth, his droll humour, and his empathy and compassion for ordinary people — vital attributes for any good reporter. Add to this a relentless determination and fearlessness (even a touch of arrogance) in getting to the truth of things, a fascination with news, a gift for spotting the riveting detail, a sense of the dramatic flourish that gilds his writing with a touch of greatness, and all the wily tricks of a reporter honed by years pounding the streets, and you have a combination that made him, in my view, arguably the finest journalist New Zealand has produced. And of course, saw him pull off the greatest feat of investigative reporting this country has seen. The following is Booth's revisiting of the long campaign in his 1997 book *Deadline*.

Behrens, J. C. (1977). *The typewriter guerrillas: Closeups of twenty top investigative reporters*. Chicago: Nelson-Hall.

Booth, P. (1997). *Deadline*. Auckland: Viking.

Booth, P. (2009). Interview with author, J. Hollings.

Jones, D. (2014). *Crewe review: Report by Independent Counsel, Mr David Jones QC*. Wellington: NZ Police. Retrieved from http://www.police.govt.nz/about-us/publication/crewe-review-report-independent-counsel-mr-david-jones-qc.=

Lovelock, A. J. (2014). *Crewe review — final report*. Wellington: NZ Police. Retrieved from http://www.police.govt.nz/about-us/publication/crewe-review-final-report

Deadline

Originally published in *The Auckland Star*. This extract is from *Deadline*, by Pat Booth, published by Viking, 1997.

April 1973. The jury of 11 shuffled self-consciously back into the jury box — one member had been excused when he became ill early in the trial. The chairman of a ratepayers' association who was foreman, the hairdresser with the high bouffant hairdo, the two middle-aged housewives, the man who chewed gum and was said to be a rugby league referee, the yachtsman, the cabinet-maker, the mechanics, the rubber-worker and the polisher— they all took care not to meet anyone's eye. Not the counsels' and certainly not the accused's.

Then came their verdict after 17 days and 436 pages of evidence: 'Guilty.'

One word set free the emotions, the tension, disappointment and anger which the solemn trappings of the court had controlled until then. The sound began as a moan and became a wail, shouts, jeers and then a solid wave of confused noise. Vivien Thomas broke from the seating, only partly restrained by friends, to run to the bar of the court and only feet from the jury. 'What sort of people are you?' she screamed. 'He's innocent.'

Behind her, Arthur Thomas' grey-haired mother, Ivy, swayed in tears as words came from a heart in torment: 'There is no justice here. '

Women collapsed, their shoulders shaking with sobs. Some fainted. Men shouted and wept angry tears. In the upstairs gallery, the sobbing and the shouting rose to match the hubbub outside among those who had not been able to find seats. Arthur Thomas, his lips moving in words no one heard, stared incredulously at the jury, his head moving slowly from side to side in obvious disbelief.

There was no risk that any of the jury would return his stare. Eleven pairs of eyes were fixed on a point above my head in the press bench opposite. Fists were waving in the public gallery as the clerk of court asked Arthur Thomas if he had anything to say. Suddenly, the noise eased and he spoke, above quiet crying from the people who stood behind him and craned to hear. He stretched out his hands, palms uppermost. They were trembling. 'Give me a lie detector test ... I had nothing to do with that horrible crime ... I am completely innocent, as God is my witness ... I was at home on the night with my wife.'

Vivien Thomas screamed: 'He was, he was.' The shouting, the screams and the weeping rose to a new intensity. Behind that noise, half-drowned by it, Mr Justice Perry passed life sentence, then hesitated as the court crier shouted for the court to stand as the judge prepared to leave the bench.

Stand, the man said. They already were, everyone, shouting, waving their arms, their anger in their voices and in their gestures. But even more on their faces, in their eyes.

Police moved in to clear the court as the judge left, as Thomas walked slowly, head bowed, down those steps and as the jury was escorted away, not risking even a sideways glance at Vivien Thomas, only a few feet away, still weeping and shouting.

That night, I wept over the Thomas verdict — for the first time, but I would do so again in the seven years ahead. That night they were tears of uncertainty and alarm. I could not know then that those minutes of such deep emotion in the court room had changed my life. I was now determined to find the truth. Ahead lay a seven-year investigation. It was as if, over all those years, I continued to hear those words I had heard repeated as I walked in the darkness away from the court building, passing Ivy Thomas, heart-broken and hunched in her grief, being supported by her family, and still repeating: 'There is no justice here.'

. . .

Arthur Thomas was right in his consistent pleas of innocence. Police witnesses lied under oath. Their evidence against him was faked and distorted. Other facts that supported his not guilty plea or weakened the Crown case were deliberately withheld to gain that first verdict and to protect it at later hearings.

This is how he was wrongly jailed for nine years.

Jeanette (30) and Harvey Crewe (29) were reported missing from their Pukekawa farm, 80 km south of Auckland, on Monday, 22 June 1970. They had not been seen since late the previous Wednesday, 17June. Jeanette's father, Len Demler, who farmed the property next door, reported finding their blood stained house and their daughter, his granddaughter, 18-month-old Rochelle, distressed and in soiled nappies, in her cot.

Despite a long and laborious search, a large team of police found no sign of the missing couple. Their first and only suspect was Demler, who was questioned frequently and closely watched.

Jeanette's body surfaced in the nearby Waikato River after flooding in September, Harvey's one month later. Both had been shot with a .22 firearm.

Again, police concentrated on Demler as their prime suspect. To test his reaction, they called him to the river bank to identify the badly decomposed body of his daughter. He gave no sign of emotion, nor had he since the first day of the mystery.

Early in October, a special conference of police and legal advisers discussed arresting and charging him with the murders. Counselled by Assistant Commissioner Bob Walton, national head of the CIB, that they did not have sufficient evidence to justify a charge and a trial, police investigators under Detective Inspector Bruce Hutton switched their attention to a new reconstruction on how the killings had occurred. Instead, they arrested and charged Arthur Allan Thomas, 32, a farmer who lived 15 km from the Crewes. Their decisive new clue was a cartridge case that had clearly been ejected from a .22 rifle owned by Thomas, a cartridge case that police said they had found in the garden of the Crewe farm four months after they had first searched it. Crown forensic scientists said the Thomas rifle was one of two that could have fired the shots from among 64 examined within an 18-krn radius.

Police suggested as a motive that Thomas, who had had a crush on Jeanette during the late 1950s, had carried a murderous obsession about her for more than 10 years and had finally killed her and her husband out of jealousy. They backed their cartridge case with other forensic and circumstantial evidence, but the cartridge was the lynch pin of their case.

Thomas vigorously denied the charge, as did his wife Vivien, who testified that he had been at home in bed with her the night police said the couple were murdered. The Crown sought to counter this by suggesting that she was involved, that she could have been a woman seen in the garden of the farm in the days before the tragedy was discovered. They produced evidence from a paediatrician that the baby had been fed, and suggested that, after her husband had murdered the couple because of jealousy, Vivien Thomas had for some reason returned to the farm to keep the baby alive.

In the last days of the Thomas trial in February 1971, a Pukekohe jeweller, William Eggleton, came forward to say that at about the time of the murder, a man he later identified as Thomas had brought a damaged, old, rolled-gold watch into his shop for repair, a watch with a cracked glass and blood and mucus on it. The Crown said Thomas had clearly damaged his watch in his attack on the Crewes and had then cold-bloodedly taken it in for repair.

The jury believed the Crown case and convicted Thomas. An appeal was dismissed in June 1971.

Arthur Thomas, his wife and family, plus the Thomas Retrial Committee, headed for years by Pat Vesey and then by David Payne, were adamant that the cartridge case had been planted and they waged a national campaign for a retrial.

In February 1972, the government asked a retired judge, Sir George McGregor, to consider both the old and new evidence. He confirmed the guilty verdict.

The campaign continued. In February 1973, after considering new forensic evidence and other testimony, including the fact that Thomas had never owned a watch of the type the jeweller Eggleton described, the Court of Appeal ordered a new trial.

In that April 1973 trial, the Crown changed several pieces of evidence. This time, for instance, police claimed — without reference to or explanation of their earlier beliefs — that the watch had been Harvey Crewe's, taken from his wrist in the killing. And since Vivien Thomas had an alibi, they now said it was unlikely that the child had been fed.

For the defence, forensic scientist Dr Jim Sprott testified that the cartridge case reported found in the garden had significant features which meant it was the wrong type to contain bullets like those that killed the Crewes. If that was true, then the cartridge case had been planted. The Crown produced evidence from the Australian makers of the cartridges that the differences he described did not exist. The jury rejected the planting theory. Arthur Thomas was convicted of the double murder for a second time.

Circumstance, coincidence, fate took me to the courtroom on verdict night. I had suggested to *The Auckland Star* that we should seek to buy the rights to the exclusive Thomas story in the event of an acquittal. Because defence counsel Kevin Ryan and his associate, twin brother Gerald, had been at Sacred Heart College with me, I suggested I should negotiate any contract. To familiarise myself with the detail, I had spent hours each day sitting in on the hearing. The more I heard, the more that I was in the strange atmosphere of the trial with its obvious win-at-any-cost attitude by the Crown, the more troubled I became.

I was driving home past the Supreme Court that evening, knowing the jury was out considering its verdict, when I made a snap decision. If there was parking, I would call in. At that moment, a car pulled out to leave a vacancy directly outside the court. Destiny had made a special space for me. Ten minutes later, the jury returned to give its verdict, prompting the most emotional episode I had ever been part of. My earlier concerns deepened further. That night, I decided to research those two trials and the whole case as the basis for a book.

Within two months of the second verdict I had established from court records, from undisclosed testimony and from my own investigations that false, manufactured evidence had been used by police to convict Arthur Thomas at both trials, that evidence that could have aided his defence had been deliberately withheld, that exhibits had been faked and planted, that judges and juries had been systematically deceived to gain those verdicts.

. . .

In manufacturing a motive for Arthur Thomas as a killer, police investigators and Crown prosecutors moved into provable fiction. Since Thomas admitted having had a crush on Jeanette many years earlier, they argued that he must have harboured an obsessive jealousy over her marriage which finally drove him to murder. The fact that he had married happily two years before the Crewes did not disrupt their fantasy.

Their scenario: that Arthur Thomas made such a pest of himself with unwanted attentions that Jeanette had given up a teaching position at Maramarua District High School and fled 'all the way to Wanganui' to escape him. That there, she had confided to a complete stranger about the problems she had. That sometime after her marriage, when he had worked on their farm as a loader for a topdressing contractor, Arthur Thomas met Harvey Crewe while having morning and afternoon tea in the farmhouse and saw the Crewes prosperous and happily married. That picture stayed in his mind and he later went back and shot them. And having shot him, he callously took Harvey's watch and had it repaired, presumably for his own use. It was a picture jury members accepted.

. . .

My inquiries showed there was no basis for the claim. Education records I checked show Jeanette had actually applied for the Wanganui job at Whangaehu school before she went as a temporary teacher to Maramarua. A Crown witness teaching at Maramarua at the time and living with her at the hostel said she had never mentioned Thomas. Her landlady for two years in Wanganui, Mrs Claire Maureen Magee, told me: 'She came to Wanganui because her best friend Beverley Willis was living here. They had been overseas together . . . she stayed with Beverley for the first few months. It was a lovely home. Her father was the local magistrate, Mr Barry SM, and Beverley married the son of another magistrate, Mr Willis SM. I don't believe she came here to get away from Thomas — it was because her best friend was here.'

Jeanette first met Harvey Crewe when she was bridesmaid for Beverley Willis and he was groomsman. Mrs Willis, the friend Jeanette went to Wanganui to be near and her host for the first months, gave evidence at the second trial but, significantly, she was never asked important and potentially enlightening questions about all this.

Nor was Mrs Magee asked for significant facts about incomplete evidence Crown Prosecutor David Morris drew from her that Jeanette had confided to her, a virtual stranger, about problems with a man in Pukekawa. Mrs Magee gave me a simple and nonincriminating explanation. She was a solo mother at the time, being pestered by someone who wanted to take her out. It was she who confided in Jeanette, not vice versa. Jeanette had told her not to worry about the situation. It had happened to her once and didn't ever last long, she said. That was not the reaction of a woman in fear.

I remember walking the darkened streets of Wanganui after this conversation with Mrs Magee, muttering: 'Those bastards, those bastards.' And I meant it, I still do.

Then there was a suggested meeting between Thomas and the Crewes on the farm where they later died. Thomas agreed that he had worked on the farm while it was owned by Jeanette's uncle, the late Harold Chennell, but had never met or seen the couple there. Morris took him back again and again to the evidence of Detective Sergeant (later Inspector) John Rex Hughes that Thomas had given him this detail in an interview shortly after the deaths.

Morris: He said you told him you had met Harvey on the farm when working for the agricultural contractors some three or four years before. Did you tell him that?

Thomas: I did not, sir.

Morris: So, if what you are telling us is correct, the detective sergeant in his evidence has given us an entirely false picture of what you told him. Is that correct?

Thomas: Yes, sir, some of it.

Later, in his final address, Morris hammered that point too. 'You may think it significant that Thomas now denies telling Hughes these things which would mean a closer association with Harvey Crewe than he is now prepared to admit and also a continuing association with the farm and Jeanette, who was no doubt present on the farm at this particular time.'

She wasn't — and neither was Harvey. Within a few weeks of that second trial, I knew that both the testimony and the counsel' use of it was wrong. And I could and did prove it.

Thomas could not have met Crewe as Hughes testified and as Thomas denied. One word in particular added to the Hughes evidence had triggered that devastating attack on Thomas' credibility.

At the two earlier hearings, Hughes had testified: 'Thomas told me (on July 3, 1970) that while employed by an agricultural contractor three or four years before he had worked on the Crewe farm. He said he had morning and afternoon teas in the Crewe homestead. He said he had met a man he knew to be Harvey Crewe and said that he appeared to be a decent type of bloke . . .' The first trial judge, Mr Justice Henry, made plain in his summing up: the evidence was that Thomas had been to the farm before the arrival of the Crewes. (He presumably had met Harvey at some district occasion later).

At the second trial, Hughes added one word and materially altered the facts: 'He went on to tell me that while employed by an agricultural contractor . . . he had actually worked on the Crewe farm. He said they would have morning and afternoon teas in the house and he met Harvey Crewe THERE . . .'

What Hughes said could not have happened and Thomas would never have said it. Thomas had worked on the farm in the years before Crewe took it over, but never afterwards. My checks on the employment records of Barr Brothers, who had employed Thomas, showed he last worked on that farm sometime before leaving the company on 19 May 1965, when Jeanette was in Wanganui and Harvey was a fat lamb buyer in Martinborough — more than a year before they married and took over the farm. The suggested meeting which, it was claimed, provoked a flood of jealousy lasting years, had never happened.

My check of their records showed that Barr Brothers never topdressed the farm for Harvey Crewe. The last time was to spread 27 tons in April 1966, two months before the couple married and 11 months after Thomas left Barr Brothers. I was the only person who had checked those records.

When the commission took up the issue more than nine years later, it compared the Hughes evidence with that of Detective (later Inspector) Bruce Parkes whose job sheet recorded an interview with Thomas on 8 September 1970: 'He would have been on the Chennell Estate (later the Crewe farm) between four and six times . . . Jack Handcock was the manager and Thomas would have eaten meals in the house while working there . . . he had not been on the property since.' And a written statement from Thomas in October said the same thing.

The commission rightly said the Hughes evidence 'assumed substantial importance . . . whether Thomas had been in the company of Mr and Mrs Crewe in their own home . . . and from the point of the credibility of Thomas in the witness box'. It accepted that Morris had believed that police checks had been made on the employment records to verify the Hughes evidence. It found no evidence that checks had in fact been made:

'The evidence of Detective Hughes concerning Thomas having been on the Crewe property and having had morning tea with them was wrong. If this was not known to be so by the police . . . it should have been and could easily have been found to be so by them . . .

'We are forced to conclude that the police preferred to leave the matter in a state which allowed the Crown prosecutor to cross-examine and address the jury as he did. Undoubtedly the matter should have been investigated and was not.

'We find the police failure to establish the truth of the matter was improper conduct.'

That was only the beginning of consistent failure to establish the truth — a failure that made nonsense of much of what David Morris told the jury about likely motive. Nonsense that clearly affected both verdicts and, in the final count, misled a total of 11 judges.

Like this from the second trial:

Morris: Do you know anybody with more reason than you to be jealous of Harvey Crewe?

Arthur Thomas, punch-drunk from hours of heavy and inaccurate cross-examination knew instinctively that if he said yes, he would be asked who? So, unwillingly, he said, 'No.'

In his final address to the second jury and to five judges later at the Court of Appeal, David Morris grossly misquoted the exchange: 'In cross examination he agreed that "no one in Pukekawa had more reason than me to be jealous of Harvey Crewe".'

The commission: 'We reject entirely the notion that any of the evidence put forward in this respect established a motive by Arthur Allan Thomas to kill the Crewes'.

The watch, the last-minute testimony that had proved so devastating in the last days of the first trial, proved all-purpose evidence, damning to Thomas whichever way the Crown used it. The first suggestion that Thomas had calmly taken his watch in for repair after damaging it in killing the Crewes was bad enough. But the second version — that he had ripped the watch off his victim's wrist at some stage of the murder — was, if anything, worse.

The Crown was forced into that fall-back position after evidence of family and friends showed that Thomas had never owned a rolled-gold watch. He had, instead, a stainless-steel model. Disregarding the fact that it had plainly misinformed the first jury, the Crown brazenly used Eggleton as a witness a second time, simply switching the watch from killer to victim. This was typical of the reasoning. Anything went, as long as it reflected badly on Thomas.

It took an anonymous phone call to prove just how unfair police tactics were, specifically about the watch. 'If you want to know about the watch, find John

Fisher,' the voice on my phone said — and then hung up. No other clues, simply a name. Amazingly, within five hours I had found him hundreds of kilometres away in Feilding. And I had almost certainly found the watch that Eggleton had talked about — and it wasn't Arthur Thomas' or Harvey Crewe's. John Fisher was a young butcher turned mechanic who had once taken his old rolled-gold watch with a cracked glass and caked with blood and mucus into Eggleton for repair. He said he had long ago given the watch to his children to play with.

Fisher had no doubts that the watch Eggleton had talked about was his. In what he remembered as late 1970, this butcher working as a mechanic in Pukekohe had killed a pig for friends. It was in the boot of his car. His father in-law had earlier chided him about the muck around his watch from earlier butchery and it had stopped. So he took it in for cleaning and repair. He remembered the occasion well. His wife was pregnant and sat in the car double-parked outside the shop. When he went back several days later to collect the watch, Eggleton tried to get him to buy a new strap for it.

The watch? Yes, he had found it in the bottom of the toy box in a jigsaw puzzle. It was old, rolled-gold and among the repair marks in it was Eggleton's, dated 12 January 1971 — six weeks before Eggleton's dramatic appearance at the first Thomas trial.

I was not the first person to hear about the incident. After reading the Eggleton evidence in a *Truth* newspaper summary of the first trial, Fisher had contacted police. Detectives had flown from Auckland to interview him and he had never heard from them again.

The police evidence was that the confusion over the date made them believe it had no relevance.

The commission did not agree. After I made the watch available and having heard evidence from Fisher, the commission held that the police should have told the defence of this evidence and allowed it to be tested in court at the second trial. Instead, they had changed their scenario to make it Crewe's watch even though no one could remember him ever owning or wearing such a watch. As the commission would later accurately sum-up: 'It is quite apparent to us that considerations of honesty, fairness to the defence and proper practice, were of no weight whatsoever to Mr (Bruce) Hutton (Inspector in charge of the investigation) in his desire to see Thomas convicted a second time.'

Soon after his arrival in New Zealand, Judge Taylor asked me to autograph a copy of my book on the case. His reading of it and the later evidence he heard which bore out my seven-year-old findings must have made him realise the relevance of the book's title: *Trial by Ambush*.

. . .

No tactic was too devious, no forensic evidence too improbable, as police defended their prize exhibit, the cartridge from the Crewe garden, to the ultimate. For good reason. As David Morris warned, when he for once accurately summed up to the second trial jury and then to the five judges at the Court of Appeal in 1975:

Discrediting the cartridge could be taken as an indication of planting by police officers involving 'a conspiracy of the most terrible kind'. It was.

In all this, in perhaps the strangest twist of all, it was a former policeman who began what grew into an avalanche of evidence which ultimately swept the Crown case away. The planting allegation was implicit from the first disclosure of the cartridge case and how the police said they discovered it.

Within a few days of deciding against charging Len Demler for the murder of his daughter and son-in-law, the police investigation made a double switch of direction — towards a new prime suspect and an entirely new theory on how the couple had been shot. The original reconstruction had been very straightforward, that the murderer had walked in through the unlocked back door and into the lounge, firing the shots inside the house. Both were killed by distinctive CAC pattern 8 bullets, easily identifiable by the figure 8 on their base. When a new addition to the investigation team pointed out in October that the louvre windows above the kitchen sink were open in first police photos of the scene taken in June, a new scenario was floated. This involved the killer standing on a ledge beside the back door and firing through the open louvres to kill Harvey as he sat in a chair in front of the fire, then going into the house to shoot Jeanette. (It was never explained why the murderer should risk this when the door was open for him to enter at will and kill both at close range.) A simulation convinced police the louvre shot was possible and it became the crux of all future events.

From that beginning, police took the theory a stage further. If the shot was fired from that position, then the used cartridge case could have been ejected into nearby garden.

Despite extensive searching and sieving of the gardens four months earlier, Inspector Hutton two weeks later ordered that a particular stretch of garden 15 feet from the louvres be sieved. He later explained that he had 'discovered this garden had not been previously sieved'.

In under an hour, Sergeant (later Superintendent) Michael Charles discovered a cartridge case that was later shown to have come from the Thomas rifle. If, as I suspect they had, police had scripted the finding of the shellcase in the garden they could not have cast a better man than Charles to find it. Honest, convincing and himself totally convinced that the shellcase he found was a legitimate exhibit, he was the ideal witness to testify as he did.

They did well too with Sergeant (later Inspector) Stan Keith, who genuinely found a cartridge with a number 8 bullet (of the type that killed the Crewes) in a box of odds and ends in the Thomas garage. He too had that justified air of honesty that the police case needed — an honesty in giving evidence and standing firm by it, which ultimately was to wreck the conspiracy of which he was not a part.

Crucially, Keith testified four times that after pulling the bullet from the cartridge, he fired the empty case in a rifle to remove the primer. He then gave Dr Nelson what the scientist described as 'a fired shellcase' and the number 8 bullet it had contained. The arrest followed a few days later.

Thomas supporters cried 'planted' from the first disclosure of this new and telling exhibit.

At the trials, the two cartridge cases were part of hundreds of exhibits and were known as exhibit 343 (the case Keith found) and 350 (the one Charles found). Later, at the second trial and all subsequent hearings, they were defined as categories three and four. In this context, for simplicity, I refer to them simply as the Keith and Charles cartridge cases.

First trial defence counsel, the late Paul Temm QC (later a judge), brought evidence suggesting that the shell case would have been more heavily corroded if it had been there in the garden all those months. Thomas Retrial supporters secretly buried cartridge cases on the Crewe property, digging them up at night months later to study the corrosion and illustrate what they saw as differences between them and the cartridge case Charles had found. As well, Temm highlighted a bloodstain directly under the chair Harvey Crewe had died in. Something like 12 other stains had been meticulously numbered by police. But not this one. He argued that this stain had been caused by blood seeping through the chair and that the chair had been moved to drag Harvey's body away. If the stain on the chair was realigned up with the unnumbered stain on the carpet, the high back of the chair would have sheltered Harvey Crewe from an unlikely marksman at the louvres. It was, in my view, a powerful point which the police could only counter by ignoring the stain below the chair.

The jury was unimpressed by Temm's submissions and convicted Thomas. When the case went back to the Court of Appeal in 1972 and then to a second trial, the defence had new evidence. Graham Hewson, one of Harvey Crewe's closest friends, had come through from Woodville as soon as the mystery was reported. He looked after the stock and helped police in their searching. He realised after the first trial that the explanation Inspector Hutton had given about that garden not having been sieved was wrong. He remembered having helped police searchers sieve there months before during the original searches. He came forward to correct that testimony despite his friendship with Crewe and solely because he thought the case against Thomas was faked: 'If he'd done it, I wouldn't want him just jailed, I'd have wanted him hanged,' he told me when I interviewed him in Woodville in 1973. A lineup of police from Inspector Hutton down denied his claim. And the second jury believed them.

. . .

Like the first, the second trial produced sensational evidence in its final stages — this time for the defence. Jack Ritchie, a retired detective, was then a 63-year-old gun-shop owner in Dannevirke. After reading detail from the first trial, in particular about the controversial cartridge case, he began checking old stock to see if he could locate similar cartridges containing number 8 bullets. In the process, his sharp eyes located a significant thing. The cartridges all had their maker's stamp on their base. But all the cases that contained the number 8 bullets had what he saw was a definably different style of lettering. In all his searches, he could not find a number 8 bullet in a cartridge case like the one from the garden. The bullets that type contained all had plain bases — no number 8. He wrote to Pat Vesey, then chairman of the retrial committee, with his theory and samples. The package was opened in the last days of the trial.

After Dr Jim Sprott had examined both the theory and the cartridge exhibits, the fired Charles case from the garden and the unfired Keith cartridge from the garage, he gave evidence suggesting that there was a difference in the ICI lettering, in particular the central C, and it coincided with different types of bullets. On that basis, he said, the case from the garden would not have contained a number 8 bullet like those found in the Crewes' skulls.

I remember the flurry of concern, the adjournment to allow rebuttal evidence to be sought, then the condescending confidence as the Crown utterly rejected the notion. Its forensic expert, Dr Donald Nelson, said he had examined the two cases, that Dr Sprott was wrong. There were no major differences in the lettering and what minor differences there were resulted because the case from the garden had been fired, the one from the garage had not. More than that, the makers of the ICI cases in Melbourne had confirmed in a phone call that there had been no change in lettering specifications in the years involved.

David Morris told the judge and the jury, 'It is plain beyond any doubt that Dr Sprott's categories are, in fact, indistinguishable and that the Charles shell and the Keith shell are indistinguishable.'

An apparent end of the argument. Next day, Arthur Thomas was again convicted. He went back to Paremoremo. Kevin Ryan remembers visiting him after the Appeal Court almost automatically dismissed his sentence. 'Never mind, Arthur, you're half way through your sentence,' he said. 'Someone else's sentence, 'Thomas snapped.

His family and the retrial committee sank back into physical and emotional exhaustion, wondering where to turn next and if there was anywhere. Jim Sprott flew out on a much-postponed overseas business trip. I borrowed the notes of evidence of the two trials from my old school contemporaries Temm and Kevin Ryan, and began my private in investigation.

The crucial stage of the argument, which would ultimately see Arthur Thomas declared innocent, was only just beginning.

. . .

The cartridge case evidence, I believed, would be a much harder issue to analyse than the disturbing and significant revelations about the Hughes evidence and the Maramarua school fiction. As a schoolboy I had been little more than a casual observer in science and maths classes. Now, as an adult, I faced the prospect of long nights of study coping with what was a complex and potentially confusing assignment. I borrowed from Kevin Ryan examples of the cartridges Jack Ritchie had sent, plus the exhibit photographs of the Charles case, and prepared for a long and laborious study.

The first stage lasted only two minutes. Perhaps it was a working lifetime's experience with type. Whatever it was, little more than a glance and then a second hard look was enough to convince me that both the Crown submissions and supporting evidence of the makers at the second trial had been wrong. There *were* significant differences in the lettering on the bases. The cartridge cases *were not* indistinguishable as Nelson and Morris had convinced both the judge and the jury.

More than that. Of the cartridges I examined, one style of case with identifiable variations in the lettering like the one Keith found contained number 8 bullets and those cases like the Charles example from the garden did not. After I had the cartridge cases photographed and enlarged in *The Auckland Star* darkroom, I could measure the differences in gaps between letters and other features. When I went back to Kevin and Gerald Ryan to show them my results, both said — as they still do — that for the first time they could understand what the Crown had rebutted and the jury had rejected. I was now convinced that the Charles cartridge case from the garden was, and could be proved to be, a fake.

Those telling photographs of cartridge cases said to be identical but clearly different were major illustrations in a high-impact section of my published investigation. Their significance hit home in high places — in particular, with Dr Martyn Finlay, the Minister of Justice in the Kirk Labour Government. He said immediately that he found the evidence I had published warranted close study and if the detail I had given could be substantiated he would refer the Thomas conviction back to the Court of Appeal. Spurred by this, the Thomas Retrial Committee suddenly and understandably found new life. A protest meeting in the Auckland Town Hall drew more than 2000 people. Others followed throughout the country.

The plot thickened considerably and quickly. Kevin Ryan met David Morris in the street not far from the *Star* building one lunch hour in the days that followed and suggested joint action by Crown and defence to clear up those Booth claims once and for all. He suggested that they take the Charles and Keith cartridge cases to Auckland University to have neutral scientists there examine them and say 'identical' or 'different'. He was surprised that Morris was so laidback on the issue. This inquiry, the Crown prosecutor said, will never get off the ground. When Ryan pressed him as to why, he said, 'You know what happens to exhibits when there is no further use for them.'

Ryan: I suppose they are dumped.

Morris: I tell you, this inquiry will never get off the ground.

Quickly back in his office, Kevin Ryan rang me excitedly. 'I think they've destroyed the exhibits.'

That afternoon I set the trap. I asked Finlay if I could have access to the exhibits for further study, in particular of the cartridge cases. He agreed. By now, I had been joined by Jim Sprott in what was going to be a seven-year partnership. Back from overseas, he had at first been guarded, as any scientist might when confronted by data from a journalist, when I told him of my findings before they were published. But within a few minutes we had established a level of respect which was the basis of our joint work over the years, and the foundation for a very deep friendship.

At my suggestion, the *Star* flew us to Melbourne to discuss the findings and to examine the records of the ICI cartridge case makers. Soon after arrival we were armed with specialist photography showing the differences I had so amateurishly illustrated. In absolute contrast with the stubborn resistance of New Zealand police, the Victorian Police Forensic Laboratory had made available experts and sophisticated equipment to help our investigation. The laboratory's comparison microscopes, for example, made nonsense of the Crown claims.

This equipment took two cartridge cases at a time, its viewing device linking the image of one half with that of the second case to match — or in this case, to clearly fail to match — the lettering. Later, an expert police witness from the laboratory would fly to New Zealand to give evidence supporting our claims. So did leading experts from the Melbourne makers.

They were astonished that there had been undetected changes in the lettering which were obvious when we pointed them out in their samples — one box from every month of production kept for 10 years. Clearly, what had happened had been an accident. As bumpers that stamped the letters into the bases of the cartridge cases wore out, others were cast and when the hobs that made them showed signs of wear, they were replaced as well. At some time in the early 1960s, an engraver had noticed what he felt was an imbalance in the positioning of the C in the lettering and had corrected it. Unofficially.

So, when ICI experts were quoted at short notice at the second trial as saying there had been no change in specifications in those years, they were right. There had been no official change — but there had been alterations just the same. And after our visit, they could identify those changes and put a date on them.

That piece of engraving ad-libbing was crucial to the campaign to free Arthur Thomas.

By painstaking checking of the boxes of cartridges in ICI samples, study of hob order forms and other documents at the Melbourne plant, plus detail on bullet production at the CAC factory in Mt Eden where the imported cartridge cases were filled, we could and did prove our argument. The Keith case could be dated to before the undetected change in letter, the Charles case came after.

There was another significant time factor. Our investigations showed that the last number 8 bullets, like those that killed the Crewes and like the one found by Keith, were loaded into brass cartridge cases on the CAC production line in Mt Eden on 10 October 1963. Our check on company and shipping records showed that the last cartridge cases from Melbourne that could have been involved in that assembly were cargo on the ship *Kaituna* which left Melbourne in August. That was five months before cartridge cases of the type Charles produced from the Crewe garden were made. The two components had never been on the production line together. Number 8 bullets had never been loaded into that style of cartridge case. Neither of the bullets that killed the Crewes could have been fired from that cartridge case. The obvious conclusion: the cartridge case had been planted to frame Arthur Thomas.

As we prepared to fly home with sworn statements and company records that documented this, there came confirmation of the destruction of the exhibits. The phone in my hotel room called me out of the shower for Valerie to tell me about Dr Finlay's announcement. The police response to a direction from him to release the exhibits to me was a sensation. They couldn't, they said. They had dumped them in Whitford Tip outside Auckland on 27 July 1973. Finlay described himself as 'desolate and deeply troubled'. Hundreds of enraged Aucklanders were already offering to search the tip and find that evidence. Without even drying myself, and leaving the shower on, I pulled some clothes on and ran down the hotel passage to Jim Sprott's room.

We were overjoyed. At that moment, able to prove that the bullets and the Charles cartridge case did not match, and with the police having destroyed the exhibits under such questionable circumstances, we believed we had won.

We had — but it would take nearly seven years before that victory was acknowledged and justice was achieved for Arthur Thomas. The Crown and the police would never concede. They would fight to the end using any tactic they believed likely to defeat us — or obscure the real issues. We were tapped, trailed, obstructed and ridiculed as our investigation went on.

The Auckland ammunition makers, CAC, were also under pressure: anonymous phone callers with the sound of machinery behind them told us of police visiting the plant wanting earlier company testimony altered to rebut our facts. Sprott and I were wholly dependent on unofficial contact with CAC. The company refused at that stage to provide us with any information while, at the same time, making every facility available to the police. It said it did not recognise us as 'bona fide representatives of the defence since no case was before the cour'. And when, seven months later, the company made records available, the condition was that I would not be present.

. . .

Bullying was common . . . At the second trial, within my hearing, Inspector Hutton threatened to arrest defence counsel Gerald Ryan for 'having posed as a policeman' when he made a phone call to the Melbourne cartridge case makers and that he had a tape to prove it. Ryan denied it. He said that if Hutton did have a tape then he, Ryan, had nothing to fear. At the Wellington Court of Appeal hearing, again in my presence, Hutton warned the Thomas barrister, Peter Williams, that unless old Mrs Ivy Thomas stopped making remarks in his hearing he would arrest her.

. . .

As Jim Sprott and I flew back from our first visit to Melbourne, just after my series was published, we crossed in mid-Tasman with Inspector Hutton and Dr Nelson on their way there in a damage-control mission, desperate for any evidence that might support an already losing cause. They did not do well. Despite their pressure on Melbourne executives and engineers at the plant that produced the ICI cartridge cases, these men refused to agree or to sign affidavits that the two types of lettering were 'identical and indistinguishable'.

Instead, Hutton and Nelson produced a new cartridge exhibit through a discovery that Dr Finlay was to describe as 'miraculous' — but which had some other descriptions attached in the years ahead. In its simplest form, the new development was this. Nelson produced from his private collection of cartridge cases. He called it 1964/2 which he said indicated the year and the month, February, when he had acquired it. It was identical to the Charles case, he said. Since it was at the CAC plant at that time, then it was possible proof that the Charles-type cases could have been there in time to be loaded with number 8 bullets and that the Booth-Sprott findings were wrong.

We weren't wrong. He was. When Sprott first saw photographs of the 'miraculous' find, he detected a major difference. It had a subtle shape difference around its base which Nelson hadn't detected. That suggested that it was a later design which included a different production process — use of 'wet priming' rather than the 'dry priming' used until the mid-1960s.

. . .

The findings totally destroyed the 'miraculous' cartridge case as evidence of anything other than more police duplicity. It was a much later case made well beyond the production years involving the number 8 bullets and the Charles exhibit. The powder in it, Accurex, was also from a much later production cycle.

. . .

The 1974–75 Court of Appeal referral, which Sir Richard Wild chaired, faced with the total rebuttal of police evidence on two key exhibits, went for cover in its findings. It 'derived no assistance from exhibit 1964/2 [the Nelson cartridge] . . . we do not think we should place any reliance on exhibit 343 [the Keith cartridge] and have accordingly disregarded it'.

So much for miraculous and significant police evidence.

A national appeal Sprott had made for .22 ICI ammunition of the period produced 26,000 rounds from all over the country, much of it still in boxes carrying the distinctive production batch number. Sorted into a progressively dated archive, none of it produced a cartridge that broke the pattern, a Charles type case with a number 8 bullet. No doubt police staged their own, more elaborate, search involving all their resources with the same result. They called in Interpol for assistance. That did not help either.

They produced a Who's Who of the DSIR to back their case to the Court of Appeal. They withheld detail of a lengthy and involved technical treatise involving 12 separate measurements of200 cartridge cases until the last of our Australian technical and Victoria police laboratory witnesses had left to return to Australia. But our case, now supported by the individual findings of emeritus

Professor of Engineering Neil Mowbray, stood firm.

Even those five judges had to agree. After months of consideration, their report found that we had proved our case, that on the balance of probabilities (the level of proof they had demanded), number 8 bullets had not been loaded into Charles-type cartridge cases. But they gave the Crown the benefit of a huge doubt. Although none had ever been found, although there was no company record that supported the theory, could not, said, rule out the possibility that it could have happened.

The following year, we flew to London and took that decision to the Privy Council. The law lords held they had no jurisdiction to review the ruling, since the Crown Law Office had cleverly sought an opinion from the Court of Appeal and not a ruling. The Privy Council does not deal with opinions.

Jim Sprott and I had to wait five more years and for that commission of inquiry before the full facts were fairly considered and assessed.

In the meantime, Robert Muldoon asked a question and got a reply that deserves reporting. Jim Sprott and I were briefing him in yet another attempt to get government action late one afternoon. I had been speaking for some minutes when I became aware that his eyes had closed. I thought he had dozed off and I had lost him. Until I mentioned the attitudes and actions of judges. One of those eyes came open and he fixed me with it. "'What do you put their actions down to — incompetence or corruption?'

I told him that given those alternatives, I would have to say incompetence. His eye closed and the briefing continued.

That reply still stands — with a degree of qualification. Incompetence is entirely justified. Corruption is too sweeping. Stubborn, with closed minds, unwilling to put aside their prejudices and to accept that their system had failed, unprepared to allow non-legal critics to be proved right, unwilling to place the rights of one nonentity from an obscure country area above the apparently sacred processes of their law, utterly deceived and prepared to allow that situation to continue — the judges were all those things.

After the Thomas pardon, the Muldoon government, pressured into an inquiry against its better judgement, tailored the terms of reference to prevent examination of the actions of judges and lawyers at the various trials and hearings. This tactic gagged evidence on aspects of the affair that cried out for investigation, both for the good of the system and the rights of often powerless individuals who are dependent on it.

The government, the justice system and the legal profession, the law society, were all ready to sweep the real issues under the courtroom carpet. Not prepared to ask the obvious questions: how could the system fail so badly and for so long? How could clearly and deliberately wrong testimony be accepted by so many so often? How could skilled professional prosecutors fail to detect the conspiracy — worse still, actually aid it through their actions? Could it happen again? What should be done to prevent a repetition? Why was no action taken against the principal named as the culprit, Bruce Hutton, by then retired from the police?

From the report of the Royal Commission to inquire into the circumstances of the convictions of Arthur Allan Thomas for the murders of David Harvey Crewe and Jeanette Lenore Crewe: 'The shellcase exhibit 350 [the Charles case] was planted in the Crewe garden by Detective Inspector Hutton and Detective Sergeant Lenrick James Johnston. [The co-accused, Sergeant Johnston, had, by then, died of cancer.] They had access to the Thomas rifle and a packet of cartridges from his farm . . . The destruction of some of the exhibits in the Whitford Tip was an improper act designed to prevent further investigation [of the Charles cartridge case] . . . Detective Inspector Hutton [later] improperly misled his superiors concerning the chances of recovering the exhibits from the tip. There was impropriety on the part of the police in failing to investigate properly the records of Thomas's employment with Barr Brothers.'

About the forensic evidence . . . 'In our considered opinion it is grossly improper for an expert witness to allow personal vanity and a stubborn determination to be right at all costs, to colour his evidence as Dr Nelson has done . . .'

. . .

The commission concluded that: 'Mr Thomas should never have been convicted of the crimes . . . our findings go further. They make it clear that he should never have been charged. He was charged and convicted because the police manufactured evidence against him and withheld evidence of value to his defence . . . we believe we are entitled to proclaim him innocent . . .'

'He [Hutton] swore falsely . . . was responsible for Thomas being twice convicted, his appeals thrice dismissed and for his spending nine years in prison, to be released as a result of sustained public refusal to accept these decisions.'

And, for me, after seven years of campaigning, a personal footnote when the commission granted Arthur Thomas nearly $1 million in compensation, other sums to his family and to Vivien Thomas and $50,000 to Jim Sprott, who had claimed $150,000 for his scientific work: 'We draw attention to the immense labour of Mr Patrick Booth in the field of investigative journalism. This was carried out as a private enterprise and at some considerable sacrifice to family life. He has formally claimed only a token $1. We are more than happy to include our recognition of the devotion of Mr Booth to this cause.'

. . .

Bruce Hutton retired from the police the same year at 47. He later farmed near Auckland International Airport and bred racehorses. Arthur Thomas used his compensation to buy a 125-hectare farm at Orini in the Waikato and later remarried. Vivien Thomas lived in Perth with her second husband.

. . .

No police inquiry was held. No charges were ever laid. I believe they should have been. If Bruce Hutton was innocent of the planting and conspiracy charges, then he should have had the opportunity of proving it. If he was guilty, as the commission clearly believed, then he should have been punished for what the inquiry described as 'an unspeakable outrage'.

CHAPTER TWELVE

Raids and racism

1976: *The Auckland Star* examines the controversial dawn raids and random
street arrests of Polynesian immigrants.

It's hard to imagine today, but there was once a New Zealand where the best
rugby teams were not heavily reliant on Pacific Islanders, where schools did
not have a strong contingent of Samoans, Tongans, Fijians and Niueans, where
people from those and other islands were not accepted and welcomed as part of
the multi-cultural mix of the country today.

Yet that was the case in Auckland in 1976, when race tension reached flash
point. Police cars roamed the streets asking anyone with brown skin for their
passport, and arresting those without them. Police squads stormed into the
houses of terrified families at dawn, yanking bedclothes off women and poking
under beds in a search for 'overstayers', the term given to anyone who had
overstayed a temporary visitor's permit.

Tens of thousands of Pacific Islanders had flooded into the country since
the late 1960s, lured by the promise of work and good pay. Many arrived on
temporary visitor's permits and stayed on illegally. Given little or no training in
English or other skills for surviving in New Zealand society, they took the jobs
and houses no one else wanted, and paid with their health.

The government response was brutal. In 1973, it had started dawn raids by
police to arrest and deport overstayers. A public outcry led the then Labour
government to end the practice. But it did nothing to stop immigration, and by
1976 numbers had almost doubled to 78,000, from 45,000 just four years earlier.

Europeans feared a crime wave as stories emerged of booze-fuelled rapes
and beatings. No one really understood the grim conditions many immigrants
were living in, or cared to know. The issue came to a head with the bizarre
arrest and prosecution of a 17-year-old Niuean factory hand, Iki Toloa, for theft
as a servant. *The Auckland Star*, under the leadership of Pat Booth, began an
investigation. It soon found out that the 'theft' was of a 10-cent plastic comb, a

reject that Toloa had picked out of a rubbish bin. The resultant publicity led the police to withdraw the charges. One university lecturer 'stole' a biro pen and presented himself at the Auckland Police Station and asked to be arrested.

But the *Star* went further. Booth sent reporter Jim Tully (later to become one of the country's best-known journalism teachers and scholars) to the Pacific Islands, and together with Samoan reporter John Paga, Tony Potter and Maggie Tully they crafted a series, 'The Islanders'. For the first time, it explored in depth the conditions faced by Pacific Islanders in New Zealand.

What those reporters found shocked many. Overcrowded homes and shockingly high rates of serious work injuries were among the facts they laid out. And crime — as Booth later wrote, 'in one month in 1976, six out of nine cases involving death in Auckland resulted in the conviction of an Islander' (Booth, 1997, p. 144). The series concluded that the government would have to be firm, and end unrestricted entry by Pacific Islanders.

The series was a smash hit, though not always in the way intended. As Tongan community leader Clive Edwards said: 'The series created an awareness of ourselves that people were blind to before. People criticized it for highlighting what they saw as bad points. But it became part of a soul-searching and self-examination process that led to a new direction' (Booth, 1997, p. 146). It also opened the eyes of all New Zealanders, and led to new efforts to help the new arrivals settle. The then Immigration Minister, Frank Gill, was quoted on the front page of the *Star* as saying that he was so impressed with the series' accuracy and depth he was going to take it on a tour of the Islands he was about to go on.

His Cabinet colleagues must have been impressed in other ways, too, because they took the series' conclusions quite literally. Only two weeks later, police resumed the controversial dawn raids. In one such raid, they entered the house of Mrs Telesia Topping at 6 a.m. The first thing Mrs Topping, who was married to a New Zealander, knew of their arrival was when a policeman entered her bedroom and pulled off her bedclothes. When the *Star* questioned the head of the Immigration section of the Labour Department in Auckland about why it was breaking the ministerial ban on dawn raids, his response was that 6.30 a.m. 'was not dawn' (Rudman, 1976).

Then, in October that year, police began the even more controversial tactic of stopping people with brown skin in the streets of Auckland and asking for their passports. Those who could not supply them were often arrested. Many Māori were detained. Embarrassed, the government at first denied that the arrests were taking place, until the *Star* flew to Wellington several affidavits of those arrested, and quoted Māori police officers who confirmed the policy and condemned it. By December, the government was beaten, and the raids and street arrests stopped.

The *Star* was first to get on to the issue of the dawn raids, and led the reporting all the way through. Ironically, the reporter who helped the *Star* get many of those scoops had been rejected just a few years earlier. While at university in Auckland, Rudman had become involved in student media, and scored a sensational scoop for the student newspaper that exposed SIS infiltration of the Students' Association. It gave him a taste for journalism, but when he applied to both *The New Zealand Herald* and *The Auckland Star* he was rejected as being 'too political', so took off to London. 'People with degrees were then looked down on in newspapers. They were taken on as cadets and then stuck on the tea trolley,' Rudman says (Rudman, 2016).

The *Star* must have been glad it had changed its mind, because Rudman's student political contacts helped him get many of the scoops on this story. He worked closely with the paper's Pacific Affairs reporter, John Paga, and says that together they led the national coverage of the issue. 'I was pretty outraged at what was going on. It was hard to believe. It was embarrassing, really, as New Zealanders, that this was going on' (Rudman, 2016).

Although he's spent a lifetime writing journalism that tries to dig deeper, Rudman doesn't really buy the term 'investigative journalist'. He points out that some of the best investigations are done as part of the routine of daily journalism work, published as news stories rather than delivered in one dramatic package. 'I enjoy digging but I have always wondered whether the investigative thing is a bit superfluous. I have always thought that was what a reporter should do. I quite like investigating stories but putting out the story as it comes' (Rudman, 2016).

The story published here is a good example. It was part of a series that won Rudman the Dulux Journalist of the Year Award (then the country's premier journalism honour) in 1976. It was also a significant element in long-running coverage that amounted to an investigation into an issue of deep public concern, that helped shift public consciousness by the accretion of revelation. In the best traditions of journalism, it did that not by telling people what to think, but by showing them what was being done in their name.

Booth, P. (1997). *Deadline*. Auckland: Viking.

Rudman, B. (1976, February 20). '6.30's not dawn, says official'. *The Auckland Star*.

Rudman, B. (2016, December 15). Interview with author, J. Hollings.

Dawn raids start again for illegal Tongan migrants: Woman tells of visit from police

Auckland Star, 19 February 1976

Dawn raids in search of Tongan "overstays" — stopped in 1974 after a public outcry — restarted in Auckland this month with swoops in South Auckland, Ponsonby and Onehunga.

Police tactics during the swoops are causing growing concern among Tongans and their leaders.

The Minister of the Free Church of Tonga, Mr P. T. Latu, said today: "Police seem to search blindly when it involves Tongans.

"I am very worried for my people. When they come I tell them their best friends are the police. If you ask them, they will help you. Now they come to me, my people, and tell me of these raids, and the way the police treat them. What can I say?"

The innocent victim of one raid, Mrs Telesia Topping of Onehunga, was almost in tears when she described to the Star a 6.a.m raid on her home on Tuesday. Mrs Topping is married to a New Zealander and has lived here 10 years. With her in the house were six Tongan relatives. She said all were on valid six-month working holiday permits granted at Mangere Airport when they arrived on November 20, last year.

Mrs Topping's home had been checked by Immigration officials in August, to ensure it was suitable, before the permits had been granted to her relatives. Jobs had also been arranged and approved.

At the airport, the relatives had entered Mrs Topping's address as their place of stay in Auckland. This is Mrs Topping's story.

"At 6 o'clock we were all asleep except for one, who had to be at work at seven. He was making breakfast when he saw a policeman trying to push up the window. He was pointing towards the door.

"As the door opened, they burst inside. Four were inside, four more outside the house. A young policeman, about 23 years old, came into my room. I'd just opened my eyes because of the noise. I asked him what he was doing in my bedroom. He did not answer.

"I was really frightened. He went into the bathroom, inspected it, came back and pulled up the covers of my bed, looked under the bed. I called out to him again what he was doing in my bedroom. He ignored me.

"He pulled open the wardrobe, fiddled with the clothing, checking everything. The same policeman went into the adjoining room where my two nephews, aged 19 and 20 were asleep.

"The policeman shone the light in their eyes, saying 'get up and get out.' Another policeman was also there. My nephews were very frightened. The police then started dragging them out to their van."

Mrs Topping again pleaded with them to stop and asked why they were there. One of them said they were taking us in because we were illegal immigrants and I told them we were not."

Papers were then produced to prove the six were not illegal and they were allowed to come back inside the house. Then police asked for Mrs Topping's passport. They finally accepted her explanation that it was with the Immigration Department because she was applying for citizenship. "They did not apologize after that. They just walked out."

Mrs Topping could not go to work for the past two days, she was so upset.

In a letter of protest to Immigration Minister Frank Gill, Mrs Topping complains about the way police can "enter and do what they like, and their rudeness and inconsideration in going about their checking."

She writes: "Would it not have been proper for them to ask for the owner of the house, to surround the house and check things out in an orderly and civilised manner?"

Mr Latu said today: "It is not fair the way they treat us. The police won't find any truth from Tongan people now. They're too scared of them. If police keep acting like this, I'm scared something must happen."

The head of the immigration section of the Labour Department in Auckland, Mr A. W. Smith, said today that they had a lot of complaints about police behaviour during "inquiries" but "they've all turned out to be false."

He said police went through a certain procedure when they went to a house, asking first whether they could come in. He said the "checks" had been intensified since Christmas "because we've been given more staff. There are a lot of places where the people are here legally — well they have nothing to worry about."

He said they acted every time they received a phone call or written note saying there was someone "illegal" at a certain house.

"We will act on an anonymous phone call," he said. "It has to be done, otherwise we'd get further calls in a week or so asking why we had not checked."

The raids had to be early in the morning, he said, as "this is the only time to catch them at home." He said there have been 30 people before the Courts since last Monday on immigration charges.

Chief Inspector A .R. Mathieson said today that the raid had nothing to do with police. "We are there only to assist immigration officials." Before he could comment on Mrs Topping's allegations against police behaviour he said he preferred that an official complaint be made to the Onehunga police.

Immigration officials said today normal procedure had been followed on the Tuesday morning raid. "We usually knock on the door and say 'We're from the Immigration Department and police, may we come in please?'", Mr Smith said.

He said he knew of no cases where permission had been refused. When illegal immigrants were present they were too busy getting out windows, he said.

The officials would not enter if permission was refused. About half the raids found nothing, he said.

Late last week six houses were raided in Otahuhu resulting in 14 arrests. On Tuesday, nine houses, including Mrs Topping's, were visited in Onehunga. Six people were arrested. On Wednesday, four houses were raided in Ponsonby resulting in three arrests.

Police wrongly arrest Tongan trio in mix-up: Boy (6) sobs as parents go

Auckland Star, 2 November 1976

A six-year-old Tongan boy was left sobbing and inconsolate in a Grey Lynn house after police arrested his parents in error as suspected overstayers.

The parents, Mr and Mrs Sione Mafi Fuavao, and a friend, Mr Sami Fuapoivaha, were released yesterday after more than 30 hours in police custody, court and prison cells. All had signed the overstayer's register.

The head of the Labour Department's immigration section, Mr Athol Smith, said the police were supplied with the register on Friday evening.

"But I have been unable to check with them what happened," he said. "It appears there's been a slip-up."

Friends in the Scanlan St house cared for six-year-old Masiu Fuavao, who woke when the police came to the house at 6 a.m. on Sunday to make the arrests.

A woman who tried to console Masiu said: "He was very upset and crying. He didn't know if his parents were going to come back, and he didn't know why the police had taken them."

The Fuavaos came to New Zealand last year for their other son Tesimoni (20) to have an operation at Auckland Hospital for a stomach complaint. The illness could not be treated in Tonga.

Mr Smith said it is department practice to pass the register over to the police on Friday evening. "This is so that if anything turns up over the weekend they can check with the register. It may have been that they had people who used different names when registering, but I don't know," he said.

Mr Smith said that in addition to supplying the police with the register, the department gives the police four private numbers of officials who can answer any queries relating to the register.

Last weekend four numbers were supplied. After their arrest the Fuavaos and Mr Fuapoivaha were taken to cells at Auckland Central police station.

Despite representations by lawyer Mr A. R. Rasheed on the Sunday, saying the Tongans had signed the register, the trio was not released and appeared in the Auckland Magistrate's Court yesterday when they were granted bail with a surety.

They could not raise a surety and were transferred to Mt Eden prison. But later the charges were dismissed by Mr H. Y. Gilliand, SM.

Mr Clive Edwards, whose legal partnership Mr Rasheed works for, said the trio came to his office at about 4.45 p.m. yesterday. Mr Edwards said: "They were extremely distressed. They were crying in my office."

This afternoon, Mr Edwards was to see Auckland police chief, Assistant Commissioner J. W. Overton, to discuss the arrests. Mr Edwards said he would discuss with the trio further action.

The secretary of the Citizens Association for Racial Equality, Mr Dave Williams, said it was a "shocking state of affairs" that people who had registered could not prove they had done so. "Everyone who is registered should be given some sort of documentation they can show the police," he said.

Editor's note

The Minister of Immigration, Frank Gill, later apologised for this incident.

CHAPTER THIRTEEN

Litany of lies

1980: *The Auckland Star* reveals crucial hidden information about the Erebus disaster.

Most New Zealanders of a certain age can remember exactly where they were on the evening of 28 November 1979. Whether watching television or listening to radio, many shared a mounting sense of dread as it became apparent that Air New Zealand flight TE901, with 257 people aboard, had disappeared somewhere over Antarctica. By the next day the worst was known: what should have been a routine sightseeing flight had turned to tragedy when the DC10, apparently in perfect working order, and in relatively calm and clear conditions, had inexplicably flown straight into Mt Erebus. Everyone aboard was killed. The crash was — still is — a tragic legacy for New Zealand, not just because it remains the country's worst disaster in terms of lives lost but also because of the bitterness aroused by the subsequent investigation into the cause of the crash.

After the bodies of the victims had been recovered, the search for answers to the mystery began. Although the obvious answer was some kind of pilot error, rumours began to circulate that pilots had been misinformed about the route they were to follow. The first reporter to investigate and confirm this vital information was *The Auckland Star*'s aviation reporter, John Macdonald.

His report, printed below, was highly significant because it revealed for the first time, in public, that something might have gone wrong in the airline.

Macdonald, now in his eighties and living in New Plymouth, remembers feeling uneasy even before the crash happened. 'Before the crash they announced they were going to run these flights. I think it was the chief pilot who got together a bunch of journalists and briefed us. There was something that didn't quite fit in. I got the feeling that the airline might have been . . . how shall I put it . . . giving great emphasis to the opportunities passengers would get to view and photograph Scott Base and McMurdo. Yet the fact that there were rigid height restrictions over the area was barely touched on. Still, we assumed it would all be sorted in time.

'When the airline's managing director Morrie Davis called a conference after the crash and became visibly upset, it was then we began to suspect all was not as it appeared on the surface' (Macdonald, 2016).

Macdonald brought a seasoned reporter's sceptical eye to the story. Born in South Africa, he'd grown up in England, then emigrated with his parents as a teenager. He spent much of his career working in Melbourne on *The Age*, before returning to Auckland, attracted partly by the *Star*'s reputation for digging deep.

'The details about the faulty navigation information came to me through a number of pilots on condition they were not identified. The pilots knew how much had happened and were angry that the airline was trying to hide much of it.

'I wrote a story and then confirmed it with a senior officer. It seemed to unravel as it went along. The more it was uncovered, the more came to life' (Macdonald, 2016).

Macdonald benefited by working with an old colleague, Graeme Kennedy. Kennedy, too, had worked in Melbourne and although rivals then, they became friends. Kennedy was now working on the *Star*'s sister publication, the *Saturday 8 O'Clock*. Both had good contacts in aviation and sometimes 'crossed paths' in arriving at a story, a competition Macdonald says helped spur him along. 'It's the main driver in getting to the bottom of stories. Kennedy and I had a feeling for going out and snooping around' (Macdonald, 2016).

The first sign of an impact from Macdonald's reportage was Air New Zealand's withdrawal of advertising from *The Auckland Star*. Then the airline tried to make sure that passengers did not read it by banning it from flights outbound from Auckland. It was a futile move, among other niggly obstructions put in the newspaper's path.

The ill-feeling continued even after the inquiry was over. After one safety story, Macdonald remembers an airline safety officer turning up in his editor's office and demanding that Macdonald reveal his sources. The editor, Ross Sayers, refused.

With questions now being asked, the suspicion of a smoking gun in the airline's drawer, and the enormity in lives lost, Attorney-General Jim McLay announced a Royal Commission under Justice Peter Mahon. Although the Office of Air Accidents was already investigating, there were doubts about its ability to ferret out what were looking like some embarrassing truths without the full powers of a court of inquiry.

The full significance of McLay's move was to become agonisingly clear when the reports of the two inquiries were compared. The first official report by the Office of Air Accidents was published in May 1980. It effectively blamed pilot error for the crash. The author, Ron Chippindale, concluded that the primary cause of the crash was 'the decision of the captain to continue the flight at low level towards an area of poor surface and horizon definition when the crew was not certain of their position, and the subsequent inability to detect the rising terrain that intercepted the aircraft's flight path'. Chippindale's conclusion suited Air New Zealand because it deflected responsibility for the crash from its management. But not for long.

Mahon's report the following year was a bombshell. As raised in Macdonald's reports, Mahon established that a key cause of the crash was a late change in the aircraft's flight path. Instead of flying the usual route safely around the mountain, the plane's computerised navigation system had been changed the night before the flight took off so that it was instead flying directly at the mountain. The pilots had not been told of this change.

As Mahon put it: 'The single most dominant and effective cause of the disaster was the mistake made by those airline officials who programmed the aircraft to fly directly at Mt Erebus and omitted to tell the aircrew. That mistake is directly attributable, not so much to the people who made it, but to the incompetent administrative airline procedures which made the mistake possible.'

Mahon also stated, 'In my opinion, neither Captain Collins nor First Officer Cassin, nor the flight engineers made any error which contributed to the disaster, and were not responsible for its occurrence' (Mahon, 1981).

Mahon concluded that Air New Zealand staff had tried to cover up the error with what he called an 'orchestrated litany of lies'. The memorable phrase lingered in the public memory long after his conclusion. After lengthy court battles, the Privy Council concluded that there was no evidence for Mahon's claims about a cover-up. But no one has successfully challenged his conclusion about the real cause of the crash.

Macdonald believes the commission would have had to happen, such was the public pressure. The work of the press prevented the community accepting the bland and easy conclusions that mark so many catastrophes and do nothing for further prevention and safeguards.

'The fact that the Erebus inquiry is considered a landmark within aviation legal circles owes much to two remarkable men, Mahon and [Captain Gordon] Vette. Both made huge sacrifices, in future prospects and health, to arrive at the truth' (Macdonald, 2016).

The report below is followed by an account written especially for this book by John Macdonald, describing the origin and progress of the investigation.

Macdonald, J. D. (2016, December 6). Interview with author, J. Hollings.

Mahon, P. T. (1981). *Report of The Royal Commission to Inquire into the Crash on Mount Erebus, Antarctica, of a DC10 aircraft operated by Air New Zealand Limited.* Wellington: Government Printer. Retrieved from http://www.erebus.co.nz/investigation/mahonreport.aspx

Navigation data changed before fatal DC10 flight
Aviation reporter

Auckland Star, 25 February 1980

Navigational information fed into the DC10 airliner which crashed on Mt Erebus was not the same as that used by the two previous Antarctic flights. But the *Star* has learnt from an authoritative source that the information used on this final fatal flight was correct. Navigation information used on the two previous flights was not accurate and the pilots knew it was not, according to our source.

The question a number of pilots are voicing is whether the captain of the crashed DC10 was told that the navigational co-ordinates had been changed — or whether he, like previous pilots, assumed they had not, and therefore made "allowances."

The chief executive of Air New Zealand, Mr Morrie Davis, when told of this today said: "You are moving into a very highly speculative area. I cannot go further than to say that the navigational information and flight plan for the aircraft which crashed was accurate and entirely in order."

Mr Davis said he could not comment on whether a change had been made to information on the final flight. "To do so would be completely improper in view of the investigation still proceeding."

The version given the *Star* was also put to a number of senior airline pilots today, and several of them said it was in complete agreement with what they knew. They said it also accorded with another fact which has just come to light.

Not long before the aircraft crashed, it descended to a height of 450 metres above the sea north of Erebus. There the machine completed a figure of eight manoeuvre before climbing out and hitting the slopes of the mountain.

The final words on the cockpit voice recorder are a call from Captain Jim Collins for more engine power — "go around power."

The figure of eight manoeuvre, pilots say, was most likely caused by uncertainty about the aircraft's position, and an attempt to identify the area over which they were flying.

The navigational information which was changed for the final flight was the co-ordinate of the McMurdo Base — the latitude and longitude refined to extremely fine limits (down to metres). These co-ordinates are fed into the aircraft's extremely accurate inertial navigational instrument shortly before take-off.

Another set of co-ordinates also punched into the inertial system's computer is the exact spot of the aircraft on the airfield before take-off. The *Star* has confirmed that these were accurate. Providing these co-ordinates are accurate, the pilots are able to read exactly where they are at any time in the flight.

But as a double safeguard pilots are given a minimum operating height (in this case it was 16,000ft), and under normal conditions are not allowed to descend below this until they pick up an identifiable beacon from the ground.

In the Mt Erebus crash flight, this beacon should have been one at McMurdo (known as a "distance measuring equipment").

Plotters of the crash flight have since found the machine descended while still out of range of the McMurdo beacon — the beacon was "shadowed out" by the mountain.

This has led to the belief that uncertainty about the McMurdo co-ordinates, and no sign of the beacon (often it is not working) led the crew to think they were over the Ross ice shelf south of McMurdo.

Air New Zealand did deny one point claimed by some pilots — that the cockpit voice recorder contained detail of an argument among the pilots about navigation shortly before the crash.

Public and corporate relations director Mr Craig Saxton said: "We know for certain this was not on because we have heard the recorder."

A preliminary report of the investigation is expected to reach the airline next week, but interpretation of the flight data recorder is still under way in the United States.

Looking back: How the Erebus investigation unfolded
John Macdonald

For several weeks after the crash there was a palpable feeling of despair around the airline. The journalism of the time concentrated on the huge difficulties of body retrieval from the ice and search for the aircraft's black boxes. These might shed light on what caused the accident. The despair was quickened by the inexplicable cause of the crash.

Aircrew and technical staff who might otherwise have shared thoughts showed a determined mood to avoid the press, even off the record. But what became clear was a general respect for the captain, James Collins, and first officer, Gregory Cassin. Both were considered good and experienced pilots, mentally well adjusted and happy. Suicide, considered these days in accident investigations, was dismissed out of hand.

To the journalist pondering the crash, the cause had to exist within one of three situations. The first was a technical failure of the aircraft, such as a break-up in the air. The next was a problem caused by some kind of natural phenomenon, a fluke of vision perhaps caused by atmospheric conditions. Finally there was pilot error, and this could only involve navigational problems.

To us, technical failure could largely be ruled out because of the situation of the aircraft — flying on a pre-determined setting up a moderately sloping ice-covered mountain flank.

The second possibility was visual problems for pilots created by the likes of the well-known polar 'white out'. This seemed to be a possibility, though it did not explain why the aircraft was flying on a programmed route towards the mountain rather than the more commonly used low-lying passage to the pilots' left.

Our inquiries did uncover some discontent among aircrew at what seemed to be a conscious lack of knowledge and training within the airline on polar phenomena. These we published.

Unbeknown to us in the press at the time, a senior Air New Zealand pilot had begun his own remarkable investigation into the visual curiosities of polar flying. The late Captain Gordon Vette had himself flown one of the previous Antarctic flights. In his own time he began seeking out scientific professionals, investigating Canadian ice flying and commissioning photographs and graphic works of the Antarctic terrain.

Vette's research came to light in the yet-to-sit Royal Commission. While it could not explain why the DC10 was on its fatal route, it provided the reason why the pilots did not realise they were rapidly closing on ice slopes ahead. Nor, despite reasonably clear weather, could they notice to their left the safe low-lying passage.

But journalists, outside the airline's innermost confines, had every reason to suspect pilot error, and that certainly involved navigational mistakes.

Then, hints, noises and other signs began to emerge, mainly out of Wellington, but also from the airline. They suggested the pre-acceptance of a pilot error verdict, despite the fact that the Royal Commission had yet to begin sitting. This would bring the whole affair to a nice tidy end, creating a blameless airline and government, perhaps saving large litigation costs.

An ominous phrase accompanied these signals: 'command responsibility'. This concept originated in the Royal Navy. In effect it meant that the blame for a ship foundering or an air crash almost automatically went on the commander. Apart from the ancient concept of falling on one's sword, in aviation (particularly military aviation) it had come to have a newer use. It suggested that no matter the circumstances, any future problem should be foreseeable by an alert commander — an idea clearly incompatible with the age of computerised technology.

At this point many pilots, though not those in management and planning, became rather more verbose when questioned by journalists. The possibility of Captain Collins and crew being unfairly judged was mentioned. No single 'Deep Throat' emerged, but a surprising amount of informative scraps could be gathered by a 'ring-around' and coalesced into a story. Few in authority would reject its authenticity.

A major feature in unravelling navigation problems is a familiarity with an instrument known as the inertial navigation system, or INS. This complex mixture of balances, gyros and sensors, put together with clock-making precision, works within a computerised framework. It had emerged only 15 years earlier. On long flights it had done away with navigators, various radio contacts and astral sightings. Embarking on a flight, the pilot simply keys in a number of geographical co-ordinates, including the destination and waypoints. Linked to the autopilot, the INS flies the machine with almost unerring accuracy on its planned path.

To me it appeared that a navigational error could only be caused by one of two things: a pilot pressing the wrong INS buttons; or a communication, verbal or written, between the pilot and flight planners gone wrong. The exception could be a route over the top of the mountain, which seemed unlikely.

Any chance of a technical problem in the INS could be ruled out with near certainty. There were three of them on the DC10, all interconnected and monitored.

The Royal Commission under Mr Justice Peter Mahon began sitting in March. Early signs of an opening for pilot error came with the report of Chief Inspector of Air Accidents Ron Chippindale. It was a solid and workmanlike report, concluding that the cause was the pilot's decision to continue on a path when unsure of the aircraft's position and in poor visual conditions.

But over the following months, the airline's planning and execution of its polar flights unfolded in a tangled complex of machinations, faulty procedures, forgetfulness, incompetence and other mistakes (including mistakes within mistakes). Scores of witnesses from the airline, civil aviation and outside experts were called before the commission. To the observer it would have been like watching the painful extraction of a mouthful of teeth; except that under Mahon it was done with civility and decorum. The judge sometimes appeared lost in thought, but could snap onto a point of evidence seconds before most. He impressed with his grasp of technical and navigation matters.

Mahon made a number of overseas visits towards the end of the inquiry, checking out and exploring points raised in evidence. One with which I travelled was to McMurdo. We flew in a RNZAF C130 exactly a year to the day after the accident. The weather, too, appeared to be the same.

Approaching over the sea from the north, the squadron leader pilot took the aircraft down to the same height and began following the same track flown by TE901. From the flight deck we watched the mountain ice below slowly closing as it slipped by beneath us. Ahead we suddenly noticed that the clear definitions of slope, rocky outcrop and mountain form was disappearing into a bland wall of cottonwool.

The pilot pulled the big aircraft around sharply and climbed away towards the clear corridor to McMurdo. Still visible, about two kilometres ahead of the track we had left, was the dark smear marking the grave of TE109. No experience could more clearly verify the Mahon conclusions on the dominant navigational mistakes responsible for the tragedy, and the Vette findings that explained why the pilots were so visually deceived and which capped the flight's final moments.

CHAPTER FOURTEEN

Chain gang

1984, *The Southland Times*: Michael Turner exposes meat union corruption.

In the early 1980s, meat production in New Zealand was soaring. Farmers had taken advantage of government subsidies to expand their flocks; sheep numbers alone topped 70 million in 1982. Farmers in turn relied on big slaughterhouses to process billions of dollars' worth of sheep and cattle a year.

To run these huge plants, hundreds of seasonal workers were needed, which over the years became highly unionised. With bad management or a militant union, or both, a plant could quickly become strike-prone.

Ocean Beach was no exception. Sited on a thin strip of land near Bluff, at the very bottom of New Zealand's South Island, it is a massive building, built to hold 1000 people dismembering 6000 sheep and cattle each day. Through the 1970s it got a reputation for poor performance, due to constant strikes.

Then, miraculously, things changed. Under a charismatic new union boss, Tony Taurima, industrial harmony at the plant improved, and production soared.

The plant's owners, British-owned CWS Ltd, saw their moment. They quickly sold the plant to a locally owned company, Alliance Ltd. Alliance had another plant nearby, at Lorneville, and saw efficiencies in owning both. It also hoped that its dynamic young manager, Tony Forde, was just the person to make Ocean Beach work (Turner, 1984).

What Alliance and Forde did not know was that CWS had been buying its way out of trouble. It had been quietly giving Taurima tens of thousands of dollars, supposedly to deposit in union funds. It also built Taurima a special office, with his own shower, and allowed him and other union officials — nominally employed to work as slaughtermen or in other jobs — to spend all their time on 'union business'.

It had allowed a culture to develop where supervisors at the plant had to ask union officials such as Taurima and his deputy Colin Manson before making management decisions, or face a strike that could cripple the plant. Taurima and

Manson, both at times members of the Communist-leaning Socialist Unity Party, saw it as a kind of industrial democracy in action.

But it was democracy only for the few. When a company newsletter innocently floated the idea that women should be allowed to work on the higher-paid slaughter line, noting that it was what the law required, Taurima demanded that the company apologise or the workers would strike. The idea was dropped.

Many plants were 'closed shops' — meaning that workers had to be union members to work there. This gave union officials considerable power, which Taurima and Manson used freely; when Manson had a heated argument with his brother-in-law John Milner in a Bluff pub, Taurima informed the management that Milner's union ticket had been 'annulled and withdrawn from the union books' — meaning that he was out of a job. (Taurima was later forced to back down.)

When Forde took over, he made it clear that the party was over. Whereas the previous management had usually buckled under the threat of strike action, he did not. The result was increasing tension. Union organisers who had kept their workers in line became union bosses who seemed determined to strike on a whim.

By early 1984, the plant was in crisis. Forde wanted changes to workers' contracts to help the plant break even, but Taurima and Manson wouldn't agree. Over the long bitter winter of 1984, Taurima and Manson rigged union elections to keep themselves in power, orchestrated a series of strikes that crippled the plant, then paid themselves and a few mates thousands of dollars from a union welfare fund set up for hard-up strikers. Finally, the end came.

Watching all this, and reporting on it for *The Southland Times*, was Michael Turner. Only 24, he had started at the paper as a cadet at the age of 16. With the encouragement of chief reporter Clive Lind, a veteran of *Truth*, he followed every twist of the story and eventually wrote a book about it. The following extract from that book is a fascinating glimpse into the inner workings of a major industrial complex in New Zealand at that time. The title comes from a T-shirt Taurima had, with the words 'No sea too rough, no muff too tough' emblazoned on the front. As Turner points out, Forde was one muff too tough for Taurima.

The extract begins early in 1984, and follows the deteriorating situation at the plant throughout the winter, until the dramatic denouement at a shed meeting of workers in October. It was truly the end of an era, because by the time it erupted into the open, a new government was in power. Over the next few years, many of the laws that had made Ocean Beach possible, such as compulsory unionism, would go.

Turner, M. (1984). *One muff too tough: Ocean Beach.* Invercargill: Sycamore Press.

One Muff Too Tough

Originally published in *The Southland Times*, 1984. This extract is from *One Muff Too Tough: Ocean Beach*, by Michael Turner, published by Sycamore Press, 1984.

The morning processing resumed at Ocean Beach after the Christmas–New Year break, on 4 January 1984. Tony Taurima called a board of control meeting.

Delegates were told the two full-time officials wished to put themselves up for re-election early. In view of 20-odd outstanding industrial issues, Taurima and Colin Manson considered it desirable to bring the election forward a month. No desire was expressed to include the third official, Vice-president Dave Sinel, in the early election.

General services delegate Bob Howley was frustrated and suspicious. The pay rates in his nine-man department had not been renegotiated the previous season and he was unhappy with some of the management's proposals for the new contract. He was not permitted by Manson and Taurima to negotiate with the company, yet they would not communicate the department's grievance on his behalf.

Howley, a long-time opponent of Taurima, decided to defy the board of control directive and take his workers out at 10.30 a.m. on 5 January. Killing was able to continue, but the action soon snowballed.

A war of words between the parties then started. The union issued a public challenge to the directors of the Alliance company to meet to discuss the problems. In declining the challenge, Chairman John Falconer said: "The directors employ management to carry out policies. There is no reason why the management and union at Ocean Beach cannot meet."

A strike or hardship fund, known as the Ocean Beach Mutual Benefit Fund, was set up on 16 January. Money was soon flowing into the hardship fund from throughout the country. Large amounts of money did not accumulate in the fund because it was paid out in food vouchers and in cheques payable to creditors as soon as it came in.

Meanwhile, Labour Department industrial conciliator Len Fortune had been sent back to Invercargill by Minister of Labour Jim Bolger to help the parties reach a settlement.

The Southland Times carried some surprising news for Ocean Beach workers on 25 January. It reported that Manson and Taurima had been re-elected unopposed. Simmering discontent about their leadership burst into the open when about 250 slaughtermen held a separate meeting. Sinel, a slaughtermen's delegate, said the men had expressed a strong desire to return to work. They had decided to request the officials call a shed meeting.

Taurima defended his decision not to call a further shed meeting. Such a meeting should only be called if it would be "purpose-meaningful and we have substantial things to say".

Fortune reported back to the Minister, who directed him to address a meeting of all Ocean Beach employees, not just meat workers, and management. On the day arrangements were announced, the Ocean Beach officials finally called a shed meeting. Taurima denied that it had been called to head off Fortune's meeting.

At a seven-hour meeting, the Ocean Beach workers passed a resolution conferring on the union officials authority to negotiate again with the management to achieve a compromise settlement. The meeting was told the company had changed its attitude, which the company later denied. Manson and O'Connor made it clear they would not attend Fortune's meeting.

When Fortune found out, he cancelled the planned meeting. He said the refusal of the branch and sub-branch officials to attend "suggests to me there is a complete lack of will to explore all avenues open to the officials to end this costly and unnecessary confrontation . . ."

On 8 February Alliance Secretary Norman Smith said the closure of Ocean Beach for the season was under serious consideration by the company. On the same day the Department of Labour in Wellington confirmed it had received a petition from about 50 Ocean Beach workers calling for an inquiry into the election.

The splinter group that had emerged at the slaughtermen's meeting was angry. They had been attempting to force a secret ballot on a return to work, but had been blocked each time. Manson and Taurima were also criticised for the information they gave the shed after the Balclutha meeting. They had gone there to seek the physical support of the other sheds, but no commitment had been given. Ocean Beach workers were not told that. Nor were they told National Secretary Blue Kennedy had recommended a return to work.

Acting Minister of Labour George Gair asked Fortune to chair a meeting of representatives of the management, the New Zealand Freezing Companies' Association and the union at the sub-branch, branch and national levels in a "final attempt" to resolve the dispute.

Smiles on the faces of the meat workers told the story as they emerged from a three-hour meeting on 14 February. On a show of hands they had voted to accept the proposal and an end to the six-week strike.

An article, based on an interview with Manson, appeared in the 23 February edition of *Socialist Action,* suggesting the link between the Ocean Beach sub-branch and the Socialist Unity Party had been renewed. The article illustrated the distortions in what workers were told.

The 1982–83 season had been marked by a number of disputes, several of them lasting up to a fortnight. "Some people could be of the opinion that these were deliberately engineered by management," Manson commented.

. . .

Money continued to be contributed to the Ocean Beach Mutual Benefit Fund until about mid-March. The fund committee continued to consider accounts for payment up until the end of March, when meat workers were informed the fund had been officially closed. About $100,000 was paid out in accounts, with most of the rest of the money used to pay accounts as an advance. Money coming back into the fund as meat workers repaid these loans boosted its total income to more than $250,000.

It was not long before the management and the union were locked in another dispute.

Chamberhands had been the most militant group of workers at Ocean Beach since Alliance took over. This time they were upset they would not be servicing the new $1 million lamb cutting department. The union approached the management with five claims relating to manning and payments. It did not want the company to take on new employees until existing employees were given the opportunity to work in the new department. They had a legitimate case to take to a disputes hearing, but they didn't do that. They went on strike.

Chamberhands would clearly be at a disadvantage under the management's plans for the new department, Taurima said later. "Clayton's chamberhands" would be doing the work and denying the 98 chamberhands their normal earnings, he said.

But the management said there was plenty of work for the chamberhands without servicing the department.

Forde gave three reasons why it was essential lamb-cutting personnel did that work — hours of work, accountability and so that throughput would coincide with the work done in the department. He hinted at another reason when he said: "The performance of the chamberhands department is totally unreliable and they have a lengthy list of strike actions to account for."

On 29 May the union put a three-point proposal to the management. The chamberhands would return to work under the "status quo", the dispute would be handed to the union's branch officials and determination of who should service the department would be decided at a level involving a third party.

After that had been rejected, Taurima said it was clear the management was prepared to "starve out" its employees in the hope chamberhands would accept losses of jobs and hourly rates of pay. The union then put forward a compromise in which the servicing of the department would be shared by the lamb-cutting personnel and chamberhands while the union invoked the disputes procedure in its award. This was again rejected by the management.

It was not surprising that the other sheds would not support Ocean Beach. Changes were taking place in nearly all meat plants and at Ocean Beach they were more positive than at other places. The new lamb-cutting department would create 40 new jobs in the near future and had the potential to employ 60 people.

Nationally the Meat Workers' Union had said its top priority was the retention of jobs. It [had] wanted to protect not only existing members' jobs, but also the number of positions available. Officials [had] talked about the union's social responsibility to preserve jobs for the pool of unemployed.

Yet the Ocean Beach chamberhands' action contradicted all that. In the final days of the season there was virtually mutiny in the union as various departments reacted to the officials' refusal to sign the contracts. In despair, some delegates literally forced the officials to sign.

Towards the end of the season, Bob Howley had heard some funny stories about payments from Ocean Beach Mutual Benefit Fund. The fact that any payments were still being made from the fund months after the strike had him thinking.

Howley had been watching Taurima for years. He saw how Taurima wanted to be in control and considered him dangerous. He had a gut feeling Taurima, who regarded any questioning of his administration as an attack on his integrity, was hiding things.

A good example was when Howley questioned workers' compulsory contributions to the union's sports fund, but Taurima turned the matter into a question of confidence in him. He cried. The meeting passed a vote of confidence in him and the fund issue lapsed.

Sinel questioned union moves openly but each time he would be nullified. The usual tactic was for Colin Manson to speak first and bore everyone to tears. Sinel would always have something to say later, but the lieutenants would ensure Taurima had the final say and countered any other arguments.

Sinel gave the impression he had much ability, but had never really chosen to use it. Those opposed to the union leadership had now turned to him to take positive action.

But before he would have to respond to that pressure, there was the Arbitration Court inquiry into the Ocean Beach election. In his decision Chief Judge Horn said there was obviously considerable dissatisfaction among a number of union members about the election and the performance of the two officials, but he was unable to hold that the result of the election was or may have been affected by any irregularity and the result must stand.

On 9 August Sinel sent telegrams to both the branch and national office expressing concern at the affairs of the Ocean Beach Mutual Benefit Fund. He pointed out there had been no board of control meetings and no financial reports. He requested an urgent investigation.

On 18 August the Times reported that the Ocean Beach management had decided to stop paying the wages of Taurima and Manson as union officials. If they wanted to retain their employment with the company, they would have to return to their former departments.

Instead of trying to ensure the plant ran smoothly, Manson and Taurima's actions heightened the conflict and disruption. As one management spokesman said: "Why should we pay them to give us a hard time?"

The battle lines were now drawn. The management obviously wasn't going to back down. Unless there was a change in the union leadership, Ocean Beach faced certain closure.

. . .

Under the heading "Union Probe Into Strike Fund", the Times reported the next day [10 September 1984] that an apparent abuse of personal authority was under investigation by the union. . . .

Particular concerns, which overlapped, named by the paper were:

- Apparent preferential treatment for some people who were recognisable as members of the "inner core" — strong supporters of the existing sub-branch leaders.
- Payments made for months after the closing date for applications for assistance — long after most members thought the fund had been exhausted.
- "Ex gratia" payments . . . to members . . . of the committee set up to dispense the fund. . .
- Availability of loans to some people, including Taurima and Manson, while union members had been told not to apply for that form of assistance.
- Use of the fund for general running costs of the union.

Initial grounds for the inquiry . . . were that the board of control was never called together to consider how and by whom the fund should be administered. . . .

Three examples summarise the abuse:
- On behalf of the committee, Terry Manson advised Ocean Beach workers on 27 February that "we are not a finance company and no personal loans will be considered". Yet such loans were subsequently made to a small number of people, including Manson himself and the officials.
- On 29 March Terry Manson advised that the hardship fund would "officially close for all types of assistance . . ." at 12.30 p.m. the following day. . . . Yet payments were still being made from the fund shortly before the internal inquiry started in August.
- On 29 March the fund committee also decided to recommend that the balance of the money be retained "in our account or at branch office" to assist with "legal requirements re Paul Mulder case".

. . .

But it was the payment of personal loans . . . that was to cause more concern.

Terry Manson took out a $300 loan on 2 March. . . . He received payments "in lieu of compo" of $150 . . . on 12 April, $150 on 13 April and $100 on 16 April. He took out a $100 loan on 27 April, a $500 loan on 7 May and two $500 loans on 29 June. One of his $500 loans was to pay Colin Manson, his brother, rent.

. . . Colin Manson received $500 loans on 4 April and 31 May. [Reg] Nicholas received a $4,000 loan . . . to put a new roof on his house. Taurima received a $1,000 loan on 15 June and John Kereopa a $400 loan on 20 June.

[Errol] Edwards, who received a $1,000 loan on 2 May, was paid $960 from the fund as rent for two meat workers living in his houses. He had a further $320 of bills paid.

Ray Bowes had earlier taken out a $1,500 loan to cover the payment of bills resulting from regravelling the drive on his property on the outskirts of Invercargill.

Mulder was paid $400 from the fund on 17 March, $1,000 as a "grant" on 2 April, $576 on 8 May to meet his legal costs resulting from the District Court appearance and $500 for accounts on 22 May.

Committee members received wage payments from the fund . . . totalling $4,325.

. . .

On 21 June members of the committee awarded themselves, except Colin Manson, $500 "ex gratia" payments. Nicholas got an extra $600, which he divided up amongst . . . supporters of the existing union regime.

. . . The Meat Workers' Union national management committee had called a meeting on October 1 to explain to Ocean Beach members the reasons for their decision to sack the two full-time union officials, including Taurima, and ban them and six others from holding union office again.

. . . [Union official] Ted Miller produced a copy of a cheque for $2,000 made out to the Bluff Squash Club on 24 July 1981 and drawn on a T. A. Taurima Administration Fund account. . . . [Fighting back tears, Taurima] told the meeting he had received nearly $60,000 from the former CWS management in payments of $20,000, $7,000, $9,000 and $20,000 in 1980 and 1981. He had spent about half the money on himself and about half helping other people.

. . .

He admitted he had written out cheques without receipts.

He told the meeting he could implicate other people present, but he wouldn't. He would take the rap himself.

"I've done some terrible things. It could be called misappropriation," Taurima said. . . .

This man, who had led the Ocean Beach union for 10 years, was telling members he had betrayed their trust. They had supported him through years of industrial turmoil, a short stable period and a succession of lengthy stoppages.

How did they react now? Jeer, boo, hiss? No. They clapped.

. . .

The day after the shed meeting Sinel and the branch officials went to the Ocean Beach union office to recover records of the various funds operated by the sub-branch. . . . Among them were the shed fund, sickness fund, sports fund, fees fund and a slaughtermen's "slosh" fund. Information relating to them was turned over to a firm of Invercargill accountants and a thorough investigation started.

. . . Taurima had returned to the union office to remove his personal effects. When Sinel, Miller and Bob O'Connor went to the office they found that . . . records of the shed fund between 1978 and 1983 were missing.

No audit had been done of the shed fund for about five years. A motion calling for an independent audit had been passed at the sub-branch annual meeting earlier in the year, to the knowledge of most workers, but that had not been done. . . .

. . . The union's bank was able to provide information about the shed fund that filled most of the gaps. [It] confirmed suspicions that the misuse of the strike fund had not been an isolated case. For example, personal payments and loans had been made from the fund. . . .

Despite requests from the auditor, information on the sickness fund had not been received to allow him to complete the audit for the year ended October 1983. The Ocean Beach Freezing Workers' Benefit Society, which administered the fund, used to be run independently of the sub-branch, but latterly Taurima had been secretary-treasurer and Colin Manson a trustee.

Taurima, Ken Jaffers and Willie Pou were trustees of the "slosh" fund, which was used to buy alcohol and send delegates away on trips — at the CWS management's expense. . . .

. . .

Naturally the Alliance company started searching the records it had taken over from CWS after Taurima's revelations at the shed meeting. Within a week three of the payments Taurima claimed to have received were traced. The first $20,000 cheque had been made out to "Union Secretary Administration Fund" and the other two had been made out to the Ocean Beach sub-branch, but all three had been banked in Taurima's POSB account. No record was found of the second $20,000 payment Taurima claimed to have received.

Bill Kirk, former General Manager of the Ocean Beach company, was one man who could hold the key to the mystery. . . .

He claimed that at no time when he managed the company were payments to the Meat Workers' Union intended for Taurima's personal use.

. . .

The following day I spoke at length to Taurima. . . .

> For some years, allegations of bribery and corruption between myself and the former management have been circulated.
>
> Until Mr Kirk had spoken, I have been unable to put these rumours down for reasons of protocol and employer–employee relationships in keeping matters relating to the parties confidential.
>
> I have never received any payments from the company other than that which is related to my employment. . . .

. . .

Many Ocean Beach meat workers were unhappy with the outcome of the shed meeting on 1 October. Some vowed they could not work alongside those implicated in the strike fund scandal and they could envisage further difficulties for Ocean Beach unless the union took stronger disciplinary action.

. . .

Tony Forde had been receiving anonymous phone calls from people reading out lists of names and warning what might happen if any one of them returned to work at the plant. He had also received a photograph of Manson with a cross through his head. Manson himself had been getting threatening calls. . . .

In any case, Forde was not about to take risks. He prevented Manson from entering the plant. "We could not guarantee his security," Forde said. "We are a management not a security force."

. . .

Tony Forde was the one "muff", so to speak, that Tony Taurima had not counted on.

Some senior union officials believed Forde's apparent lack of experience in a top managerial position, his relative youth and his impetuosity were contributing to the problems at Ocean Beach. In fact, the difficulties were not due to any weaknesses he might have, but to his strengths. He was the first manager Taurima had struck who confronted him and kept on confronting him. Forde, unlike his CWS predecessors, was fortunate to have a local board of directors and a tide of change in the industry behind him.

It was only because Taurima could no longer deliver to union members that they, eventually, started to question him in any numbers. Under CWS, Taurima rarely had to justify the reasons for strikes — they were usually short and successful from the union's point of view. But the opposite was the case under Alliance.

. . .

Taurima knew at least by the start of 1984 . . . that, unlike the previous management, Forde would not cede his management responsibilities to a third party. Taurima had no apparent desire to end the strike.

Why?

There is little doubt Taurima was strongly motivated by his Socialist Unity Party involvement in the mid-1970s, yet he did not have a lasting philosophical commitment to the cause.

When the opportunity for increased status was effectively offered by the CWS management from late 1978, Taurima seized the opportunity with both hands. . . . an income approaching $40,000 a year, a boat, a new car and a leisure pursuit such as flying did not fit in with his earlier communist affiliation.

But when Forde came to Ocean Beach and the disruption of earlier years resumed, the SUP link appeared to be renewed. Taurima needed that connection as a justification for what was happening.

The impression Forde soon gained from Taurima was that he had the existing management personnel under control and didn't want any additions to the team. Not surprisingly, just about every step Forde took to run an efficient plant mucked things up for Taurima.

For Taurima to be able to carry out his assurances of industrial harmony he needed a work-force under his control and a management, at that time, that was willing to pay. In some respects, the T. A. Taurima Administration Fund . . . was the link between the two.

He could use the money in the fund to buy off the delegates and ringleaders in the more militant work areas. This was done in subtle ways — they might be sent away to union conferences or money might be loaned to them. As long as Taurima had the loyalty of delegates, he was likely to have the loyalty of their departments.

Money was also loaned from the shed fund. There was a high demand for such assistance to pay court fines and for travel to attend funerals and so on. It was not so much the union lending money, but Taurima, and the recipients were unlikely to stand up and oppose him at a shed meeting.

With the lengthy stoppages under the Alliance management, the demand for such assistance from union funds grew. The loyalty Taurima required previously to ensure industrial harmony was still needed, but for a different reason. He had merged his own interests with the interests of the union. This was to lead to his downfall.

Forde took the control away from Taurima and his inner core. The new contracts ate into the higher-paid departments that had done extremely well under Taurima's stewardship. Restrictions were placed on the union's use of the company computer to make automatic deductions from wage payments to repay loans. His restrictions on the officials and delegates' previously uncontrolled movements changed the lifestyles of powerful people. Much of the industrial disruption resulted from measures such as these.

Taurima appeared to become more isolated during 1984. He told me in August he believed Alliance wanted to close Ocean Beach down and use him as a scapegoat. That was an unusual thing for the company since it had paid more than $11 million for the plant, spent about $6 million upgrading it and lost about $8 million running it.

. . .

Forde has achieved much at Ocean Beach. When the plant operated smoothly in the autumn of 1984 it was the most cost efficient in Southland. That was not done by ruthlessly hacking away at wages, but by efficient management. . . .

But Forde's ability as a manager cannot be acclaimed finally until the plant processes two million head in a season and it runs at an operating profit. There are some who doubt that his style of management, exhibited so far, will ever be accepted by the racial mix at Ocean Beach.

. . .

Dave Sinel regards himself as a strong unionist, who is not about to lie down and let the employer beat him over the head with a stick. . . . But he also recognises times have changed and tactics used ten years ago are no longer acceptable.

. . .

But there will not only be changes in the union–employer relationship. The way in which the union's affairs are run will also change.

. . .

Within a few days there, Sinel received numerous requests from workers for financial assistance from the union. "Those days are over," he told them. No more loans would be made from the shed fund.

CHAPTER FIFTEEN

Disgraceful conduct

1987, *Metro*: Sandra Coney and Phillida Bunkle expose an unethical experiment on women with cervical cancer, which leads to a shake-up of medical ethics.

In 1987 two women wrote an article for *Metro* magazine. According to the then norms of journalism, the article should probably have disappeared without a ripple. *Metro* was a relatively new publication, not especially well known outside Auckland, and not especially widely read within it. Neither Sandra Coney nor Phillida Bunkle were full-time staff writers, although Coney was an experienced professional journalist. The long, highly technical piece about a particular form of cancer and its treatment did not seem made for a national scandal.

Yet no story has had more impact on medical practice in New Zealand. Its revelations led to a Committee of Inquiry, sweeping changes to the way in which medical practice is regulated, and a revolution in the relationship between doctor and patient.

The 'unfortunate experiment' story was the result of many months of work by Coney and Bunkle. Perhaps because neither was a staff writer on a mainstream publication, they brought to the story fresh eyes that saw injustice where others didn't. Both were the same age, and shared a commitment to feminism: Coney co-founded the feminist journal *Broadsheet*, and Bunkle, teaching at Victoria University in Wellington, began New Zealand's first Women's Studies degree. They also had the vital signs of true investigative journalists: expert knowledge of their field, the capacity to spend many months mastering the technical detail of cancer treatment, a determination to get the story right, no matter how long it took, and a burning sense of the importance of the story in order to save the lives of the women at the centre of the debacle (Coney, 1988).

The article is the story of a bizarre set of experiments performed on unwitting women at National Women's Hospital in Auckland in the two decades leading up to 1987. It showed that hundreds of women from throughout the North Island known to be at risk of developing potentially fatal cancer of the cervix were not being told of that risk, and were not offered treatment that could save their lives. They were not being offered treatment because a prominent gynaecologist, Dr Herbert Green, was conducting an experiment to prove a theory he had developed: that abnormal cells on the cervix would not develop into invasive cancer. Worse, hospital authorities had been warned that he was putting patients at risk and had done nothing to stop him (Bunkle & Coney, 1988).

The way Coney and Bunkle came across, and then developed, the story is textbook investigative practice. Through Coney's editing of *Broadsheet,* and both her and Bunkle's help on the class action on the Dalkon Shield disaster [the Dalkon Shield was an intra-uterine contraceptive device marketed in the 1970s, which was later found to have caused severe injuries and infection and, in some cases, death], both had developed expertise in investigating health issues. They had good contacts at the University of Auckland Medical School, and one of these told them that a statistician colleague, Peter Mullins, was working on a paper relating to Green's work which he described as 'dynamite' (Coney, 1988). Coney got in touch with Bunkle, with whom she had been working in the women's health group Fertility Action, and together they started to follow the story.

Realising that the story needed a patient's perspective, they began interviewing women and were introduced to Clare Matheson, who was involved in a medical misadventure case against her GP. Clare, who was to be known as Ruth in the subsequent story, at that stage believed her GP was to blame for her lack of treatment, and thought that Green was on her side. It was only after she went through her notes with Bunkle and Coney that the full enormity of what Green had been doing dawned on them.

'When she turned up with her file, we realised she was one of the women who was part of Green's study. She had got the wrong end of the stick,' says Coney (Coney, 2017). The inclusion of Clare's story, and the skilful way in which it is woven throughout the chronology of Green's decades-long experiment and the often highly technical discussion of cervical cancer diagnosis and treatment, gives the following piece much of its emotional power.

'She was a really strong woman and was already taking her case against her GP. She had developed cervical cancer and had had treatment, the final outcome of which remained uncertain, and she was already pretty committed to wanting to hold someone accountable' (Coney, 2017).

Clare's account, and testimony at the later inquiry, was the core of the story. At the inquiry, many women came forward to testify on behalf of Green: some then realised that they had had no idea what was really going on, while others clung to the belief that Green had their best interests at heart.

'They were there to tell us how wonderful Professor Green was. A lot of those people were ordinary working people. For some, getting this attention from Green, who was a top person in National Women's, they were thinking they were getting special treatment. Once they knew what was really going on, it took on a more sinister aspect. One woman thought she was getting special treatment because Green [had] arranged leave from her factory work for her to show her untreated lesions to visiting gynaecologists. She thought she was important because she would be brought in to show these [cancerous] cells to visiting gynaecologists. She was told she was an "odd bod"' (Coney, 2017).

Coney believes that a big factor in her and Bunkle's success was their meticulous, but open, approach.

'We were incredibly thorough. We taped everything and we were very open about what we did. We interviewed Bonham and Green, and they had every opportunity to explain what was going on. We asked for a lot of documents from within the hospital. We did an incredible amount of reading around the issue. We contacted cancer specialists from overseas who had been to National Women's during the period this was going on. It's hard to think what more we could have done. We knew how serious this was, the power of the profession and the reputations that were at stake' (Coney, 2017).

Unlike some of the journalists featured in this collection, who came to their stories with a professional interest and then later developed the emotional investment needed to sustain them through the long months of inquiry, Coney and Bunkle were driven by emotion from the start — but channelled that with a professional devotion to getting the detail of the story right.

'We were very motivated by the fact that we knew that there were women out there who still needed treatment. We had that history . . . we had both [had a lot of experience in working on women's health issues] so there was a background that we brought to it that kept us going. A lot of that did come from that campaigning perspective of wanting to bring about change, it's not just that we wanted to break the story. We had our feminism to motivate us. We were probably more [journalists] in the Nicky Hager mould' (Coney, 2017).

Although they met resistance, they also had a lot of encouragement from people within and without National Women's, including doctors, not all of whom were prepared to put their names to the story. 'We found that people all over the place knew about it. We were getting a lot of encouragement to keep going. The big breakthrough was Dr McLean, who said everything we were saying was right. We got the whole inside story and key documents from him that showed we were on the right track' (Coney, 2017).

Metro was the perfect vehicle for the story. Founded only six years earlier, it was irreverent, stylish and opinionated. Furthermore, it was under the leadership of Warwick Roger, a former *Dominion* reporter who was himself an investigative journalist and who had the vision to judge the article on its quality, not on the lack of reputation of its writers. The story was ideal for *Metro* — it struck at sacred cows, it was new, it was long and detailed. It was a story that only a magazine format like *Metro*'s could do justice to, and it was set in Auckland. Most of all, it was outstanding journalism, as can be judged from its impact.

The month it was published, the government announced an inquiry into the claims, led by District Court Judge Silvia Cartwright. After seven months of hearings, the examination of hundreds of patient medical records, and hearing from numerous local and overseas witnesses, her report confirmed the most important points in the *Metro* story. She recalled a number of women for further treatment and recommended major changes to the way patients were consulted and managed by medical professionals. Many of the recommended changes were based on a second submission of evidence to the inquiry, compiled by Bunkle with input from Coney and Dr Forbes Williams. Its key, internationally innovative recommendation was to recognise patient rights as fundamental human rights and therefore remove patient complaints from internal professional bodies and place them under the jurisdiction of human rights (Bunkle, 2013). Bunkle feels that this was her biggest contribution (Bunkle, 2017).

As a result, the government established a Health and Disability Commissioner, effectively taking the policing of medical malpractice away from doctors, and introduced a code of patients' rights that enshrined in law the principle that patients had to be properly informed about treatment before consenting to it. Health boards were required to set up independent health ethics committees outside hospitals, and a national programme of screening women for cervical abnormalities was established.

Green was never charged with misconduct, due to ill-health, but his superior, Professor Denis Bonham, was found by the Medical Council to have engaged in disgraceful conduct (Coney, 1993).

After the *Metro* article was published, both Coney and Bunkle maintained an interest in health, and particularly consumers' rights. Bunkle became a Member of Parliament and eventually Minister of Consumer Affairs, before leaving Parliament to pursue further study. Coney has written more than 16 books and served as an Auckland councillor. Clare Matheson, the rock around which the story was built, retired from teaching and is now part of a women's health Cartwright Collective with Coney and Bunkle (Coney, 2017).

Looking back, Coney says it is definitely the story of which she is most proud, and that she wouldn't have done things differently, although she had not predicted the degree to which it would consume her life. The story didn't lead to more work in journalism, as she had thought it might. 'It became very difficult for me as a freelance journalist. I became untouchable. We were seen as very controversial. It certainly wasn't particularly helpful to me' (Coney, 2017). Instead, she found herself drawn into long hours helping the Committee of Inquiry, unpaid.

There was initially no money to pay the costs of Coney and Bunkle's research or communication, or, most importantly, their lawyer, Rodney Harrison. Fortunately, women around the country began sending money to support their work. 'We used to have women from the Country Women's Institute at little towns in the South Island send us $64 they got from a trading table. A lot of trade unions also sent us money' (Coney, 2017).

As public support grew, the Ministry of Health agreed to pay their legal bills. In cross-examination, 'one of the lawyers tried to suggest we had done it for the money but when we told the inquiry how little we got for the article, their mouths dropped open' (Coney, 2017).

Almost 30 years later, the story continues to generate controversy (TVNZ,

2010). There have been claims that the story was a feminist witch-hunt, and University of Auckland historian Linda Bryder argued that there was no experiment and the practices at National Women's were not unusual for the time (Bryder, 2009). However, a study by Otago University medical researchers in 2010, which reviewed all patient notes and the original smears, found that 127 women denied treatment by Green had a 10 times greater risk of developing potentially fatal invasive cancer. Of this group, eight had died (McCredie et al., 2010).

Like many good investigative stories, its reputation has grown with the passage of time. In terms of impact, and public interest, it must rank in the top two or three pieces of investigative journalism published in New Zealand. As is often the case with important, controversial and truly shocking stories, the story did not gain the recognition it should have within journalism at the time. It takes time for people to recognise that the shift in reality they imply is credible.

'Maybe because it was written by people who weren't staff writers, and because it was so controversial. Maybe if it had been in the *Herald*, it would have been different. But I like the story and how we put it together. It was very difficult to write, because Phillida was in Wellington and I was in Auckland . . . it's a miracle it all came out as well as it did' (Coney, 2017).

For Coney and Bunkle, most satisfaction seems to come from what the article achieved, rather than the craft. Bunkle suggests that it achieved an enduring shift in public consciousness because it made visible experiences that many patients around the country recognised (Bunkle, 2017).

Coney concludes: 'The cervical screening programme has been very successful in terms of reducing deaths from cervical cancer — it has saved many lives. I think the medical profession really took on board the main issues and delivered on them. Informed consent is embedded in medical practice in New Zealand; that has been one of the biggest successes. We are not just expected to be compliant and do what the doctor says, but decide about our own health care.'

Bryder, L. (2009). *A history of the 'unfortunate experiment' at National Women's Hospital.* Auckland: Auckland University Press.

Bunkle, P. (2013). Feminist input into the development of patient-centred healthcare in New Zealand. *Women's History Magazine, 17,* pp. 12–22.

Bunkle, P. (2017). [Email to author].

Bunkle, P., & Coney, S. (1988). The unfortunate experiment. In P. Bunkle (Ed.), *Second opinion* (pp. 13–190). Auckland: Oxford University Press.

Coney, S. (1988). *The full story behind the inquiry into cervical cancer treatment.* Auckland: Penguin.

Coney, S. (1993). *Unfinished business: What happened to the Cartwright Report?* Auckland: Women's Health Action Trust.

Coney, S. (2017, January 30). Interview with author, J. Hollings.

McCredie, M. R., Paul, C., Sharples, K. J., Baranyai, J., Medley, G., Skegg, D. C., & Jones, R. W. (2010). Consequences in women of participating in a study of the natural history of cervical intraepithelial neoplasia 3. *Australian and New Zealand Journal of Obstetrics and Gynaecology, 50*(4), 363–370.

TVNZ. (2010). *Unfortunate experiment led to eight deaths.* Retrieved 2014, July 21 from TVNZ. http://tvnz.co.nz/health-news/unfortunate-experiment-led-eight-deaths-3577366

An 'Unfortunate Experiment' at National Women's

Originally published in *Metro*, June 1987. This extract is from *Second Opinion*, by
Phillida Bunkle, published by Oxford University Press, 1988.

Part One

In October 1985, Ruth (not her real name for reasons that will become clear later
in this story) returned from National Women's Hospital and told her workmates
she felt as if she'd just been to Auschwitz. 'I feel as if they've been experimenting
on me,' she said. Ruth's fellow schoolteachers thought she was being ridiculous
and said so, and so she pushed these doubts to the back of her mind.

It was over twenty years since Ruth had made her first visit to National
Women's Hospital. She had not been a teacher then, but a twenty-seven year old
suburban mother of three small children. She had failed University Entrance
and with 'the disadvantage of no education' remembers herself as 'the sort of
patient who meekly did what she was told'. She had been referred to the hospital
by her general practitioner after a 'suspicious' cervical smear. Having a cervical
smear means that cells are collected from the surface of the neck of the womb
with a sort of ice-block stick, then smeared in a thin film across a glass plate so
that their structure can be seen through a microscope.

At the hospital Ruth was told that although her smear was 'suspicious',
nothing more serious was going on. She came home and reassured her husband
that she did not have cancer and that there was nothing to worry about. 'That',
she remembers, 'was the frame of mind they put me in from the beginning.'
Six months later she had an examination of her cervix with the colposcope, a
powerful magnifying instrument, and a single punch biopsy removed a fragment
of tissue the size of a rice grain for scrutiny in the pathology laboratory. In the
space of six months, Ruth had three colposcopies and three smears were taken.[1]
She felt confident that she was being carefully watched.

In mid-1965, Ruth became pregnant. Her GP was surprised when she told
him about the pregnancy. 'What do they think at National Women's?' he asked.
Ruth told him the doctor she saw at the hospital said it was fine and her GP
agreed that he must know what he was doing. In March 1966, Ruth gave birth to
her fourth child, a healthy eight-pound baby girl.

The doctor Ruth saw at National Women's Hospital was Associate Professor
Herbert Green. What Ruth didn't know was that Green was experimenting on his
patients and that her case had already been written up in a medical magazine.[2]
Herbert Green was an expert on cervical cancer. He was on the world circuit,
attending conferences and publishing frequently on the subject in prestigious
gynaecological journals. From 1956 to 1982 when he retired, he saw virtually every
woman at National Women's Hospital with invasive cervical cancer and many of
the women who had earlier or 'precursor' stages, a total of some 1800 women.[3]

Green was born in Balclutha in 1916. He qualified from Otago Medical
School in 1945, where he had won his rugby blue. A Southland representative

cricket player, he was a powerfully built man who towered over his colleagues. In 1948 he took a position as house surgeon at National Women's Hospital in Auckland. He immediately became involved in the treatment of cervical cancer. National Women's Hospital was at that time in its infancy. It had opened in 1946, in premises that the American army had vacated in Cornwall Park, a sprawling network of buildings with innumerable rooms opening off immensely long corridors. A staff member of the time vividly remembers the perpetual thunderous tramp of people traipsing down the passages.

National Women's Hospital had opened to provide for the post-war baby boom.[4] Auckland had been short of beds for maternity patients, the Hospital Board providing only a ward in Auckland Public Hospital and two small maternity units in Warkworth and Waiuku. With the soaring post-war birth rate the problem had become severe. The board had come under pressure to live up to its obligation under the law to provide maternity services for women of the region. After a Government election promise to provide a major obstetrical and gynaecological unit in Auckland, the Board capitulated and set up temporary premises in Cornwall Park. The first baby was born at the new hospital in 1946.

The powerful Obstetrical and Gynaecological Society, wishing to consolidate its power by controlling the teaching of obstetrics and gynaecology, pushed for the establishment of a Post-Graduate School based at National Women's Hospital. With the support of the Auckland business community it endowed a professorial chair. An Australian, Harvey Carey, took over this position in 1954. Carey's contemporary, Dr Stephen Williams, remembers him as a 'bit of a brash bulldog'. Carey was liberal in his views, and would ultimately fall foul of the obstetricians by advocating less medical interference in childbirth and opposing a specialist monopoly of the planned unit. Dr Williams was one of Auckland's first cytologists. Cytologists use a microscope to look at the structure of a smear of cells collected from body surfaces. They can detect abnormal changes in the cells and therefore allow early treatment of a disease. In 1954 Carey was keen to test the use of cytology in the detection of cervical cancer. National Women's Hospital had inherited responsibility for the treatment of cervical cancer from ward four at Auckland Hospital. It took cases from the whole of the northern half of the North Island and by 1954 a specialized clinical team had been set up.[5]

Invasive cervical cancer is described as 'the most miserable of cancers'. In the days before cytology it was not always detectable until at an advanced stage when there would be unusual bleeding from the uterus or a visible growth on the cervix. The only treatment was by deep ray or radium, although in the early fifties surgery was introduced at National Women's Hospital as an additional treatment. Invasive cancer was thought to go through earlier or 'precursor stages'. These stages were called dysplasia, or abnormal cells, the most abnormal cell being called carcinoma *in situ* or CIS (pronounced kiss). CIS was believed to progress finally to invasive cancer. A smear from the cervix might reveal cell changes in the earlier stages. The theory was that if cancer could be detected before it reached the advanced invasive stage, it might be possible to remove it and cure the disease.

Carey knew that at nearby Green Lane Hospital Dr Stephen Williams' cytological smear tests of sputum had been successful in detecting unsuspected lung cancer. He knew too that in New York, Dr Papanicolaou, inventor of the 'Pap smear', was 'booming away about his cause'. Carey went to Williams, and as Williams recalls 'begged him' to do a trial run of 1000 cervical smears of women entering the hospital for other causes: 'Of course long before we had done 1000, at about the two hundredth specimen, we had turned up an extraordinary smear of carcinoma *in situ* with cancer cells spread right across the smear. There had been not the slightest sign of cancer on her cervix. Carey was dumbfounded. We did a biopsy tissue test of the cervix and discovered loads of CIS in the tissue.'

With this success the programme did not stop at 1000 smears. It continued and a full-time cytologist was appointed to National Women's Hospital to set up a laboratory and train staff. He was sent to the United States to study cytology at first hand and on his return the Papanicolaou grading sequence was introduced. By 1957 the 'Pap smear' was offered to all doctors in New Zealand. Carey was evangelistic in his belief in the benefits of screening: Williams remembers, 'Carey raced around like a bee in a fit. He wrote an article for *New Zealand Woman's Weekly* saying that cervical screening could save lives. He concluded that he could save five lives for every 1000 smears, a wildly exaggerated claim as it turned out.'

By 1964 the hospital cytology service was seeing 20,000 specimens a year. The year before National Women's Hospital had shifted to new purpose-built premises, erected for a cost of three million dollars in Claude Road, Epsom. It also had a new head, Londoner Dennis Bonham, elevated to the status of professor from a position as lecturer at University College Hospital, London. A new cytology block was put out to tender in 1964, but by this time Herbert Green had stepped in and said he was having doubts. Green had joined the cervical cancer clinical team in 1955. He and another colleague had done a limited number of smears in 1948, but he had been out of the country when the major initiatives on cervical cancer were taken. He was not convinced of the idea of progression of the disease, that carcinoma in situ developed into the potentially fatal invasive cancer. He argued that invasive cancer was probably a quite separate disease. If there was little or no progression, then CIS was not a harmful disease, and screening for cervical abnormalities would not lead to a reduction in the incidence of invasive cancer. These were the hallmarks of the position he would express for the next two decades.

Part Two

When Ruth first visited National Women's Hospital in August 1964, she had no idea there was any debate about cervical cancer or that her doctor held controversial views. She was quite sure she was in the best of hands. She was put on the waiting list for a cone biopsy, an operation which removed a cone-shaped core of the cervix which could be checked to see that all abnormal tissue had been taken. But the day after her admission for the cone biopsy, after preparations for the operation had been made, Professor Green had told her that he had decided against operating and she was discharged without any treatment. Every few months after this Ruth was recalled to the hospital where she had further smears, colposcopic examinations, and occasional punch biopsies.

The purpose of a punch biopsy is to diagnose what the disease is and how far it has gone. It enables the pathologist in the laboratory to scrutinize a small section of the cervix under a microscope, look at the cells, and say what they are doing. Very occasionally a punch biopsy can cure CIS, but it is most unlikely, the sample taken being so minute. It has never been regarded as a treatment for cancer. Treatment involves more extensive surgery to remove the cancerous cells; the object of any treatment is to return to a negative (normal) smear later.

Ruth's first punch biopsy in 1965 showed carcinoma *in situ*, a diagnosis which would be consistently entered on her records for fifteen years. Her smears were almost invariably positive (abnormal), the reports describing the cells as 'suggestive' or 'strongly suggestive' of malignancy. But this Ruth did not know. Many years later, in 1985, Ruth would see her hospital file and finally know that from her first visit she already had carcinoma *in situ*. In 1964, and over the years, the words were never mentioned.

By May 1967 the colposcopist entered in her notes that he had observed that the abnormal area on Ruth's cervix had increased in size in the two years since the first colposcopic examination. By the end of that year he recorded 'progression both in extent and degree'. Throughout 1968 and 1969 Ruth's smear reports were 'conclusive for malignancy'. But still nothing was done. In March 1970 Ruth was admitted for a curette of the uterus (a scraping out of the lining of the uterus) and wedge biopsies. A wedge biopsy takes a rather larger piece of tissue than a punch biopsy, but it is also used mainly for diagnosis although rarely it can be a cure. Ruth's pathology report showed carcinoma *in situ* in all the specimens and in one 'microinvasion of the cervix'. This is the first sign that the cancer is penetrating deeper layers of cells and becoming invasive. Despite this, Ruth was again discharged. She returned for smears right through 1970, each one showing cells still 'strongly suggestive' or 'conclusive for malignancy'. Ruth still had the disease and still did not know it.

Ruth was not the only patient Professor Green was studying. Between 1962 and 1974 he wrote numerous papers for the medical journals detailing his experiences with women with CIS and cervical cancer at National Women's Hospital. It was experiences with young childless women that started Green asking questions about the current diagnosis and treatment of cervical cancer.

By the early sixties, the idea of the progression of cervical cancer through precursor stages was generally accepted in the medical community. However, the disease was not completely understood and there was room for argument. The causes of cervical cancer were not known. How often it progressed and how quickly were the subjects of debate. It was strongly argued that widespread screening programmes would reduce the incidence of cancer by detecting it earlier and the large programme underway in British Columbia, Canada, was being watched with interest.

Women with abnormal smears were customarily investigated further by biopsy to diagnose more accurately the stage of the disease. The standard treatment for the precursor stages was cone biopsy. Cone biopsy is described as a 'nasty operation': haemorrhage needing emergency treatment is not an uncommon problem; the woman's chances of conceiving afterwards can be significantly reduced; and the cervix can be so scarred that menstruation can become difficult and very painful. For carcinoma in situ the standard treatment was hysterectomy, a major operation involving removal of the uterus or womb, which therefore rendered the woman sterile.

Twenty-five years later Professor Green can remember in vivid detail some of the cases that distressed him most. A young poet had her university degree conferred in a ceremony in ward nine a week before she died of cancer of the cervix. 'When you see a young attractive woman who'd make a wonderful friend for a man a little younger than myself, when you see her die, it's not nice. That's why I've been so vocal. This is bad for mankind. I realized at the time she wasn't the only one under thirty, there were four.' It was another patient, Shirley B, who gave Green the clue that formed the basis of his theory. He calls her 'the little girl who put me on the right track'. Green performed a biopsy disclosing CIS, but Shirley 'refused a hysterectomy'. 'Two years later she had a baby. She's still alive, living somewhere around Whenuapai.'

Green was concerned at any reduction in women's fertility. He was an opponent of abortion and with his gynaecologist colleagues, Dr Patrick Dunn and Dr William Liley, later played a leading role in the early days of the Society for the Protection of the Unborn Child (SPUC). He took such an uncompromising view of abortion that he was used to present the extreme anti-abortion view to Auckland Medical School students and at one stage caused a furore at National Women's Hospital by refusing to work with doctors performing abortions, whom he called 'murderers'. He also held conservative views on sterilization. He could see virtually no grounds for it, medical or social, arguing that abstinence would lead to the desired result. Once sterilized, he said, a women had 'thrown away a unique possession'.[6]

Professor Green became a man with a mission. He wanted to avoid mutilating surgery and save women's fertility. To do so he had to prove what at first he had suspected, but then came to believe: that CIS was a harmless disease which hardly, if ever, progressed to invasive cancer. His belief led him to treat some patients less extensively. He stopped performing routine hysterectomies in women with CIS, instead performing cone biopsies, but checking by pathology (tissue diagnosis) that the complete tumour had been removed. By 1962 he was able to report that no patients treated this way had progressed to invasion.[7]

Time has shown that Green was correct in arguing for more limited treatment of CIS patients. Many women were saved from unnecessary hysterectomies and by the mid-sixties cone biopsy for CIS had become standard treatment.

Having made a breakthrough and producing what looked like support for his hypothesis, Green pushed the limits of his theory further. Many other authors had published papers in the fifties and early sixties estimating that CIS progressed to invasion in a variable proportion of cases. Green proposed 'to show the lesion is probably benign in the great majority of cases' and to question the view that screening programmes could eliminate invasive cancer.[8] He began to treat small groups in unorthodox ways. At least five women, and possibly as many as sixteen, had hysterectomies without prior biopsies to diagnose what was happening to the cervix. Green had only looked at the cervix with the naked eye and taken a Pap smear. While a Pap smear can reveal an abnormality, a biopsy is necessary to say accurately what stage the disease is at. Earlier, Green had always argued that biopsies were vital for proper diagnosis. In these cases he omitted this step. One result was to provide him with intact cancer lesions to study in the laboratory.

In Green's words, these patients formed a 'special series wherein invasive cancer has been ruled out as far as possible by clinical [looking and listening to the patient] and cytological methods before hysterectomy; serial section studies of lesions thus undisturbed by biopsy are being made and will be reported separately.' There were two dangers in performing a hysterectomy without biopsy. Firstly, a healthy uterus might be removed mistakenly. Secondly, and possibly fatally, if the woman, in fact, had invasive cancer, it would be difficult to treat optimally with radiation therapy after a hysterectomy. In this treatment, radioactive rods are inserted through the cervix to sterilize the uterus and adjacent tissue. With the womb removed, the rods could not be put in place.

Because in these cases Green had not done biopsies before surgery, the only way to detect the seriousness of the disease and see if more treatment was needed, was to examine the excised wombs in a pathology laboratory immediately. Before this could be done, Green took some of the wombs with him to New York when he left in 1962 on a year's prestigious Lederle Scholarship. Two months later, National Women's Hospital received a note from New York. Green was reporting that one of the wombs had shown the woman actually had invasive cancer at the time of her hysterectomy. Despite more extensive surgery, she died two years later.

In other groups of patients the abnormal tissue was not completely removed, or Green 'temporized', that is, delayed further treatment despite positive smears continuing after cone biopsies. This, he acknowledged in writing, 'may appear foolhardy to those who believe in a high chance of progression of the disease to invasion'.[9] Although it is clear from Green's writing that he knew his was a minority view and that he was providing unorthodox treatment, he did not think the patient should be the one to decide: 'If we are uncertain about the natural history of the disease which cytology has revealed in her, how can we possibly expect her to make what is really our decision?'[10] Green justified his unusual handling of cases by insisting that he always rigorously excluded the possibility of invasive cancer before deciding on limited treatment.[11] He also produced his results in vindication of his methods. For much of the sixties he insisted that not a single case had progressed to invasion.[12]

In April 1963, Green embarked on another study. Between this date and June 1965 the rate of cone biopsy at National Women's Hospital doubled, peaking at 140 operations annually before falling to below forty in 1966. Green wrote '200 [cone biopsies] were performed by the author as a special study' one of the aims being to 'estimate in a consecutive series' the correlation between the grade of the prior smear with the later histology (tissue diagnosis) report. In nine women, the smears had showed nothing wrong. Their cervices were coned only because they 'looked suspicious'. In fact the postoperative histology reports showed that five of these women had only cervicitis, a mild inflammation of the cervix in no way requiring such drastic treatment.[13]

By the mid-sixties Green was so convinced that CIS was harmless, he even argued against the necessity for cone biopsy, a proposition he decided to test on women. This was the probable reason for the sudden cancellation of Ruth's cone biopsy in 1964. In June 1966 Green formalized his experiment and gained permission from the hospital medical committee to manage a group of women 'conservatively', that is, to withhold conventional treatment of cone biopsy or hysterectomy.[14] The women selected were under the age of thirty-five and the possibility of existing invasive cancer was excluded by a punch biopsy performed by a colposcopist looking at the magnified cervix.

Colposcopy was introduced to National Women's Hospital in the mid-sixties. The colposcope sharpened the view of the cervix, enabling abnormal cells to be seen in a way that they could not be by the naked eye. The site for biopsies could then be carefully chosen, rather than the more random method of the past. In the women Green managed 'conservatively', the lesion was to be damaged as little as possible by the biopsy, and despite continuing abnormal positive smears, the women were to get no further treatment. Other women who had abnormal smears after initial treatment, such as cone biopsy or hysterectomy, were also to receive no more treatment. According to a paper by Green, by the end of 1966, some seventy-three women with evidence of persistent, uncured CIS were being 'followed'. Twelve of these had diagnosed microinvasion of the cervix. Sixteen had only a punch biopsy.[15]

Differences of opinion over the best treatment for CIS were one thing. There was always unanimity in the medical community about the object of treatment — to return to a negative or normal smear. A positive smear was a sign that treatment had not been successful, there was still disease present and there had been no 'cure'. In such cases, further treatment was called for, until the smear became normal. This was never the intention in the National Women's Hospital experiment. Some women with evidence of disease were to be left. They would be 'followed', that is, brought back for regular smears and possibly more biopsies, but there was no intention to cure them.

The dangers of this are many. If initial diagnosis was inaccurate, women might be unwittingly harbouring an advanced stage of the disease. Women might ultimately need unnecessarily extensive treatment to cure invasive disease. They might even die, for once the cancer has become invasive, treatment will not always halt the disease. In addition, if they failed to attend for follow-up, missed appointments, or moved overseas, they were at serious risk. But by watching these women, Green hoped to observe the natural history of the disease and prove his thesis, that untreated CIS rarely, if at all, led to invasion. The words 'natural history of the disease' are important and need to be emphasized. 'Natural history' means what the disease will do if it is not interfered with by medical treatment. Many of the overseas researchers interested in cervical cancer would very much have liked to study the natural history of cervical cancer, but it was considered unethical to do so. If you believed in the progression of the disease, as they did, you could not risk women developing the potentially fatal form by not treating its precursors.

When asked recently to comment on this study, Leopold Koss, Professor of Pathology at Montefiore Medical Centre and Albert Einstein College of Medicine, the leading world authority on cytology, wrote:

> ... there is excellent evidence that not all of these precancerous lesions progress to cancer hence a large number of them may be presumed to be unnecessarily treated. Dr Green stresses this point repeatedly in his papers and as far as this issue is concerned he is completely correct. On the other hand, neither he nor anyone else can predict which one of the precancerous lesions will progress to cancer and which will not. Therefore all must be treated. I would rather not comment further on Dr Green's reputation because he is a senior and generally respected gynaecologist who is a well known contrarian. I must stress though that most serious observers of the cervix cancer scene do not agree with his views.

Dr David Boyes, Director of the Cancer Control Agency of British Columbia and author of the studies that have convinced the rest of the world of the efficacy of cancer screening, makes a similar comment:

> ... unless the whole lesion was removed, it was not possible to know whether there was some beginning invasion. We have never considered that it was appropriate in man to study the natural history in this fashion because one never knew what one was dealing with unless the whole lesion was removed.

Ralph Rickart is Professor in Pathology and Chief of the Division of Obstetrics and Gynaecology, Pathology, and Cytology at Columbia University College in New York and another luminary on the cervical cancer scene. Described as a 'flamboyant' character, his comments are more forceful. He does not think the study should ever have been started.

> *By the late fifties, and certainly by the mid-sixties there was little*
> *debate on the fact that CIS progressed. The weight of evidence at*
> *the time was that CIS was a precursor. Others had conducted long*
> *term studies on the disease but had used CIS as an end point. It*
> *was absolutely unacceptable and unethical to follow people past*
> *that point.*

Rickart believes that most cancer lesions progress if the women live long enough for that to become evident. 'At best,' he says, '75 per cent will progress within ten years.' There *was* debate about progression in the sixties but the debate in the rest of the world was about the progression *rate*, not whether it did or did not progress.

In one of his papers, Green quotes the famous New Zealand gynaecological specialist, Professor Stallworthy, Professor of Obstetrics and Gynaecology at Oxford University, as having said in 1966: 'To regard carcinoma *in situ* as not being a killing disease is comparable to giving a stiletto to a paranoic'[16] In another paper Green quotes the opinions about the rate of progression held by others at this time: Dunn et al. (1959) 100 per cent; Lange (1960) 33.3 per cent; Boyes et al. (1962) 60 per cent; Graham et al. (1962) 10–20 per cent; McGregor and Baird (1963) 33.3 per cent; McGregor (1966) 100 per cent.[17] These figures are quoted here to show that Green was out on a limb, his opinion was not shared by the medical community and he knew it. A 1970 paper in an Australasian medical journal was headed 'An Atypical View'.[18] Green said that by 'commonly accepted standards, many *in situ* lesions have been almost disdainfully under-treated',[19] and that 'It is clear that the author's experience with cervical carcinoma *in situ* is at considerable variance with that of the great majority of others.' He called others' belief in progression a 'dogma', which had become 'immutable and almost unchallengeable' and so he set about challenging it.

Professor Green described the purpose of his experiment:[20] 'The only way to settle finally the problems of what happens to *in situ* cancer is to follow indefinitely patients with diagnosed but untreated lesions. This is being attempted.' Discussion of the ethics of the study never appeared in his papers. It never seems to have occurred to Green to worry about medical ethics because he believed so absolutely that women with CIS would not develop invasive cancer. Green has written: 'If the physician does not worry too much about the disease then neither will the patient.'[21] Consequently, patients, like Ruth, did not know they were being studied, nor that they were being treated in an unorthodox way.

In his paper 'The Natural History of Cervical Carcinoma *in Situ*' Green described the arbitrary manner in which women were selected: 'No clear pattern of selection is discernible, and subsequent treatment was most often a matter of chance, dependent on the views of the consultant under whom the patient was admitted — and, therefore, really on what day of the week the patient was referred to the clinic.'[22] It has been impossible to discover whether all the patients given limited treatment were Herbert Green's. Neither the present medical superintendent of the hospital, Dr Gabrielle Collison, nor the head of the Post-Graduate School both then and now, Professor Dennis Bonham, could answer this question, although Bonham said other doctors referred CIS cases to Green 'because of his interest'.

In answer to a question about whether women were told there were differences of opinion about the methods of treatment, Green replied, 'I suppose not'. In answer to the same question, Professor Bonham said 'I wouldn't know, you would have to ask each individual doctor who treated patients.' There was no hospital plan to seek the agreement of the women to their unorthodox management. Thus, like Ruth, they were unaware they were getting anything other than standard management for their disease.

In 1966 there was no ethics committee in the hospital. At that date, no hospital in New Zealand had one. The study was passed by the hospital medical committee of which Bonham was chairperson. However, despite the lack of an ethics committee, international standards for human experimentation did exist. Ethical standards for human experimentation had been set by the Nuremberg Code in 1947. The code was the first serious attempt to produce a universal code of conduct for doctors and scientists engaged in medical research involving human experimentation. It formed the basis for all subsequent codes, most notably the World Medical Association's Declaration of Helsinki, first issued in 1964 and revised in 1975. Its central principle is an unequivocal statement of the need for informed consent (see appendix). The National Women's Hospital experiment, it appears, violated most articles in the code.

Part Three

In 1971 Ruth attended the National Women's Hospital colposcopy clinic where the colposcopist, Dr William McIndoe, observed 'dramatic changes' in her cervix. The abnormal area visible under the microscope had increased. McIndoe arranged for Ruth's admission for a cone biopsy, which Green performed a month later. The histology report showed microinvasion of the cervix and that the tumour had not been completely removed.

When Ruth returned eight months after the operation for a further colposcopic examination, McIndoe was worried about a small area of unremoved abnormality extending into the vaginal wall, and her continuing positive smear. 'I would be more satisfied clinically and scientifically,' he wrote, 'since this should be quite possible, quite safely and readily, to remove this small area which remains.' Green was out of the country and McIndoe performed the operation himself.

The tissue he removed showed carcinoma *in situ*. In 1971, for the first time in seven years, Ruth's next smear was relatively normal with no evidence of malignancy, although this would not last. By the end of the year, she was once again showing evidence of malignancy. Despite this, for some reason, Ruth had no colposcopic examination by Dr McIndoe after 1972.

By 1971, Dr Bill McIndoe was a worried man. He did not like what was happening at National Women's Hospital. The first person in New Zealand to use a colposcope, he has been called the father of New Zealand colposcopy. For more than ten years after he arrived at National Women's Hospital he was the only colposcopist in New Zealand and he trained many practitioners of the new speciality in his clinic. From the time he arrived he worked closely with Associate Professor Herbert Green and was the colposcopist for all the women being studied. He was in the position of observing lesions that in any other hospital would have been removed.

Cytologist Dr Stephen Williams describes McIndoe as 'professionally very careful, exact, and accurate. He was a worrier to some extent and at times he was in an enormous dilemma about all this business.' According to a later colleague: 'He was worried sick about it. He could see people dying under their hands and that the standard wisdom being taught was wrong.' Bill McIndoe is called by those who knew him, 'very religious', 'a lovely bloke', and 'shy'. He died in late 1986, of a heart attack, aged sixty-eight.

For twenty years Bill McIndoe opposed what he saw happening at the hospital. On June 20 1966, when Green put forward his proposal to study the natural history of cervical cancer on National Women's Hospital patients, he objected. At the senior staff meeting to which he spoke at length he outlined his fears in a memorandum: 'At our present state of knowledge rather than swing to an extremely conservative position with respect to treatment, I feel the correct measure would be to aim to remove tissue responsible for the positive smear . . .' He called Green's management 'inadequate' both from the point of view of diagnosis and treatment.

However, McIndoe was not a member of the hospital medical committee, the élite group that controlled practices in the hospital. The committee was chaired by Professor Bonham and comprised the superintendent, Dr Algar Warren, Green, leaders of the hospital's clinical 'teams', the radiologist and the head pathologist. Later in the day of 20 June 1966, the committee approved the Green proposal. McIndoe did not get a chance to express his views at this meeting, views that apparently were supported by at least some of the medical staff not on the committee. However, not everybody had McIndoe's clear vision of the implications of the proposal.

The dangers McIndoe saw were twofold. Firstly, that by limiting diagnostic biopsies a smouldering invasive cancer could be missed. Secondly, that by delaying treatment or not completely removing abnormalities, risks were being taken with the women's lives. It was an unequal battle. At this stage McIndoe's was a lone voice. McIndoe is described in his obituary as a 'kindly self-effacing man of complete integrity [who] could not abide sham or hypocrisy in any form. He was a good man whose high principles showed up strongly in his whole life . . .' Had he not believed so passionately in the wrongness of the National Women's Hospital experiment, he would have been content to work behind the scenes, developing the scientific basis of cytology and colposcopy. He had come late to medicine, after training as an electrician, and when he arrived at National Women's Hospital he never quite fitted into the powerful inner group that ran the hospital. Yet it was this unlikely person who challenged the awesome figure of Associate Professor Herbert Green.

Almost everybody, supporter or opponent, comes up with similar descriptions of Herbert Green. 'Domineering', 'belligerent', and that he could not bear criticisms, are the opinions of his detractors. But a member of the non-medical staff who described Green affectionately as a "kind, cuddly teddybear of a man' also talked of his propensity for 'getting on his high horse': 'He was right, and everybody else was wrong. He always had the last say.'

McIndoe's struggle to end the experiment is called by a friend 'the battle of his life'. His attempts became more desperate as the tragic scenario he predicted unfolded in the cancer clinic. It was McIndoe who was operating the colposcope, who could see through its powerful magnifying eye the troubling abnormal patches on the cervices of the women he examined. When these women were brought back again and again, without the treatment he could see they needed, he could not bear it. Green was the consultant and had responsibility and ultimate control over treatment. McIndoe could not interfere directly in the consultants' clinical judgement. 'I have been powerless to intervene,' he wrote.[23]

Although McIndoe found the 'vocal' and 'dogmatic' Green 'difficult to cope with', he persistently challenged him in memoranda and in person. In 1969 in a long memo he discussed disagreements about specific cases. Later, in 1972, he and Green locked swords on five occasions, once prompting Professor Mont Liggins to interrupt them by asking 'Are you two still at it?' McIndoe described these confrontations as 'vigorous interrogations'. On one occasion he said 'I was goaded into calling him [Green] irresponsible in his attitudes and management of patients.'

The response, said McIndoe at the time, was that Green 'not only will not, but does not, listen to any comment which does not suit him. I have endeavoured by all means possible in a mature and dignified manner to make my feelings plain . . .' Some time in the late sixties, McIndoe began keeping a list of patients 'who were causing concern'. As the years went on, the lists grew longer. By March 1971 there had been a death. A full year had elapsed between the date that this woman's punch biopsy had shown CIS and the date she was brought back for a more extensive biopsy that showed invasive cancer. Despite a Wertheim hysterectomy where the internal organs are irradiated before the uterus, ovaries, and upper vagina are removed, she died. 'It is very difficult', McIndoe wrote in a memo, 'to maintain a high standard of reporting of the cytology work in such a climate. What can I say to a technician who misses an obviously malignant slide at the screening stage who replies, "What difference does it make anyway, they are not going to take any notice of the result."'

In 1971 the National Women's Hospital tumour panel was established with Bill McIndoe as convenor. It is not clear exactly who was responsible for the institution of the panel, but the purpose was to open up to discussion particular cases of gynaecological cancer. By this stage McIndoe had been joined in his campaign by Dr Jock McLean, the chief pathologist at the hospital. McIndoe's unhappy role in colposcoping the same untreated women over and over again was matched by McLean's experience in the subterranean laboratories of National Women's Hospital. Under the microscope he viewed thin slivers of tissue taken by biopsies and he was aware that he was viewing the same tumours in the same women again and again. When he reported that the specimens showed CIS, or microinvasion, or suspected invasive cancer, he was aware these alarming reports were not always acted upon. In other hospitals such reports would have resulted in prompt treatment. In addition, there had been conflicts between McLean and Green about diagnoses from pathological specimens. Green would ask for particular slides to be brought to his room where he would sometimes write his own diagnosis beside McLean's, in spite of the fact that he was not a trained pathologist.

McLean calls cancer 'an appalling enigma. Even 1.6 per cent of the best treated females will develop another cancer. A woman who has CIS is at risk of developing something nasty. Positive cytology is a red light at a corner. Continuing positive cytology always requires treatment.' At National Women's Hospital the red light was not always being heeded.

McLean says that junior resident doctors came along to the tumour panel meetings to be entertained by hearing Green, McIndoe, and McLean slugging it out. Any staff member could come to these meetings and anyone could introduce cases. As far as McLean was concerned this was 'progress': 'It meant controversial cases could be brought out into the open and discussed. It protected the patients and ensured they could be treated in an orthodox manner. At one point one of the professorial people introduced an amendment that cases could not be introduced by the pathologist only by clinical people, but it was defeated by a majority of the hospital medical committee.'

The tumour panel, however, was not a complete answer. Cases could only be discussed one at a time. It was, says McLean, 'like Lord Shaftesbury. We could not get everyone out of the mines at once.' In 1973 McIndoe decided to take more formal action. Eight years had elapsed since the institution of the study and his attempts to prevent limited treatment of patients had met scant success. He wrote a memorandum to the medical superintendent, Dr Algar Warren, asking for 'a reappraisal of policy' for cancer patients. There were women, he said, who because of 'limited biopsies' were in danger of having hidden invasive cancer go untreated. He outlined seven cases to illustrate his point.[24]

McLean's accompanying memorandum to the superintendent outlined fourteen cases where limited treatment, he said, was 'not soundly based'. All the women were eventually shown to have invasive cancer. McLean contended they had probably had it from the beginning, but because of inadequate biopsies, it had been missed; 'In my opinion,' he concluded, 'these patients have had what can be termed varying degrees of delayed and inadequate treatment for a disease (invasive carcinoma) that is generally considered to warrant urgent hospital admission for adequate diagnosis and definitive treatment.'[25] For instance, in one patient's case, McLean talked about inadequate diagnosis and 'excessive delay'. CIS was diagnosed in October 1967, but she received no treatment until six months later when a cone biopsy showed microinvasion with possible invasive cancer nearby. More than two years elapsed before this woman had a Wertheim hysterectomy for invasive cancer of the cervix and vagina. In another patient the biopsy showed CIS but possibly invasive cancer. No action was taken for a year when another biopsy showed invasion. McLean called this 'an example of delay in definitive diagnosis and treatment through failure to heed the warning of the possibility of invasive cancer in the initial biopsy.'

In his reply, Green insisted that other clinicians were also following his mode of treatment and that other staff were implicated in the policy of limited treatment. He said that by studying the natural history of the disease 'calculated risk that invasive cancer could be overlooked' was always present but he denied that delayed treatment affected survival rates. For early invasive cancers, he said the ten-year survival rate was 96 per cent so that patients whose cancers were 'overlooked or treatment delayed' were not 'at a disadvantage'. He cast aspersions on the quality of colposcopy and pathology and complained that McLean kept 'the best diagnostic slides from many cases in his own private collection under a disease index only,' preventing him from having access to them. He regretted that 'Dr McIndoe's indecision and doubt could cost a long lead in the elucidation of the problem of the natural history of *in situ* cancer.'[26]

Dissatisfied with Green's response, McLean and McIndoe again approached the superintendent, McIndoe listing 100 women whose cases were causing him concern[27] and McLean concluding with a clear statement of the issues at stake for the women:

> When patients are admitted to a public hospital they put themselves
> in the hands of medical staff with the explicit understanding
> that they will be provided with at least adequate, and preferably
> optimal treatment for their complaint. Clinical studies and trials to
> [establish] optimal management are at times necessary. However,
> when in the course of a trial it becomes apparent that patients
> are at risk, there must be a reappraisal of the trial. Despite what
> Professor Green may say, the consensus of opinion at present is that
> any delay in the diagnosis and treatment of invasive carcinoma
> puts the patient at an increased risk. A survival rate of 96 per cent
> for Stage 1a carcinoma of the cervix is very good at a statistical level
> — but not for the four or so women who die from the disease. At
> our present state of knowledge no one can deny that there is every
> possibility that with earlier diagnosis and treatment, these four or
> so patients could be alive.[28]

By this stage Warren too had become concerned. With him, McLean and McIndoe attempted to take their complaint outside the hospital to the controlling authority. They approached the medical superintendent in chief of the Hospital Board, Fred Moody, who discussed it with the Board's chief executive. Despite the fact that the complaint came from the medical superintendent and two such senior doctors, Moody declined to act. 'The whole thing', remembers McLean, 'was thrown back to the hospital to sort out.' The hospital medical committee set up an investigation committee of three senior gynaecologists, chaired by Dr Richard Seddon (now professor at Otago Medical School). The resulting report, issued in 1976, vindicated the policy of conservative treatment: 'It is the firm opinion of this committee that all staff members involved in the implementation of the policy concerned with this conservative management of carcinoma *in situ* have acted with personal and professional integrity.' The 1971 death that had so concerned McIndoe and that had intensified his efforts was put down by the committee to a 'colposcopic miss', the responsibility for which, of course, lay with McIndoe. By this time even Algar Warren, who had been initially reluctant to act, was calling the report a 'whitewash'.

The unease was spreading, and more doctors were coming to see the validity of McLean and McIndoe's views. Dr Bruce Grieve, a member of the hospital medical committee, supported further investigation and suggested that McIndoe and McLean give reports to the committee. As time passed, says McLean, 'the better was our case. More and more ladies were coming back with invasive cancer because of the conservative treatment while Green was going on with his mode of management. Doctors stopped transferring patients and Herb's reservoir of cases diminished.' The reports were accepted and 'we felt Green had been completely discredited'.

Despite McLean's belief that their objectives had been achieved, in all the interviews we conducted in the course of writing this article no one could give us an assurance that this experiment ever ended. It was never formally stopped. No instructions were issued to doctors to abandon practices that by now had clearly been shown to be dangerous. Dr Gabrielle Collison, who came to the hospital as medical superintendent in 1983, in answer to our questions referred us to Professor Bonham who, as chairman of the hospital medical committee, then the ethics committee, and head of the Post-Graduate School throughout this time, had ultimate responsibility.

It is very difficult to discuss the National Women's Hospital experiment with Bonham because he does not concede that it ever took place. Despite the consensus we encountered with other interviewees that this experiment was to study the natural history of CIS, and despite Green's documented assertion in paper after paper and in memos which went through Bonham's hands that that was what he was trying to follow, Bonham insists that the subject of the study was quite different.

We must refer here to a problem we encountered in interviewing Bonham, which made clarifying his views difficult. He has a curious tendency towards circumlocution, that is, several viewpoints can be contained in the same answer to a question. To take an example, when we asked if in some patients 'there had been a deliberate leaving of part of the lesion, the excision of only part of the lesion', Bonham replied: 'No, no, no, not deliberate at all. Not deliberate leaving of it, that sounds, that's misinterpretation. They were taking enough to biopsy. We could call it a deliberate leaving if you like.'

About one thing Bonham is clear. The experiment was not to study the natural history of the disease. It was, he says, to study 'colposcopic control', 'to treat the patients by minimum interference so long as the colposcopic control was adequate'. In 1966, he says, 'it was suggested that it was time we treated people with either less than a hysterectomy or a full cone biopsy. And the offer came from Dr McIndoe that he would be willing to provide colposcopy.' It was McIndoe's offer, says Bonham, which made the experiment possible: 'The theory was at the time that you could adequately follow it [the disease] with colposcopy. That was McIndoe's theory.'

Where others define colposcopy as a diagnostic tool, Bonham refers to its use as 'treatment'. Of course, if colposcopy is 'treatment', then it is not possible to claim that any patient went 'untreated' for all had colposcopic examinations. 'McIndoe,' says Bonham, 'could have gone on biopsying until he had taken all' of the abnormality, an absurd proposition, for they were not his patients and he was known to abhor the practice of some clinicians overseas who subjected women to a great number of biopsies without anaesthetic.

It is certainly true that McIndoe did not oppose Green's plan as strenuously in 1966 as he did a few years later, when he could see starkly the reality of its consequences, nevertheless only a very imaginative interpretation of events could claim that the experiment was to test a theory held by Bill McIndoe. In fact, McIndoe objected to his role in the experiment from the start. In 1966, he wrote:

> . . . inadequate tissue diagnosis, which can be the only description
> of the type of biopsy I at present perform (if this is to be the only
> biopsy done) and follow-up only taking the further steps if there
> is clinical or colposcopic evidence of invasion, would seem to me
> the type of care that should not be followed . . . If Professor Green's
> proposal is accepted I would feel it very difficult to take seriously
> any cytology reporting or colposcopic assessment.[29]

Although McIndoe was therefore clearly unhappy about the limited colposcopically directed biopsies Green expected him to do, Bonham still blames him and not Green for the 1971 death of a woman in the study. 'I had the notes out on that one . . . and I am sure that one case that died then was a colposcopic miss. I think the biopsies were taken from the wrong part. And I think the person who did that colposcopy is now deceased.' This version of events not only unfairly blames McIndoe as the colposcopist, but ignores the fact that the biopsy showed CIS for which no treatment was undertaken. Bonham calls the sixties and seventies a 'developmental stage' in the treatment of cervical cancer. Although American cancer specialist Ralph Rickart was of the opinion that the study should never have been started, other cancer specialists have said that in the mid-sixties, the proposition was probably acceptable. There was general agreement, however, that by the early seventies, when McIndoe could point to dozens of cases that were causing concern, when a great many women given only limited treatment had returned with invasive cancer and when one woman had died, the study should have been stopped.

Bonham cannot give a date for the time when the study stopped. When asked who could have stopped Green's research, he replied: 'I think it would have been stopped jointly by the hospital medical committee at that time.' Throughout this period Bonham was the head of that committee, and after 1977, of the hospital ethics committee, but he took no action to end the study. The study, he now says, 'merged into general treatment. It stopped being a study and became general treatment.' This was perhaps the most disturbing thing that Professor Bonham said. It puts in question the treatment of all the cervical cancer patients who have attended National Women's Hospital over the last twenty years.

McLean thinks that 'peer pressure forced the study to come gradually to an end'. He is 'pretty certain' the limited treatment of women stopped. McIndoe, however, believed 'it never came to an end'. He said that 'Green carried on with varied managements to the end of his days'. In the light of Bonham's equivocal statement about the fate of the experiment, McIndoe may well have been right. This view is lent support by what was happening to Ruth in the late 1970s.

Part Four

After five years of smears suggestive or conclusive of malignancy, Ruth was abruptly admitted in 1976 for a ring biopsy, a shallow biopsy removing only the surface cells. All the tissue samples showed CIS and the pathologist reported that 'the tumour reached the upper cut edge in several slides'. Despite this report no further action was taken. Over the next three visits to the hospital clinic, Ruth returned normal smears, reports which a clinician would usually view with scepticism in view of her history.

Ruth was brought back in 1977 but not for treatment of cancer. This time it was because her scarred cervix had stenosed, or narrowed, so that menstruation had become painful. The operation was to stretch open the cervical canal. She was still returning normal smears but the histology report of scrapings of tissue from inside the uterus showed 'fragments of carcinoma . . . probably carcinoma *in situ*'. After her next visit in 1977, Green commented on Ruth's case notes that 'the histological report is somewhat surprising'. Nevertheless, after one more visit in 1979 Ruth was discharged from the cancer clinic into the care of her general practitioner giving her a clean bill of health. In his letter to her doctor, Green concluded 'she has no more chance than the next person of now developing carcinoma of the cervix'.

By the date of her discharge in 1979 Ruth had visited National Women's

Hospital thirty-four times, she had had twenty-eight cervical smears, and five biopsies, four operations under general anaesthetic, and ten colposcopic examinations, but as the final histology clearly showed, she still had cancer. But this Ruth did not know when she was discharged. 'I and my family were delighted. We believed that Professor Green had monitored my condition and that I had never approached any condition that looked like cancer.'

Green could ignore Ruth's pathology report showing cancer because he did not believe that pathology was an accurate science. He placed primary value on what the gynaecologist could see with his naked eye during an examination and on his questioning of the women. He thought an abnormality should be defined by what it did over time, rather than what it looked like under the microscope.

In 1966, the year the cancer experiment officially started at the hospital, Green repeated a test he had heard about overseas. He sent sample biopsy slides to five Auckland pathologists and in only three cases was their verdict unanimous. Twenty years later he quoted this experience to us in support of his long term distrust of pathology:

> How can you base a theory on such impractical proofs? Tradition demands that the pathologist's opinion be accepted, but he is just as likely to be in error as the clinician. Diagnosis is so uncertain and open to dispute by other pathologists. One man's cancer is another man's normality. Countless women have been subjected to unnecessary diagnosis and treatment. I've resisted the opinion of the pathologist in many cases. Sometimes I've been right and sometimes I've been wrong.

Because he doubted so strongly the accuracy of diagnoses given by pathologists, Green disputes cases which have been identified as progress to invasion. He asks 'Who said they became invasive? I could dispute every one of them.' We asked, 'When would he accept that there was invasion?' 'When you have an obvious ulcerating or fungating lesion,' he replied, 'or the woman dies of the disease.'

The year after the experiment started, Green wrote that of 503 patients not one had progressed to invasion. The reason for this, he said, was that invasive cancer was 'excluded as far as possible at the outset' of the experiment.[30] Two years later, Green reported in the *International Journal of Obstetrics and Gynaecology* that one case had appeared among the women being studied, but he went on to say that this was to be expected since it was within the normal incidence for the disease. Another case, he predicted, would 'probably appear in 1972'. He postulated that his results differed from overseas reports because of his 'insistence on the adequate exclusion of invasive cancer at the outset'.[31] By 1974 there had been a dramatic change. In a paper in the *New Zealand Medical Journal*, Green said of his previous prediction that it was 'perhaps over-stated and must be modified, not because of the "rash" of invasive cancers [six since 1970] but mainly because of inability of present methods to exclude adequately invasive cancer at the outset . . .'[32] This was a profound about-face from his confidence of previous years about the hospital's thoroughness in excluding invasion. Nevertheless it provided a means of avoiding the more unpleasant conclusion — that his theory was wrong and he had endangered women's lives.

Green discussed seven cases. In only two does he accept there has been 'true' progression and both these had had negative smears after his conservative treatment. In all five other cases where the danger signal of continuing positive cytology had been ignored, Green reinterprets the evidence. 'From the above case-reports it can be seen that the issue of progression or not to invasion cancer is clouded by inadequate initial exclusion of invasive cancer . . . and possible over-diagnosis of invasion . . .'[33] Thus he attributes the apparent invasion to either under or over diagnosis by pathology. So-called 'under diagnosed' cases could be dropped from the study thus improving the final figures. The one death he discusses (not included in the seven cases) is blamed on a mistake of colposcopy.

This bold rewriting of events implicates Drs McIndoe and McLean, both of whom were at the time actually protesting about Green's actions. McIndoe was clear about what Green was doing: 'He believed that CIS is not a cancer. When it does become a cancer, then either it was at the beginning or it isn't now. He plays with the categories of diagnosis.' By the same date McIndoe had more than Green's seven cases. His list included thirty cases that were now invasive.[34] Even if it upset his predictions, Green seemed unperturbed by cases of invasion. He wrote: 'It does not seem that it is a very dangerous lesion if only one in sixteen incompletely treated lesions progresses to invasion.'[35] Green virtually ceased publishing after this paper appeared. Ralph Rickart says that 'after Dr Green was finally silenced, when he didn't publish any more or get on the lecture circuit, I didn't hear anyone doubting that CIS progressed to invasion.'

Green's explanations about under and over diagnosis point to the ultimate folly of the whole experiment. Professor David Skegg of the University of Otago Medical School has given a concise summary of the problems with what he calls 'the unfortunate experiment at National Women's Hospital':

> Green tries to dismiss the results as being due to either inadequate exclusion of invasion at the outset or over diagnosis of invasion later. The latter explanation is hardly credible in the case of those women who have died from their disease, and the whole argument betrays circular thinking. If the experiment was incapable of falsifying Green's hypothesis, why was it carried out? Moreover, if invasion could not be excluded confidently at the outset, were the patients warned of the risk that was being taken?[36]

Why did Green persist in the face of the increasingly depressing reality in the cancer wards? Professor Green's answer would be that he believed what he believed and he needed to convince the rest of the world. As Dr McLean says: 'I have no doubt that in his own view Herb was acting in good faith. He believed that CIS was not of any consequence. He felt in his conscience that he was not doing any harm to his patients.' A member of the administrative staff recalls that Green was very kind to patients in the cancer ward: 'He saw young women coming in and dying and he would be very, very unhappy. He took time and talked so nicely to the husbands and relatives.' Green himself prized his ability to talk to his patients. He retold with pride that at his retirement the medical superintendent said that Professor Green's patients 'think he walks on water'.

An observer might say that Green had invested so much in his theory that he was incapable of changing his mind when it became overwhelmingly clear that he was wrong. For twenty years this quote was written on his office blackboard: 'Don't confuse me with facts — my mind is made up.' Cervical cancer had consumed his attention since the mid-1950s. He had written paper after paper on it, had initiated one of the biggest studies in the world, which was to be the cornerstone of his career. Had he been right, he would have been a world leader. By the early 1970s he was over fifty and it was too late to carve out a career in a different direction. Already disappointed when as acting head he had been passed over as chief of the Graduate School in favour of Dennis Bonham, he was never made a full professor.

In 1987 Herbert Green still cares deeply about cervical cancer. In his retirement years he has over 2000 cases filed on his home computer and spends much time writing papers that are rarely published. Not only does he doubt cytology and pathology, he now rejects other modern technical advances in the management of cervical cancer. He calls colposcopy 'the most undignified procedure for a woman'. He hates doing it: 'They want to colposcope everyone now. They want to up-end all the women in New Zealand. It's a horrible position for a woman.' Of the recently introduced laser which allows less destructive treatment he says: 'It's a toy, a gimmick.' Underlying his attempts to prove his theories, there seems to be a kind of fatalism about life and a medical nihilism. He sees a need to accept the inevitability of suffering and death. 'We've got to accept cancer. Cancer in our culture has become a dirty disease. We must cut it out, burn it out, abolish it. We are asking for prolonged life.'

However, if Green could not accept the evidence why was he allowed by others to go on? Professor Green was not the only player in the tragedy which unfolded at National Women's Hospital. But from Professor Bonham downwards no one but McLean and McIndoe would take him on. As McLean said, 'For many years I felt isolated. I kept away from the clinicians. I felt an antipathy against me. They feared I would open my mouth too wide. They have spoken behind Herb's back but they won't confront him. Have you tried arguing with him? Herb's an absolute bastard when stood up to.' People were too frightened of him. 'When McIndoe and I tried to stand up to him Green reacted by doing nothing and saying nothing. He's a bigoted zealot. He's like a missionary who thinks he can do no wrong.' Another scientist said 'I learnt early you produced data and didn't discuss it. There was no point in talking to him. You couldn't discuss scientific validity.' McIndoe said 'it wasn't possible to get the medical profession to take this fellow on. He had a Muldoon personality.' But unlike Prime Ministers, women do not get a chance to elect their gynaecologists.

Professor Bonham views the struggle between McIndoe and Green as merely a personality clash:

> *McIndoe and Professor Green didn't get on terribly well together
> ... if there had been greater harmony among the individuals
> involved in this group things might have happened a little sooner
> ... Bill McIndoe was a charming chap but he did have a vicious
> streak. Which made it very difficult — you can't talk about this
> really, about someone who had died, but it made it difficult.*

Professor Bonham believes that,

> *in an academic scene you need a few free thinking people to
> stimulate in various directions ... Herb Green was a unique sort
> of free thinker. I had to live with him for a lot of my life. Though
> it was sometimes difficult because of his fairly free ideas, he fitted
> into the department extremely well and we didn't have problems.
> No one would be unhappy with the way he managed the patients
> with cancer. He really looked after them fantastically.*

Part Five

When Ruth noticed slight bleeding between her periods two years ago she was not unduly worried. 'I was approaching forty-nine and thought this could merely indicate the onset of menopause. When I visited my doctor about a painful shoulder, I suggested that I should have a smear test, since I had not had one since leaving National Women's at the end of 1979.' Her smear was suggestive but not conclusive for malignancy and she was referred to a specialist. 'I took the liberty of reading the referral letter before the appointment. On reading it my husband and I were alarmed that it mentioned carcinoma *in situ*. We looked up this term in a medical dictionary and were disturbed to realize that I been seen for a condition which without treatment could lead to truly malignant cancer.'

The specialist told Ruth that her National Women's Hospital records revealed that earlier smears had shown carcinoma *in situ*. She had, in effect, 'been sitting on a time bomb'. The biopsy he performed showed that Ruth had invasive cancer.

> *I was now facing the reality of cancer. I felt angry and frustrated.
> First Professor Green had never informed me of my condition
> over the years, nor did I feel that my treatment from 1964 to 1979
> had been satisfactory. I had had a ring biopsy performed on me
> in 1976 when I was forty years of age. I could not see the point
> of continuing with biopsy treatment at that age. I had not had*

a child since 1966 and had had no intention of starting another
pregnancy in 1976, when my career as a secondary school teacher
was well under way. At no time had I been fully informed or given
any say in the treatment I received.

In October 1985, Ruth entered National Women's Hospital. For two days she lay behind lead shields with caesium rods inserted in her cervix. Six weeks later she returned for surgical removal of the uterus, tubes, and ovaries. She spent New Year's Eve in Hospital and was discharged in January 1986.

Ruth was the first of five women to return to National Women's Hospital with invasive cancer after the publication of a study of the treatment of CIS at the hospital. It was not written by Green. The authors of the study were McIndoe, McLean, Ronald Jones, a clinician at the hospital, and Peter Mullins, a statistician at the medical school. It was published in *Obstetrics and Gynaecology*, the journal of the American College of Obstetricians and Gynaecologists, in October 1984.[37] The authors had gone back to the tissue samples and smear tests for all the women who had been diagnosed as having CIS at the hospital since 1955. The raw data for 948 women was analysed, making it the largest study of its type in the world.

The study divided the women into two groups: 817 who had normal smears after treatment by 'conventional techniques' and a second group of 131 women who had continued to produce persistent abnormal smears. This second group is called in the study the 'conservative' treatment group. Some had only biopsies to establish the presence of disease and no further treatment. Others had abnormal smears after initial treatment, and were not treated further. For example, one woman had twenty-two malignant smears over sixteen years after a hysterectomy, but no further treatment. She eventually developed invasive cancer of the vaginal vault.

A most significant finding was that in only 5 per cent of the 'conservatively' treated women in group two did CIS disappear. Ninety-five per cent continued to have CIS, or worse: twenty-nine (22 per cent) of these women developed invasive cancer of the cervix or vagina. In contrast, of the 817 group one women who had normal cytology after treatment, only twelve (1.2 per cent) progressed to invasion. Those who received inadequate treatment were twenty-four times more likely to progress to invasion compared to those who were treated. Such enormous differences in outcome demonstrated beyond a shadow of doubt that women with continuing abnormalities ran a very high risk of developing invasive cancer. Twelve of the total number of women died from invasive carcinoma: four (0.5 per cent) of the group one women, and eight (6 per cent) of the group two women who had limited or no treatment. Thus the women in the limited treatment group were twelve times more likely to die as the fully treated group.

There is one small group of women in the study that deserves special attention. Twenty-five women had only a diagnostic punch or wedge biopsy and no further treatment, including eighteen who received only a single biopsy 'with minimal disturbance of the lesion'. These twenty-five women were the ones who could most clearly show 'the natural history' of CIS. Ten developed invasive cancer. Worse, almost all of the women who had continuing abnormal smears after the biopsy developed invasive cancer. There were ten women in this group, and nine of them developed invasion. The authors concluded the study by saying that 'it is, therefore, impossible to escape the conclusion that patients with continuing abnormal cytology . . . run an unacceptably high risk of developing invasive carcinoma compared with women with continuing normal cytology'. The women with abnormal cytology, that is, the group two women, had an 18 per cent chance of developing invasive carcinoma of the cervix or vaginal vault at ten years, and a 36 per cent chance at twenty years. The study had clearly shown that 'CIS of the cervix had a significant invasive potential'.

Green's thesis that CIS was a harmless lesion and invasive cancer a separate disease had been disproved by his own data. When interviewed, Green disputed the findings of this study on the basis that the pathology was incorrect. He could not accept that all the invasive cases really were invasive. On three occasions during our interview with him, Green raised the subject of the deaths of the women.

Unasked, he said, 'It's unfair to accuse me of studies which led to deaths, when they were part of it.'

'But we haven't said that to you,' we replied, 'Who has?'

'I had it from McIndoe before he died.'

Eight of the 131 group two women died. If the death rate in this group had been the same as the group one women, none would have died. The scientific method depends on the publication of results which disprove as well as those which prove a hypothesis, but Green never completed his study or published the final results himself. McIndoe and McLean decided to work on and publish the study because they wanted to bring what had happened out into the open. It was drafted and redrafted over several years and statistician Mullins was brought in to 'provide a stronger statistical basis for making the statement. They wanted to nail it down more firmly.' 'We tried to make it impersonal,' says Mullins, 'so we couldn't be accused of a witch-hunt. The ethical issues were drawn out and highlighted.' Green's name is not mentioned in it.

McLean had given some of the data at an international pathology conference in Sydney in 1982:

> *I got very good feedback from the top gynaecological pathologists in this field. One of the top gynaecologists in the UK came to me afterwards and the first word he said was 'litigation'. He thought there would be some. Because of the efforts on the part of some staff here to sweep the thing under the table, we wanted to bring it out into the open and let our peers judge. They'd tried to cover it up and shut me up. The findings vindicated us. We didn't make it too public in the hospital that we were working on it at first, but in general the clinical staff were supportive. They were too frightened to stand up*

> *themselves but were quite happy to let someone else stick their necks*
> *out. It's like penguins on [an ice-floe]. They push one in first, and if*
> *he doesn't get eaten by the killer whales, they all jump in.*

The authors of the study hoped the academic media would pick it up and were disconcerted when it did not, as Mullins puts it, 'make more of a splash'. 'There were some reprint requests from overseas', says Mullins, 'but none from New Zealand.' If overseas doctors saw the issues, it was not so clear to the New Zealand medical fraternity. Although he agreed that in general scientific findings should be published, Bonham was critical of the paper. 'They were unethically describing Green's cases to some extent and poking the finger a bit at him. There are innuendoes in that paper that shouldn't be there.' Bonham had outlined his concerns in a letter to the medical superintendent in November 1982 before the publication of the study:

> *I have heard a rumour that Dr McIndoe, and possibly another*
> *specialist, have been reviewing cases of carcinoma* in situ *that*
> *have been managed in the hospital. I have no recollection of*
> *approval being given for review of* in situ *cases belonging to other*
> *consultants and I wonder if they have been reviewing cases by*
> *courtesy of Miss Owen, [the secretary of the clinic] without the*
> *approval of the clinicians concerned. This may only be a rumour*
> *but I think it may be worth while your having a look at it in*
> *the first instance because any publication emanating from this*
> *hospital must be acceptable to the staff of the hospital before it is*
> *submitted for publication, as I am sure you will agree.*

Mullins said that McIndoe was motivated most to write the paper by concern for the future if Green's attitudes continued to have influence. 'He thought Herb Green's theories would fade away and Dennis Bonham would change his mind.' A friend of McIndoe's told us that he 'went through agonies over writing the paper. He didn't think anything would be served by pillorying Green, but he worried about the future particularly about the effect on doctors trained at National Women's who would not keep up with the research. Green's teaching was still being followed out there among the GPs.'

Part Six

While Ruth was visiting her specialist before her hysterectomy, he had mentioned that her National Women's Hospital records showed that she had had a cervical smear in 1982. 'This threw me a little,' remembers Ruth, for she was quite sure that she had not had another smear test after being discharged from the hospital in 1979. When Ruth was admitted for her operation, the house surgeon also mentioned that the hospital had received smear reports from her GP: 'I told him that I would like to see one of those reports. He passed me my file. On it I saw clearly in print on two occasions: "Alive and well — with evidence of cancer." I asked how in the hell my GP could say that when he was not doing smear tests.' The house surgeon told Ruth that her GP should have been performing a smear test annually. This he had not done. What he had done, however, was fill in the hospital cancer clinic follow-up forms as if he had, and return them to the hospital. This he did in 1980, 1982, and 1984. He even provided dates when the non-existent smears had taken place.

When Ruth realized the full enormity of the mismanagement of her case she decided to take some action. She had the choice of proving medical misadventure through the Accident Compensation Corporation and thus recouping some of her sick leave, or taking a case against her GP to the Medical Disciplinary Committee. 'I had to decide between ACC, which would have been good for me personally, or protecting other women by exposing my doctor.' Ruth decided on the latter course. She describes the disciplinary hearing as a harrowing experience. The hearing was conducted like a trial with lawyers, people sworn under oath and cross-examinations. A panel of five males, three doctors, a legal assessor, and an ex-serviceman would make the decision. The hearing lasted from ten in the morning till quarter to four in the afternoon. Ruth was cross-examined in the witness box for 'what felt like twenty-four hours. The lawyer tried to put words in my mouth. His main thing was that at National Women's I would have been told I should have follow-up smear tests. I got to the stage I thought I couldn't take any more. Then, thank God, he stopped.'

Apart from her lawyer, Ruth had no support in the courtroom. 'They went through all my personal files from the hospital and from my GP. I can only liken it to a rape case, I felt so exposed and vulnerable.' Ruth's lawyer called a National Women's Hospital cervical cancer specialist, Dr Murray Jamieson, to question him about the hospital's handling of Ruth's case. The committee also wanted to know why the hospital had not acted on the GP's report of continuing cancer. Jamieson replied that many doctors filled the forms in improperly, and, anyway, it was assumed that if there was evidence of continuing cancer, the doctor should have done something about it. Responsibility, then, was laid at the door of the GP.

Four weeks after the hearing, Ruth's lawyer received the committee's written decision. Her GP was found guilty of professional misconduct and censured, but in mitigation the committee noted that Ruth had not asked for a smear after being discharged and said that her doctor had been 'influenced by the over-optimistic opinion' of the National Women's Hospital specialist. The GP was ordered to pay the court costs and $1,551 of Ruth's legal expenses. This left her with a bill of $1,500 in legal fees to pay, but she did not have the satisfaction of helping other women because the committee also ordered that there should be no publication of the doctor's name in the *New Zealand Medical Journal* and no publication of details of the findings 'in such a way as to identify either the complainant or the doctor' in any other media. For this reason Ruth has been unable to use her real name in this article. 'I felt the whole thing had been a bit contradictory. In no other court in the land does a person found guilty have their name suppressed without a very good reason. Why should doctors be immune from the normal laws of society?'

On the surface, this further sad chapter in the mismanagement of Ruth's illness could be seen as just bad luck. Perhaps Ruth was unfortunate to be under the care of a sloppy GP. There is another more likely explanation. The attitude of Ruth's GP suggests that the whole climate of training about cervical cancer has been affected. Ruth's GP had done his post-graduate training at National Women's Hospital in 1976. He may have felt justified in not taking further smears if he had been taught that smears were inaccurate, of limited value, and cervical cancer relatively unimportant. He may have felt justified, especially when he read the letter of referral from Green, which said that Ruth had no more risk of developing invasive cancer than the next woman. It seems that Professor Green's attitude has spilled over into a negative, sceptical attitude to cervical screening among doctors.

The investigation for this article met with great discouragement from doctors contacted for comments. With one or two exceptions, doctors said to leave it alone, it was in the past and no good would be served by revelations in the lay media. It was seen as a matter for the medical profession, not the public. Most doctors refused to talk at all; others were encouraging, but declined to be quoted. We began to feel a little like Dr McLean's penguins who would be pushed off the [ice-floe] to test the water. Eventually we were forced to seek comments from cancer experts overseas who were more forthcoming in their opinions. They all knew about 'the unfortunate experiment' at National Women's Hospital. It was not necessary to explain to any doctors, local or overseas, what the experiment had been about. Yet whatever their personal views, the New Zealand medical profession closed ranks to protect the reputation of their fraternity.

'The unfortunate experiment' is not an issue of the past. It has continuing repercussions for the women, like Ruth, who were part of it, who have to live with cancer now or in the future. However, it also has implications for the treatment of cervical cancer today, and for the future of New Zealand's long overdue cervical cancer screening programme. The cervical cancer rate has dropped in countries that have a programme of screening women by systematically taking cervical smears, but in New Zealand which has no population screening programme, the number of cases has not declined. The rate of deaths from cervical cancer is gradually increasing, and some doctors talk about an alarming 'epidemic' of the cancer among younger women who rarely showed cancer in the past.

Many women in New Zealand do have cervical smears taken by general practitioners, family planning clinic doctors, or during antenatal care, but the coverage is haphazard and the groups most at risk are the least likely to have regular smears. Of forty cases of invasive cancer at Wellington Women's Hospital in 1986, fourteen had had a previously abnormal smear that had been ignored. Others had been treated for gynaecological problems, but had not been given a smear test, while, shockingly, several women had asked for an examination and been refused.[38]

New Zealand lags behind the rest of the world in every area of the management of cervical cancer. Some of the country's major diagnostic laboratories still use the outmoded Papanicolaou grading system which has been abandoned in more advanced parts of the world. The care of women with cervical abnormalities is haphazard and casual. Women are brought back endlessly for repeat smears when they should be referred for colposcopy. There are under twenty colposcopes in the country where there should be twice that number. Consequently, at Middlemore Hospital 'older' women are not referred for colposcopy after an abnormal smear, but proceed straight to a 'blind' cone biopsy, a practice frowned on by cancer experts. There are only two lasers, the treatment technique that is least damaging in many cases. New Zealand women have been sold short in this crucial area of their health care. As Wellington colposcopist Dr Graeme Duncan said recently, 'I'm sorry for the ladies that have got cervical cancer. We, collectively, are years behind the game.'

American cancer expert Richard Reid, guest speaker at a symposium on cervical cancer at Auckland Medical School in late 1986, was 'incredulous' at attitudes expressed at the symposium. His wife said she had never seen him more angry than when he arrived back at the hotel after the meeting. He said: 'I was surprised by the lack of conviction about the benefits of screening expressed at the meeting, and surprised that in New Zealand there had been no decrease in mortality. Everywhere else in the world has had a two-thirds reduction in deaths.' Skilled in the use of the laser, he was sufficiently concerned to offer to train at no cost New Zealand doctors who could get to his clinic in Detroit.

National Women's Hospital is the primary teaching hospital in gynaecology, it controls undergraduate teaching in gynaecology at the Auckland Medical School and is the home of the Post-Graduate School of Obstetrics and Gynaecology where doctors are trained in the speciality. Professor Green controlled the teaching on cervical cancer until he retired in 1982. In his view 'screening is the biggest hoax ever perpetrated on New Zealand women'. He thinks cervical smear tests for screening are a waste of time and money. He contends that more women will die from complications of unnecessary hysterectomies because of false negatives than if they had been left to die of cervical cancer. The only way to prevent cervical cancer, he says, would be to stop 'fornication'. When we asked how you would detect CIS before it became invasive without screening, he replied, 'You won't. All you can do is reduce the effects [of invasive cancer] by early diagnosis.' He emphasizes the importance of taking histories, asking women about any unusual bleeding or discharge, which can be signs of invasive cancer. These symptoms, however, only usually appear once the cancer is invasive and the woman's prognosis worse than if the cancer had been detected at an earlier stage.

Green believes there are 'vested interests' in the current push to set up a nationwide screening programme for women. There are academic careers to be built, he maintains, and he talks of the 'colposcopic empire' — gynaecologists motivated by the prospect of a great increase in expensive colposcopic examinations. This contention is contradicted by the fact that most colposcopes in New Zealand are in public hospitals where no private financial interests are involved. Twenty colposcopes hardly constitute an empire. Green is undismayed that his views are regarded as idiosyncratic outside National Women's Hospital. He also believes that cigarette smoking and lung cancer are not linked and smokes at Cancer Society meetings.

Green's successor as teacher and head of the cervical cancer team was Dr Murray Jamieson. The son of a Nonconformist minister, he became a Rhodes Scholar, but also went as a surgeon to Vietnam after a stint in the territorials. Later, he became Green's registrar at National Women's Hospital. Jamieson is one of the new generation of 'baby boom' doctors. It is rumoured he is being groomed by Professor Bonham to be his replacement when he retires. At his invitation we attended one of Jamieson's lectures on cervical cancer. It was impeccable and taught the generally accepted position on cervical cancer screening. Jamieson said he had always taught this way. However, only two years ago, the head of one of the hospital's other clinical teams was so disturbed at one of Jamieson's lectures, he stood up and presented an alternative pro-screening view.

There is evidence of what appear to be recent anti-screening statements. In an *Auckland Star* article of September 1986, Jamieson is described as an 'opponent of the nationwide screening programme'.[39] Like Professor Green, Jamieson prefers early diagnosis of invasive cancer to prevention by screening. There is an 80 per cent cure rate for invasive cancer, he says, 'a great deal higher than any other cancer'. The other way of looking at this, of course, is that at least one in five women with invasive cancer will die, women who might have been saved by earlier treatment.

In August 1985 Jamieson and Petr Skrabanek, a Hungarian working at the University of Dublin, published a letter in the *New Zealand Medical Journal* entitled 'Eaten by Worms: A Comment on Cervical Screening',[40] in which they quote classical and biblical beliefs that sexual misconduct was the cause of genital cancer. They say '... some southern authorities have promised New Zealand an epidemic of that disease. Every woman should be screened. We are told cervical cancer is a sexually transmitted disease ... True, the victims are not eaten by worms, but gnawed away by cancer (or fear of it) they are. The wages of sex is a positive smear.' In the thirty years from 1953 to 1982 'no more than an average of ninety women a year have died of cervical cancer, compared with almost 2000 persons who died in 1982 from accidents, poisoning and drowning, or to the 364 suicides and forty-one homicides in that year'. The letter concludes that screening is therefore hardly worth the considerable effort involved:

> *Why then do we fuss so much about cervical cancer? Every woman*
> *should have a smear, correct? Every woman should be reminded*
> *that there is a danger? Why? Is it because the fear of being eaten*

by worms is a healthy fear? Should one million New Zealand
women over the age of nineteen live in daily fear, though only
0.009 per cent of them will enter the final statistics? Listening to
and asking leading questions of a patient is far, far better than
screening in the control of cervical cancer.

Dr Jamieson says this letter is not evidence that he is opposed to screening. He dismissed it as a joke, suggesting it was intended as a lampoon. Although Professor Green described himself and Jamieson as particularly 'close', Dr Jamieson was quite certain that at National Women's Hospital he practised and taught the 'standard line'.

Dr Jamieson and Professor Bonham both express identical attitudes to screening. They felt that a national register would be unacceptable to New Zealanders;[41] they believe that because of the low proportion of abnormalities detected, the medical industry will gain more from the business than women; they fear that the false negative and false positive rate make it an impracticable test which will not lead to a reduction in deaths, but which will cause unnecessary worry to women; and above all they believe that the importance of cervical cancer must be seen against the much larger risks of breast cancer, motor accidents, suicides, and so forth. Both Dr Jamieson and Professor Bonham deny that theirs is an 'anti-screening' attitude. Like Green they both offered us an apparently unpublished article by Skrabanek, which questions the figures that show that screening programmes have been effective. They say that they compare cervical cancer to much larger risks, like smoking, not with the intention of undermining the value of cervical cancer screening, but to put the problem into proportion. As academics they feel obliged to point out this and the limitations of the test. Says Bonham: 'We are trying to teach people to be in proportion. If a patient comes to you at the moment because she has read the propaganda from the American Cancer Society or recently, the New Zealand Cancer Society, and she comes in and says, "Doctor, I have come for a cervical smear". Now, most doctors take off their pants and do a cervical smear: I say, you have to check their breasts as well.'

It is presumably in the spirit of academic enquiry that a debate entitled 'Cervical Cytology Screening — Is It Worthwhile?', chaired by Murray Jamieson, was held in the hospital just over a month ago. Nevertheless, Professor Bonham said that the widely held belief that National Women's Hospital is opposed to screening was 'an absolute falsehood'. He explained that he had always supported screening and had indeed pressed for research to prove its value. As evidence he said that four years ago he had made 'an impassioned plea' to the Auckland Cancer Society 'to let us set up a study, and go and screen everybody in Northland'. Professor Bonham hoped that it would finally establish the usefulness or otherwise of screening. 'But it was blocked. The Cancer Society refused to do it.' Professor Bonham believed that the scheme was defeated by the GP representative at the society because it would threaten GPs' business.

'The GP chap, Dr Barham, thought it would be cutting across the general practitioners' interests. That's why he was against it.'

Dr Phillip Barham of Auckland Medical School has no memory of an 'impassioned plea'. According to him, Professor Bonham made a verbal mention of the idea to a member of the society's education committee which decided the idea was 'not in their ambit'. This account is corroborated by Alan Spence, chief executive of the Auckland Cancer Society, who writes that 'at no time did the Society receive a formal proposal for any funding from the Professor.' Such a proposal might more appropriately have been made to the scientific committee of the national cancer society, but its chairperson Professor Gavin does not recall such a proposal being made and certainly not an 'impassioned plea'.

The most up-to-date statements about screening attributable to Professor Bonham are found in the most recent issue of the *Australia and New Zealand Journal of Obstetrics and Gynaecology*. Bonham was asked to comment on a paper on cervical cancer from Melbourne Royal Women's Hospital. He invited Professors Liggins and Green to join him in replying, an action which suggests a concurrence in Bonham's and Green's views. 'Annual cytologic screening for cervical cancer is uneconomic,' they say, 'unless an individual woman's life is valued at NZ$420,000 or more.' They ask whether,

> *the huge capital investment involved in screening for the detection of a cancer which causes only 0.4–0.5 per cent of all deaths in Australia and New Zealand makes economic sense? Against a possible gain to society and a certain pecuniary one to all the diagnosticians involved, must be placed only a minute chance of personal good accruing to the individual woman — and at the expense of appreciable anxiety and physical morbidity resulting from protracted diagnostic and therapeutic procedures.*

It is difficult not to see these views as anti-screening.

Even Dr Gabrielle Collison, the hospital's medical superintendent, talks of 'two camps' in the hospital, a 'pro' and an 'anti-screening camp'. Professor Green says the 'pro' group consists of the part-time clinicians; the 'anti' group of the professorial school. However, Professor Bonham insists that doctors who see National [Women's] as anti-screening have all been reading 'bunkum from Skragg' [sic] whose views he calls 'false and libellous'. Professor David Skegg, an epidemiologist from Otago Medical School, has been one of a number of doctors not connected to National Women's Hospital who have been trying to persuade medical opinion of the need for a screening programme. He is the author of the Skegg Report, published in the *New Zealand Medical Journal* in 1985,[42] which reviewed the evidence for the effectiveness of screening and provided a model for a possible programme in New Zealand. While in many countries it might not be necessary to review the evidence, says Skegg, in New Zealand it was 'because National Women's Hospital, which is very influential, has over about fifteen years contained some people who have been very anti cervical screening, and I think it would be impossible to overestimate the effect that has had on medical training'.

Richard Reid said the situation in New Zealand was unique: 'There's nowhere else in the world where the benefits of a screening programme are doubted.' Ralph Rickart was blunt when asked if there were doubters elsewhere: 'It's inconceivable. I'm serious. I don't know of any informed person who would doubt it. The data is overwhelming.' Some New Zealand doctors talk about the National Women's Hospital 'party line'. Dr Ian St George, a lecturer in General Practice at Otago Medical School, said that through National Women's role as a teaching hospital Green's theories have had a 'profound influence' both on practice and on the lack of screening in New Zealand. If doctors were to be educated about the value of screening, he says, it would be necessary to 'address the issue of Herb Green and the influence his teaching has had in New Zealand, and show that it was wrong; there are still plenty of people who rationalize their lack of effort in taking cervical smears on that opinion'.

Dr Allan Gray, medical director of The Cancer Society of New Zealand put it more strongly:

> They are totally up a gum tree. It's like belonging to a political party. Teaching at National Women's is not authoritative on this issue. It's a big disaster area. All the teaching at one medical school is totally out of date and incorrect. They've taught several generations of doctors the wrong thing. A lot of practitioners won't do smears because they don't believe in them. They have been taught that it's useless.

It is clear, then, that National Women's Hospital is a crucial factor in the success of any nationwide cervical screening programme. But no one has been prepared to confront its power directly. Even doctors who want screening avoid rather than confront the problem of National Women's Hospital. Some of the comments about National Women's Hospital included in this article were taken from the published proceedings of a Health Department meeting, which none of the participants apparently expected to be transcribed and published. It was only an accident, therefore, that they became public. Although National Women's Hospital deals with by far the largest number of cervical cancer cases in the country, none of the doctors involved was asked to this first major meeting on cervical cancer. Rather than tackling the problem of the hospital the doctors were simply left out. Professor Bonham reprimanded the Department for what he called this 'specific act of parochialism'. He insisted that Professor Skegg's remarks about the hospital in the published report 'must be removed' if the Department wished there to be 'a unified scheme in New Zealand'.

The cervical cancer symposium held at Auckland Medical School in 1986 was organized specifically to counteract the National Women's Hospital influence. 'The Cancer Society', says Allan Gray, 'paid for the two overseas speakers in the hope of bringing in a glimmering of light.' Once again, this sidles round the problem. Similarly, no one was prepared to publicly confront Professor Green about 'the unfortunate experiment'. He retired with his career intact. A eulogy written by his colleague Professor Liggins in the *Auckland University News* only praised Green: 'His views on its [cervical cancer's] natural history which were condemned in the 60s as revolutionary and dangerous were largely vindicated in the 70s to the extent that as he retires he has the satisfaction of seeing worldwide acceptance of his conservative approach . . .' Not a word of criticism passed Professor Bonham's lips when we interviewed him. Professor Green still chairs the hospital's tumour panel.

The silence stems from the medical profession's rigidly enforced loyalty among its members. Doubtless the doctors who did talk will be condemned by some of their brethren for breaking ranks, but it could be argued that they are the only ones who have demonstrated any personal and professional integrity. Ruth's lawyer encountered that same silence when he tried to find a doctor who would testify to normal handling of a disease like hers. He was refused by several doctors. Professional solidarity is always a priority for the medical profession because it is basic to their power. There are many penalties for those who violate the code. Such doctors are marginalized and their careers stalled. Covered by his medical insurance, Ruth's doctor only suffered a day's embarrassment for his life-threatening negligence. Had his crime been against the profession and not the patient, he might well have suffered a more severe outcome.

Autonomy is crucial to the power of the profession. Doctors are fanatically jealous of any encroachment on this autonomy. The profession is entirely self-regulating and beyond scrutiny. Doctors are accountable to no one but each other. To preserve this autonomy, the public must learn as little as possible about medical bungles. Left to them the story of 'the unfortunate experiment' would have been buried with the victims. The right of the doctor to treat his patient as he wishes is absolute. The dangers of this are demonstrated by the case of Professor Green. For over twenty years, no one interfered in his treatment of patients. Eventually, new cases were not referred to him; but no one intervened on behalf of the women he was already handling. In the medical system, there is no effective voice for the public interest.

With no public scrutiny possible, regulation is supposed to come from peer review, that is, evaluation by others in the trade. Some doctors say that such a calamity could not happen again because peer review is now so widely practised. 'The bad old days of the consultant as tyrant are gone,' Dr Collison told us. Most hospitals now have ethics committees to monitor practices. However, ethics committees are invariably dominated by doctors, and all members are appointed by the hospital with Hospital Board approval. They are not publicly elected. At National Women's Hospital the ethics committee consists of doctors, one nursing and one lay member. It is chaired by Professor Bonham. Although the committee was instituted in 1977, it appears it failed to investigate or definitively terminate the experiment begun in 1966. Doctors' autonomy on ethics committees ensures that they protect the profession. They are the gatekeepers of the institutions. They decide who can research practices in the hospital.

There has been no fundamental change in the rights of health consumers. In many hospitals anaesthetised women are used to train groups of medical students in vaginal examination without the women's prior consent or even knowledge. The patients' bill of rights used in some hospitals has no legal standing. The consent forms protect only the doctor. Those used in the Auckland Hospital Board area provide blanket consent to any procedures thought necessary by any doctor. Not even the treating physician is specified. Patients can complain to the Auckland Hospital Board, but the outcome of such complaints is often decided within the Board by the executive. They will not necessarily come to the attention of Board members, the elected representatives.

Ruth was never informed or consulted about her condition or treatment. If Ruth had been aware of her situation instead of being dismissed from hospital without a word of explanation, she could have made sure that she had adequate regular smears. Although she was an educated, professional woman, she was never treated as a responsible person capable of making decisions about her health. Her understanding of the situation was seen as irrelevant. Ruth's own priorities were cast aside. She was most concerned with her own safety. Had she been given the choice, she would have had a hysterectomy to cure the disease years before a more extensive operation became necessary. Professor Green wrote on her records in 1968: 'She is a sensible patient and knows all the ins and outs of the situation.' Ruth is adamant she received no explanation about her illness. She only knew she had cancer when she saw the records in 1985. When asked why Ruth's situation was never discussed with her, Professor Bonham replied: 'You'll always find people who will say that.'

A concept of informed consent that can be legally enforced by the consumer is vital to patients' rights. It is not a reality in present-day New Zealand. There is little legislative control on human experimentation in New Zealand. Research on human subjects comes under the Medical Research Council, a powerful doctor-dominated body in which the public has no say. A subcommittee of the Council, the Scott Committee on Therapeutic Trials, must approve experimentation involving unregistered drugs; however, its proceedings are secret. The public, even subjects of trials, have no right to know what drugs are currently being tested. The committee is not charged to consider ethics or the issue of informed consent. The research worker is trusted to consider the ethical issues.

There is no statutory requirement for trials involving registered drugs, or, like the National Women's Hospital experiment, no drugs, to go through any approval process. If they are based in hospitals, this is left to the hospital's ethics committees. The only ethical standards are the codes derived from the Nuremberg judgement and they are not enforceable by consumers. The only redress for a person used in a human experiment without permission would be civil, and the person would have to prove harm had been done. What this adds up to is that in present-day New Zealand individuals have no absolute right not to be used in an experiment without consent. There are actually more legislative controls on animal experimentation than on humans. Since the passing of the Accident Compensation Act, which effectively removed consumers' right to sue for medical abuse, no one has succeeded in bringing a negligence action against a doctor. The act has contributed substantially to the peculiar legal immunity of the medical profession.

There is another reason why action is urgent. During this long investigation, no adequate reassurances were given that all the women like Ruth have been brought back and treated. The medical superintendent, Dr Collison, said 'I really don't know if all the women have been recalled.' Professor Bonham felt that because of the hospital's follow-up system, women would have been treated in due course. However, the hospital apparently saw no need to alter its system to ensure the women were found and treated. 'I don't think I can tell you about each individual patient,' he said. 'Individual people [doctors] managed them according to their own lines.'

Ruth's experience shows the dangerous gaps in this approach. She was discharged with evidence of disease. She was not warned to have continuing smears. Her GP took no steps to monitor her condition and the hospital did not act on reports that she still had cancer. Only her own action saved her life. It is vital that any women at risk be identified and their cases reviewed. Advocates for the women and doctors independent of National Women's Hospital must be part of those reviews so the women can have confidence in the process. The women who were experimented on must also be made aware of their legal rights, as must the families of women who have died unnecessarily.

Could 'the unfortunate experiment' happen again? The whole horrifying saga demonstrates the failure of the internal processes that doctors prize. 'Keeping it all in the family' offers no protection to patients who are asked to have blind trust in their physicians. There is little more protection for patients in 1987, than there was in 1966, or 1976. Only an independent evaluation of hospital practices by non-medical people will reveal whether these fears are well-founded. This is certainly called for.

Appendix
The Nuremberg Code
Permissible Medical Experiments

1. The voluntary consent of the human subject is absolutely essential. This means that the person involved should have legal capacity to give consent; should be so situated as to be able to exercise free power of choice, without the intervention of any element of force, fraud, deceit, duress, overreaching, or other ulterior form of constraint or coercion; and should have sufficient knowledge and comprehension of the elements of the subject matter involved as to enable him to make an understanding and enlightening

decision. This latter element requires that before the acceptance of an affirmative decision by the experimental subject there should be made known to him the nature, duration, and purpose of the experiment; the method and means by which it is to be conducted; all conveniences and hazards reasonably to be expected; and the effects upon his health or person which may possibly come from his participation in the experiment. The duty and responsibility for ascertaining the quality of the consent rests upon each individual who initiates, directs, or engages in the experiment. It is a personal duty and responsibility which may not be delegated to another with impunity.

2. The experiment should be such as to yield fruitful results for the good of society, unprocurable by other methods or means of study, and not random and unnecessary in nature.

3. The experiment should be so designed and based on the results of animal experimentation and a knowledge of the natural history of the disease or other problem under study that the anticipated results justify the performance of the experiment.

4. The experiment should be so conducted as to avoid all unnecessary physical and mental suffering and injury.

5. No experiment should be conducted where there is *a prior* reason to believe that death or disabling injury will occur; except, perhaps, in those experiments where the experimental physicians also serve as the subjects.

6. The degree of risk to be taken should never exceed that determined by the humanitarian importance of the problem to be solved by the experiment.

7. Proper preparations should be made and adequate facilities provided to protect the experimental subject against even remote possibilities of injury, disability, or death.

8. The experiment should be conducted only by scientifically qualified persons. The highest degree of skill and care should be required through all stages of the experiment of those who conduct or engage in the experiment.

9. During the course of the experiment the human subject should be at liberty to bring the experiment to an end if he has reached the physical or mental state where continuation of the experiment seems to him to be impossible.

10. During the course of the experiment the scientist in charge must be prepared to terminate the experiment at any stage, if he has probable cause to believe, in the exercise of the good faith, superior skill, and careful judgement required of him, that a continuation of the experiment is likely to result in injury, disability, or death to the experimental subject.

The following footnotes are taken from extensive notes compiled by Sandra Coney for the Cancer Inquiry.

. . .

Note: All quotes attributed to people in this article are taken from interviews with them conducted by the authors.

1.   All medical details of 'Ruth's' treatment are taken from the summary of her case from the cervical cancer clinic.

2.   G. H. Green, 'Pregnancy Following Cervical Carcinoma in Situ: A Review of 60 Cases', *Journal of Obstetrics and Gynaecology of the British Commonwealth*, vol. 73 (December, 1966) 897–902.

3.   This figure was provided by Professor Green in the interview with him conducted by the authors on 27 November 1986.

4.   See J. Donley, *Save the Midwife!* (New Women's Press, 1966) 65–77 and the files on National Women's Hospital, Auckland Public Library.

5.   W. A. McIndoe, 'The Contribution of Cytology to the Diagnosis of Invasive Carcinoma of the Cervix in a "Medical Climate" Somewhat Critical to Cytology Population Screening', (undated circa 1972) 3.

6.   G. H. Green, 'Tubal Ligation', *New Zealand Medical Journal of Obstetrics and Gynaecology*, (1958) 470.

7.   G. H. Green, 'Carcinoma in Situ of the Uterine Cervix. Conservative Management in 84 of 190 cases', *Australia and New Zealand Journal of Obstetrics and Gynaecology*, vol. 2, no. (2 June, 1962) 49–57.

8.   G. H. Green, 'Cervical Carcinoma in Situ: True Cancer or Non-Invasive Lesion?' *Australia and New Zealand Journal of Obstetrics and Gynaecology*, 4: 165 (1964) 165–73.

9.   G. H. Green, 'Cervical Cytology and Carcinoma in Situ', *Journal of Obstetrics and Gynaecology of the British Commonwealth*, vol. 72 (February, 1965) 19.

10. Ibid, p. 19.

11. See Green (1964) footnote 8.

12. See Green (1964) footnote 8.

13. G. H. Green, 'Cervical Cone Biopsy with Octapressin', *Australia and New Zealand Journal of Obstetrics and Gynaecology*, vol. 6 (1966) 259–65.

14. G. H. Green, 'Invasive Potentiality of Carcinoma in Situ', *International Journal of Obstetrics and Gynaecology*, (August, 1969) 157–71 and W. A. McIndoe, memorandum to the Medical Superintendent 'Diagnosis and Management of Precancerous Lesions of the Cervix' 10 October 1973.

15. See Green (1969) footnote 14.

16. G. H. Green, 'Cervical Carcinoma in Situ: An Atypical View', *Australia and New Zealand Journal of Obstetrics and Gynaecology*, 10 (1970) 41–8.

17. See Green (1969) footnote 14.

18. Green (1970) footnote 16.

19. Green (1969) footnote 14.

20. Green (1970) footnote 16.

21. Green (1969) footnote 14.

22. G. H. Green and J. W. Donovan, 'The Natural History of Cervical Carcinoma in Situ', *Journal of Obstetrics and Gynaecology of the British Commonwealth*, vol. 77, no. 1. (January, 1970) 6.

23. McIndoe memo, 14 December 1973.

24. McIndoe memo, 10 October 1973.

25. McLean memo, 18 October 1973.

26. Green memo, 7 November 1973.

27. McIndoe memo, 14 December 1973.

28. McLean memo, 10 May 1974.

29. McIndoe memo, 20 June 1966.

30. G. H. Green, 'Is Cervical Carcinoma in Situ a Significant Lesion?' *International Surgery*, vol. 47, no. 6 (June, 1967).

31. Green (1969) footnote 14.

32. G. H. Green, 'The Progression of Pre-Invasive Lesions of the Cervix to Invasion', *New Zealand Medical Journal*, vol. 80, no. 525 (9 October, 1974) 283.

33. Ibid, p. 284.

34. McIndoe memo, 14 December 1973.

35. Green (1974) p. 285, footnote 32.

36. D. C. G. Skegg, 'Cervical Screening', *New Zealand Medical Journal* (22 January, 1986) 26–7.

37. W. A. McIndoe, et al., 'The Invasive Potential of Carcinoma in Situ of the Cervix', *Obstetrics and Gynaecology*, vol. 64, no. 4 (October, 1984).

38. G. Duncan. 'The Role of Colposcopy in the Diagnosis of Early Cervical Cancer', at the Symposium on Cervical Cancer and its Precursors, organized by the Colposcopy Society of New Zealand, Auckland University School of Medicine, 19 November 1986, and G. Duncan, 'Smear Tactics', paper at National Summer Update Conference of the New Zealand Obstetric and Gynaecological Society, Auckland, 26 February 1987.

39. A. Storey, 'The Modern Woman's Plague', *Sunday Star* (14 September 1986) A10.

40. Petr Skrabanek, and Murray Jamieson, 'Eaten by Worms: A Comment on Cervical Screening', *New Zealand Medical Journal* (14 August, 1985) 654.

41. See L. Dyson, 'Testing Times', *More Magazine* (March 1987) 117–127.

42. D. C. G. Skegg, et al., 'Recommendations for Routine Cervical Screening', *New Zealand Medical Journal*, vol. 98, no. 784 (14 August, 1985) 639–9.

CHAPTER SIXTEEN

A slow killer

1992, *The Evening Post*: James Hollings investigates the contamination of blood supplies with the fatal liver disease hepatitis C.

Hepatitis C is a slow killer. Unlike the other forms of hepatitis, it isn't spread so easily — it usually requires coming into contact with the body fluids or blood of someone infected. But what it lacks in agility it more than makes up for in lethality. Although many infected people will have no symptoms, those who do may notice jaundice, stomach pain, nausea, or fatigue. About three-quarters of those who get hepatitis C will develop a chronic form, and eventually, as it continues its assault on the liver, they will develop liver cancer. Nowadays, there are effective treatments. Back in 1992, the choice was either a long and expensive course of interferon treatment or, possibly, liver transplant. Neither was a sure cure, even if you could get it.

When I started work at *The Evening Post*, in 1992, as health reporter, I hadn't heard about hepatitis C. By the end of that year, I knew a lot more. That is because I had reported on what was arguably the biggest scandal to hit the New Zealand health sector since the 'unfortunate experiment', and possibly since. Until the *Post* began running stories, New Zealanders had not known that they were knowingly being transfused with infected blood.

I came across the story when following up on a small story that appeared in the *Waikato Times* in March of that year. It was about Cherie Beard, who had contracted hepatitis C after a blood transfusion. I didn't smell a rat; I was simply curious how someone could contract a disease like that from a transfusion. After making enquiries, it became clear that I wasn't the only one who was curious: there was widespread concern in the blood transfusion service that repeated warnings about the safety of the blood supply had gone unheeded.

The *Post* ran several stories over the next few months, each unearthing a bit more about the bureaucratic bungling that caused this disaster. Eventually public outrage forced the government to hold an inquiry into what had gone wrong.

The following story is a summary of the issue, published shortly after the inquiry's findings were announced. That inquiry cleared the then Minister of Health, Simon Upton, but he didn't escape censure. Growing public concern over the direction of the government's highly unpopular health-sector reforms (especially the introduction of user charges for patients in public hospitals) saw him replaced as Health Minister less than a year later.

Bureaucracy gives the kiss of death
The Evening Post, 22 December 1992

Imagine you are in hospital and doctors say you need a blood transfusion. You know it may give you the potentially fatal liver disease hepatitis C and refuse it, but the doctors insist, to save your life.

Three months later you are tired and moody, and have abnormal liver function. Tests confirm the worst: you caught the disease from the transfusion. You face a lifetime of sickness, and possibly death from liver cancer.

Later you learn that you would probably not have caught the disease if the Government had followed Australia's example and started screening all blood donations for the disease in early 1990 — as it was told to at the time by medical experts.

That is exactly the situation faced by an unnamed 25-year-old Whangarei woman, who learnt in August that she had the disease.

According to Health Department estimates she is one of 163 people still alive who will develop chronic hepatitis C from a blood transfusion in the 2½ years between a test becoming available and screening being introduced last July.

If she is lucky she will be one of the 130 who have only "minimal disruption to daily living". If not she will be one of the 33 who "will develop aggressive liver disease with cirrhosis and some may develop cancer."

This point is worth restating: 33 people may well die as a direct result of a 2½-year delay in introducing screening of blood donations for hepatitis C. Medical Association chairman Alister Scott believes this is a conservative estimate — the real figure might be higher.

There has been publicity about this issue, but it faded after the Government introduced screening. It flared again last month when it was revealed that though most of the population was made as safe as medically possible from July, about 15 uninfected haemophiliacs continued to be exposed as late as November, due to their use of a contaminated blood product.

The ensuing scandal brought calls for Health Minister Simon Upton's resignation, as he had apparently been warned in a letter in July that haemophiliacs continued to be at risk.

An inquiry was set up by Health Department Director-General Chris Lovelace. It was conducted by former Labour Cabinet Minister Stan Rodger and

Australian Dr Sue Morey, Chief Medical Officer, New South Wales Department of Health. A censored version of its report was released last Friday.

Predictably, the report found no one person was to blame. Rather, there was a kind of systems failure. Though the department's director-general was warned as early as April 1990 that screening should be introduced — the transfusion advisory committees repeated this warning to the department in July that year and the Minister, Helen Clark, was told in August that screening would be cost effective — "the fact that the department was undergoing a number of major restructures during the period and that there was no medical or epidemiological input from within the department at decision making level, no doubt contributed to the delay in screening."

It adds: "It is clear that from early 1990 there was a view commonly held by departmental managers that the first generation test was not reliable enough. It appears to the inquiry that the concepts of sensitivity and specificity of tests were not well understood, and that considerable emphasis was placed on the number of false positives rather than on the fact that screening would enable 86 percent of the cases of hepatitis C to be eliminated from the donor pool."

The department still denies it gave bad advice. Officials say they were worried that the number of false positive tests could waste blood donations, and cause unnecessary worry to blood donors.

But the report says the managers' view was "contrary to that of the Blood Transfusion Advisory Committee, the Communicable Disease Centre Advisory Committee, the Atlanta Communicable Disease Center, as well cost effectiveness studies produced in New Zealand . . ."

They would have been more aware of the level of concern among medical experts "if a senior medical member of the department's staff had been assigned the responsibility for broad oversight of the operations of the Blood Transfusion Advisory Committee".

It is probable managers were given legal advice in 1990 that they were unlikely to be sued for not introducing testing, but this cannot be confirmed — a section relating to it was censored from the inquiry report.

When the department finally did advise Mr Upton in July 1991 that screening should be introduced, he approved it the same day. But it took a further year before screening started, due to bickering over money.

Mr Upton says he did not immediately order area health boards to find the $1.6 million needed in the 1991–92 year because "I was reluctant to place [them] under further [financial] pressure."

But he was part of a Cabinet which took $4.5 million from the boards in that year to fund the National Interim Provider Board, which advised on health reforms.

Last May Treasury turned down his request for extra money, and area health boards were told to start in July and pay for screening themselves.

He stands by his decisions: "To this day I have no formal means of weighing the many unfunded priorities that are put to me. The Core Service Committee process and a refocused department will in future be better able to provide advice about priorities . . .

"Naturally I have had to exercise my judgment on issues such as funding and priorities. On that score there is nothing I would not stand by."

The report also found that on the narrower issue of why haemophiliacs continued to be placed at risk as late as last month, neither Mr Upton nor senior departmental officers had been "specifically alerted" to the ongoing risk. This claim is questionable, but it enabled Mr Upton to say the report exonerated him.

Even if Mr Upton had known, the report says no completely satisfactory alternative was available — but it also states Britain has been making a hepatitis C free Factor 9 product since 1985.

The report makes a number of recommendations for bureaucratic reform which the department says it is now moving swiftly to address.

But it leaves begging the larger question of why the department was so disorganised. That, among other things, has led Haemophilia Society President Mike Mapperson to label it a whitewash.

"Who instigated the reorganisations? . . . He [Mr Upton] did. He is ultimately responsible for the failings that went on."

He added: "Is this what we are to expect from the reorganisation of the health service away from something providing a service to something that makes a profit?"

In fact only two of the four reorganisations in the past four years were under Mr Upton's tenure. It was one under Labour's Michael Bassett which began replacing doctor-managers with non-doctors.

The report rightly makes the point that blood screening can never be 100 percent safe. Even now the hepatitis C test is only 98 percent effective, and there is still a risk that some as yet undiscovered virus is slipping through.

The report blames media coverage for causing unnecessary alarm, but admits that action on the haemophiliac issue came as a direct result of media coverage.

In its narrow focus on bureaucratic solutions, the report raises more questions than answers:

- If repeated restructurings let this fall through the cracks, in what other matters has the system failed that we do not yet know about?
- Why did no one in the department speak out publicly? Many of those involved were medical doctors. Were they concerned about the delay? If so, why did they put their duty to their employer ahead of the 160 people now suffering from hepatitis C?
- Where are the checks and balances to stop this happening again? Until July 1991 the public could have pressured their local elected area health boards for action if the Government did nothing.

In fact, Otago's head of blood transfusion services, Jim Faed, was so concerned by November 1990 about the lack of action on hepatitis C screening that he told his board he could no longer be responsible for patient safety. This apparently forced Otago Area Health Board to make enough money available to introduce partial screening for hepatitis C in the middle of last year.

But the elected boards were sacked at that time and replaced by Government appointees by Mr Upton as part of the health "reforms".

Regrettably, it was to be another year before screening was introduced nationwide. The national cost will be $1.6 million.

If all 33 patients the department estimates will develop "aggressive liver disease" require liver transplants, it will cost the Government $2.64 million. This is assuming the current $80,000 subsidy is maintained. It does not take account of the costs of Interferon treatment ($4000 a patient), possible legal action, or of the inquiry itself.

A Health Department spokeswoman said on Friday no one had resigned, or would resign, over the issue.

CHAPTER SEVENTEEN

Our national shame

1992, *Metro*: Lesley Max tells the story of the two-year-old who was tortured and killed by her parents, and lifts the lid on child abuse in New Zealand.

This story of how a gentle, defenceless two-year-old girl was tortured and killed at the hands of her mother and her mother's boyfriend may well be one that you find, as I did, almost too painful to read. But you should read it. More than any other, this is the story that opened New Zealanders' eyes to perhaps our greatest national shame. The short life and sad, painful death of Delcelia Witika is a story that has become emblematic of our saddest secret.

From the early 1990s, New Zealanders began to become aware that their children were dying, in increasing numbers, from something entirely preventable. Not from disease, or hunger, or accidents, but from something far more mundane: their parents and relatives. We became aware, many of us for the first time, that New Zealand — the country we often told ourselves was the best place in the world to bring up kids, the country that gave the world Plunket, the family benefit and a raft of social welfare reforms aimed at helping families, the country of beaches and school sports, of free milk in schools and free education — was also the place where children were more likely to be beaten, stabbed, strangled or simply starved to death than almost any other OECD country.

To put some figures on that: a UNICEF study of child death rates from physical abuse or neglect between 1971 and 1975 found that we were ninth best out of 23 OECD countries, with 0.9 child deaths per 100,000 population. Only 20 years later, that same rate for the years 1994 to 1998 was 1.2 children per 100,000 population. New Zealand had slipped to twenty-fifth out of 27 countries. In other words, in just 20 years our child abuse death rate had gone up 30 per cent. Only the US and Mexico were more dangerous (Connolly & Doolan, 2007).

We became aware of this staggering statistic not through diligent browsing of official reports, but because the police and government agencies responsible for child welfare started to take those responsible to court. In the nine years to 2000, 91 children died. Almost two-thirds of them were under five. As their killers went through the courts, a succession of children's names became grimly familiar as their eulogies were written in prison sentences. Names such as Craig Manukau, 1992. Riri-o-te-Rangi (James) Whakaruru, 1999. Saliel Aplin and Olympia Jetson, 2001. Chris and Cru Kahui, 2006. Nia Glassie, 2007. Moko Rangitoheriri, 2015 (Dalley, 2011).

We also learned that these children had died in conditions of horror. Often they had been beaten for days, weeks or months. Photographs of the children's battered bodies, presented as evidence at trials of their killers, began to appear in newspapers and magazines. What started as a trickle of stories became, if not a flood, at least a stream. Even more disturbing, for those who wanted to blame the new awareness on the media, was that this roll of dishonour was not a media creation. The problem was not a result of increased perception; it *was* actually getting worse. And nothing seemed to be helping.

What was the effect of all this coverage of a hitherto unknown tragedy? In the late 1980s, partially in response to another high-profile death, that of a child known as Baby C, the government had passed the Children, Young Persons and their Families Act. According to historian Bronwyn Dalley, this aimed to reinforce a trend that began in the 1970s as the state moved away from taking at-risk children from their families and making them wards of the state. Instead, it tried to reinforce the role of families and whānau by introducing family conferences with social workers, known as family group conferences (Dalley, 2011). By the 1990s, however, there was already concern that this system wasn't working as it should. The public, outraged by a seemingly undiminished flow of child deaths, blamed the government agencies responsible. Social workers, labouring under high caseloads, said that they simply couldn't make the system work. One expert, Mike Doolan, says that it became a downward spiral as government attempts to grapple with the problem, by doing reviews of each high-profile case, caused more media coverage, which in turn did harm:

> Reviews became a source of official information that exposed the phenomenon of child homicide to the New Zealand community. Throughout the 1990s the news media provided the community with stories of children who had died in the most horrifyingly violent circumstances, and this built to a crescendo of alarm about child abuse in the latter half of the decade. Publicity around these deaths was often associated with an examination and criticism of statutory child welfare agency practices and perceived failings. While health, education and police professionals faced criticism, the most sustained and critical scrutiny focused on statutory child-welfare professionals.

> Where the agency itself had intended case reviews to provide an opportunity to improve practice, the media saw the reviews as

*the means of linking child death to instances of professional error
or incompetence. In what Ferguson (2004) refers to as 'scandal
politics', media pressure called for accountability from the
staff concerned and the agency that employed them. We believe
that this has been critical in the emergence of more risk-averse
practices by child-welfare professionals, which may, paradoxically,
increase the level of risk for highly vulnerable children . . .*

*Increasingly, it seemed, the statutory agency charged with caring
for our society's most vulnerable children became the agency not
only associated with, but also arguably held responsible for, child
deaths by the community. (Connolly & Doolan, 2007, pp. 14–15).*

One case, though, could not be blamed on government officials; nor could
it be passed off as the product of a blame culture fuelled by media interest.
More than any other, the case of Delcelia Witika showed that something was
fundamentally wrong — because in Delcelia's case there had been no state
intervention before she died.

The stories about Delcelia Witika were written by freelance journalist
Lesley Max and were published in *Metro* in 1992. Max grew up on Auckland's
North Shore. In a curious parallel with another journalist featured in this book,
Nicky Hager, she was born into a family acutely aware of the thin line between
security and disaster. Max's father, Maurice Shieff, was a successful clothing
manufacturer, as was Nicky's father, Kurt Hager. Both Hager and Shieff were
Jewish, and both had lost family members in the Holocaust. Like Nicky Hager,
Max believes that much of her social conscience developed from an early
awareness of the sudden calamity that could befall families. She also had a
natural curiosity. 'One of my teachers said: "Lesley always wants to know the
why and wherefore of everything", so I suspect I could see journalism was a
natural path for me to pursue' (Max, 2017).

In a way, Max had been waiting all her life for this story. She had been
concerned about the vulnerability of children at least since the birth of her own
children, when she had witnessed first-hand the lack of help for a solo mother
leaving hospital. She had already written several features for *Metro* about the
care and protection of children. One of her earlier pieces led to an invitation to
write a book: *Children: Endangered Species?* was published by Penguin in 1990.
It was an impassioned call for action to protect vulnerable children. As someone
with a powerful social conscience, Max decided that she needed to do more
than just write about the problem. With the aid of the book, she and others got
funding to set up the Pacific Foundation, dedicated to setting up programmes to
support at-risk families.

The programme had been going for barely a year, and it must have seemed
as if she had left journalism behind, when Max got a call. A friend told her that
a man named Eddie Smith was about to be tried in a particularly appalling case

of child abuse. Smith, the friend said, had already abused another woman. The decades Max had spent thinking and writing about the problem of at-risk children suddenly crystallised into a powerful intuition: this was a story that had to be told. 'I had a gut feeling this was going to be very important' (Max, 2017).

As research on investigative journalists has shown, gut feelings like that do not come out of nowhere (Ettema & Glasser, 1998). They are the result of years of getting to know an issue, and developing the knowledge and context to know when something is truly extraordinary.

Max persuaded the Pacific Foundation board to give her leave from her position as chief executive, and went down to Auckland High Court to cover the trial. That time in the courtroom, every day for five weeks, gave her the access she needed to do the story. 'One of the things [about covering trials] is the intimacy generated by people being around the same place for five weeks. There's a kind of familiarity that builds up. I saw them, they saw me, you know enough about them to be able to make an approach.

'Some of the relatives were just so horror-stricken that they were quite pleased to talk, almost as a way of releasing some of their own feelings about that situation. Tania's sister, Eddie's sister, they were very forthcoming.'

She also got to know the police officers involved in the case, who gave her Tania's diaries. Those diaries, and the photos of Delcelia, give the articles their terrible power. But Max has received some criticism for the way she treated the story. Some have said that the articles were too intrusive, or took advantage, or portrayed Tania Witika too sympathetically. 'Yes, I did have some qualms about using them [the photos]. More from the point of view that they would be intolerable for people to see. I thought they couldn't do any further damage to this child than had already been done. I didn't think they could have posthumously degraded her.'

She also thought it important to include not just the photographs of Delcelia's injuries but also one of a moment of happiness. 'She was sitting on the knee of Eddie's mother . . . And I thought it was important to see her dressed and cared for and looking reasonably secure, to balance that terrible horror. It was some kind of balm to me to know [she had times when she was comforted and cared for].'

Likewise, Max still believes that the diary entries are justified. 'To see the degree to which Delcelia was present in her thoughts. And the answer was very, very little. So while she [Tania Witika] could be reflective about many things she was very little reflective about Delcelia. It did shed some light on her capability of feeling shame and remorse at what she had done to Delcelia. I just thought they were hugely illuminating.'

Some of the police officers involved, who she says were heavily emotionally invested, felt that Max had been too light on Tania. At the same time, she's aware of criticism that her treatment of Tania failed to take enough account of her being trapped in an abusive cycle of violence. While she deplores what Tania did, she did find herself developing some understanding of her. 'Tania and I wanted the same things in life: a good relationship, someone who loved us, and some satisfaction in life. You can see yourself sometimes in a person who is standing in the dock. My circumstances have been so [much more] fortunate than hers, but I don't know that I'm morally better. I have been more fortunate' (Max, 2017).

One of the strengths of the two stories reproduced here, apart from the extraordinary glimpse it gives into the lives of Smith and Witika, is the attempt — sometimes, in retrospect, a trifle heavy-handed — to look for meaning. Max does not simply voyeuristically recount the horror. Instead, she tries to give an understanding of the context, first by looking at the upbringing of both Smith and Witika. 'I would tell the story and attempt to get as much understanding of not only the [details of this case] but [also of] what lay before. I do believe in going upstream. [Looking at] Tania's early life and the biological father of Delcelia; not only his early life, but [also] his mother's life. . . . The mystery of course was Eddie. The rest of his family were highly respectable. I never felt that I entirely understood the enigma that was Eddie' (Max, 2017).

Another strength of Max's coverage is that she tried, in a follow-up piece a month later, to draw out lessons. 'I was wanting to say this is an atrocity where a small child was the victim but we have to look at how do such things happen and how can we help prevent them.

'I didn't want it . . . to be a salacious wallowing in horror. I wanted it to say, "Look this is as bad as it gets. What are the policy lessons that we need to learn?" And Warwick Roger, being the superb editor that he was, provided me the opportunity to do that.'

She also takes comfort in knowing that the articles did achieve something. Max received a Churchill Fellowship, that enabled her to visit successful intervention programmes in Hawaii, and advocated for the establishment of a similar programme here, called Family Start.

The stories were also attached to a 1992 proposal to the then National government to extend to more suburbs the Family Service Centre model she had created to support at-risk families. At a time when much welfare was delivered by central government, the idea was novel. Also, times were tight — the infamously hard-nosed Minister of Finance Ruth Richardson had just delivered her so-called Mother of all Budgets, which slashed welfare spending. The prospects weren't good. However, some angel was on Max's side. While in the supermarket, Richardson had picked up a copy of *Metro*, read Max's piece, and cried. Minister of Social Welfare Jenny Shipley, was also moved. And it was Ruth Richardson, as Minister of Finance, who approved the creation of the Family Service Centres.

Max is hugely satisfied that Family Start has also grown, and is helping myriad families with at-risk children. 'That's one of the outcomes which can be very clearly related to the publication of this piece. . . . Cases such as Delcelia's could very well have been raised. Or it's possible that [families like hers] can now come along to such a place and it could have been a different outcome for

Delcelia, as it has been for untold children.

'All the time I was driven by my experience of sitting in that courtroom watching these people, interviewing the friends and relatives, and exploring the issues, motivated by a sense that things can't just go on as they were. . . . At least we can say that while it's little comfort, some benefit accrued to some other children as a result of this story being told.'

And, despite the continuing roll-call of abuse cases, there have at least been attempts at change, for which Max, and these stories, can claim a share of credit. Besides the Family Start programmes, the spiral of child deaths led to a succession of government reviews and reforms throughout the late 1990s and early 2000s. In 1999, child protection was brought into a new government agency, called Child, Youth and Family. In 2004, the Care of Children Act was passed, reinforcing the safety of children. In 2007, what became known as the 'Anti-Smacking Bill' was passed. It removed from the Crimes Act the statutory defence of using 'reasonable force' to correct a child, meaning that parents could no longer claim this as a defence against a charge of child abuse. In 2017, after yet more deaths and yet more reviews, Child Youth and Family was replaced by a new agency, the Ministry for Vulnerable Children.

For Max, the struggle to protect children goes on. She was awarded an MBE in 1994 and was made Dame Companion of the New Zealand Order of Merit in 2010 for services to the community. At the time of writing, she had stepped back from her role as chief executive of the foundation she helped found, now called Great Potentials, to take up the role of Founder and Senior Advocate, and was envisioning a new initiative, also aimed at supporting at-risk families.

She still thinks of Delcelia, often. 'We don't live that far from where she is buried. I have a few times gone and stood there and thought thoughts. She's very real to me. I just feel that, and this is what I felt when I was writing my book . . . these instances of cruelty towards children, the only thing that can make it tolerable for me to write it, was I can write about it and I can help people put in place better programmes to help children.'

Connolly, M, & Doolan, M. (2007). *Lives cut short: Child deaths by maltreatment*. Wellington: Dunmore Press.

Dalley, B. (2011). Child abuse. In Te Ara — the Encyclopedia of New Zealand. http://www.teara.govt.nz/en/child-abuse

Ettema, J., & Glasser, T. (1998). *Custodians of conscience: Investigative journalism and public virtue*. New York: Columbia University Press.

Max, L. (2017). Interview with author, J. Hollings.

Delcelia's Story

Metro, May and June 1992

. . .

DELCELIA PETRINA WITIKA was born on December 28 1988 to Tania Gaye
Witika, the youngest daughter, adopted, of Annie and Lou Witika of Otara;
youngest sister of Aroha (Girl), Lee (Dingo), Evelyn, (Yantoe), Louis, Thomas,
Hinewai and Puawai (Honey) Witika.

Delcelia's father was Peter Lafaele, the son of Anna Lafaele, the eldest of
her family of three children. Peter and Tania had met at a spacies' parlour and
soon begun to live together. Tania quickly became pregnant, despite the teenage
parents-to-be having neither home nor jobs.

The baby's name was decided before her birth, once a scan had revealed
that a girl was expected. The name Delcelia was composed of Celia (Aroha's
second name) and Dallas, the name of Aroha's partner. The second name was a
compliment to the teenage father.

The baby was born at Warkworth maternity home near Annie Witika's
Wellsford farm. At the time, Annie and Lou had been separated for about 10
years. After a few days with Annie, Tania and Peter took Delcelia to Auckland to
stay with her father, Lou Witika, in Otara.

Tania herself was born in September 1969 at St Helen's Hospital, where she
was abandoned by her mother. She doesn't know who her birth father is. She
was adopted by her birth mother's sister and brother-in-law, Annie and Lou
Witika, and became the youngest of eight children.

Tania maintains that she had a happy, secure childhood, with affectionate
parents who encouraged her both at school and sport. Discipline was apparently
in the form of smacks and growls, never abuse, though Aroha concedes that her
sister did get slapped on the face, though it was "very rare".

When Tania was eight, her parents separated amid much argument and
the child thereafter shuttled back and forth between her mother, at first in
Papatoetoe, and her father in Otara. When she was 11 or 12 she ran away from
her father's house after her sister Evelyn had thrown a chair at her. Tania rang
the Citizen's Advice Bureau, who contacted Social Welfare.

From this age she spent periods in foster homes. In 1983, a complaint was
laid against Lou Witika, the complaint was admitted, and Tania was placed
in a girls' home. She was 14 and had alleged physical abuse by her adopted
brothers and sisters. She was reported by [the Department of Social Welfare] to
be frightened and barefoot, though adequately dressed. In Tania's words, "Then
Dad took me to Bollard [Girls' Home] because I kept running away from home.
Then I went to Weymouth Girls' Home and then to Allendale Girls' Home." She
liked Allendale because it was an open home. She went to school there, having
previously gone to Hillary College. When she was in the fifth form she went
up north to stay with her mother's sister in Kaikohe and attended Northland

College, but she ran away because there was "a breakdown in communication" and stayed with another family.

After working for a short time at an oyster farm in Russell, she returned to Auckland in 1986, staying first at the Baptist Children's Home in Manurewa, then returning to her father's. She got a sewing job.

Then she met Peter Lafaele and soon Delcelia was born.

PETER LAFAELE, Delcelia's father, is New Zealand-born, of a Samoan mother and Pakeha father, a well-built, macho 19-year-old, roughly dressed, with long hair in a pony-tail and a moustache, who speaks in monosyllables.

Peter's mother, Anna, had been taken out of school at 10 or 11 to care for the younger children in the family, so that her mother, widowed at 30, could go out to work. "I was an adult before I was a child," she recalls.

Social Welfare took Anna for a while, after she was found malnourished, with sores all over her and with rotten teeth. Before long her mother got a boyfriend and Anna got a live-in sexual abuser. At 18 she was pregnant with Peter. By the time he was five he had a stepfather who beat and abused and demeaned him verbally, and sexually abused his younger sister. Peter was bright at school, his mother recalls, but when he brought his reports home, he'd be belted across the face and compared with his stepfather's own son.

Peter learned to stay silent, to drink, use drugs and his fists. At the trial of Tania Witika and Eddie Smith, Peter Lafaele was on leave of absence from his own High Court trial for, in the words of his girlfriend, "punching a guy over and taking his car". He told TVNZ reporter Ian Sinclair about his violence towards Tania. "I had light fists. Anything she'll say will start me off. I'll hit her."

His sister, rescued by Anna from the streets from stripping and prostitution, is at 17 the mother of a baby boy.

Peter's new girlfriend has been a strong support to him, helping him, along with his mother, through a suicidal phase following his daughter's death. She's also got hopes that Odyssey House will help him with his drug problem. His mother says he's being helped in prison. Anna hopes for better times, but she's deeply sad at what has happened to her, her son and daughter and her granddaughter.

OMINOUS SIGNS FOR Delcelia were not long in coming, despite her arrival, in the words of the Warkworth midwife, as a "healthy babe". However, Ayala Nicholas, the Whangarei Plunket nurse, felt that Tania was distant from the child, holding her away from her and not talking to her "in a relaxed attitude". The nurse considered this to be a result of postnatal depression.

But in court, at her sister's trial, Aroha said that in Delcelia's first couple of months, while Tania and Peter were staying with her, "Sometimes I couldn't wake [Tania]. I just got pissed off and did baby myself. It was less hassle. Tania and Peter slept most of the time."

Before Delcelia was three months old, Tania and Peter had left her in Whangarei to return to Auckland. "It was supposed to be for a short time," Aroha recalls, "but she stayed away too long and she was frightened to come back and face us."

In the first year of her life, Delcelia spent no more than three months with her mother and was never the sole responsibility of Tania. There was always another person, Anna Lafaele, Peter, Aroha or Lou Witika, who either physically cared for Delcelia or kept an eye on her. While Delcelia was with Aroha and Dally in Whangarei, for much of the period between February and December 1989, Peter visited her but Tania did not. She has no explanation for that. She could have visited. She chose not to.

A family meeting at the beginning of September 1989 when Aroha was too unwell to cope with both her own son Hone and Delcelia, gave Delcelia to Tania, though, in fact, she spent most of her time in Anna Lafaele's care.

Whenever Tania had Delcelia for a while, then returned her to Anna, the child was in a bad condition, according to her grandmother. "She used to be so dirty, she actually smelled like a dog."

At first Tania's sister Evelyn thought that Tania was going to be a good mother to her first child. "She was good to her at the beginning, till she and Peter broke up and she met Eddie Smith. We all noticed, she got so violent towards Delcelia. She hit her so hard, as if she was an adult, in front of us. We all noticed it. My Dad tried to talk to her about it and so did I, but all she said was, 'It's my baby.'

"She gave her really good hidings, before she was even one, if she just grizzled or didn't eat her kai. It wasn't 'cause Eddie was beating her up. She just didn't want anything to do with Delcelia. End of story. She just wanted to have a good time. Having her daughter around her made her sick. She couldn't stand her. That girl, she was very frightened of the mother."

Aroha is a curly-haired woman of 31 who could well pass for 40, perhaps because of toothlessness. She is the mother of five children to three different fathers, and has also acted in a mother role to her younger sisters, Evelyn and Tania.

Despite her irritation about Tania and Peter's "rotten lifestyle" Aroha considered that Tania "seemed all right with Delcie". Yet Peter Lafaele remembers that in Delcelia's first six months, Tania had less patience with her than he had. "She'd growl at it as if it was a grown-up child. She'd smack it on the back of the hands."

When Delcelia was about five months old, the teenage idyll, such as it was, was over. Peter and Tania were by then living with Peter's mother in Papatoetoe where Anna Lafaele remembers Tania's lack of interest in caring for Delcelia: "It was always, 'Get in here, Pete! Do that baby!'"

Soon, Peter's eyes were wandering in the direction of a girl named Rose. There were arguments. Tania took off and returned to her father in Otara.

Peter admits to having hit Tania, but according to her it was the other-woman factor rather than this that caused her to leave.

The day after their son Hone was born, Aroha and Dally brought Delcelia to Auckland where two family meetings were held to decide on her future, and it was agreed she should go to Peter and his mother.

Tania had by this time met Eddie Smith, a handsome young man, son of a Pakeha father and a Cook Island mother. Aroha had heard about their lifestyle, "on dak (cannabis) and getting on the piss and that".

Aroha also remembers that Tania and Peter "were arguing over who was going to claim money for her. That's what all the arguments were about." They both wanted the benefit, even if they couldn't live together. On one occasion Tania took the baby, her clothes and her birth certificate to go to the Housing Corporation.

Delcelia took up more or less permanent residence with her mother from the time of her first birthday, which doesn't sound, from Tania's cryptic diary entries, that it had much to do with the child. January 5 1990 reads: "Had Delcelia's 1st birthday party. And it went for the whole weekend." January 6: "1st Birthday!" January 7: "Recooperating".

IF THERE'S ONE central motif in the early months of Tania Witika's diary which covers the time Eddie Smith and she lived at her home, with her father and various brothers and sisters, it is the phrase, "had a few beers". Whether it's a birthday or a funeral or a dull day at home, the beer flows. An aunt is buried. "Returned back to the marae, had a big feed, big clean up, then it was PARTY — HEARTY!" The next day the formalities continue: "Later on had a rage at Evon's house." The next day: "Me, Eddy and Hinewai went back to Dad's. Their were still quite a few people raging when we left."

The next day, February 1: "Baby started walking. Me, Eddie and Baby stayed home and watched videos. Had a few beers to."

February 2: "Stayed home watched videos and had a few beers."

February 10: "Me, Dad, Hinewai, Walter, Dingo and Eddie had a barbecue. Then we went and got six dozen."

February 11: "I woke up with a hangover."

A year later, with two children and pregnant with a third, it was the same.

February 4: "After all the beer had gone we all had a feed and went to bed."

February 15: "Left to go around Toe's [Evelyn's]. Didn't stay very long because they only had six bottles."

November 9: "It was Mum's birthday so we put down another hangi. Then we all got on the piss again."

It was a style of life not particularly different from that of tens of thousands of New Zealanders. It was a life in which a child was quite peripheral. The diaries, which were a key element in the evidence, and extensively read out in court, make it crystal clear who was central in Tania's life. It was Eddie Smith.

. . .

SAYS HIS SISTER NGAIRE: "When Eddie was around 14, he came home from school one day and found his father, then about 73, dead. After that, Eddie had far too much freedom. My mum worked full time. He got a bit cocky, I reckon.

Used to getting what he wants, doing what he wants.

"The thing that really knocks me is that he's an intelligent person. He always thought he'd be number one. He left school at 15, idiot! He worked hard at his first job, bought a section at Totara Heights, at 16 or 17, paid it off, then he sold it and bought the takeaway bar.

"He had everything going for him. He had plenty of money. Plenty of friends that Mum never liked. Too many hangers on. Girls used to fall at his feet. He wasn't fat then. [But he was] the big guy with the business, the van, the fast life. We watched him becoming irresponsible.

"Mum and my daughters and my sister and me, we all went over to help him [in the takeaway bar]. He was his own worst enemy. He was too young to have responsibility. He'd get lax — off to the nightclub and wouldn't open up the next morning.

"Finally he had to sell it. Things started going down and down. When I went to see him in the cells at Otahuhu, he's become a fat slob, no pride in himself. That happened over the last few years.

"As for Tania, she seemed all right, not extra bad. We never knew for months that she had a little girl. I really can't say anything bad about her. The pair of them liked their booze too much. The buggers used to drink all the time. Come back absolutely planked so you'd wonder who on earth would be looking after the kids, cause neither of them could."

The mother of a pre-Tania girlfriend of Eddie's remembers her then-23-year-old daughter's excitement when she met him. "I've met this guy and he's so positive, he's like a magnet!"

It wasn't long, however, before the daughter phoned her parents to say Eddie was bashing her. Her stepfather would go over to the girl's home, where she lived with her two-year-old daughter, but Eddie would be gone. After several such occasions, including one where the young woman's nose was broken, the stepfather warned Eddie: "You want to get some help before you do real damage, before you end up in a lot of trouble." On two occasions the police were called, but on neither did the young woman want to lay a complaint.

Eddie tried to avoid the parents, to the extent that the stepfather, a gentle man who works "in the helping industry", was finally driven to an uncharacteristic act: writing on Eddie's fence, "Eddie Smith is a woman beater."

He was also sometimes very rough with the two-year old, picking her up by the arm, and verbally abusing her. (The child, several years later, remembers him with horror.) Her mother, with difficulty, finally severed the relationship.

The "magnetic, positive" young man was by then being described by her as a werewolf, a reference to his piercing, feral stare.

In the witness box at his trial, Eddie Smith emerged as a young man who could control his temper perfectly. He never lost his civility. He emerged instead as remorseless. He neither expressed nor evinced regret for any brutality inflicted on either Tania or Delcelia. Eddie is clearly a person who can neither feel nor respond appropriately to another's pain.

There's the paradox: Eddie the keen student, Eddie the provider for his family — "I saw myself as the head of the family. Father. That's my family. I wanted to provide for them." — Eddie the good kiwi joker, the rugby league player, wonderful with his hands, building outdoor furniture, Eddie the good mate to his friends; Eddie the young man who wanted to get ahead, who bought a section at 16, who worked steadily for several years as a storeman at Dalgety's and as a fork lift driver, who worked nights in rubbish collection, who was in his second year of study at Manukau Polytechnic, pursuant to being self-employed: Eddie, the youngest of five, whose brothers and sisters are all married, hard-working, stable citizens.

EDDIE AND TANIA met in a pub on June 8 1989 and the chemistry was good right away. "When you meet someone it always starts off pretty good at the beginning," Tania remembered. Two weeks later he ripped her dress and punched her "just for talking to another guy. At the time I thought he liked me, so I didn't do nothing about it."

Tania was to receive many such demonstrations of Eddie's affection. For several months, though, they lived contentedly, as far as her diary records, at her father's home in Pearl Baker Drive, Otara, apparently enjoying life as part of her large, disordered family.

At around her 20th birthday, at a time when Eddie came to live with her at her father's, after a terminated pregnancy and at the beginning of a new pregnancy, Tania took possession of Delcelia, who had already, at nine months of age, taken on the role she was to have in her brief life, that of the parcel in Pass the Parcel.

Aroha said, "I thought she'd be all right, 'cause she'd be living at the old man's."

In April 1990, however, Tania, Eddie and Delcelia went to live in the house Tania acquired in Cornwall Rd, Mangere. Ngaire recalls, and the diaries indicate, that they began their life there with real hopes for future happiness. Tania revelled in cooking good meals, Eddie gardened, and Delcelia shuttled between Whangarei and Auckland.

Eddie was soon to have his own child. On March 5 [1990] Tania had written: "Went to the hospital yesterday. Found out I was caring twins. I know Eddie was happy and I'm glad. I love him alot and his really happy, that his going to have two boy's. I gave up smoking as well." The romantic dream of so many emotionally needy young women was alive again.

Meanwhile, there was still Delcelia. Nowhere in her diaries, nowhere in her police interviews and nowhere in her court testimony did Tania express any convincing enthusiasm for Delcelia. Asked by the police whether there was any reason she didn't more often take care of Delcelia herself, she said, "No. If someone wanted her, I'd just give her."

Instead there was this:

20/8/90 "I hit Del-C really bad yesterday. It gave me a real fright. And that's when I knew I had to stop hitting her; not for my sake but for hers."

21/8/90 "I'm really happy with myself; cause I'm learning to control my anger and that's good cause I'm not hitting Del-C out of anger. And I don't want to anymore either, only for a good reason."

28/12/90 "Delcelia's 2nd birthday. Went and picked up Del-C had a bar-b-que and a few beers." [This was the only night in a four-month period which Delcelia spent with Eddie and Tania. Next day, when Aroha took her north, she noticed fresh bruising on her face.]

5/2/91 "Del-C starting to get use to going to the toilet now. But she still needs a hand to get on it. She's 26 months old now and she doesn't seem to be getting any bigger. But she's still in her baby stage. As for little Eddie Junior, he's getting bigger every-day. He eats alot too. But that's good, cause at least we know we aren't starving him. [Delcelia was found to be suffering from malnutrition.] He's a strong, clever and contented baby as well. Everyone say's he looks like his father (and Eddie [does] as well) but as he grows bigger and older as he grows up I can see some of me in him."

2/3/91 ". . . Got up and gave the kids there lunch and played with them. They behaved themselves really well. I watched Del-C and son play together."

Those are the sum total of the meaningful diary entries involving Delcelia. The centrepiece of the diaries is her relationship with Eddie.

. . .

7/3/90 "Got a bit lonely during the day because I was missing Eddie. But he'll be back from work soon."

14/3/90 "Got a hiding with a steel bar from Eddie. I left for a few day's cause I had to protect the baby I was carrying and Delcelia. Got a lot of bruises on my bum."

15/3/90 "Went over to Mere's for a drink with Yantoe. Met Eddie and Walter over there. Went home at 4.30pm."

16/3/90 "Ring Maori Affairs in Ponsonby about loan. Got the loan for mine and Eddie's house. Eddie and I got engaged. We stayed home. He brought me a gold ring."

19/3/90 "Went into Middlemore Hospital because I was getting contractions. Found out I was going into premature labour . . ."

21/3/90 "Still in hospital and missing Eddie. Can't wait to go home to him. I've been crying for him since I've been in here. But I wont' tell him. Cause he's got enough on his mind as it is. And so have I."

22/3/90 ". . . It was Eddie's birthday today and I think the best present I can give him, is giving birth to his kid's and loving him . . ."

28/3/90 "I've been missing Eddie a lot. It's like that everyday for me, mainly from Monday to Friday cause he's working. And with the hour's he's doing the only chance we get to ourselves is the weekend. I love him so much. He's the best thing that's come into my life."

29/3/90 "Yesterday Eddie asked me if I think we'll last! I know we will? But why doe's he ask me that question? I hope he's not seeing someone else! Please God don't let it be true, if he is."

30/3/90 "I can't stop thinking about what Eddie said to me! If there's one thing that I don't want to happen, is for our relationship to end!! Maybe it's because I'm not a Pakeha girl? He's always talking about Pakehas, and Maoris are useless. Well I'm sorry I'm one. But I have feeling's too. Maybe I'm not his type."

10/4/90 "Rise in my benefit . . . Haven't been too happy lately cause there's alot of thing's on my mind that are really bugging me. I wish I had someone to confide my feeling's to. I always listen to everyone elses problems, but no-one listens to mine!"

3.8.90 "Eddie and I had an argument. He gave me a hiding. He started talking about Pakeha's this; and Pakeha's that. I just wish he'd I've told me he wanted to be with one. I think the only reason he loves me is cause I had his baby, but I know he doesn't love me cause he lets it show."

4.8.90 "I feel like taking my own life; in my own hands I know he don't love me and neither does my family."

5.8.90 "I wish I was dead then no-one will have to listen or love me! I don't want to see tomorrow or the day after that!"

6.8.90 "I've lost all my feelings for Eddie since he beat me. I just wish he would of told me how he felt about Maoris; before we got seriously involved with each other. I reckon the only two things he appreciates that I have done for him is having his baby and sex!"

7.8.90 "I've really grown scared of Eddie. And it's because of the beatings he's given me. And my body reacts differently to him. And things are not the same between us, and I don't sleep with him no more because of this."

16/16.9.90 ". . . next thing you know he had me on the floor in the hallway and he was kicking me in the face, head, body, and my private parts. And from it all I got a damaged face, sore jaws, big bump and bruise just above my right eye, and a black eye, and a very sore vagina with a bump on it. And its bleeding. And I hate him for what he has done to me. I've had hidings from him but this is the worst one."

24-26.9.90 "Eddie did his thing this morning, then then started calling me a slut, black Maori, and Maori this and that. Broke the blinds in the room. Sometimes I wish he'd just leave me. Cause I'm sick of it and I don't think I can take much more of it. I'm sick of his abusive language and it makes me repulsive towards him. I have never met anone that hate's Maoris so much that they always carry on about there; useless, dum, no brain's, good for nothing, lazy, slut, black bastard. All the names under the sun. Eddie has said them all to me. Everyone I've met thru him say his good with his hands. If only they knew how good he is with his mouth as well. And I can see our relationship slowly falling or slipping away. I just wish he'd leave me. Then I won't have to listen to his abusive language and making me feel like nothing."

27-29.9.90 "We haven't had sex for a week and 02 days now. Not that it bothers me, I'm quite happy about that! It's quite good for me really. In a way, ever since the beating Eddie gave me that's what turned me off about him. And our relationship is really failing. Nothing seems to be the same between us like it was before. We had a argument yesterday early hours of the morning because Eddie doesn't like it when son cry's. And I'm getting really sick and tired of Eddie. When son crys he yells, swears. And I'm just about reaching breaking point and when I do I think I'll just up and go cause there's just problem after problem. And he expects me to carry it all on my own. And its a waste of time talking to him, cause all he says is if you want to fight I'll fight you. When all I want to do is talk. But talking to him is fighting so if l can't talk to him I might as well carry the burden myself alone."

2.11.90 "Eddie ripped all my clothes up the whole lot and smashed the sliding door window. Last night at Matts he said that men are better off without women. Well he can have it that way. I have had enough of his shit."

11-13.12.90 "Called around Eddie's Mum's. He makes me really sick at times. He got some photos and cards from his Mums. I didn't mind the photo's, but the cards from his old girl-friend is a different story. He reckons they have been sitting in his draw all that time just so he can bring them here. I guess that's why he gives me shit. Her name was the same as mine. He reckons I'm only being stupid. I wonder how he'd feel if I did that too. Not that I would anyway. But I suppose some people can't leave there past behind like Eddie."

5.1.91 "Got a hiding with the pooltable stick from Eddie. Not much of a day really."

4.2.91 "Since Eddie and I have met things have been good. I wouldn't say a bunch of roses. When he runs me down about my race, colour and upbringing it really tears me apart . . . but we've got a lifetime to work on it . . . One thing I'm really happy about is Eddie hasn't hit me for a while, not that I urge him on to do it any more. With him I can reach a fantastic orgasm."

5.2.91 "Sometimes I think Eddie thinks that I don't love him or even enjoy making love to him cause he's fat! Well, it doesn't worry me. I love him just the way he is . . . I've never tryed to change him (not that it would do any good), but you don't try to make or change them into what you want them to be. Like you see in books, down the street or on television. You just except them for *who* they *are* and *what* they *are*."

21.2.91 "Eddie can be a real pig at time's. I went to the shop to get some milk and when I came back Delcelia was crying. "When I asked him nicely what happened he yelled back at me, and said, "ask her, I don't fucken know"! So seeing little Eddie was asleep I said Id take Delcelia for a walk. Then Eddie yells out to me to come back. "When I did, he threw my bank-book at me and said "go and get your fucken money out of the bank, so I can spend it."! Then he threw a bottle of twink at me, but luckily he missed!

So Delcelia and I went to get it and came home. Now after Eddie had a sauna and shower, he's gone to Tom's for a beer. I do everything in this house and all I get in return for it is Eddie's shit!

He goes to tech every Monday and Wednesday and all he does for the whole week is study in his room (and he's in there all the time). Then he moans and complains for just about everything.

When I ask him to watch baby for me while I'm sweeping the floor, dishes, etc, and he says "you do it, I'm studying."!

All it takes is 10 minutes or so, and he can't even do that. Is that so much to ask for! And most of the time he's in his room studying, working-out, or having a sauna.

Or just lying around. He never asks me how I feel, or how the kids are. It's like the only thing he wants me to communicate and know about, is himself, and his Penthouse books he keeps in his room. And of course his studying. What sort of relationship is that! And he seems to forget that I stay home look after the kids, clean and cook. Everyday! And what do I get for my reward. *Nothing*! He's the only one that deserves them, as far as he's concerned. Well that's just fine, cause one-of-theseday's I'm gonna prove to him that I'm more that just a *Maori girl* he can shit on, and tell, when to jump and sit at his every command.

Everyday he doe's, it draw's me away from him, and not any closer!

I've never written about him like this before, but I'm sorry Diary! You were the only one I could tell. Cause your alway's here with me, in my up's and downs. Sharing my deepest thoughts and feelings. That I can't tell Eddie cause I don't think he's interested anyway.

And your the dearest companion and friend that I can tell."

22.2.91 ". . . Eddie and I had another argument. I think the problem with us is, we are no good drinking together. Whether it's at friends house, Dad's, the pub. Anywhere really.

And the unreal thing about it is he blame's me. He say's all I want to do is drink, and forget about the kids. What a whole lot of *bullshit*. And he uses that same techinque everytime we argue, when we are drinking. Sometime's we are alright but, at other times we are not. That's why I would rather us drink separately in the future. Him with his mates, friends, or my family and the same with me. That way, we can have a good drink and enjoy it without arguing."

24.2.91 ". . . We haven't had sex lately. Now we just have it once a week. I'm not one to complain (not that I tell anyone, or even Eddie) but I wouldn't mind having it three times a week. I don't know what's happened with us. Sometimes when we go to bed, I just want to roll-over to him, and do it. That's happened for quite a while now, in the past month or so. Now all I do (to save myself from being hurt, from his refusal. Is sleep on it.) And I don't tell him.

Sometimes I think to myself, he gets off on himself, more in his sauna than with me. But I don't say that to him. Cause it's none of my business. And I know he won't tell me anyway!!

Made baby's bottles, had a shower. *Good-night!!?!!*

3.3.91 "Today I just feel like writing about Eddie. Sometimes he can be really sweet, funny and good company. But at other times, he can be really abusive, like the devil himself! His mood's change like the weather. Like when I woke up from a sleep. And I was checking Del-C over and then he says, go an do tea (when he had already started doing it!) When I was getting the kid's tea out, to warm it down. He say's to me is it ready, and I said yes twice. And he thinks I'm being smart. Then he starts calling me a dog, fucker, black-bitch. I really don't understand him, one bit.

The entry for March 4th mentioned her soaking Delcelia's hands and foot in cold water, "cause she was burnt", then went on to Tania's sexlife with Eddie "starting to wear off".

THE DIARY STOPS on March 6, three days after the probable date on which Delcelia was first burned. On March 21 she was dead.

It is hard indeed to reconcile the love and acceptance of Eddie, and the hope of a future together, and the desire for more frequent sex between them, with the clear, detailed accounts Tania gave in court of Eddie's beatings and the brutal sex he would force on her afterwards. The hidings were for "reasons" such as being home late from shopping, his not being able to find his wallet or her not cleaning a spot off the microwave. Sometimes the "reason" was even more spurious, a matter of his provoking a quarrel so that he could put into practice ideas gleaned from his "bondage and discipline" magazines in his home-made sauna.

In court, Tania professed a disgust for these practices and for Eddie. Yet her diary confirms her continuing desire for him. And a letter she wrote to Eddie, following the worst beating in September 1990, demonstrates the skill and sensitivity with which she tried to advocate for herself. It is not known whether the letter was given to Eddie.

"Eddie. I'm writing you this letter because of what you've done and made me feel . . . The only thing that's changed is my face. When I got up and looked in the mirror, man, I freaked out . . . and I knew Delcelia and I have to go. You've given me hidings before but not this bad and I know I have to leave before it gets worse. I feel like a prisoner in my own house . . . Next time you might kill me . . . At your Mum's you kicked me in the head, face and in my vagina and it's very, very sore. It's been bleeding ever since. I don't blame you for your anger . . . but no girl deserves to be kicked down there . . . I knew all the work you're doing causes you a lot of stress . . . but you've bitten off more than you can chew and it's paid off on me . . .

I did a good clean-up last week . . . and all for what? For you to beat me up because you're under stress? . . . You're not the only one with mixed emotions . . . I wish you would put yourself in my shoes . . . the pain you've caused within me and the anger. That's why I need to go away from you. Tania."

. . .

ON MARCH 21 1991 an ambulance was called to 1/4 Cornwall Road, Mangere.

It is possible the ambulance officers were expecting something strange. The despatcher had just taken a call from a young woman phoning from a video store, a young woman who reported that her child was dead and sounded less distraught than many a woman might sound who was reporting that her washing machine was broken. It wasn't the tone of a person numb with shock and grief. It was a polite, conversational tone. "She's two . . . Been out for a couple of hours . . . Excuse me [to the video shop worker], do you have a phone number? . . . Can you make it [the ambulance] quick, please?"

What the ambulance officers and then the police officers found was a small child, lying dead on a plastic sheet, on a mattress that was heavily stained with urine, blood and faeces. She was naked except for a woman's singlet, cut up the back, straps knotted.

The pathologist, Dr Jane Vuletic, reported that Delcelia Witika weighed 11kg at two years, three months. The catalogue of injuries was difficult to credit in a child who measured no more than 88cm. There was hair loss and hyperkeratosis (thickening) of the surface of the skin of the scalp; thin, poor quality hair; ulceration where her ears joined her face; on the corners of her mouth and inside it; an ulcer in one ear; numbers of bruises, abrasions, contusions and ulcers on her forehead and cheeks.

Her upper jaw was fractured and the frenulum torn, an incisor tooth was missing — all consistent with "repeated blunt trauma". On her neck were multiple marks which counsel for the Crown and for Eddie Smith would suggest were adult fingernail marks.

Her arms and legs and trunk were extensively bruised, the bruising even extending over the burnt flesh of the buttocks. There were multiple "circumscribed" marks on her legs, suggestive to a witness of cigarette burns.

The hymen was absent and there was a large vaginal opening for the age of the child. There was an area of apparent old bruising at the posterior aspect of the vaginal opening.

Examination of the alimentary system revealed a severe peritonitis.

Wrote Dr Vuletic: "Postmortem examination has revealed evidence of multiple injuries of varying ages and types in a child who was severely malnourished. The immediately fatal injury is blunt abdominal trauma resulting in rupture of the small intestine and leakage of faecal contents into the peritoneal cavity resulting in peritonitis . . .

"The second major injury is the injury involving the buttocks, abdomen, left hand and left foot. The appearances of the injury are those of a hot-water scald. Most of the burn involves total skin loss and the total area of burning is approximately 10 to 15 per cent of the total body surface.

"In my opinion death resulted from peritonitis following blunt trauma to the abdomen, in a child who has sustained a recent hot-water burn and multiple injuries as a result of blunt trauma, in association with malnutrition."

The pain in peritonitis is particularly severe, so that the person would lie very still since any movement such as crying would cause even more pain. The bowel stops working, so one would not want to eat, but would be nauseated and vomiting. Peritonitis, untreated, is always fatal.

The burns over much of the body would probably have been inflicted within 10 days or a week of the death, at least a week before the blows to the abdomen. They would have caused shock and required pain relief and intravenous fluid therapy. The burns could not have been accidental. "The pattern is consistent with and absolutely typical of a child being placed in water, being held under the shoulders and knees and placed in water. They could not have arisen in any other way," wrote Vuletic.

As to the sexual abuse, it was most probably a prolonged episode, as indicated by quite severe inflammation of the vaginal skin, the likely cause being continual penetration of the vagina. The purple colour of the vaginal bruising indicated it was most likely that it had been inflicted within three to four days of death and therefore probably after the massive burn. All the injuries in and around the genital area indicated that Delcelia had been the victim of chronic sexual abuse.

As to the age of the injuries, most of the bruises were inflicted somewhere between one week and six weeks before death. The injuries to the mouth were sustained over months or longer. The loss of hair and thickening of scalp skin were sustained over months. The child's poor nutritional state had existed over months at least.

DELCELIA'S SECURITY and custody was entrusted, following her death, to a police officer, the first time this child, so grievously in need of care and protection, was ever officially granted it.

For the police and ambulance officers, the horror of the scene — the tortured body, the vomit, faeces, blood — was compounded by the strange behaviour of the two adults. Detective Constable Caroline Fisher says she can never forget cool Tania sitting in the back of the police car, asking for a cigarette, outside the house in which her daughter's body lay.

Eddie Smith's behaviour at the scene was so detached that some thought he was merely a passer-by who had come in to see what was going on with the ambulance and police cars. The detachment continued at the police station that night as Eddie was questioned by Constable Christophe Dunn. The following extracts give the flavour of his statement:

"I'm unemployed. She's on the benefit. [Delcelia] spewed up today. She always mimis the bed, poohs her pants. She hasn't eaten for two weeks . . . Everyone looks after her [in response to a question as to who is responsible for her care].

"That's my missus slapping her around. She gets lots of smacks. She gets baths twice a day. She gets quite a few hidings. She gets a whack for bedwetting. Today she had a bath because she'd mimied the bed and spewed up — with Dettol in the bath. She wouldn't eat breakfast. We just put her back to bed, left her. We went to Mum's, Barney's. When we got back, my missus found her dead . . .

"She's been pottytrained. She's had scabs since she came back from up north.

A lot of the family got them . . . She got slapped around [in answer to questions about the marks on her forehead], toilet training. She was still wetting the bed . . . Just a few whacks on the burn . . .

[In answer to questions about whether she'd been taken to the doctor with the burns.] "No, it was all right. The skin peeled in the morning. I got some stuff from the chemist. . . .

"She fell over the front steps [in answer to a question about her tooth].

Meanwhile, Tania, still composed, was being questioned by Detective Constable Fisher and a male colleague.

THERE IS NO ROOM in this article to enter into speculation as to which of the two accused were responsible for which particular injury. The court was satisfied that each was guilty of manslaughter. What is more to our purpose here is to consider the attitudes to child-rearing of this not-extraordinary couple of young New Zealanders, as revealed by their own statements.

First, however, it's appropriate to try get some picture of Delcelia. Was she a particularly unlikeable, difficult, hard-to-love child? No. There is not one shred of evidence to support this. Delcelia was loved by her extended family — Witika, Lafaele and Smith — but not effectively protected by them. Evelyn saw Delcelia battered, holding her arms up, pleading, but Tania yelled at her to shut up. Eddie's family were horrified at her bruises. They all mourn her. They loved her. But they did not save her.

There was fear. There was Tania and Eddie's hostile denial. And for some there was undoubtedly acceptance of the "norm" that babies get hidings.

Every person who has commented on her speaks of her lovable qualities, her easiness, despite all. There are a few family photos showing Delcelia with her Witika, Smith and Lafaele families, though never with Tania and Eddie. She's smiling out of the photos as she's held by Lou Witika or Julie Lafaele, or securelyin the midst of the Smith family's Christmas.

The best picture of Delcelia can be gained from the home video shot at McDonald's, at a birthday party.

A month earlier, in October 1990, Ngere Smith, Eddie's mother, a nervous little woman, who was terrified of her son, had taken the bruised, frightened child from the back of Eddie's van, where she was frequently concealed, when she wasn't left in the house alone. Mrs Smith kept Delcelia for three months.

It was the happiest time of the child's life, and ended three months before her death. In the video, Delcelia is seen sitting quietly, secure between one of Eddie's sisters and Mrs Smith, whom she called Mum. She looks neat and clean in a pink track suit. She's noticeably quieter and more tentative than the other children. Kind adult voices can be heard above the chatter: "Show Bruce what you've got. That's your curl! Show him." And Delcelia feels her topknot for the camera. Two women help her on the slide, making "Whee!" noises of encouragement. Children call "Delcie!" Someone puts her on a little "horse" in the shape of a hamburger. A voice calls "Heigh-Ho, Silver!" In her tentative, wondering smile you can see the gap of the missing front tooth. Later, when the party moves home, Delcelia is seen walking quietly around, holding a balloon, then, fascinated, gently playing with a white kitten. The camera watches her, sitting cuddled on Mrs Smith's knee.

How many such days did Delcelia have?

TANIA MADE THREE separate statements to the police, each videorecorded.

In the first, recorded on the night of the death, she accepted responsibility for all the injuries to Delcelia. "I did it. Everything that's on her. I just hit her all the time." In the second, recorded two days later, and the third, a few days after that, she changed her approach and blamed Eddie for the major injuries.

The reason for the change, according to Tania, is that Eddie had threatened her so menacingly to take the blame that she initially did, but changed her mind after hearing postmortem information about the sexual abuse and because she agreed with Detective Constable Fisher that she wouldn't be able to live with herself unless she told the truth.

Tania said she'd smacked Delcelia on her non-burnt hand and on her mouth on the day she died. "Just when she didn't eat or didn't drink, that's what annoyed me the most. Just her lips started bleeding in the corner . . . I smack her on the mouth, yeh, but I don't smack her on the head. I'm not saying there's a difference. I just don't smack her on the head."

In the third video, Tania admitted to punching Delcelia, with a closed fist, about twice a week.

In the second interview, where she laid the blame on Eddie, she said the injuries started "when we were living in our own place in Mangere, when she wasn't going to the toilet properly . . . Eddie would smack her, and when she wouldn't listen."

Q: What would you smack her with?

"My hand, or a plastic spoon."

Q: Where?

"On her hand, or on her bum, or her legs."

Q: You'd do that yourself?

"Yes."

Q: And Eddie?

"He'd do the same, only harder and more times, on her hands, her side, her back, her bum, her legs."

Q: How did the bruising come about?

"Through Eddie and myself."

Q: How was the tooth knocked out?

"Eddie punched her in the mouth with his fist, then he threw her across the floor."

Q: Why?

"I don't know why."

Q: How is it that she has hair missing?

"Sometimes he'd lift her by her hair and lift her off the floor."

Q: How often?

"Sometimes three times a week."

Q: And the hitting with the spoon or punching?

"Any time she didn't listen or was on the toilet or was eating . . . a couple of times a week?"

Q: The forehead and skull abrasions and grazes?

"Eddie would make her walk around in circles in the lounge. If she stopped he'd push her and she'd fall and whack her head on the floor. Tears would roll out of her eyes. He'd push her or punch her over."

Q: Where?

"In the arm and in the chest and in the leg."

Q: This little game was regular, was it?

'Regular. Even after the burns she had.'"

Tell us about the burns.

"It was her hand, the first time he burnt it, about a month ago. The right hand. I looked at her hand one day and it was peeled. When I went to bathe it under cold water she just screamed. I heard Eddie coming home in the van. I says to him, 'Look at this.' He went to the chemist and came back with this tube called Afterburn. I bathed her one day. The back of her head felt really soft, like the bottom of her brain from when he pushed her over, really hard. I said to him, 'You've got to stop it. You'll braindamage her.'"

The next burns?

"Saturday, last week. When was Crocodile Dundee on? That's when he did it. I'd said, 'Would you watch son in the bath for me while I cook tea?' [Eddie refused.] I said, 'Fuck you' and I went out — I thought I'd break. I just sat in the bus shelter for a few minutes. When I got back he was waiting at the front door. 'Are you ready for your hiding, bastard?' [he said]. I said, 'I just want you to help me with the kids, Eddie.' He just drove off in the van. After tea Eddie must have thought she needed a bath and he took her in the bathroom and shut the door and I heard the shower running and I was still cleaning up after tea and I just heard this scream and I could hear him yelling 'Shut up! Turn around and shut up!' When he brought her out I noticed that she was hot. I towelled her down really softly and the skin came off in my hand. She looked at me. There were tears in her eyes but she wouldn't cry. I says to him, 'You burnt her! You can't do this no more! She's had enough, Eddie.' Then he'd whack her with the plastic spoon. She was shaking. Her whole body would shake. Her hand would bleed. Those are those bloodstains on the carpet. He'd constantly keep hitting her on the arm with the burned hand.

"He said to me, 'You're a dog and she's a dog.' And I said, 'Just leave us. Just leave us alone. Go.'"

Is there any reason why you didn't take the baby to the doctor?

"Scared."

Of what?

"Eddie."

Tania was asked if she could make any comment on the evidence of sexual abuse.

"No."

She was asked about the stomach injuries and recalled that on Tuesday or Wednesday she'd heard a "whump" noise and found Delcelia on her back in the lounge, out of breath. Eddie said she'd fallen over. "She'd find it hard to stand up on her feet and she'd fall back again. She was so slow, as if she was handicapped . . . She walked so slow, she'd be panting. Even going from the lounge to the kitchen. She'd stand and look at me as if she was in another dimension. She'd just fall. Eddie would yank her back up."

Tania stated that Eddie stomped on Delcelia's stomach and punched her. "He'd given her another bath. He was punching her guts because she wouldn't put her hand in the water. He was punching her directly into the stomach. And when I looked at her, tears rolled. She wouldn't make a crying noise. Just tears rolled."

On the morning of the Thursday, the day Delcelia died, and she'd been found in the morning dirty with vomit and faeces, "Eddie gave her a cold shower. She was shaking. She was kneeling down, using one hand for support, purple in the face. Her lips were purple. Her burnt hand was all purple from the cold. I put the shower on again on warm. She was crying in silence. [Tania took her into the kitchen.] She wouldn't eat. She just dropped on the floor, her bum started bleeding. Her mouth was shaking. She wouldn't take nothing. I put my blue and white singlet on her, I took her in her room and laid her down on the plastic and I stayed with her and I was crying, crying so Eddie wouldn't hear . . . We went out about 10 o'clock. We left Delcie unattended after that time."

Tania said she wanted to stay with Delcie, "but Eddie said no, you can come with me."

The police questioned Tania about her not taking Delcelia to a doctor. "I'd get a hiding . . . He would have taken off with my son. He'd have just disappeared . . . He'd just waste me to a pulp and he'd take his son."

SERGEANT RUSSELL Lamb interviewed Eddie on that same Saturday, two days after Delcelia's death, and after Tania's interview. Eddie was asked to recall the day of the death. He recalled that in the morning "Tania was screaming at her because she couldn't stand up or walk. I heard her cry, because she hasn't cried for a while because we haven't been smacking her that much because of her bum." He said they didn't get her medical help because they were scared on account of their living together and both claiming benefits.

How many times did you leave her alone?

"A dozen times."

There followed a question about her need for care.

"I didn't think about it."

He said, "Delcie's getting hidings from my missus. I've been unhappy. Last time I told her she was mad. Our relationship has suffered because of this. I've given Delcie some good hidings, but nothing like she does. I told my brother Ernest about it. [When Delcie stayed with his mother] she don't get no smacks or anything there. My mother's done a good job with all of us . . . I've given her some good hidings, mate. I gave [Tania] a good hiding because she doesn't look after the kids."

Eddie was asked about Delcie's tooth. "Tania said you punched her in the mouth."

"That's bullshit."

She says you make Delcelia walk in circles in the lounge and if she stops you punch her.

"That's bullshit."

She says it's you who takes Delcelia into the bathroom.

"That's bullshit. Anything you say is bullshit."

So, there it is. Belsen, Auschwitz. In Mangere. In 1991.

Smith and Witika were found guilty on five counts: manslaughter; willful ill-treatment; neglecting to provide medical care; omitting to provide medical care thereby committing manslaughter; and willful ill-treatment in a manner likely to cause unnecessary suffering. Each was sentenced to 15 years and seven months imprisonment.

. . .

THE KILLING OF Delcelia Witika demands a facing up to a number of uncomfortable issues, rather than taking a witch-burning approach. Tania Witika and Eddie Smith don't belong in some gothic horror comic. They are far from unique products of contemporary Auckland and their doubles can be readily found. Expunging them, while it might be satisfying to some, would not in any way improve the situation of battered and frightened children. Rather, the case points out the tragic vacuum in our planning for healthy children and families. It exposes the lack of prevention of abuse and the lack of adequate response to dangerous family dysfunction among us.

It points up the need for a rational balance to be struck, in our extremism-prone society, between the rights of the parent and the child; between the benign and restrictive state; between taxpayers' rights and beneficiaries' rights; between answering need and encouraging responsibility.

It is time to accept as simplistic the view that all parents want the best for their children and that only unemployment, poverty, racism and sexism prevent good child rearing: that if you look after the social structure, the children will do fine.

It is time to accept as naive the view that if you simply supply more services (desperately needed though they are), all parents will make use of them. Dr David Geddis, medical director of the Plunket Society and expert in the prevention and treatment of child abuse, says that many abusing parents feel no need for help. Dr John Newman, director of child health services at Auckland Hospital says that 90 per cent of child abuse is committed by otherwise caring but not coping parents, while 10 per cent is done by sadistic parents.

It is time too to grasp some nettles, one being the role and function of the state with regard to benefits. This case revealed the ugly spectacle of a child treated as valueless by her parents, yet nevertheless being of high monetary value, as the means to both house and income.

I was puzzled throughout this case why Eddie Smith was so determined to retain in the house a child he loathed and despised, a child he didn't value in the least. Could it have been because the child *did* have value for him — monetary value?

There is the need to re-think issues of rights, civil liberties and compulsion. As taxpayers, we are compelled to pay our taxes. I would pay cheerfully towards the upkeep of a woman and her children who had fled a brutal husband. I pay less cheerfully towards the upkeep of people who give no thought whatsoever as to whether they should have a fourth or fifth child, in the knowledge that "the state" will provide. Tania Witika didn't "believe" in contraception. She didn't need to.

And I am extremely unhappy to pay parents who burn or beat or otherwise ill-use the child to whose upkeep I am contributing.

Tania's diary offered a picture of people who see the Department of Social Welfare as a kind of indulgent parent with bottomless pockets.

26.3.90 "Went with Honey and Hinewai to Social Welfare to get a check of them for a lounge suite for Dad's house."

It was at Dad's house the month before that "me, Dad, Hinewai, Walter, Dingo and Eddie had a barbecue. Then we went and got six dozen." A couple of months later, the family members were each expected to give $500 for their father's 60th birthday party.

Is it appropriate for Social Welfare to pay for a lounge suite for a man who has been employed all his life and has sunk a huge amount of whatever he has earned in alcohol?

15.10.90 "Went to get an advance of Social Welfare."

15.11.90 "Called around Eddie's Mums to see her and Del-C. Him and his Mum went to Social Welfare to do his accommodation benefit."

6.12.90 "Went to Social Welfare to get some money off them for our TV."

There's a sense of having it all — a lifestyle many careful New Zealanders could never dream of. Hiring three videos at a time, endless beer and appliances. "We went and lay-byed a fridge-freezer and a Gentle Annie automatic washing machine."

The rip-off factor is one thing. What is of over-riding concern is the fact that while the indulgent department, like a profligate parent, is handing out this largesse, the child is being progressively brutalised, and it is never anyone's role even to lay eyes on her to ensure that she — the supposed beneficiary — is receiving some benefit from the benefit. In other words, that there is at least a modicum of accountability for the receipt of public money, as there is in virtually every other sphere.

If this is not done, the danger, particularly in tough economic times with diminished job prospects, of a child being seen as a voucher for a house and income is quite real. As things stand, we have put in place a system in which it becomes a viable career option, and a means to independence from an unhappy home, to have a baby.

The Domestic Purposes Benefit started as a humanitarian response to the cruel need of unsupported mothers. In 1974 it was paid to 17,000 women and in 1992 is paid to around 100,000, at a cost of over $1000 million for the year.

In 1962, eight per cent of births were ex-nuptial. In 1990, the figure was 34 per cent. It is not a peripheral matter. We have to meet the humanitarian imperative and provide for those who, through misfortune or disability, cannot provide for themselves. We must provide the means to independence for a woman and children leaving a violent relationship. But somehow it has gone far beyond that. Among the disadvantages to the child that frequently, though not necessarily, accompany this situation is the increased risk in living with their mother and a stepfather. This can be a dangerous situation, markedly raising the odds for abuse. A just-released Otago University survey on sexual abuse has ascertained that a child is 10 times more likely to be sexually abused by a stepfather than by a biological father.

In an article I wrote in *Metro* [April 1991] on the growing phenomenon of stepfathers who kill, I quoted a brief passage from *Children: Endangered Species?*, a book I wrote to explore the situation of New Zealand children today. Anyone who followed the Witika case would recognise how apt that passage remains. I quoted an American paediatrician who told a New Zealand medical conference that "Fathers will abuse their own children, but it is unusual for a father to kill his own offspring. Mothers' boyfriends don't bond in the same way with another man's child. The abuse rarely begins and ends with one occasion, but more often has been insidious for a while . . . The thing that amazes me is that the mother stands back and lets it happen . . . the mother's need for a relationship outweighs her need to intervene and protect her child."

Several years on there still remains no public level of awareness of the hazards facing at least some of the thousands of New Zealand children who experience serial stepfathers.

Delcelia Witika was not the first unfortunate small girl with whose mother Eddie formed a relationship in which both mother and daughter were ill-treated.

In a few years of research I have been staggered at the number of instances I have found where violent men have ricocheted into and out of the lives of women and children, hitting, abusing, destroying and moving on to the next needy woman.

ANOTHER KEY ISSUE that emerged from this case was the acceptance of violence by the strong against the weak. There was never a suggestion in the story of Eddie, Tania and Delcelia that a man who hits a woman, or an adult who hits a child, would be ostracised or not tolerated. The police were called on at least four occasions when Eddie beat his former de facto or Tania. He was never charged.

Mike Pomare, a community health worker and criminal counsellor based at Carrington Hospital and a friend of Eddie Smith for 12 years, told me, towards the end of the trial, after all the ghastly revelations, that he still didn't see Eddie as violent, though Tania, in her evidence, claimed that on more than one occasion he had witnessed it. On the night of Lou Witika's 60th birthday, which Tania wanted to attend, they went to Pomare and his partner's house where, according to Tania, Eddie beat her and threw Delcelia across the room. Yet the friendship continued.

One of the most lasting troubling issues in this case was the use, by judge counsel, the accused and reporters, of the word "discipline", both as noun and verb. The inference has been that hitting small child is permissible and may even be evidence of parental responsibility.

It *must* be asked: In what circumstances is hitting a baby acceptable? Does the word "discipline" legitimise extreme cruelty?

Criminologist Gabrielle Maxwell states that it is rare to find a violent criminal who has not experienced a great deal of harsh physical punishment in childhood. Researchers Jane and James Ritchie have demonstrated conclusively, over years of study of New Zealand childrearing, an excessive reliance, in all social strata, on hitting children. They have campaigned energetically for legislative action to "spare the rod".

One simple but significant step, which might signal a more appropriate attitude to rearing children to develop a strong moral sense, would be to remove the following sentence from Section 59 of the Crimes Act: "Every parent . . . is justified in using force by way of correction." This would not outlaw corporal punishment of children, but it would remove an automatic sanction.

This should be backed up by a vigorous campaign to show parents alternative means of managing children's behaviour and clear information about stages of development.

So long as hitting a baby can be legitimised as "discipline", and the letters to the editor columns and the talkback stations are full of advocacy for "a good hiding" as the answer to crime and violence, there will be a vast iceberg, nine-tenths submerged, of child abuse, while cases such as Delcelia's will represent the sharp tip.

A grave error is made by those who assume that this case was a total aberration, a gothic horror that happens once in 100 years. The fact is, between 1976 and 1989 there were 30 cases of child abuse leading to death in the Auckland region. I have details of many infants being beaten, kicked, stomped and thrown, sustaining multiple fractures, lacerated duodenum, head injury and perforated stomachs. Many, probably most, were returned to those parents.

WHAT ARE WE GOING to do to prevent more killings of more Delcelias?

Let us not, for God's sake, create another talkfest. We already have the knowledge. We need the will to act. We could turn this country around. Or we could spend the next decade beefing up our burglar alarms and putting bars on our windows and lamenting our moral decline. We need to ask ourselves a simple question: how do we produce healthy, secure children who will grow into positive, stable, productive adults?

We need to learn two simple facts, here expressed by Professor James Ritchie and Dr Greg Newbold, respectively: ". . . the functions of parenting are not instinctive in the human species to any significant degree." ". . . a lack of effective parenting is crirninogenic."

We need to be clear that prevention is not only more humane, but also cheaper than dealing with the consequences of a lack of prevention.

We need to understand that it is beyond the scope of any one ministry to assume responsibility for producing healthy families. If each relevant "Vote" contributed a modest sum to specific preventive work, the payoff later, in reduced drain on that Vote, would be substantial.

As an example, the expenditure of the Justice Department on courts, penal institutions, probation and psychological service for the year ended June 1990 totals nearly $35Sm. If it contributed 1% to an inter-sectoral prevention programme of what it normally spends for the trial and incarceration of the neglected, abused, ill-educated, semi-deaf children who, grown large, form the bulk of the prison population, it should, within 10 years, reap major benefit.

Let's take the image of a safety net to prevent children from falling into abuse, neglect, crime or even death. Imagine that safety net as being strong in parts but with a great many of its threads fraying and weak, and several areas where there are no strands at all, so many children fall through the holes. Repair is needed, as well as the construction of new sections.

Any safety net requires a strong framework if it is to perform its supporting function. The legislative framework protecting children in this country is feeble. This is the challenge facing us — to produce this two-part structure that will support children and their families within firm boundaries.

Let's look at some things that could have been done — and still could be — if we decided to act.

- We could institute a nationwide maternal screening and support programme at an annual cost of around $20m, or $6 on our individual tax bills.
- We could build on the success demonstrated by the Dunedin and Nelson Acorn Clubs that provide appropriate support for the 9% or so of women who are shown by simple screening to be at risk in child rearing. Tania would almost certainly have registered as at risk and therefore in need of practical and emotional support, before and after the birth of the baby.

The success of this well-researched programme can be judged by the fact that in several years of operation in Nelson, no Acorn Club family has had to go to the Women's Refuge and no child has been admitted to hospital as the result of abuse.

Inexplicably, in over a decade, this proven approach had never been seriously considered in the Auckland region. In April, the Pacific Foundation held a seminar featuring the Acorn Club, to promote the idea of coordinated maternal screening and support. For the 100 health and community workers present, a key fact was that it costs the same — around $70,000 — to keep Eddie Smith in Paremoremo for one year, as it does to pay salary costs for the Nelson Acorn Club for one year.

An Auckland manifestation of maternal support is the teenage mothers' support group, Te Kaha O te Rangatahi. Had it been in existence at the time Tania was pregnant with Delcelia, she may have been referred to the group, which was the joint creation of Plunket and the Cot Death Society. Peter Lafaele's sister, a mother at 17, is part of the group.

But even a group such as this, for all its strengths, cannot work miracles in the face of damaging life experiences and the natural self-absorption of youth. Anna Lafaele has fears for her grandson. "It's not really sunk in that she's the mother of a baby. I know what it's like — I was a young mother myself. I had Pete at 18."

Te Kaha o te Rangatahi targets pregnant teenagers — mainly Maori and Pacific Island — from Otahuhu to Pukekohe, seeing them through pregnancy and the infancy of the child. Its headquarters is a house in Papatoetoe, staffed by a group of Maori women, Plunket nurses and other health workers. The atmosphere is low-key and warm, within a strong Maori framework, so that the intensely practical (baby-care, accident prevention) is supplemented by the spiritual and cultural.

If the group had existed at that time, and if Tania had been referred to it, and if she had agreed to attend, she would have been shown, through discussing and modelling, ways of managing children other than hitting them. She would have had some opportunity to learn about managing her own anger. She might have been helped to cut down on her drinking. If she'd wanted to smoke, she'd have had to do it outside.

She'd most definitely have learned about contraception. Eddie's sister Ngaire says that "Tania didn't believe in contraception", a conclusion easy to reach, judging from the fact that she had had three children, one miscarriage and one termination before her 22nd birthday.

DELCELIA SLIPPED through the net of family, friends, neighbours, Plunket, Middlemore Hospital and GP, partly because it was nobody's specific job to make sure she was alright. In fact, during the later stages, she was deliberately hidden. She appears to have received no health care in Auckland at all — no checks, no immunisations, no treatment.

Six years ago a large and distinguished group of Christchurch paediatricians and other health and welfare professionals made a submission to the Ministerial Task Force on Income Maintenance, recommending that child-related benefit payments be contingent on preventive health care.

Such a system would require the computer entry of the name of every child born in New Zealand, or arriving here as an infant. An agreed schedule of well-child health and development checks and immunisations would be established. A range of recognised child health agencies would be computer-linked to the central databank. If any child were not presented for health checks and immunisations, "alarm bells" would ring in the computer system and the child would be located to enable him or her to be seen by a recognised health worker.

There would be a provision for "conscientious objectors" to immunisation, who would have to sign a declaration to the effect that they had made a considered choice on the matter.

Countries such as France, Austria, Japan and the Scandinavian countries operate similar systems, and all outstrip us in child survival.

Such a suggestion receives support from such people as Pat Seymour, New Zealand president of Plunket; Dr Anne Kolbe, director of paediatric trauma services for the Auckland Area Health Board and June Mariu, former president of the Maori Women's Welfare League. It also received strong support in two major surveys of parents.

It would not, however, receive universal approbation. Dr Michael Watt, Auckland paediatrician who sees many child abuse cases, says, "The kind of computerised system you suggest sounds absolutely right to me, but people have got shot down for suggesting it in the past."

They have. But I detect a difference now. There seems to be a recognition that the more generalised, trickle-down approach is not sufficient. And there seems to be an acknowledgement that, much as many adults have an innate resistance to such systems, the time has come to protect children a good deal better.

There's recognition that, without this kind of structure, in a region of high mobility, children simply get lost, and those most in need receive least.

There's also a realisation that truancy is out of control. There are significant numbers of children who drop out of the school system, not moving on to the next school, or not making the move from primary to intermediate, or from intermediate to secondary. They will be the bag people of the future, and it's nobody's job to know who or where they are, or whether or not their fundamental right to health care and education has been afforded them.

We could institute such a system, or we could continue to leave children to their fate in the big Lotto game of life.

If there were a preventive health campaign aimed at child abuse prevention, as there has been on smoking, drink/driving, eating a lowerfat diet and other issues, perhaps Eddie and Tania might have tempered their behavior to some extent. Each had absorbed heath messages — Eddie the danger to the unborn child (his!) of the mother's smoking and drinking and Tania the message to cool burns for 10 minutes in cold water.

Finally, New Zealanders have never been exposed to an unequivocal message — Don't hit small children. New Zealanders have never been exposed to the message — A baby is not a band-aid.

It's time for a campaign both to inform and change behaviour; to reinforce the better instincts that even the Tanias and the Eddies have.

There has never been any adequate attempt to provide even the basics of parenting messages, in a form in which they'll be received, to a nation in which a lack of parent education has been identified again and again as a major problem.

All of these, and most particularly the failure of any member of any of the families involved to take decisive steps to save Delcelia, formed holes in the net that might have supported her.

THERE ARE STUMBLING blocks obstructing the way for New Zealand children to have safer and healthier childhoods. One is an inequitable share of resources. Another is an ideology that lacks sympathy with children.

As to resources, consider the Witika case. Add police and ambulance time, DSIR and pathologist's time, the cost of six lawyers, add in the cost of the depositions hearing, applications to the Court of Appeal, the High Court trial which occupied five weeks, plus judge, stenographer, clerk, cryer, jury, court police, witnesses' expenses, prison service staff, custody of the accused, and then consider the custodial care of both convicted people for 16 years, probation service and the Department of Social Welfare. The cost can be estimated at around $3m.

Conflict in ideology is a major barrier. Dr Michael Watt confirms this. "I'm biased," he says. "By training and inclination I take the view that the child comes first. That's not a view that's fashionable at the moment. Current ideology makes it very difficult. Through the position our [hospital] team took — a child-centred one — we were seen as elitist and racist. We had to modify our views or we would have had no referrals. We had to accept the fact that children were going to suffer and die before the community's thinking would come around to protecting that group of children who need it. It's amazing how widespread fear of the ideologues is."

THERE IS NO shortage of ways to protect children better and to support their families more appropriately. The problem lies largely with the Department of Social Welfare which "owns" child protection and with the legislation shaped by it and within which it works, namely, the controversial Children, Young Persons and their Families Act, 1989.

This act virtually sanctifies "the family", in effect, sacrificing the paramountcy of the child's interests. On its passage through Parliament, the thenMinister of Social Welfare, Michael Cullen, said: "The guiding principle . . . is that the family group should be recognised as the fundamental locus of responsibilities in all matters relating to the care and protection of their children."

The corollary of this statement is that of Maarten Quevooy, senior programme officer in the CYP and F area, who stated to a 1991 conference on child abuse, "It is not the role of the state to make every child safe."

The recent report of the Commissioner for Children states, "Children need their own family, no matter that they have been ill-used by it . . ." The act is deeply flawed, both in its provisions and its administration. For example, while the law allows for the removal of a child from the family where he or she is in risk of serious harm, no less a person than Dame Silvia Cartwright, Principal District Court Judge, has acknowledged that the act is as yet too new for cases to have gone to the High Court or Court of Appeal to provide guidelines as to what constitutes "serious harm" to children.

The fact is that children are routinely left in situations that are damaging to them, because of the view that it is the parents' rights to enjoy undisturbed possession of their children.

More disturbing is the fact that children are routinely returned, after abuse, to the very parents who abused them, without any realistic plan for ensuring their safety.

Professional intrusion is rarely allowed to mar the pristine purity of the chief goal of the legislation — family empowerment. This means that the adults of a family decide what happens to the child, whether they have the skills to deal with abuse or not.

"But child abuse is no place for amateurs," says Dr David Geddis, medical director of the Plunket Society; and the chairman of the now-disbanded National Advisory Committee on the Prevention of Child Abuse which had strongly condemned the current legisation, pointing out that it created an imbalance in the competing interests of child protection and family autonomy. Geddis contended that the concept of family group conferences was "basically untried and untested prior to its statutory introduction", having been piloted with a total of six families. "Since this approach also increases the likelihood of wrong decisions being reached, the outlook for the seriously abused child is indeed bleak," he added.

With the DSW's theoretical monopoly of, yet inactivity in, child abuse prevention, the plight of children in clearly dangerous situations remains in noman's-land. Thus, the children of children — mothers of 13 or 14 or 15, living with their boyfriends, often in a situation of poverty, alcohol, solvent and drug abuse, fighting and general chaos — are nobody's business.

Similarly, the children living with violent, psychiatrically disturbed parents are nobody's business. The children living with parents who are violent criminals are nobody's business. The child, Delcelia, born to a girl who has spent much of her youth in "girls' homes", patently in need of care, is nobody's business.

The other legislative pillars that should hold up the supporting net are changes to the CYP and F Act, to reinforce child paramountcy and to strengthen the provisions for prevention and for care and protection.

THE DEPARTMENT of Social Welfare was never involved in Delcelia Witika's life. It cannot be blamed for her death. But her case clearly demonstrates the lack of foundation for the DSWs blind faith in "the family" in the face of serious child abuse.

Delcelia's extended family actually operated in textbook fashion, exemplifying DSWs most dearly-held principle: They held two formally-structured family meetings on the subject of her future. Informal arrangements were made within the family for her care, as DSW strongly prefers. A senior member of the family was designated to "keep an eye" on her when she was returned to her mother's care. But she was still neglected, semistarved, rejected, sworn at, beaten, burned and ultimately punched to death by her mother and stepfather.

Why?

Families, quite simply, have their limitations when it comes to protecting children from abuse. This is not to belittle or blame families. It merely recognises that human beings normally behave in accordance with their own interests and needs, and within their own limitations. Serious child abusers are often very angry or disturbed people. To confront them with the issue and try to intervene will certainly be unpleasant and may well be dangerous. Therefore, despite concern and love for the abused child, relatives did not, or could not, or felt unable to, take the actions that were necessary to protect her.

Eddie's mother, Ngere Smith, recounted taking Delcelia out of the back of the van, in October 1990. The child was, she recalls, "very nervous, very frightened. Someone been giving her hiding. Round her body, round her tummy, round her leg, round her bottom. All bruise." She was asked if she asked Eddie and Tania about the bruising. "No, I'm scared."

Understandably. Mrs Smith was 69 years of age, maybe around five feet tall and perhaps eight stone in weight. She was well schooled in the consequences of making Eddie angry. Holes in her walls, broken glass, a thrown headlight, pots and axe, the attacks on Tania — all bore testimony to his temper.

What Mrs Smith did do was to take in the little child of her son's de facto (a young woman she disliked), and looked after her with love and patience. She even made an attempt to get Delcelia back, at one stage sending her daughter-in-law around to Eddie and Tania's to bring her back. But they said she was up north, as she might have been on that day.

Aroha Witika told TVNZ journalist Darryl Passmore: "We couldn't read the signs at the time. We see it clearly now, but it's too late."

Aroha should not have to flagellate herself. She did so much so right. She loved Delcelia, she cared for her, she confronted Eddie with her suspicions and was unwillingly persuaded when he took Delcelia on his knee and poured out tears, in protesting his innocence.

Anna Lafaele, Delcelia's grandmother, was barred by Tania from contact with the child, seeing her only when Aroha smuggled her over.

What can't be overlooked, though, and what is central to the whole matter of relying on families to protect abused children, is that abusers tend to come from troubled families where there is often domestic violence, involvement with the police, a hostile attitude to outside help, and alcohol and drug abuse. How can such families, overwhelmed by difficulties and tensions, be deemed a safe or therapeutic environment?

June Mariu, who has worked with such families in a lifetime of teaching, Maori Women's Welfare League and now the Waipereira Trust, says flatly, "The Delcelia case blows the whanau idea right apart. Of course there are families that are wonderful, but there are lots of others where you just cannot leave children.

"For myself, I would not hesitate to interfere to save a child. I'm not too worried about the whanau having the last say. The safety of the child is paramount. Then you start working with the family. But there needs to be some control, along with all the support, or the families can just humbug their way out of responsibility. 'Oh yes, we'll change; we'll go off the booze or the drugs', but they don't. They come to the first meeting, and that's all.

"We've got to be real, to face facts, or there are going to be more and more Delcelias."

Paul Barrowclough, the detective, who, with his colleague Caroline Fisher, devoted months of his life to Delcelia's case, is entirely determined about two things. One is that the people of New Zealand should be in no doubt that Delcelia's sufferings were not unique, and, secondly, that she should not be seen just as a symbol, but as a person who deserves to be understood now, in death, as she was not in life, and deserves to be remembered for herself.

We might also think of 21-month-old Rachel Waerea. She is the third child of 21-year-old Deidree Wickcliffe, who also has a four-year-old and a three-yearold. Rachel lived with her grandmother for much of her life, because Deidree hit her.

Six weeks after Rachel was returned, her mother got angry because the child wouldn't go outside, so she "ran her around" the house till she fell over, then trampled on her chest, having earlier hit her on the head several times with her son's plastic cricket bat.

Rachel suffered a stroke. She's partially blind and partially paralysed.

CHAPTER EIGHTEEN

Too close to the police

1996, *Sunday Star-Times*: Donna Chisholm details the misuse of DNA evidence and helps free a wrongly convicted man, David Dougherty.

There haven't been many cases of wrongful convictions in New Zealand. Perhaps a dozen, or maybe a few more. That's if you judge it by the number of convictions that are actually overturned, and prisoners that are set free. There are even fewer in which journalists have played some kind of a role. This book highlights three of them — Arthur Allan Thomas, Teina Pora, and this one, David Dougherty.

Of course, the actual number of convictions overturned is no reliable guide to the safety of the rest; as has been pointed out, if overseas trends are anything to go by, it is likely that there are more cases of wrongful convictions that have not yet been found. The justice system is human, and makes mistakes, sometimes despite the best of intentions.

This story is about one of those mistakes. In hindsight, it all seems pretty obvious: Dougherty could never have done the rape he was accused of. The DNA evidence was clear, as long as you looked at it the right way. But at the time, it wasn't so clear. The system had investigated, tried him, convicted him and locked him up.

Donna Chisholm was already an experienced journalist when she came across his story. She had worked on *The Auckland Star* during its investigative heyday in the late 1970s and '80s. Like many others, she credits deputy editor Pat Booth with fostering a sense of moral purpose: that journalism could be there to help people, as well as inform and entertain. Two years out of journalism school, in 1977, she was given a chance to help when reporting the trial of a young Samoan charged with stealing a comb from his employer. She remembers rushing back to the newsroom. 'Pat was the one who shared the sense of outrage and put it on the front page for three days in a row. And he was the one who made sure there was momentum from that.' That sense of outrage, and that belief that journalism should help people, has stayed with her. 'It's motivated by a sense of trying to put things right or do the right thing by people' (Chisholm, 2016).

However, it wasn't just a desire to help that initially got Chisholm interested in the Dougherty case. She was alerted to the story by a lawyer, who told her about an interesting case of possible wrongful conviction involving DNA evidence. Back in 1996, DNA was still new, and, as she puts it, 'sexy'. But what may have started as a professional interest, as a journalist tracking a new development in justice, eventually became a personal crusade when she realised that Dougherty was innocent.

Her reporting did not free Dougherty. That was achieved, most of all perhaps, by the scientist Arie Geursen, who noticed the flaw in the Crown interpretation of the DNA evidence. Chisholm believes that her greatest contribution to Dougherty's case was helping raise public awareness of the case, and gain him nearly $870,000 in compensation in 2002 for his wrongful conviction and imprisonment. Campaigning aside, her reporting did unearth important facts, which helped build the case for his innocence. In particular, she highlighted doubts within ESR, the Crown laboratory that was supposedly impartially assessing the DNA evidence, about the ESR's own interpretation of that evidence. What Chisholm showed, and what was particularly disturbing, was that here was a scientist who was too close to the police.

It is easy, in hindsight, and now that such stories of scientific fallibility are commonplace, to overlook the difficulty that confronted those who questioned the science in those days, before the internet made Google Scholars of us all. But these stories were ground-breaking in that it was the first time in New Zealand that the wonder-science of DNA evidence was seriously questioned.

The two stories here are from 1996, the year in which Dougherty's conviction was finally proved wrong. The first is an account of his time in prison, the second highlights concerns about the evidence in the case.

Chisholm, D. (2016). Interview with author, J. Hollings.

Now hear my screams
Sunday Star-Times, 25 August 1996

DAVID DOUGHERTY leaves his hotel door open to a howling gale on Tuesday night and realises, finally, that he is free.

In jail, it is 9 o'clock lockup, but now, for the first time in more than three years, he watches the open doorway — the symbol of his freedom — almost with disbelief.

"That's when it sunk in," he says later. "But I couldn't go out. It didn't feel right to me — it was almost as though the chain was still around the ankle of the elephant."

For someone who was dragged to prison from the dock, screaming his innocence to the court that had just convicted him, the 40-minute drive to the hotel after he is bailed is strangely quiet.

A call to his mum to say he is out and on his way. Then, a silence, broken only by radio news bulletins announcing his release.

Even when he speaks, Dougherty's voice is often barely audible. Almost as if he's used to no one listening. "I have been screaming in the darkness. Now, I am getting a chance to have my screaming heard," he says.

"The first night after the trial I was locked in a round room in a special unit because they thought I was a suicide risk. I went crazy. I was locked up against my will for something I know I didn't do. It wasn't that I planned to kill myself. It was just that I didn't know how to cope with the hopelessness of how I felt and the situation I was in. Nothing could give me comfort."

His fear was compounded by the knowledge that in jail, alleged child molesters are regarded as fair game.

"I rang my brother and I was crying on the phone. I told him: 'I'm going to die, man, I'm not joking'."

He was, his then lawyer recalls, like a man at the gates of hell. But within 24 hours, all that changed.

"The next night, I cried out to the Lord and said: 'I can't handle this'."

From that moment, he says he became a devout Christian. His bitterness faded and his strength returned.

He pulls from his suitcase a much-thumbed *Bible*. On almost every page, line after line of meaningful passages are highlighted with ballpoint rules. He recites verses at will, the result of daily hours of study and weekly attendance at church services.

God became his closest confidante. In jail, he says, you usually don't bother protesting about your innocence because so many others are saying the same thing.

Sentenced to seven years and nine months jail in June 1993 and having his first Appeal Court case dismissed a year later, Dougherty will be retried after DNA evidence — of someone else's seminal stain in the complainant's underwear — raised doubts about his guilt.

His faith was tested after that first Appeal Court hearing. He had had high hopes for his case to be reopened; his blackest moment was hearing he had been turned down. "I have always felt there was hope apart from that time. I was living on a knife edge."

But within a month, lawyer Murray Gibson called offering fresh hope of a new appeal based on another scientist's interpretation of DNA evidence in the case.

For Dougherty, preparing for a pre-Christmas retrial on the 1992 child rape and abduction charges, prison routines are hard to break — even at the resort hotel where he spent several days after being bailed.

At breakfast, he cleared his own plates. "I felt as if I should be the servant."

Within hours of his release, he was on the phone to Rangipo Prison, where he has spent the past 18 months, trying to call prison officer "Ron M", a man he regards as a friend — "a primo dude".

"The prison officers at Birch Camp were as closely supportive as people in their position could be — not only of me, but of the whole camp. The camp was a place you didn't need to wear a mask. In some places, you have to look bad and tough or you are considered weak. If you look happy or open or inviting, they consider it weakness. But at Birch, there was a relationship of mutual respect."

Most of his sentence has been served in a "harmony unit" in segregation and he has never been beaten or even threatened by other inmates despite the charges on which he was convicted.

But Dougherty challenges the public perception of the prison as a holiday camp.

"People say we're getting better fed than people outside struggling on the poverty line; that we've got a good feed every day and a bed to sleep in. But the whole concept of imprisonment is not whether you are in a hole with bread and water seven days a week or pampered with bacon and eggs. It's the fact that you know at 9pm that night you will be locked up and you won't be unlocked until 6.30am. There will be no variation on that.

"Once the door closes, the scary reality of being locked up against your will, separated from your loved ones, hits you."

He remembers watching the Mt Ruapehu eruption, gathering the ash that coated the compound. One of the boxes he carried from Mt Eden Prison contains a bag full of it that he couldn't leave behind.

Yes, it was awesome to watch, he says, but little looks beautiful when you're looking out from a cell.

There's a verse in an old western paperback that Dougherty set to music a little while back. He sings it now, softly:

> There are bars across my window,
> and bars across my door
> and bars across my heart
> because I see you no more
>
> For what is the sunshine
> and what are the stars
> if you only can see them
> through steel prison bars?

Rangipo's 1995 karaoke champion sounds a bit like Kenny Rogers, but reserves most of his singing for hymns these days.

He plans to record a video to send to mates still inside. The release of a close friend always wrenches the hearts of those left behind, he says. As he speaks, he strokes the bone and paua carving around his neck, a treasured gift from a friend transferred with him from Mt Eden to Paremoremo to Rangipo in the past three years.

"The night before I left, I found it hanging on a noticeboard in my hut," says Dougherty. "I just looked at it and said: 'You are too much, bro'."

He had admired the piece when his friend, who learned to carve in prison, completed it months before. "I said to him then: 'Buddy, this is the best yet.' It was a prideful and joyful thing for him."

Dougherty says prison discipline has changed him. He no longer drinks — shunning even champagne to celebrate his freedom.

"I'm now more of a look, wait and see person. Before, I was more flamboyantly open and giving of myself. Now I just melt into the background. I can just sit and listen. I look at the cover a lot longer before I decide to open the book."

For a man who spent much of his time alone — he usually went to his cell each night at 6pm — renewed contact with society has been a jolt.

"All these people . . . people everywhere. In the bush, you just didn't see people. On the motorways, I just think: 'Far out, this looks dangerous'."

Although he left school early, Dougherty is highly articulate.

"I've learned a lot about human relations. I've been everywhere. I've gone down all these deadend streets and when I went into jail, it was as if the car had broken down and I had to look into the glovebox for the manual. The manual showed me the easiest and safest way to reach my destination was God. Like a lot of other people, I had thought I could get there under my own steam until something forced me to take a greater look outside myself and say: 'Hey man, I'm not the centre of the universe'."

Dougherty, who will live north of Auckland with his partner, Jo-Ann, hopes to start work soon with a home renovation company and regrets that, at 29, he is not established in a trade.

Today, though, that does not worry him. He is concentrating on the new trial. "Praise God I am free but it is not over yet."

Accused sent through the gates of hell

Sunday Star-Times, 5 May 1996

IT TOOK eight hours for a jury to find David Dougherty guilty of the rape and abduction it now seems he did not commit.

When the foreman delivered the verdicts, Dougherty started at the jury, let out a piercing cry — "I didn't do it" — and had to be carried, thrashing and screaming, to the cells.

"It was a numbing experience," his then defence counsel Robin Brown recalls. "He was like someone at the gates of hell. He was berserk."

From the moment he met Dougherty on what seemed like just another legal aid assignment, Mr Brown was convinced of his innocence.

"The first thing he said to me was, 'You might have acted for people you think are guilty. But I swear to God you are looking at someone who is not.' I take what people say with a grain of salt, generally, but I had to be touched by that. I believed in his innocence from the word go and I have never wavered from that."

He was impressed that Dougherty went to the police station after hearing that police wanted to talk with him about the rape, and immediately volunteered to have body samples taken. "You don't do that if you're guilty," said Mr Brown.

ESR scientist Susan Petricevic told the jury that seminal fluid was found on the crotch of the girl's underpants and her pyjama pants, but that there was insufficient material to allow traditional DNA profiling.

But a new test, introduced shortly after Dougherty was jailed for seven years and nine months in June 1993, enabled the ESR to amplify the DNA by about a billion times. It revealed the DNA in the seminal stains on the victim's underwear was not Dougherty's.

Scientists in Auckland and overseas consulted by the defence believe the way the ESR reported the DNA findings to the Court of Appeal may have misled the court when it rejected his appeal the following year. His lawyer, Murray Gibson, has now petitioned the Governor-General to return the case to the Court of Appeal for a re-hearing.

The jury had to rely on the unequivocal identification evidence of the young victim — his 11-year-old neighbour — who said Dougherty took her from her bedroom about midnight — gagged, bound and blindfolded — to a nearby property where he raped her.

She was a strong and convincing witness, said Mr Brown. When cross-examined, she denied that she was blaming the wrong person to protect someone else that she knew.

"I thought to myself, 'Good God, Robin, you have your work cut out for you here'," he said. "It is very hard defending people where the evidence is ostensibly overwhelming and when you have a young complainant and there is a great deal of sympathy in her favour. These sort of trials are the most stressful. If we had had the DNA evidence, we could have raised a reasonable doubt."

Even without the DNA findings, however, there were pointers at Dougherty's trial which raised doubts about his guilt.

There was clear medical evidence the girl was raped. But what no-one has even tried to find out is that if Dougherty did not leave the seminal stains in the girl's underwear, who did?

1. The locked ranchslider

Police alleged the rapist gained entry to the girl's bedroom, on the bottom floor of her three-storey west Auckland home, through a ranchslider door. But there was no evidence of forced entry of this door or any other door of the house.

The victim said she checked the ranchslider and her window before she went to bed and they were shut and locked.

Police constable William Taylor, who examined the girl's bedroom, tried to open the ranchslider, using "average force" from both the inside and outside when it was locked and was unable to do so.

There was no evidence that tests for fingerprints were taken on the ranchslider or window surrounds.

2. The identification

The victim told the court she woke because "David" was beating her up. Asked how she knew it was David, she said she recognised his voice and "he said he was David".

Why, after identifying himself, did her assailant then blindfold her?

At the depositions hearing, the victim said she asked him if he were David; at the trial she said she did not ask.

She said she was sure her assailant was clean shaven. Dougherty had a moustache.

When the man was taking her away, she said she could see his face for about 20 seconds when a security light came on. Under cross-examination, she said she could see only an outline of him at that time.

3. The blindfold

In her original statement she said the blindfold was removed and a sock gag taken out of her mouth after the rape. In court, she said the T-shirt was removed before the rape, "but he told me to keep my eyes shut"; then that he took the blindfold off after the rape and told her to look away as he dressed.

4. The grass clippings

Clumps of grass were found in the victim's room. Her father said he always used a catcher when he mowed his lawn but David Dougherty did not and he presumed the grass had come from his section. But although it was early October and the ground was wet and boggy, no footprints were found on the grass outside the house, even though her father checked as soon as she reported the rape about 7.30 the following morning.

5. The lighting

The girl told the court her assailant took her to the New Lynn Bowling Club where he tried to unlock a brown gate. When a security light came on he said, "this is no place for us" and took her across the road.

But a technician who installed the lights said there was no chance anyone could reach the gate without activating the sensor light at the entry to the carpark at least 20m away.

6. The alcohol

The victim told police her assailant gave her a pill and alcohol when they reached the property, where he raped her. In court, she said she was given the pill and drink after the rape.

7. The incident

The assailant, according to the victim, told her that if anyone saw them, she was to "act as if he was my brother". When her hands were bound with a shoelace, she was gagged with a sock and blindfolded with a T-shirt? Whey did he take her, in such a state, on roads with the risk of being seen by passing traffic or from houses?

8. The rape report

The girl told police that when the rapist released her she went home and went to her brother's room before returning to her own room where she stayed for the rest of the night.

She reported the rape about 7.30am after seeing Dougherty leave his house.

At the trial, when asked where she went when she got home, she said "Into my bed".

After she reported the rape to her parents, her father phoned the police. He said he told them he "wasn't 100% sure if this had really happened". He decided she was telling the truth when he saw the scratches on his daughter's neck. He said "at first the story sounded so unbelievable I thought she must have been sleepwalking again. She does have trouble with sleepwalking, but she's never gone out of the house."

Her father later said he was sure his daughter would not be capable of making up such a story.

9. The medical evidence

Despite evidence of abrasions and bruising at the girl's vaginal entrance, the hymen was not torn, indicating complete penetration might not have taken place. The significance of this became apparent at the Court of Appeal when the judges questioned why, if the seminal fluid in the girl's underwear was from the assailant, it was not also present on swabs from her genital area.

Editor's note

In 1998, then Minister of Justice, Doug Graham, referred Dougherty's case to Queen's Counsel Stuart Grieve for review. Grieve requested further testing of the DNA samples, which showed the profile of another man. In 2000, Grieve found that Dougherty was, on the balance of probabilities, innocent, and recommended compensation. The next year, the government paid Dougherty $868,728 for his wrongful conviction and imprisonment. In 2003, Nicholas Reekie was found guilty of the abduction and rape of Dougherty's neighbour.

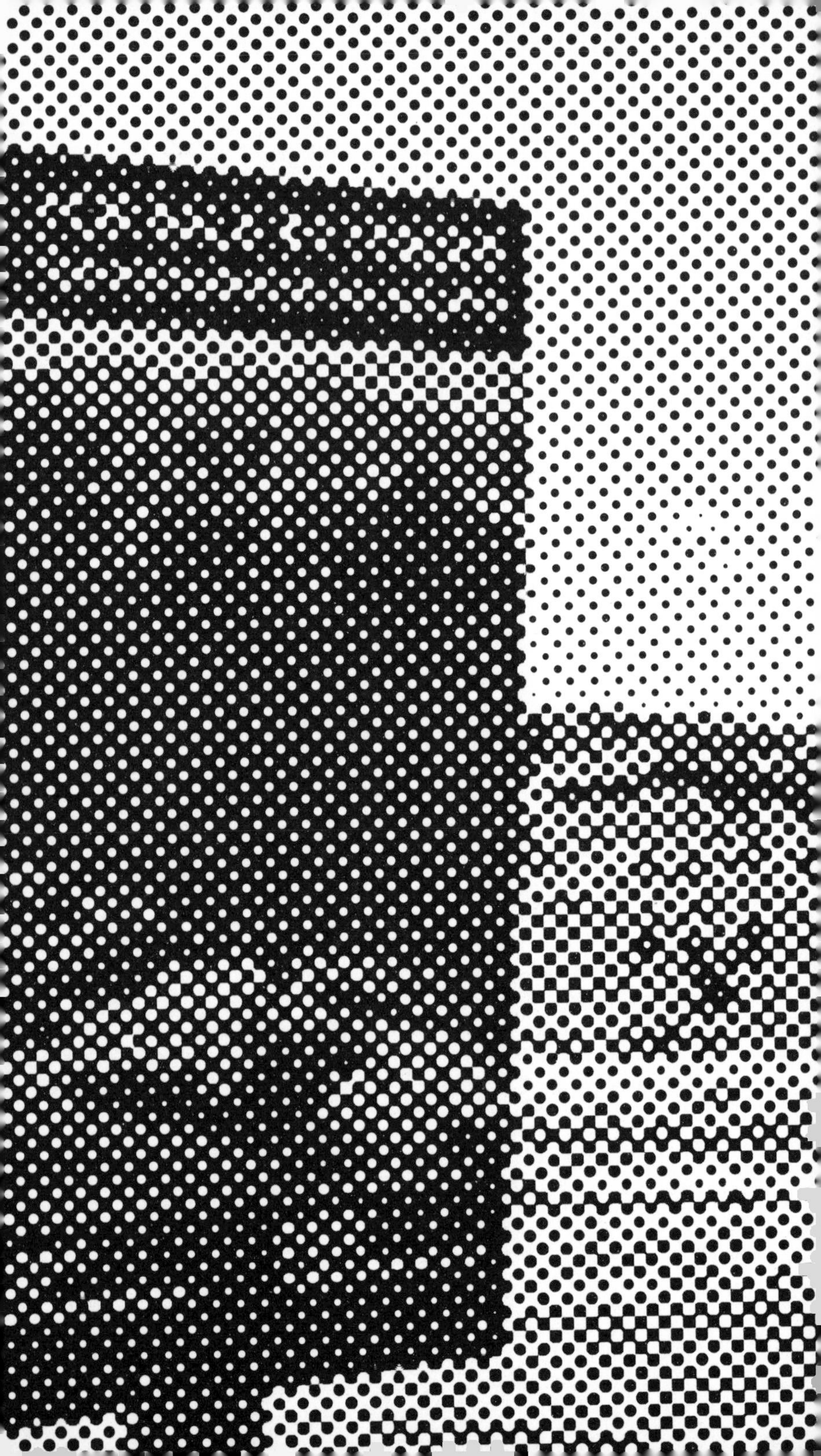

CHAPTER NINETEEN

High-country sell-off

2002, *New Zealand Listener*: Bruce Ansley examines the sale of New Zealand land to foreigners.

In 1990, the New Zealand economy was struggling. The free-market changes introduced in the late 1980s, which had cost thousands of jobs as factories formerly protected by the state had closed, had yet to produce much economic benefit. That year, a new government, led by the conservative National Party, looked to foreign investment as a golden goose to help turn the economy around. It quietly scrapped long-standing rules limiting foreign ownership of land, effectively hanging out a 'For Sale' sign on some of our most iconic landscapes in the South Island high country.

Wealthy foreigners saw those signs, and came calling. Lured by the beauty, the privacy and bargain prices, hundreds of foreign buyers started snapping up farms, high-country stations, beaches and islands. The new owners often appeared to have little time for the Kiwi tradition of equality of access to beaches and rivers. Too often, one of their first acts was to put up 'No Trespassing' signs, fence off pathways that had been used by trampers and hunters for decades, and employ hard-faced managers to frighten away locals. Amidst the many crises gripping the country at that time, no one seemed to be paying much attention to this quiet invasion. Only one small lobby group, the Campaign Against Foreign Control of Aotearoa (CAFCA), was raising a voice, and compiling a database of land sales.

Journalist Bruce Ansley had noted the CAFCA's work, but had not so far followed it up. But after hearing that the Member of Parliament for Nelson, Nick Smith, and his family had been thrown off a beach on Pepin Island, near Nelson, which had been bought by an absentee German industrialist, he began to make enquiries. What followed was a succession of revelations that made many New Zealanders very concerned. Over the next 15 years, Ansley doggedly dug through land-sales records, pestered government officials and tracked down some of the most significant foreign buyers, many of whom had probably hoped they would not be noticed.

In a succession of stories for the *Listener*, Ansley showed that the government agency that was supposed to be scrutinising foreign buyers — the grandly named Overseas Investment Commission (OIC) — was in fact little more than a rubber stamp for anyone with a chequebook (Ansley, 2002, 1995, 1994). Of 471 applications made by foreign buyers between 1991 and 1994, it turned down none. Although charged with ensuring that foreign buyers were of good character, it waved through an application by a convicted German fraudster to buy Pakatoa Island, and then approved the sale of an iconic high-country station to Tommy Suharto, son of the Indonesian dictator Suharto, despite him having had convictions for political corruption and having being charged with murders in his home country.

'How could anybody who read a newspaper say he was of good character? It was just a rubber stamp,' says Ansley. 'I described them as that in one article and was called by the head [of the OIC], who said he was going to ban me from their office. It was of no consequence to me as I never got anything from them anyway' (Ansley, 2017).

Ansley's stories did what investigative journalism is supposed to do — they held power to account. The government certainly noticed. Its response to the growing concern was to pass a new law making it a criminal offence — with fines of up to $100,000 — to publish details of an application to the OIC.

Over time, though, public pressure for change grew, and successive governments have moved to tighten the monitoring of foreign buyers. Ansley is pleased that his work has had an impact. 'I think I did a good job in as much as there was very little being done on it at the time. So I was the first to peer into that subject. The more I did, the more others got involved and it became appealing to politicians. It became a political issue and developed its own momentum.'

For someone with such a long and distinguished career in journalism, Ansley's path into it was almost accidental. After growing up in Christchurch, in the beachside suburb of New Brighton, he'd just finished a degree at the University of Canterbury and was wondering what to do next when he noticed a job at a small newspaper in Hawke's Bay. Despite having no journalism training he thought he'd give it a shot, and got the job. 'I worked for them for two years and got this amazing background in journalism, covering everything from sheep sales to flower shows.' After that, he worked at the *Dunedin Star* and the *Otago Daily Times*, and helped found Radio Otago before heading to the UK. In London, Ansley swung night shifts at *The Sun* before returning to New Zealand for a long stint at *The Star* in Christchurch. He joined the *Listener* in the early 1990s, serving as a senior writer until he left in 2006. Ansley now lives on Waiheke Island and writes books. His most recent, *Islands: A New Zealand Journey*, explores many of the same themes that occupied him at the *Listener*: those affecting the fate of our natural beauty.

While Ansley is pleased that the OIC's successor, the Overseas Investment Office, has taken a more active role in monitoring foreign land sales, he is not sure that it goes far enough. 'Whether it's adequate, I don't know. . . . I believe, personally, that our rights aren't being looked after by our own agencies. While we have progress, is it enough to satisfy the public interest? Is an American who buys a high-country farm more or less as a bach of good value to New Zealand? I don't think that's been answered.'

Ansley, B. (1994). High country sell-out. *New Zealand Listener*, 16 July.

Ansley, B. (1995). Rolling out the red carpet. *New Zealand Listener*, 13 May.

Ansley, B. (2002). This land is your land. *New Zealand Listener*, 2 March.

Ansley, B. (2017). Interview with author, J. Hollings.

This land is your land
New Zealand Listener, 2 March 2002

Of all the views in all the world Jean-Francois and Gwen Taquet liked this one. It looks over the glorious country around Lake Wakatipu. Superlatives are currency around here, magnificent, breathtaking, awe-inspiring and so on, but for my money the Taquets have the best of the best. You can stand at their place and look over the Remarkables, the Crown Range, Coronet Peak, Lake Wakatipu, Lake Hayes, and all the juicy bits in between.

Taquet is a French chef who went on to open two restaurants in Philadelphia. He visited New Zealand in 1995 and liked the place so much — "welcoming people, clean air, pristine water" — that he bought quite a lot of it. "As soon as we came here the first time, we were amazed," he says. "We flew to Queenstown, drove to Auckland, saw an immigration lawyer and decided to move."

The Taquets now own Glencoe Station, 9315ha of terrace, tussock, high hills and river valleys. It runs from Arrowtown to the Crown Range Rd, the skiers' road between Queenstown and Wanaka so famously difficult that many insurers won't cover cars taking the route. Then it runs north, skirting the Cardrona skifield to Mt Cardrona, returning down the Arrow River. It is seriously spectacular country, "the perfect piece of land", says Taquet. "I am from a very small village in the southwest of France with only 600 people. Gwen is from a little lakeside town in New Hampshire with only 4000 people. For us, Arrowtown is not remote at all."

You get to Glencoe Station by taking the steep zigzag up to the Crown Terrace, a broad flat shelf lying between the valley and the mountains, then turning off on what is little more than a track, grass growing along its middle and ending in a basin with the old wooden homestead in its middle. The Taquets' married couple live there. The Taquets themselves have a big new house on the edge of the terrace, with the choicest of views.

Soon they will be surrounded by other big new houses, for the Taquets are developing what they call the Glencoe Estate.

They propose 17.8ha sections on 332ha of land, with the balance to be covenanted for no more residential development. They expect to see "luxury homes", each site "landscaped to blend with the natural surroundings", and Taquet promises that they will be very expensive. This is because he needs, he says, millions of dollars for the rest of his development plans, and "I'd prefer fewer, more expensive houses to raise the money".

They eventually intend building a luxurious lodge. Homeowners and hotel guests will enjoy what will be a huge organic farm, for the Taquets intend converting the entire station to a certified organic operation by 2004. They plan to restore historical sites on the station, the old school, stonewalls, sheds and homesteads. They are reducing stock numbers to encourage vegetation and, says Taquet, to "revive the environment of the high country".

Taquet is a stocky man who exudes energy and is forceful enough to make you want to take a step or two back. He has a successful track record and he is planning to spend a lot of money on his developments and around Queenstown, you can't argue with that.

He is the very model of foreign investment, adventurous, visionary, committed to the country, the kind who brings on backslapping at the Overseas Investment Commission (OIC).

But locals complain that although most — 8500ha — of Glencoe Station is pastoral lease with the Crown as landlord, Taquet won't let them across his property.

This hurts. Glencoe Station is among the best tramping country in the region. The same views that Glencoe Estate homeowners will pay hundreds of thousands, perhaps millions for, can be had by any member of the public with a pair of walking shoes and a little breath in their body.

"This is completely false," Taquet protests. But as he goes on it is evident the he is uncomfortable with the New Zealand tradition of public access. He talks of people leaving rubbish, leaving gates open, stealing, starting fires, saying they will be in one place then going to another, letting dogs run, disrupting livestock and wildlife, trespassing, the full panoply of problems between landowners and public. "Sometimes we have to say no, for our own reasons," he says. And: "Most of the time I let them stay. For the moment I have a pastoral lease and the land is private property. Just like your own home or private property."

So the Taquets have become part of the new conundrum facing the high country. They're entrepreneurial but exclusive.

The high country is a big part of our legend, like the Australian outback, or the Swiss Alps. Most of us are never going to get up there outside a skiing trip or a scenic flight. But we like to know it's there if we want it. It's ours. We don't like the thought of it being sold off to foreigners, but that is what is happening.

We celebrated the old high-country station-owner, along with musterers, merinos, swaggies, Swannies, snowlines, huts with smoke curling from tin chimneys.

Of course we found holes in the tale. High-country stations were running superb country dry to make a bob, leaving a legacy of soil degradation and rabbits. So many thought. And cantankerous high-country cockies were a legend of their own, running their territories like fiefdoms, letting people in or kicking them out on a whim. So many thought.

But the 1990s changed everything. Back in 1994, the *Listener* reported an incipient trend: six high-country stations had been sold to foreigners in the previous three years. Some 70,000ha of our finest scenery was now controlled by overseas interests. In 2002, the figure is 220,000ha and counting.

The new owners, generally, are interested in farming only as part of diverse land use. Like the Taquets, they plan subdivisions, hotels. They see guided tours, exclusive hunting and fishing, and the fear is that when they're charging people to hunt and fish and tramp they're not going to let New Zealanders do it for nothing.

Like their predecessors, they are jealous of their turf. But it's one thing to be told to bugger off by a New Zealand station-owner. Quite another to be ordered off by a foreigner — especially when he is ordering you off publicly owned land.

In the new legend the old cockies have become nostalgic figures, kindly folk who helped trampers across fences and made them cups of tea. "We once used to be able to wander virtually anywhere we liked," says the Federated Mountain Clubs' (FMC) Mike Floate. "Now access is often denied, more by foreign owners who don't have that tradition. They see they have trespass rights and use them. And they run businesses, so they want to keep exclusive rights for their clients."

The sins of New Zealand owners are forgotten, almost. The new owners of Erewhon Station, deep in Canterbury mountains, put up a sign that is probably there still: "Forgive those that [sic] trespass? Not me. I shoot the bastards."

But at least part of the growing complaint rings true. People who have had to pay for a stretch of trout river, or write cheques to shoot almost tame stags on some of our so-called game parks, or who have guards on their gates back home, are from a different culture. "Foreign owners are not necessarily evil," says Ross Millichamp, Fish and Game's Canterbury manager. "But it comes down to a culture where if your land adjoins the river, you own the river. They bring that culture to New Zealand. They expect control over the river, and public access comes as a shock."

The South Island's superb high country is what most foreigners see first. Cities, geysers, beaches, trees, birds . . . well, nice to visit, but who wants to live there. What would a marketing campaign, tourist drive, poster, television commercial or *Lord of the Rings* be without the high country?

It is not surprising that when foreigners come to see the scenery and find it's for sale, they reach for their wallets. They want the showiest places, of course, the best peaks, finest lakes, rivers, bush.

But that is exactly where New Zealanders most want to go, too.

The government originally resolved the tension by creating pastoral leases: the high country remained in public ownership, the state landlord and farmers tenants.

Stubborn owners presided over some runs, but the general rule was that farmers allowed public access except during lambing.

That tradition stood for a century and a half, almost surviving privatisation and the market economy.

For three things have happened.

First, tourism shifted the focus of many high-country stations. Fine wool, merino, was once the main earner. But more and more station-owners are realising that they have something visitors want. They're branching into tourism, horse trekking, four-wheel-drive adventures, hunting safaris, fishing. They are immediately in conflict with the public. The public wants in, but the owners want exclusive use.

Second, through the OIC successive governments have encouraged foreign ownership in the name of investment.

Third, the exchange rate has done the rest. The high country is a good investment for overseas owners. They buy the farm, set up a business, and they get the views, too.

The new owners are unencumbered by the New Zealand tradition of public access. In many cases they've brought their own: they own the land, or at least control it, and the natives can take a hike. "There used to be a lot of goodwill among high-country landowners who believed the public had the right to be there," says Millichamp. "A lot of roading was put into high-country stations, for example, for deer or possum control, but it went in by the easiest route rather than the legal road and we're now finding that if the formed road doesn't run along the paper road the landowner often denies access, and that's frustrating when it was paid for with taxpayer money."

"This is going to get worse," promises Les Cleveland, chair of the Otago Conservation Board. "It's an emergent problem."

We're talking a lot of New Zealand here. The six million hectares of high country comprise 20 percent of the South Island. Half of this is conservation land, half a million hectares is freehold, and the remainder is in some 365 pastoral leases. Those leases cover nine percent of New Zealand's land area, or close to 2.5m hectares. Bill Rosenberg of the Campaign Against Foreign Control of Aotearoa (Cafca) has analysed OIC records and listed all rural land sales to foreigners between January 1991 and the end of last year.

The figures are not comprehensive because the OIC, for its own arcane reasons, sometimes keeps transactions secret.

The Royal Forest and Bird Protection Society has examined Rosenberg's figures in turn, concluding that more than 220,000ha of high country, most of it pastoral lease land, is now owned by foreign interests. This, Forest and Bird analysts Eugenie Sage and Sue Maturin point out, is the equivalent of more than seven Paparoa National Parks.

Forest and Bird is calling for a moratorium on the sale of pastoral leases to overseas interests. It says the ban would prevent the alienation of leases with high conservation value, and protect the public interest in the high country. It wants the government to direct the OIC that, as a matter of government policy, the sale of pastoral leases to foreigners is no longer in the public interest.

Pressure on the government to keep the high country for New Zealanders is steadily increasing.

A week ago the Otago Conservation Board took its case to the New Zealand Conservation Authority. The board argued that the OIC's criteria for approving sales to farmers needed to be widened. Sales to overseas buyers under current criteria must be in the "national interest", a vague term that is clearly tied only to economic benefits. Surely, says the board, this should include recreational and social values to meet the broader interests of New Zealanders. Says Cleveland: "Farmers who've been on their land for generations build up a rapport with the community. Queen Street businessmen have none of that and certainly foreign owners don't have that tradition. Traditional goodwill is giving way to more commercial and entrepreneurial activity. Shouldn't we make sure some other values are protected in the process? We've got to change the OIC's rules."

Public Access New Zealand (Panz) has been hammering away at the problem for years. It wants reserves along all water bodies, and access to them, to be made a condition of sale by the OIC. "Water frontage is a key marketable commodity," says Panz's Bruce Mason. "If reserves were excluded from the sale, it would take away some of the incentive to shut out the public."

Federated Mountain Clubs wants it made mandatory for high-country properties to go through tenure review before the OIC approves their sale to foreigners. These and other groups are finding traction in wider support. An editorial in the conservative *Otago Daily Times* last December began: "Something very special about New Zealand is seeping away like a tarn in a drought. Our access to the wide open spaces is slowly but surely drying up. A combination of hardening attitudes, the freeholding of Crown leasehold land and increased foreign ownership is placing barriers in the way of our freedom to roam."

Will the OIC change its ways? Unlikely. Its chief executive Stephen Dawe has said it won't, because New Zealanders are as much to blame as foreigners in denying access to New Zealanders; besides, both natives and foreigners are subject to the same rules. Access questions, he said, are better dealt with by other agencies.

Dawe echoes Finance Minister Michael Cullen's view. Cullen favours the status quo, he says, because it "provides an appropriate balance between public concerns and the promotion of economic development". Nor, says Cullen, does he encourage farm sales to foreign investors. The government's encouragement of foreign direct investment is aimed rather at "new job and technology-rich activities".

Of course, this does not bear scrutiny in an environment that encourages foreign investment without distinction. The OIC has turned down only a handful of applications from foreigners to buy land here; it has approved hundreds. And the public, through its various user groups, clearly does not think any "appropriate balance" has been achieved.

Farmers are split on the issue. Some, especially in Southland, are bitter that absentee owners are buying up farms and gutting local communities. Others want no restrictions on who they sell to. Foreign buyers not only have larger wallets, but they have pushed up prices — the value of the farmers' assets — too.

Cullen at least recognises some public concern. He says this is reflected in a "new, tighter regime".

The innovation, New Zealand First-inspired, is a new regulation that came into effect in January. The only real change it makes is the demand that land be offered on the open market to New Zealanders before its sale to foreigners can be approved by the OIC.

This feeble measure pleases few. Federated Farmers says it is ineffective and will both increase the costs of a sale and create uncertainty for potential buyers. If a deal has already been struck, all the seller needs to do is keep it quiet until the property is advertised, leading others into an expensive charade.

Says FMC patron Allan Evans: "It's bloody ridiculous. It's not going to stop foreigners outbidding New Zealanders. It's just a sop."

Lilybank started it. The formerly famous and later notorious sheep station at the far end of Lake Tekapo was sold to the infamous Hutomo "Tommy" Suharto, a son of the former Indonesian dictator, in 1992. He makes nonsense of the obligation on the OIC to ensure foreign buyers are of "good character". Suharto has since been convicted, then on appeal acquitted, on graft charges in his home country, where he is now in custody awaiting the outcome of murder inquiries.

Some 25,500ha of the 27,500ha station was supposed to be given back to the Crown under a deal struck in the late 70s: taxpayers paid to improve the better, lower country on the farm and were to get the land in exchange. But Suharto fought the deal and only relinquished the land in 1996 — and before he did it his managers burnt down three huts beloved of trampers, hunters and musterers for 70 years. Throughout the 90s, constant friction marked Lilybank's relations with the public.

The station and the luxurious lodge built by Suharto were sold to his Singaporean business partner Alan Poh in 1999 for $1. In June last year a sale to American interests fell through and the lodge went on the market for $7.2m. It was described as a private paradise. It has since been withdrawn from the website advertising its sale, and its current status is unknown.

How this deal advanced the "national interest", as it is required to do under OIC rules, remains puzzling. Certainly official correspondence obtained by Cafca indicates considerable government embarrassment.

Nothing matches the bizarre Lilybank story for sheer audacity.

But tramping and mountain clubs, environmental groups and the Department of Conservation (DOC) can produce a long list of sensitive properties.

Glenhope Station was bought by American interests in 1998. The station accommodates what was described to the OIC as the biggest professional guiding operation in the South Island. Since then, Forest and Bird has complained that a traditional walking track was fenced off, Fish and Game fought difficulties over public access to rivers and DOC may have to move a trampers' hut.

Glenhope is adjacent to St James Station, near the Lewis Pass National Reserve and Nelson Lakes National Park. St James Station and the neighbouring Rainbow have 18 recognised tramping routes entirely within their boundaries. The New Zealand-owned St James has the well-named Rainbow Rd, which runs through the station. It's a wildly beautiful, rough drive through the mountains from Canterbury to Nelson.

According to a briefing paper prepared for Prime Minister Clark for a flight over the high country last year (subsequently cancelled), and obtained under the Official Information Act, three local authorities — Tasman, Marlborough and Hurunui — want to upgrade the road and make it legal as an alternative route. But the landowner denied them access by locking his gates. Ironically, Rainbow, owned by an American, seems frictionfree, but environmentalists tremble over the future of this sensitive area and want the government to buy St James at least. The briefing paper agrees that the Crown's best guarantee of certain public access is to buy selected properties as they come onto the market, but Land Information NZ (Linz) says it does not have the money.

Ryton Station, in the mountains west of Christchurch, featured in the *Listener* last year when the sports association that has run ice-skating at Lake Ida since 1948 found themselves locked out of the access road. Trespass notices were served. The 14,600ha station has gone heavily into tourist ventures, offering everything from fishing and mountain-biking to golf and, of course, ice-skating. It is 90 percent owned by the chief executive of international company SGS, a Swiss who appears to hold both British and NZ citizenship as well.

Coleridge Downs Station was bought by the Hawaiian-based Erdman family and in a deal with the then-Electricity Corporation of New Zealand acquired shelter belts and walkways around Lake Coleridge village that homeowners regarded as reserves. They remain nervous.

At Wyuna Station, 11,945ha on Lake Wakatipu, the American owners are said by local interests to have pulled out of the tenure review process. This is denied by DOC. "The worry is," says the FMC's Mike Floate, "that with the lodge there it could become an exclusive hunting area with the owners as pastoral leaseholders invoking their right of trespass."

Many stations are in sensitive areas with plenty of potential for friction.

A half interest in Mt Creighton, 15,824ha around Skippers Creek, Queenstown, was bought by American and Hong Kong interests in 1999, although no details were then released by the OIC. Last year, the Mt Creighton owners bought the neighbouring 33,000ha Branches Station, too. That station includes two areas subject to QE2 open space covenants, Lake Lochnagar and the MacKay Falls.

The list goes on.

A huge land swap creating a vast new conservation estate is now shifting gear in the high country. Pastoral lessees can volunteer for the tenure review process. Essentially, they agree to hand back part of their property to the Crown in return for freeholding the rest of their leasehold land.

Linz estimates that one million hectares, or 40 percent of the land held under pastoral lease, could be returned to the Crown and become conservation estate. Thirty-six pastoral lessees have already negotiated deals under the tenure review process, and more than 100 others are now being negotiated.

Tenure review is acclaimed on all sides. It gives much of the high country back to the public, while farmers keep the better country below. It should end friction over access once and for all.

But of course, nothing is that good. Tenure review has been embroiled in the usual concoction of controversy, venality and outright cock-up.

Top of the list in the last category is a change in the law. The 36 tenure reviews signed up were completed under the Land Act of 1948. That act was superceded in 1998 by the Crown Pastoral Land Act, which contained a flaw: it had no provision for carrying over tenure review negotiations from the old regime to the new.

This meant that all the deals still in the pipeline before the 1998 law was passed had to be scrapped and started all over again. It led to a frustrating nexus for farmers, government agencies and interested groups.

So Murray and Jacky MacMillan of Mt Pisa Station have been waiting *seven years* for a result. Mt Pisa is one of the tenure review deals that will create a new Pisa Range Conservation Park. "That's 10 percent of my life expectancy and I'm getting pretty near the end anyway," says Murray MacMillan. "We're a lot wiser, a lot more frustrated — and a lot older."

He should also be a lot richer. On the other side of the Clutha River separating them lies Bendigo Station, one of the first properties to undergo tenure review. The *Listener* reported in 1994 that the station owners, John and Heather Perriam, were to keep 7997ha of their 11,289ha property in the land swap, including freehold title to desirable lake-front land on the then newly created Lake Dunstan. Financial details of these transactions are kept secret, but the *Listener* reported, on good authority, that the price of winning the freehold was only $100,000.

Many feel the agencies involved — DOC and the Commissioner of Crown Lands — are driving a poor bargain on behalf of the public in deals that make station owners rich but still provide insufficient public access.

"As tenure review proceeds, and more lower country is freeholded, access to the high country is increasingly difficult," says the FMCs' Mike Floate.

The tenure review process is voluntary. Lessees can sit on existing arrangements if they like. If the terms don't suit, lessees can simply pull out. It's a potent negotiating tool, although there have been hints that the process could become compulsory. Certainly MacMillan believes so: "If the government wanted to take it, I think in time we'd lose it anyway," he says.

What will be done with the land?

Whole stations will need to be bought to link it together if it is to be made into coherent public conservation parks. Conservation groups have long urged the government to buy back pastoral leases with outstanding natural features. But the memo to Prime Minister Clark indicates that all available cash is being used for the land swaps, although Linz is trying to wring more money out of Treasury for outright purchases.

Jean-Francois and Gwen Taquet like it here. They plan to look after their land. Certainly, some of that land will be well outside the price range of most New Zealanders; it's likely that more foreigners will enjoy the exclusive views from the Crown Range. But making a buck is what it's about.

The Taquets bought their delectable station on December 7, 1999. Taquet says on December 15 that year he was offered the same figure as they paid for it — but in US dollars, doubling the price. A month ago, he got a cash offer for two and a half times what they paid.

Not many in this country will ever afford that. Face it. Once they're sold, they're gone.

A private sex club

2004, *The Dominion Post*: Philip Kitchin investigates the police officers who abused teenager Louise Nicholas.

When I first met Philip Kitchin, I was reminded of one of those gunslingers from an old Western. He had come in from his farm, somewhere in the back country of Hawke's Bay, for an interview. He greeted me with a gritty handshake and a flinty-eyed look, and after a few preliminaries he sat down in front of the camera and answered my questions in a measured drawl, fingering his takeaway coffee like a Colt. The impression of the reluctant lawmaker come to clean up town is reinforced when you look at his work. He's spent a lot of his career investigating crime; first in Hawke's Bay and then, as his reputation has grown, nationwide (Kitchin, 2008).

He didn't seem at the outset to be a promising candidate for a star reporter. His first attempt to get into journalism school, at Wellington's polytechnic, was turned down. But he persisted, and became probably New Zealand's most successful practising investigative reporter on a mainstream newspaper. Like many good investigative reporters, he got the taste for the craft on the police beat, while covering Hawke's Bay for *The Dominion*. There he built up a network of contacts that later helped him turn out local stories with national impact.

In New Zealand, police reporting is often given to younger reporters — a strange practice, since it requires experience and resilience to do it well. Police reporters need the mental toughness to cover grisly accident and crime scenes, the sensitivity to talk to victims and gain their confidence, the shrewdness to know whether criminals and those accused of crime are telling the truth, and the independence of mind to maintain good relationships with the police while also maintaining a healthy scepticism. All police reporters, after they have been in their job for a while and after they've got used to covering the routine stories, such as the car accidents, crime scenes and so on, start to build up contacts. After a few months, or probably a year or two — once they decide the reporter can keep a secret — the contacts may start to tell the reporter the real gossip, the inside stories that are going around. These are the hard stories. They require a lot of digging, and often turn out to be untrue or exaggerated. One difference between a competent beat reporter and a great one is their willingness to risk their time chasing these will-o'-the-wisps, sorting fact from fantasy. But they also need something else: the independence of mind to sometimes cover stories they know that some of their contacts will not like.

A famous study of Canadian police and court reporters described this difference between police reporters, labelling them 'inner-circle' and 'outer-circle' reporters. 'Inner-circle' reporters end up identifying more with the groups they are supposed to be reporting on than with their readers, whereas 'outer-circle' ones manage to retain their independence (Ericson, Baranek, & Chan, 1989). New Zealand, with its tendency to put young reporters into the police round, and perhaps due to its small-town culture, has found it hard to generate reporters who have both the experience and contacts and the independence to become true outer-circle reporters. Perhaps that is one reason why the police force, and its inevitable lapses, have remained a closed shop in New Zealand.

Another reason is the willingness of politicians to give the police protection from media scrutiny. The Police Complaints Authority, which is charged with investigating police misconduct, is one of the few organisations in New Zealand (along with Parliament and the courts) that are exempt from the Official Information Act. Like any large organisation, the police force in New Zealand has had its share of incompetent and occasionally corrupt and criminal staff, but this combination of official protection and news media apathy has meant that the public usually only hears of police misconduct when the police hierarchy chooses to put it before the courts. This unhealthy lack of scrutiny has meant that stories about police misbehaviour are rare in New Zealand; and when they do appear, they have a disproportionate impact on a public encouraged to have unrealistic ideas of what is possible from a large, and ultimately human, organisation.

On the last day in January 2006, *The Dominion Post* led with one such story. 'Police raped me' was the headline. Philip Kitchin's story about Louise Nicholas was the result of years of investigation into a group of police officers who had run their own private sex club. The allegations were harrowing, and the impact no less devastating.

The story of how Philip Kitchin heard about, and eventually broke, the Louise Nicholas stories is best told in the book he and Louise wrote, *Louise Nicholas: My Story* (Nicholas & Kitchin, 2007). It's a classic example of investigative technique — the vague, tantalising, anonymous tip about an unnamed woman, then years of phoning, asking, chasing and digging. Eventually, another tip came from another anonymous, clearly terrified source that mentioned a particular court case. A long battle with an obstructive court official ensued, to obtain access to the records of that case and to find Louise's name. Then came the delicate process of gaining Louise's trust, and the long process of corroborating her story. Finally, dramatically, a sting operation in which Louise wore a concealed microphone and caught her so-called protector, former CIB Chief Inspector John Dewar, in an admission that helped send him to prison.

It is worth noting that it was only after being let down by three statutory bodies — the police, the courts and the Police Complaints Authority — that Louise Nicholas finally agreed to talk to a journalist. It is an important reminder of the fact that journalism can sometimes do what official bodies cannot. It was, in this case, a court of last resort.

Kitchin believes that one reason for the immediate and dramatic government response to the story was because it was the result of a collaboration between television and print; in this case, TVNZ and *The Dominion Post*. Such collaborations are more common now, but in 2006 it was unheard of. Kitchin believes that the combined power of both media gave the story impact that could not be ignored, nor the response delayed. He is very grateful for the backing he had from two courageous news executives — Bill Ralston at TVNZ and Tim Pankhurst at *The Dominion Post* — who took the decision to publish. 'It would have been very easy for them to say let's drop all the names out of this. They backed me.' (Kitchin, 2016).

What makes Kitchin such an effective reporter? First, his tenacity: he is determined to find the truth and is prepared to dig, often for years, until the story is done. He is not afraid of a challenge — where many reporters would write off a potential story because of a lack of evidence, he keeps going until he finds the evidence, or at least proves it isn't there.

Second, his rigorous method — like a good detective, he is not satisfied with one account until it has been verified by another. A former senior police officer who worked on the case, Rex Miller, told me that Kitchin reminded him of a good detective because of his thoroughness in corroboration (Miller, 2009). Kitchin is also fiercely independent — he describes himself as an 'old-fashioned' reporter, in the sense that he prizes detachment and neutrality. This story was a challenge for him because, more than any other, he developed an emotional attachment to one side of the story.

'There were many times doing the story and right the way through where we were . . . crossing the line between old-fashioned investigative journalism and . . . crusading.

'I admire many crusading journalists. There's a place for that in society, but it wasn't a mould that fitted me so I was always trying to avoid that. So it was very unusual to have that experience' (Kitchin, 2016).

He says he tried to deal with this as carefully as he could, but on a story like that it was impossible not to become involved. 'You can't pretend that you are entirely detached. You can try and be as detached as you can, but you are fooling yourself if you think you are. You would have to be a robot' (Kitchin, 2016).

As well as tradecraft, and the mental resilience to persist with stories where others wouldn't, Kitchin's rock-solid personal ethics have enabled him to win the trust of some very vulnerable, frightened people. When he said he would keep a secret, he did. When he said he would never lie to them, he didn't. When he said he would keep them informed every step of the way, he did. It was this demonstration, over a period of time, that he was reliable, honest and independent that gave people such as Louise Nicholas the confidence that it was worth taking the risk of telling their story; that here was a reporter who would not stop until he had found the truth, regardless of who it hurt (Nicholas & Kitchin, 2007).

Lastly, for someone who holds himself to high standards, he has compassion for the downtrodden. Together with a droll sense of humour, this helps him connect with people from all walks of life.

To work at that level, on stories with such high stakes, is mentally very intense. Not only is there the worry of getting things wrong, but the sheer amount and nature of people contact, over several years, becomes draining. 'It's hard to get time away from the phone. Even now, years later, people still ring me [who have had something to do with the story]. It has profoundly affected them, so you have to listen to those people.

'It's a hard job. But it's rewarding' (Kitchin, 2016).

There are many stories of Kitchin's that could sit well in this collection. His exposure of Donna Awatere Huata's fraudulent misuse of public funds was the first time that a serving MP had been convicted of fraud. Again, it was the result of patient detective work, and of gaining the trust of whistleblowers who provided the corroborating evidence needed.

But I believe that this story is his finest work. The example here was published the day the story broke. It is Louise's account of being raped by serving police officers. It was the first of many revelations in this story, as Nicholas's example encouraged many other women to come forward with similar stories. Although brief, the story conveys the vulnerability and helplessness of a young woman being preyed on by men in uniform.

In response, the government announced a Commission of Inquiry into police misconduct, chaired by Dame Margaret Bazley. After taking evidence from many women who alleged abuse, her report was scathing of police culture and led to wide-ranging reforms. It also led to a criminal investigation, which resulted in some of the officers named in the stories being convicted of sexual offences and jailed. Dewar was jailed for four and a half years for obstructing justice, for deliberately derailing the rape trials in which Louise Nicholas was attempting to bring her tormentors to justice.

Above all, this and the other stories that followed led to a wide-ranging debate in New Zealand on sexual abuse. The story of Louise Nicholas showed, in a way that had not been done before, the importance of actual, genuine consent, and what that meant if sex was not to be rape: a victimised person not saying 'No' was not the same thing as a non-victimised person saying 'Yes'.

Just as importantly, Louise Nicholas broke the hidden consensus that rape victims had to be silent. The law in New Zealand gives automatic name suppression to rape victims. One unfortunate side-effect of this well-intentioned law has been to perpetuate a culture of shame and isolation for rape victims. By telling her story, Louise Nicholas showed that she was not ashamed of what had been done to her. Since then, several women have obtained court orders allowing them to waive name suppression and tell their stories.

Kitchin feels that this is the story's lasting impact: the vastly more accepting response from the public to victims of sexual abuse now. 'That is some testament to what we had achieved. If you dig deeper, things are set in stone now.'

Ericson, R., Baranek, P., & Chan, J. (1989). *Negotiating control: A study of news sources*. Toronto: University of Toronto Press.

Kitchin, P. (2008). Interview with author, J. Hollings. [Video recording]. Wellington: Massey University School of Communication, Journalism and Marketing Archive.

Kitchin, P. (2016, December 12). Interview with author, J. Hollings.

Miller, R. (2009). Interview with author, J. Hollings.

Nicholas, L., & Kitchin, P. (2007). *Louise Nicholas: My story*. Auckland: Random House.

'No, I don't want this'
Dominion Post, 31 January 2004

THE woman at the centre of rape allegations against three men including a police assistant commissioner says she knew before they touched her what was about to happen.

The incidents began, she says, in Rotorua when she was walking home from work one day in about 1986.

She alleges Bob Schollum, a former friend of her father, offered her a lift home but instead took her to a house she had never been to before. Louise Nicholas says she recognised Clint Rickards and Brad Shipton at the house but did not know a fourth man wearing a police shirt but mufti trousers.

"The next thing I can recall about this incident is being in a bedroom . . . the room was dull, possibly because the curtains were closed, but I could still clearly identify the people who were in the room with me. Schollum and Shipton were wearing shorts but I'm not sure what Rickards was wearing.

"I protested vigorously about being in the room with them because I knew what was about to happen. I was saying, 'No, I don't want this, guys.' I remember pleading more with Schollum because I knew him better. All three started to abuse me sexually . . . all three had intercourse with me."

Mrs Nicholas said Mr Shipton brought out a wooden police baton and she protested, saying, "No way."

She says the baton was put into her anus while she was made to perform oral sex.

"It was so painful. I remember saying, 'No more, no more,' and rolling away.

I picked my clothes up off the floor and Schollum told me to go and have a shower, which I did."

Mrs Nicholas says she cried as she was driven home and Mr Schollum said, "I'm sorry, Lou," when she was dropped off at her nearby flat.

She did not tell anyone about the incident at the time because "I felt no one would believe me because they were police officers."

She said: "It was around this time that Rickards and Shipton from time to time would call around to my house uninvited. They would insist on having sex with me . . . the sex would occur on the floor in the lounge and it was usually two on one . . . they wanted me to perform indecent acts on them.

"The lounge had big French doors with net curtains. You could see out the French doors but people could not see into the lounge because of the curtains. There was a clear view of the driveway and anyone approaching from outside.

"They would normally drop their trousers and remove any lower garments I was wearing. I never physically undressed them or myself.

"There was never an occasion when they visited and didn't insist on having sex. The sex was the only reason they were coming around and it was not at my invitation.

"As soon as I saw these two on my doorstep my heart skipped a beat and I would think to myself, 'Here we go again.' I never ever gave any consent to any of these people. It was always taken for granted."

Mrs Nicholas says she tried complaining about the three police officers to Trevor Clayton, a policeman she knew through her family and whom she hoped might persuade his colleagues to leave her alone.

Mr Clayton, who subsequently left the police, died last year.

"He knew all about it because I did tell him . . . he was a good mate of my brother's."

In a record of an interview made during an investigation of Mrs Nicholas' complaints, Mr Clayton admitted doing nothing about her allegations, and being prepared to lie about her in court, in order to protect his "mates".

Mrs Nicholas said that, once she met her husband and began a relationship with him, the visits stopped.

The Dominion Post asked her why people should believe that she was raped on several different occasions when she had not fought, run or made a formal complaint at the time.

She said she did complain to police [to Mr Clayton], and to the alleged rapists. "I would say to them, 'No. C'mon guys, just no. I don't want it. Just don't.'

"It meant nothing. It just went in one ear and out the other — if in fact it got that far."

She says the authority and power of the police intimidated her and, when she complained, she was told no one would prefer her word to a police officer's.

"Sure, I didn't scream and I didn't fight and I didn't do what people would think you should do.

"I was shit-scared. And I don't know how else I can explain it. You just go . . .

you just fold into yourself when all these things are happening. You are not even there. You just go away from your body and you are just not even there. You just close your eyes and think of other things."

CHAPTER TWENTY-ONE

The big lie

2005: Nicky Hager reveals the cynical electioneering behind the National Party's race-based election campaign strategy.

Nicky Hager's house is perched on the slope of one of those impossibly steep Wellington hillsides. You get to it down a path and then a long flight of steps. Way down, in a shroud of native trees, there it is — a small, two-storey wooden dwelling, nestled into the side of the hill. He told me, with some pride, that he built it himself, on a platform chiselled out of the hard Wellington greywacke. There's no way to get a digger down, so he dug it out himself, by hand. It took him six months (Hager, 2009). Most people would have chosen an easier site to build their first house. Not Nicky. Where others see insurmountable difficulty, he just sees an intriguing problem.

He's taken the same approach to journalism. If anyone tries to tell you that the only way to become an investigative journalist is through years pounding the streets as a reporter on a newspaper or radio or television, go and see Nicky Hager. The way in which he taught himself to become one of the country's most penetrating investigators without ever setting foot in a newsroom is the exception that proves the rule that a professional education is the best route to excellence. He is a classic example of the New Zealand do-it-yourself 'number eight' ethic — the notion that a good keen man or woman equipped with a piece of number 8 wire can tackle just about anything.

Hager was born in New Zealand, the son of Jewish refugees who fled Vienna when the Nazis took over. Within a few years of arriving in New Zealand, the Hagers had created a successful textile manufacturing business, run on socialist lines, in Levin. With many of their family in Europe devoured by the Holocaust, Hager inherited their passion for social justice and their belief that a democratic society requires its members to exercise constant vigilance.

And he, more than any other journalist in New Zealand, has kept vigil over those who are supposed to be watching on our behalf. His tenacity and industry has produced a body of work that has made him New Zealand's best-known investigative journalist. His first investigation, *Secret Power* (1996), was into the Echelon spy network run by the so-called Five Eyes — the UK, US, Canada, Australia and New Zealand. It was the first detailed description of that network, and in particular the extent to which it was collecting and sharing intelligence, at a much greater level than previously known. Former Prime Minister David Lange wrote in a foreword to the book that some of its contents were an unpleasant surprise to him (Hager, 1996).

Several significant investigations followed, into a government-backed spying and black propaganda campaign against conservation groups (*Secrets and Lies*, 1999), and then into a cover-up of the introduction into New Zealand of genetically engineered seeds (*Seeds of Distrust*, 2002). In 2011, in *Other People's Wars*, Hager turned to the long-running and under-reported role of New Zealand in the war in Afghanistan.

Hager's best work is classic empirical research. He observes, drawing on intuition to find a topic; usually something that he finds curious, or surprising. Then, in his own phrase, he 'becomes an expert', finding out everything he can, before getting down to analysing his data and inducing a theory. His strengths as a reporter are his patience, the capacity of his mind for detail and his naturally scientific approach, combined with strong personal ethics that have enabled him to build trusting relationships with sources from all sections of the political spectrum.

Hager is motivated by a strong sense of social justice, something he says he got from his parents and their parents before them. But it's not just that which drives him — he genuinely enjoys the work. 'I love research. It's a game for me — the research is the fun part of the work — and the harder the better' (Hager, 2016).

Of his earlier work, two investigations with undeniable impact are *Secret Power* and *The Hollow Men* (Hager, 2005). *Secret Power* foreshadowed the revelations of the mass surveillance by Wikileaks and Edward Snowden. It spurred the European Parliament to hold an inquiry into the Echelon network (Hager, 2009).

But as an exposé of the behind-the-scenes tricks of an election campaign, this chapter from *The Hollow Men* is the more gripping read. Published in 2005, just before one of the dirtiest, most cynical election campaigns New Zealand had ever seen, *The Hollow Men* helped finish off the electoral hopes of Don Brash, the arch-conservative who had recently become leader of New Zealand's mainstream conservative party, the National Party. Backed by a secretive group of rich neoconservatives, Brash's team resorted to an array of sordid tactics and murky dealings to try to sway voters. These included a secret pact with an extreme religious sect, the Exclusive Brethren, which mounted an advertising campaign on National's behalf. To the embarrassment of many in the party, it also played the race card, in a cynical attempt to whip up fear and paranoia about Māori special privileges. One particularly vile example was the creation of billboards that suggested Māori would soon close public beaches to non-Māori.

It was the notorious Orewa speech, delivered in the summer of 2004, for which the campaign will most be remembered. In that speech, which engendered a surge in popularity that very nearly put him into power, Brash professed to be genuinely worried about a creeping Māori takeover, by a privileged minority with 'a birthright to the upper hand', with 'greater civil, political [and] democratic rights . . . than any other New Zealander' (Hager, 2005, p. 88). As this chapter reveals, through leaked emails from inside the Brash machine, it was a speech based on what could be described as a calculated and cynical plan to appeal to the dark side of New Zealand politics. Once the darker side of Brash's strategy was revealed, through Hager's reporting, any credit that Brash retained with the more mainstream elements in New Zealand society was lost. Shortly after he lost the election, he resigned as National Party leader and the party returned to a policy of trying to build consensus on Māori and Treaty issues.

Hager, N. (1996). *Secret power: New Zealand's role in the international spy network*. Nelson: Craig Potton.

Hager, N. (2009). Interview with author, J. Hollings.

Hager, N. (2005). *The hollow men: A study in the politics of deception*. Nelson: Craig Potton.

Hager, N. (2016). Interview with author, J. Hollings.

The big splash at Orewa: The strategies behind the speech

The Hollow Men: A study in the politics of deception, by Nicky Hager, published by Craig Potton Publishing, 2005.

Brash and his advisers decided that his first major speech as leader, timed for 27 January 2004 at the Orewa Rotary Club, would be about 'racial separatism'. It was not a cautious address. It presented a highly negative version of Maori history, questioned the very idea of being Maori and characterised political consultation with Maori as a 'deeply corrupt' process that 'allows people to invent or rediscover beliefs for pecuniary gain'. Most powerfully, he aroused feelings of resentment and envy by describing a greedy 'grievance industry' in which 'the minority has a birthright to the upper hand', and vowed to put an end to 'special privilege' for Maori.

The speech is now remembered not so much for its content as for the extraordinary effect it had on National's poll results. After a long period stuck in the low 20s, the party's support leapt to about 45 per cent. The wave of emotion that drove up the polls lasted only a few months, but that one speech put Brash and National in a position where they were seriously challenging the Labour-led government and within reach of winning the 2005 election.

Brash was immediately branded as a racist by his opponents and likened to Australian Pauline Hanson and her One Nation party. But Brash was not driven by racism. The speech marks his descent into unprincipled politics because of the motives and political calculation that lay behind the decision to make that sort of speech at that time.

Publicly, Brash claimed to have noble motives. 'In many ways,' he said, 'I am deeply saddened to have to make a speech about issues of race.' But 'I believe in plain speaking' and the risk of 'disaster' had required him to be 'blunt'.[1] Was it a courageous speech, as Brash's supporters claimed, or was he just cynically playing the race card to capture voters off other parties, as his detractors argued? That question can now be answered. The internal National Party communications before and after the speech give a clear picture of what was in the minds of the people responsible.

It was no surprise that Maori rights were on the agenda in early 2004. Controversy was still raging over the foreshore and seabed issue, which had been sparked by a Court of Appeal decision allowing Maori organisations to make claims over coastal waters and shorelines and continued when the government introduced and passed legislation restricting those rights. Brash became National Party leader when the topic was hot. Much of his initial advice on this subject came from freelance speech writer and strategist Matthew Hooton.

A few days after the leadership vote, Hooton sent Brash a five-page communications strategy plan entitled 'Internal vs External Audiences'. . . . Hooton argued that people who identify themselves as left or right 'are the most interesting people to share dinner with, but they are not important to us politically, because they vote one way or the other. The people who count would be described by a political scientist as "centre".' The paper, which described how Brash could appeal to these centre voters, is an excellent example of the thought process of a Beehive spin doctor. Hooton summarised his plan as:

- Keep the [right-wing] base happy, but do this below the threshold, with nods and winks, and private functions . . .
- In association with the wider base, unify the party at all costs.
- Use the highest-possible quality research to identify potential groups (eg, superannuitants) who could switch votes, what they think about you, and what they want to see from you.
- When developing strategy, appointing an office, communicating — in everything you do — be informed by the need to reach across the divide and touch base with the audiences identified from research.
- Be surprising but not confusing.
- Buy some light-blue shirts![2]

A couple of days later Hooton elaborated on the 'be surprising' part. His paper had used the example of George W. Bush inviting Muslim clerics to the White House, noting that no one thought Bush had gone soft on Muslims but that it seemed intriguing and attracted media attention. He suggested that Brash could do something similar by engaging constructively with Maori.

According to Hooton's plan, which was very different from the subsequent aggressive strategy behind the Orewa speech, 'the surprise comes from constitutional/Treaty/Maori issues'. The idea was to surprise and interest the public by National responding sympathetically to Maori concerns about the foreshore and seabed. 'If we can surprise everyone on these issues,' Hooton argued, 'we will:

>Eliminate perceptions Don is only about economics
>Eliminate perceptions Don is hard right
>Surprise urban liberals and make them consider us
>Pick up conservative Maori votes, and
>MOST IMPORTANTLY put the shits up Labour and force them into a more radical 'pro' Maori position and pick up red neck votes as well.'[3]

Hooton's advice was born of political manoeuvring more than strong principle — how to use the issue to Brash and National's advantage — but it was also much more in accord with the traditional National Party approach to Maori matters than the final Orewa speech would be. Later that week Hooton spelt out the case against a more confrontational approach, unknowingly anticipating some of the flaws in the Orewa speech. 'Be very careful with the use of "separatism". What does it mean? Are you really against Maori communities in the Far North from being able to run the local school based on Maori culture? No? What about health clinics in Kaeo? No? What about a Maori ONLY private boarding school getting vouchers? Maybe. But it seems to me you can't be for devolved delivery of social services and community autonomy and against "separatism", whatever that means in a modern context.'[4]

. . .

He offered to discuss these ideas with Brash in more detail.[5] . . .

In late November 2003 Hooton gave Brash another piece of advice that was highly relevant to the decisions that followed. After Brash became leader National's opinion poll results had risen, then sunk again in the following weeks during messy struggles over the deputy leader position. Hooton had some undeniably sound advice for Brash on the link between poll results and his ability to control the caucus and thus National Party strategy.[6]

. . . '[If] you don't take big bold moves based on leadership preference, you'll go down in the polls and won't be able to take any initiatives in future. You'll become a prisoner of the caucus. I figure you have the next few weeks to establish which one it will be.' The Orewa speech, which [Peter] Keenan began work on shortly after, would be a perfect example of a big, bold move that would establish Brash's control over the leadership and party.[7]

[Bryan] Sinclair wrote to Brash and Keenan, who had just arrived in the office, saying he agreed with Hooton.[8] . . . Keenan replied that he could draft a 'good speech' and 'have it delivered at whatever opportunity is the highest profile'.[9] Brash responded: 'Thanks guys. We need to review communications strategy soon, perhaps on Monday morning.'[10]

At this stage, early December 2003, there was still no hint of plans for a confrontational stand on Maori issues. This is clear from a Brash email on 5 December, where he reacted to New Zealand First leader Winston Peters circulating a leaflet critical of Asian immigrants. Earlier that day Richard Long had emailed Brash about Maori television, urging him to be more aggressive: 'You need to get a little more populist on some of these issues, even controllably angry. If we make our policies too bland . . . we are not going to get traction.' But that evening Brash emailed his closest staff and several National MPs about Peters exploiting racism for political gain, exclaiming 'Peters is a totally cynical politician of the worst kind'. They should find arguments to attack Peters and 'expose his total cynicism'. 'Might it cost us votes? Possibly, but I don't want the votes of the totally bigoted . . . that is what Peters is trying to attract.'[11]

In mid-November the *National Business Review* had reported 'Brash lifts National's hopes with strong party-vote poll'.[12] *NBR* owner Barry Colman had sent the poll results to Brash the day before with a note saying, 'This is the shot in the arm we've all been praying for'.[13] But the following month's *NBR* poll showed National dropping.[14] . . .

. . .

That morning Peter Keenan sent a briefing note to Brash about the poll. 'What is the message from the NBR Poll?' he wrote. 'Basically the Peters immigration stunt.' . . . Keenan argued, however, that the shift [to New Zealand First] would 'not [be] enduring if we react appropriately'.[15]

This note contained the first suggestion that they might use the Orewa speech to counter Peters. Referring to the New Zealand First leader's successful exploitation of the immigration issue, Keenan said, 'There is no quick fix on this; we will always be vulnerable to Peters on these issues until we can credibly position National as being aware of and concerned about these issues. We can include some of this in the Orewa speech.'[16]

Bryan Sinclair replied to Keenan's note agreeing with 'the analysis of the NBR story' but stressing . . . '[the] party's prospects are very much linked to Don Brash. The vote is won on the stage not in the backroom. That's what moves public perception. It's like New Zealand First — that issue was a Peters-based issue. No issue National is plugging at the moment is a Brash-based issue. . . . Don is being painted as lacklustre and unfortunately this is the feedback that he's getting from those close to him outside of this place. This public perception will concern him greatly, particularly when it's even started coming from our "friends".'[17]

Keenan emailed back to Sinclair [that] ' . . . It would be great to have a big issue', . . . or to 'manufacture one like Peters', and he concluded that 'the only real prospect is the Foreshore issue'.[19]

The next day, 13 December, a Saturday, Keenan wrote a long email to Brash on the subject, headed 'Some thoughts re a speech on the foreshore'. 'Don,' it began, 'I know all sorts of people are pressuring you to get up and make some strong statements on the foreshore, or any other issue, to keep some profile, maintain momentum etc etc. Sometimes I feel we are surrounded by panic merchants. They need to get a grip.'

He pointed out that the fortnight before Christmas was a hopeless time for Brash to gain public attention. . . . 'So, thinking about the time to make a speech that would make a big splash, the Orewa one is probably the best time. It will come after a summer with demonstrations on beaches, so that should set it up well. To be done well, this sort of speech needs some serious time to work on — it needs to have an elevated tone, not day-to-day politics. If we knocked up something in the next few days it would not be very good, and would be lost in the noise of politics and Xmas in any case.

'What I have in mind,' he concluded, 'is a major speech on race relations in this country, dealing also with the immigration issues that Peters has manipulated, delivered at Orewa.'[21] Since Brash's election as leader, his staff had been identifying the need to target the approximately 15 per cent of centre-right parliamentary seats held by the New Zealand First and United Future parties.[22] This had become more urgent with support moving in the other direction.

Brash deferred to Keenan's advice on timing. 'Peter, thanks for that sober reflection. Certainly there are a number of my colleagues urging that we "MUST" raise National's/DTB's [Brash's initials] profile before everybody heads off to their barbecues. And I have some sympathy with that view. But you may well be right. Let's work on the assumption that we will not do a big speech on race issues pre Christmas.'[23] Keenan began work on the 'major speech on race relations' for delivery in January.

The 'elevated' tone Keenan planned for Orewa might not sound much like what eventuated, a speech that National Party historian Barry Gustafson would describe tactfully as 'oversimplifying and polarising the issue of the Treaty and the place of Maori'.[24] But remember that Keenan had a particularly cynical attitude to the public. This is the man who quoted with approval United States Republican strategist David Horowitz: 'Political war is about evoking emotions that favour one's goals. It is the ability to manipulate the public's feelings in support of your agenda.' In this war, he argued, 'the most potent weapons' were anger, fear and resentment.[25] . . .

The change from Hooton to Keenan advice on race issues is evident shortly after the big-splash email, when Hooton contacted Brash with his latest strategy idea on 15 December 2003 after public criticism of the government's foreshore and seabed plans that morning by the 'powerful iwi Nga Puhi and Ngai Tahu'. He proposed a Brash media statement attacking Deputy Prime Minister Michael Cullen's 'mishandling of the issue', including the message that 'You don't tell iwi leaders that their most cherished beliefs are worthless, as Dr Cullen is reported to have done'.

Hooton suggested that Brash note that 'National's experience with aboriginal rights and Treaty issues under Prime Minister Jim Bolger and Treaty Minister Sir Douglas Graham in the 1990s had taught it the importance of maintaining an open mind and treating all involved with respect. The goal had to be to find innovative solutions that met the expectations of all New Zealanders, Maori and non-Maori.' He proposed that Brash say, 'There is no room for smugness and poll-driven politics on an issue that is about our history and our future.'[26]

Until now Brash had been reasonably receptive to similar advice from Hooton. But things had changed. When Hooton wrote this draft press release it was just three days since the *NBR* poll that had shown National Party support dropping. Poll-driven politics was at the front of their minds. Brash politely declined Hooton's suggestions. . . . 'As I mentioned on the phone last night,' Brash said in an email, 'I don't see how we can exploit the divisions in the Labour Caucus without running a big risk of offending our traditional non-Maori supporters.'[27] . . .

In a follow-up email to Brash on 13 December, Keenan cemented his strategy dominance. He gave qualified support to Sinclair. . . . He was scathing, however, about Hooton. 'By the way, frankly, I think Matthew Hooton is an idiot. I had a long chat with him and his wife (she seemed much more sensible) and Bryan. Matthew is totally full of himself, and not half as good as his own self-image. He tries hard to impress, with over-the-top enthusiasm — an actor. He would be massively disruptive around here.'[29] For months Hooton had been writing Brash's speeches and advising him almost daily on media and tactics. But these comments appear to have been the end of his prospects of getting a full-time job in the leader's office, and also the end of the less aggressive approach to Maori issues.

From this point on, a small group of close Brash allies worked on the Orewa speech. The change of direction over race relations was not shared with the wider caucus until just before delivery. Keenan prepared the first draft, which was more strident than the final speech. Then he passed it to Brash's friend Michael Bassett, who had long held bitter and angry views about Maori history and Treaty issues, which he wove into the speech. MP Murray McCully, another with strong opinions about Maori issues, also reportedly had input.[30] Brash would later name other people as being involved, but they were consulted at the last minute, and were not architects of the speech.

Back in 2002 when Brash was campaigning for Parliament he had made some populist public statements about Maori issues, using the ACT Party's language about a Treaty 'gravy train'.[31] But as he pursued the party leadership he had adopted a much softer line. . . .

In his first speech as leader, Brash had said that National was proud of its record in Maori development. 'In the 1990s, we promoted Maori self-management in education, health and social policy, just as we encouraged other communities to have more say in their schools, and their health and other services.'[33] In the Orewa speech only weeks later Brash would attack these Maori services as being 'separatist' and 'special privileges' and declare 'there can be no basis for government funding based on race'.[34]

A Wellington PR company client newsletter written in November 2003 by television producer Richard Harman had discussed precisely the tactics that the Orewa speech would employ. Under the title 'Dog Whistling, a handy tool for aspiring leaders', it advised: 'Dr Brash's tactics must be to win as much of the Winston Peters vote as he can without doing a Bill English and losing

National's core vote in the process. This is where some "dog whistling" could come in handy.'[35] Dog whistle politics is the term associated with Australian prime minister John Howard and his appeal to so-called blue-collar voters on anti-immigration and race issues. It refers to political actions and rhetoric that, while superficially appearing reasonable, contain language, claims and racial stereotypes designed to excite the prejudices of certain target audiences, in the same way that dogs will react to a high-pitched whistle that humans cannot hear.

Brash's advisers had decided that he needed to be seen 'on the front foot showing strong leadership on something in the next few weeks' so they made very sure that the Orewa speech would have maximum impact. National's media staff talked up the speech in the weeks before delivery, promising a 'stinging attack' on the government's policies, 'more trenchant' in its criticism than Bill English had ever been.[36] Deputy leader Gerry Brownlee would say later that a key reason for the speech's success had been 'conditioning work' to fire up the media in advance.[37] . . . As a result there was a large crowd of journalists present on the day to hear the most explosive speech in New Zealand's recent political history.

The initial media reaction to the speech was cautious, almost shocked, with headlines like 'Brash's risky Maori strategy'[38] and editorials questioning its divisive style. But the dog whistle had worked. Within days the headlines changed to 'Readers back Brash speech' and 'Strong support for Brash's race relations speech'.[39] The greatest impact was exactly where they had been aiming: low- to medium-income men and the elderly. After years trailing Labour badly in the polls, this one speech catapulted National into the lead.

The speech had been skilfully worded to evoke the Horowitz feelings of anger, fear and resentment. Anger was encouraged by painting Maori as 'mischievous minds' who interpreted the Treaty of Waitangi to 'suit their financial purposes' and 'invent or rediscover beliefs for pecuniary gain'. Fear was evoked using a negative picture of 'conflict', 'corruption', 'stand-over tactics' and 'tragedy' — and by promoting a sense that 'non-Maori' New Zealanders were somehow becoming second-class citizens in their own land. Resentment was fanned by talk of a privileged minority with 'a birthright to the upper hand', who had 'greater civil, political [and] democratic rights . . . than any other New Zealander' and 'power to veto' development projects 'which could provide us all with jobs'. 'Non-Maori' who supported 'the Maori cause' were a treacherous 'fifth column'.

It is not hard to see how these words could raise feelings of injustice and envy in people who were not wealthy and powerful themselves. Although the 5000-word speech covered many issues, the part that resonated with the most people and was remembered longest was the idea that Maori were enjoying special race-based privileges — an idea that grates in a society that sees itself as egalitarian. Because the message was coming from the respectable Dr Brash, it was easy for people to forget, at least temporarily, all the competing evidence telling them that privilege and wealth are located elsewhere in our society. . . . It was a classic exercise in manipulating the feelings of the 'political middle ground'.[40]

To avoid going too far or leaving Brash open to accusations of racism, Keenan and Bassett peppered the speech with a few uplifting statements and legitimate challenges to conventional thinking: 'The indigenous culture of New Zealand will always have a special place in our emerging culture and will be cherished for that reason'.[41] . . . But each positive comment was like a drawing of breath before the next attack.

Keenan had explained the thinking behind this style in an email to Richard Long. 'I think it is essential that every time we talk tough on [Maori] issues, we also run hard with a compassionate line — otherwise we fail the political hygiene test.'[42] This concept came from a British Conservative politician, Robert Darwell, whose writing on this subject had been sent to Don Brash by Ruth Richardson shortly before.[43] Darwell argued that the way to stop the public feeling uncomfortable with radical policies that might harm disadvantaged people was to 'over-compensate' by sounding concerned and wanting the best for those people.[44] The positive elements provide political cover; the negative bits are what most listeners remember.

And the speech was overwhelmingly negative. Business journalist Rod Oram took issue with the argument that there were 'widespread [Treaty] abuses starting to destroy the country' and concluded that Brash's view was wrong on four counts.

> First, the [abuses] are exceptions, not the rule; second, they are
> not confined to Maori (Pakeha are just as capable, for example, of
> exploiting the Resource Management Act to extract compensation
> from their neighbours or to stop a competitor's project); third,
> junking the Treaty, as he advocates, once historic grievances are
> settled, would make a mockery of the settlement process. Fourth,
> the view of Maori — as expressed in his speech — was disparaging
> about Maori behaviour and values. Literally, only one sentence in
> a 10-page speech had anything positive to say about recent Maori
> economic, cultural, social and political progress.[45] . . .
>
> . . .

Having generated public reaction and outrage from the subject of race-based privilege, Brash's staff found themselves being asked by journalists for evidence and examples of the supposed widespread abuses. . . . Instead, the internal communications show them urgently trying to bat the enquiries away. The power of the speech had come from emotional lever pulling and button pushing, not factual accuracy. As soon as the media started asking about the facts, the staff started dodging and ducking.

For instance, a couple of weeks after the speech, Brash's media staff received an email from *New Zealand Herald* reporter Ruth Berry who was writing a backgrounder on 'race-based funding'. She asked National to say what it meant by this term and to name the top ten examples of race-based funding which it would prevent. Instead of being pleased, Richard Long was immediately defensive. He forwarded her email to Peter Keenan and Murray McCully saying, 'Can you confer? We need to come up with a credible holding answer for these, that will avoid "National gone to ground and can't answer" type articles. . . .'

Long proposed that they say the information was not yet ready or available — 'Something along the lines of this week we commissioned the first in what could be a series of professional reviews of legislation to judge the full extent of the infiltration and what needs to be done to remove/correct etc. This will not be hurried and we are not prepared to address this in a piecemeal fashion.'[48]

. . .

The next day press officer Jason Ede drafted a reply to Berry saying that it was hard to 'disentangle' race-based from needs-based funding and it would take a National government its 'first year or two' to do so. Ede also tried to shift onto more defensible ground: 'there are areas where race-based funding might be acceptable', such as Maori teacher training. This directly contradicted Brash's black and white stand in the Orewa speech: 'There can be no basis for special privileges for any race, no basis for government funding based on race'. Ede said, 'The reality is that there are examples all along the spectrum: from clearly unjustified, through the merely debatable, to those that are justified and effective programmes.'

. . .

Murray McCully subsequently took over, writing to Berry: 'Ruth, No, I can't provide detailed responses on the issues you have raised. Two weeks ago, Don Brash made a speech which will shape the direction of our policy for the next election. But being very thorough people, it is normally our practice to spend more than two weeks going through a consultative and deliberative process before announcing policy.'[51] Richard Long, pleased with McCully's response, sent it to all Brash's staff to use. 'Attached is a reasonable response we can make to the nitpickers demanding instant detailed policy answers from us,' he wrote.[52]

After the staff had wriggled out of that one, Brash was broadcast on TV One that very evening trying to throw more fuel on the race-based privilege fire. His example this time was universities providing access quotas for Maori medical and law students, which, he suggested, resulted in their being not properly qualified and competent for these jobs. Like the other claims, this sounded initially convincing. Then the universities replied that quotas are common — for instance for mature and rural students — and that all Maori students had to pass exactly the same exams as other students from entry to graduation. The standard of Maori degrees was exactly the same as others.

Rather than back down, the National media staff came up with a clever answer to deal with media calls the next day. 'Don's comments on TV One,' Jason Ede wrote as a guide, 'were related to perception.' The Maori quota had 'the potential to leave the perception among non-Maori that Maori students have favourable treatment and may be less qualified'.[53] Ede seemed to have forgotten his own statement days earlier that some race-based programmes were 'justified and effective', for instance where Maori teachers were needed — which sounds very like the point of quotas for Maori doctors and lawyers.

. . .

Long had written to Brash advising him how to handle the Maori quota subject in future. 'When questioned, as you will be, about the education comment,' he said, 'you should explain that you were basically talking about perceptions.' It might be 'a good idea . . . to slip into example/anecdote mode . . . that came across well in the NZ Herald today. . . .'[57] . . . [Brash] could be seen following this advice in subsequent interviews, often using the same anecdote over and over and, when challenged about inciting prejudice, claiming he was discussing only perceptions.[59]

This ignored the obvious point that Brash himself was helping to create the perceptions by repeatedly raising the issues and by choosing unrepresentative and inflammatory anecdotes. The idea of Maori having special privileges had always been at best exaggerated and at worst malicious.

Having written the Orewa speech, created the big splash and reaped the poll rise, Keenan confided during the election year that 'I hate the "race based privilege" line'. National was still milking the 'end race-based privilege' slogan, which was one of six main election messages selected for endless repetition. But Keenan told Sinclair he thought this was 'ludicrous when Maori are largely at the bottom of the heap'.[60]

Keenan seems to have been admitting that, when all the 'elevated' rhetoric was stripped away, the speech he drafted was based in part on an unpleasant lie. Brash had told his well-heeled Orewa audience that much of the 'non-Maori' tolerance for the Treaty settlement process was based on a 'perception of relative Maori poverty'. In other words, he was denying that many Maori were at the 'bottom of the heap' . . .

There was no shortage of research to inform Brash and Keenan of the facts. For instance, three studies by the University of Otago's Wellington School of Medicine and Health Sciences plotted how differences between Maori and Pakeha health and life expectancy diverged dramatically from the early 1980s. The 'clear and disturbing' results showed that at the end of two decades of diverging incomes there was a ten-year difference in life expectancy, whereas in the 1960s and 1970s they had been getting closer.[62]

The Orewa argument about Maori poverty — coming from Keenan, Bassett and Brash — was particularly distasteful because this poverty increased dramatically in the 1980s and 1990s as a result of the free market reforms championed by them and their colleagues.

. . .

The morning after delivering the Orewa speech, Brash was interviewed for a television documentary. The programme recorded his discomfort about whether he had written the speech himself. 'I don't have any regret at all about the content of the speech,' he said. 'I looked at it very carefully. I read it, of course. Wrote it.'[63] The missing 'I' was telling.

Once the Orewa speech's claims about race-based privilege were firmly planted in the public mind, Brash was willing to admit that this potent argument did not actually amount to much financial benefit for Maori. He told *Mana News* reporter Carol Archie: 'I don't think the financial benefits to Maori from having funding formula based on race, not need, are enormous at all. And I never suggested they were. I just think they are very damaging, indeed, to race relations in New Zealand.'[64]

By then Brash was riding high and, at least for the audiences he was targeting, he had already won the point. . . .

Brash had spoken of being 'deeply saddened' at having to speak about 'issues of race', but now his mood was more one of elation. He wrote to Matthew Hooton two days after Orewa: 'The speech got a fantastic reception — better than I dared hope.'[66] . . . 'As Hirohito [Japanese emperor during the Second World war] might have said, the war is not going quite as well for Labour as the PM might have hoped!'[68]

Columnist Jane Clifton described other National MPs strutting in Parliament, 'engorged' by the high poll ratings. Deputy leader Gerry Brownlee got carried away and called one Maori MP a 'black fella'. Brash's staff used facetious kia oras to each other in their emails and after a protester hit Brash with mud during the February Waitangi Day celebrations Bryan Sinclair joked, 'Hahaha, I was in disguise'.[69] The then National Party senior whip, John Carter, was captured on a television documentary telling Brash that the mud-throwing incident should be worth a good three or four points in the polls.[70] National staff and MPs appeared far more interested in their political achievement than in the supposedly grave and pressing issues that had required the painful but necessary 'plain speaking'.

. . .

After the election the Orewa policies were challenged from within the National Party. Only two weeks after the votes were counted, MP Bill English gave a speech at Auckland University about 'Treatyology' that advocated a 'more constructive way ahead' than one constrained by rigid 'ideological advocacy'. The language of blame, debt, separation and guilt, he said, needed to be replaced by a new language built on the foundation of justice. No one doubted he was talking about Brash's Orewa speech.

At the same time a group was formed called Nationals for the Treaty. The spokesperson, National's Waitakere branch treasurer Michael Kidd, said many National members were concerned about the party's stance. . . . The group aimed to return to the party's roots of working co-operatively with Maori.[71] National Party historian Barry Gustafson, commenting on the new group, said that National's race policies during the 2005 election campaign had been the work of the 'radical right'. 'From time to time, the more free market ideologically driven radical right manages to seize control' of the National Party, and this had been one of those times.[72] By then, for most New Zealanders, the Orewa themes that had seemed so urgent and important in January 2004 now seemed extreme and negative. The fever had passed.

1. Don Brash, 'Nationhood', address to the Orewa Rotary Club, 27 January 2004.

2. Matthew Hooton, 'Internal vs External Audiences', 1 November 2003.

3. Matthew Hooton, email to Bryan Sinclair (for Don Brash), 3 November 2003.

4. Matthew Hooton, email to Bryan Sinclair (for Don Brash), 5 November 2003.

5. Ibid.

6. Matthew Hooton, email to Don Brash, 25 November 2003.

7. Ibid. Hooton also advised that 'in taking initiatives . . . you should however inform (note, inform not consult) the front bench and others with an interest in the issue'. Brash followed this advice. His caucus colleagues had no say on the policies in the Orewa speech and were informed of it only a few days before.

8. Bryan Sinclair, email to Peter Keenan and Don Brash, 25 November 2003.

9. Peter Keenan, email to Don Brash, 25 November 2003.

10. Don Brash, email to Peter Keenan and Bryan Sinclair, 29 November 2003.

11. Don Brash, email to Peter Keenan, Bryan Sinclair, Wayne Mapp, Pansy Wong, Richard Long, Murray McCully and Gerry Brownlee, 5 December 2003.

12. 'Brash lifts National's hopes with strong party-vote poll', Graeme Hunt, *National Business Review*, 14 November 2003.

13. Barry Colman, email to Don Brash, 13 November 2003.

14. 'Poll bashes Brash', Nick Smith, *National Business Review*, 12 December 2003.

15. Peter Keenan, 'NBR Poll', 12 December 2003.

16. Ibid.

17. Bryan Sinclair, email to Peter Keenan, 12 December 2003.

18. Peter Keenan, email to Bryan Sinclair, 12 December 2003.

19. Ibid.

20. Peter Keenan, email to Don Brash, 13 December 2003.

21. Ibid.

22. For example: 'I do believe that we need to do some focus groups on what middle NZ (I'm talking United, Don't knows and NZ First) think about Don's strengths and weaknesses.' (Bryan Sinclair, email to Matthew Hooton, 3 November 2003.)

23. Don Brash, email to Peter Keenan, 13 December 2003.

24. Barry Gustafson, interviewed by Simon Pound on 95bFM Radio, 29 September 2005.

25. Peter Keenan, email to Anne Small, 3 November 2003.

26. Matthew Hooton, email to Don Brash and draft press release, 15 December 2003.

27. Don Brash, email to Matthew Hooton, 15 December 2003.

28. Matthew Hooton, email to Bryan Sinclair, 17 December 2003.

29. Peter Keenan, email to Don Brash, 13 December 2003.

30. 'I have a nightmare', Gilbert Wong, *Metro*, April 2004.

31. 'Brash serves up a portion of politics at business breakfast', Simon O'Rourke, *Daily News*, 20 June 2002.

32. Don Brash, 'A Nation in Peril', address to the ACT Upper South Island Regional Conference, Christchurch, 27 September 2003.

33. Don Brash, address to the New Zealand Chamber of Commerce Annual Conference, Hamilton, 8 November, 2003.

34. Don Brash, 'Nationhood'.

35. 'Dog Whistling, a handy tool for aspiring leaders', Richard Harman, Political Update, Busby, Ramshaw Grice, 11 November 2003.

36. 'Brash ready to come out swinging', John Armstrong, *New Zealand Herald*, 17 January 2004.

37. Gerry Brownlee, email to Don Brash, 8 November 2004.

38. 'Brash's risky Maori strategy', Colin Espiner, *Press*, 28 January 2004.

39. 'Readers back Brash speech', *Dominion Post*, 30 January 2004; 'Strong support for Brash's race relations speech', Colin Espiner and Tim Hume, *Press*, 31 January 2004.

40. Two good analyses of the speech are Gilbert Wong, 'I have a nightmare' and Jon Johansson, 'Orewa and the Rhetoric of Illusion', *Political Science*, Vol. 56, No. 2, Victoria University of Wellington, December 2004.

41. Don Brash, 'Nationhood'.

42. Peter Keenan, email to Richard Long, Don Brash and Murray McCully, 5 December 2003.

43. Ruth Richardson, email to Don Brash, 11 November 2003.

44. Don Brash, email to Gerry Brownlee, Simon Power, Murray McCully, John Key, Richard Long, Peter Keenan and Bryan Sinclair, 23 November 2003.

45. 'The folly behind Brash's words', Rod Oram, *Sunday Star-Times*, 7 March 2004.

46. Don Brash, 'Nationhood'.

47. Confidential source.

48. Richard Long, email to Peter Keenan and Murray McCully, 16 February 2004.

49. Phil Rennie, email to Richard Long, Peter Keenan and Murray McCully, 16 February 2004. Rennie was a former Young Nationals president and went on to work for the Sydney Centre for Independent Studies.

50. Jason Ede, email to National Communications Staff, 'Subject: This must go to Ruth Berry today, but Murray has sign off on it first', 17 February 2004.

51. Murray McCully, email to Ruth Berry, 19 February 2004.

52. Richard Long, email to National Leader's Office staff and Murray McCully, 19 February 2004.

53. Jason Ede, email to all National Party staff, 20 February 2004.

54. Jason Ede, email to Colin James, 2 March 2004.

55. Colin James, email to Jason Ede, 2 March 2004.

56. Jason Ede, email to Richard Long and Peter Keenan, 2 March 2004.

57. Richard Long, email to Don Brash, National Communications Staff and Murray McCully, 21 February 2004.

58. Don Brash, email to Richard Long, 21 February 2004.

59. For instance: *Carol Archie: You have talked about public perception that Maori who have earned degrees in law or medicine by entering through a quota system, have second-rate degrees. Is that your perception?*
   a. Don Brash: No, it is not. Though having said that, I had an anecdote only yesterday which makes me uncomfortable about that situation.
   b. Carol Archie: The degrees they get, though, you would agree they are the same?
   c. Don Brash: Yes I do. I am talking about perception. Perceptions are quite substantial. . . .
   d. Carol Archie: Some think you are trading on the public's ignorance and their prejudices. Do they have a point?
   e. Don Brash: No, I think the public do have inevitably some prejudices and some biases, and what I am saying is that affirmative action programmes tend to accentuate those prejudices. (Don Brash, interviewed by Carol Archie, *Mana News*, 5 April 2004, recorded by National Party staff media.)

60. Peter Keenan, email to Bryan Sinclair, 27 April 2005.

61. Gilbert Wong, 'I have a nightmare'.

62. Tony Blakely and Bridget Robson, 'Decades of Disparity', University of Otago's Wellington School of Medicine and Health Sciences, 2003–2006. Similar results were available from earlier studies.

63. Television New Zealand, *Hurricane Brash*, broadcast 12 April 2004.

64. Don Brash, interviewed by Carol Archie.

65. 'The Rotarian's idol', Anthony Hubbard, *Sunday Star-Times*, 22 February 2004.

66. Don Brash, email to Matthew Hooton, 29 January 2004.

67. Don Brash, email to correspondent, 12 February 2004.

68. Don Brash, email to Matthew Hooton, 30 April 2004.

69. Bryan Sinclair, email to Cameron Brewer, 10 February 2004.

70. Television New Zealand, *Hurricane Brash*, quoted in Johansson, 'Orewa and the Rhetoric of Illusion'.

71. 'National members bid to soften race policy', Ruth Berry, *New Zealand Herald*, 26 September 2005.

72. Barry Gustafson, interviewed by Simon Pound on 95bFM Radio.

CHAPTER TWENTY-TWO

Death of a teenager

2007, *Sunday Star-Times*: Tony Wall asks why a teenager was beaten to death in a prison van.

Tony Wall grew up in Christchurch, and took the traditional route into journalism. After doing the journalism course at Aoraki Polytechnic in Timaru, he worked his way up, via the *Ashburton Guardian*, the *Waikato Times* and *The Sydney Morning Herald*, to *The New Zealand Herald*, and then to a position as senior reporter on the *Sunday Star-Times*. There he's built a reputation as a reporter who can 'do pavement', as Carl Bernstein would say.

'I love the detective work involved. Wearing out shoe leather and knocking on doors, going to corners of the country, going somewhere remote and shining a light on it. It's a fascination thing, really. It's not a great professional desire to reveal the truth. Sometimes that can be over-egged. I'm a little bit selfish; I do it a little bit for my own pleasure. It's fun, and it's interesting. Those are things that drive me' (Wall, 2015).

Unlike many of the other journalists in this book, Wall is not particularly interested in rooting out government failings. He points out that stories about people, that shine a light on a little-known world, can take just as much effort and be just as much in the public interest. One story, about the homeless of Auckland, took him to three nights of living rough on the streets of Auckland. 'In some ways that's the story I'm most proud of, because it uncovered a whole world.'

A hallmark of Wall's work is his writing. Perhaps the best example is his account of the death of Liam Ashley, presented here. Told using fictional techniques, using the point of view of the main people in the story, it has a painful immediacy that makes it at times hard to read. Wall didn't break the Liam Ashley story, but his account helped fuel the public outcry that led to changes in how prisoners are transported.

'Mine is more people stuff, because that's what interests me. If I could uncover a great government story, of course I would, but my bread and butter is more human interest. I like to just do unusual things and tell a great yarn.'

Wall, T. (2015). Interview with author, J. Hollings.

Collision course
Sunday Star-Times, 28 January 2007

THEY ARE five hours Lorraine Ashley will never get back. Her youngest child, Liam, was alone for that time, brain-dead in a hospital bed, after he was strangled and bashed in the back of a prison van. No one had contacted his family.

Finally at 10.30pm on August 24 last year, two police officers knocked on the door of the Ashleys' clifftop home in Beach Haven, on Auckland's North Shore.

Lorraine's husband Ian had gone to bed and the 46-year-old Scottish immigrant was pottering in the kitchen. Out the window she could see across Waitemata Harbour to the flickering lights of west Auckland.

Her first thought was, "It can't be about Liam, they've already got him."

The 17-year-old had been taken into custody several days earlier on a string of charges — breaking into the family home, stealing his mother's Honda, doing wheelies inside the grounds of Long Bay College and carrying a pipe to smoke his favourite drug, marijuana.

As the whole nation would soon learn, Liam's family had decided not to bail him, to give him a shock that would hopefully turn his life around.

But one of the officers said: "There's been an incident involving Liam, he's in Auckland hospital."

On the drive over the harbour bridge in the police car, Lorraine and Ian, 47, begged to know whether Liam was going to live or die. The officers said they knew nothing.

At the hospital, the Ashleys were told there was no hope.

His face was covered in blood, there was foam coming out of his mouth, his eyes were fluttering and there were tubes everywhere. Ian and Lorraine and their other children, Bailey, 25, Downee, 21, and Logan, 19, held Liam's hand, talked to him, and washed him. In the morning, his life support was turned off.

Lorraine had known Liam was different since he was born, and she had spent 17 years fighting to get him the specialist help he needed. Now her "gorgeous boy" was dead and she felt it was her fault.

A COUPLE OF nights later in a Housing New Zealand high-rise in Onehunga, south Auckland — a world away from the relative privilege of the North Shore — Denise Boynton's phone rang just as there was a knock at the door.

She took the phone call first. It was her 25-year-old son, George Baker, calling from prison.

"Mum, are you sitting down?"

"No, George, there's someone at the door."

"Don't open it. You need to know something."

Boynton, 46, wondered if George knew about the prison van death of Liam Ashley, a case fresh in her mind as she had seen it on television the night before.

"You're a witness, aren't you?" she said. "You give evidence, you tell. I know you guys don't like narks, but you tell."

Baker said: "Shush mum. Mum it was me, I did it."

Boynton dropped the phone. She opened the door in a daze. A reporter thrust a microphone in her face — her son had killed a boy and it seemed she was the last to know.

George had been in trouble with the law since he was 11 or 12. She had spent years struggling alone to get help for her youngest, fighting state departments, never giving up hope of a brighter future for her boy. In her own way, another mother grieved.

GEORGE BAKER told prison psychologists he was possessed by the spirit of his great, great grandfather on his mother's side, Tuhoe prophet Rua Kenana.

When Kenana declared in World War I that the Germans would win, police moved to arrest him and his followers for sedition. Two people, including Kenana's oldest son, were shot and killed. Kenana spent nine months in Mt Eden prison in Auckland.

Baker learned a lot about his whakapapa in the same prison, and reported that he heard Kenana's voice urging him to be violent to others and destructive to himself.

When Baker was seven, Boynton left the boy's father, also Maori, because of his violence. Baker never got over it, and his mother believes the lack of a strong male role model is the root of his problems. Baker told psychologists his wild behaviour growing up was an attempt to get his parents to reconcile.

His father, George Thomas Baker, was a former army officer and body builder who now works transporting youth prisoners in Queensland. He and Boynton separated when the family, including Boynton's oldest son Adrian to another man, was living in Australia.

Boynton, who worked in factories in Sydney, says her husband beat her. She got a "hiding" when she announced she was pregnant with another child, Thomas, who died soon after birth.

Boynton moved back to Whakatane in the Bay of Plenty with her boys about 1990. Adrian was a "good boy" (he has become a painter-decorator and has a partner and two children), but George still harboured a well of anger.

Soon after they arrived back in New Zealand, Boynton said to him: "George, if you want to tell me you hate me, or slap me or yell at me, then do it, let it out."

Baker told Boynton he hated her for leaving his father.

His behaviour worsened. He was enrolled at several Whakatane primary schools, but hardly attended, preferring to sniff lighter fluid with a cousin and steal from his mother, once selling her television to the Black Power for cigarettes.

When he was about 11, Boynton went to Child, Youth and Family for help. Baker, by now a tall, strapping lad and well on his way to his adult height of 199cm (6ft 3in), was taken into Social Welfare custody and placed in a succession of foster homes.

Baker later told prison psychologists he was sexually and physically abused by relatives and caregivers over several years and as a result found it almost impossible to trust people.

As a teenager he tried to kill himself by jumping off a bridge into shallow water, cutting his wrists, taking pills and drinking methylated spirits. His mother says it was a "cry for help".

He was placed in secure youth homes in Christchurch and Auckland and spent time in psychiatric hospitals. He continually escaped.

When he was 12 or 13 he was put into the care of Tuhoe activist Tame Iti, against his mother's wishes. She contested the decision, but lost. Boynton says her son was frightened of Iti and ran away several times.

Iti says Baker was basically dumped on him by CYF with no proper plan or funding for his care. He says CYF "stuffed up from the beginning" by failing to diagnose Baker's mental health problems and get him the treatment he needed.

Boynton says she would leave CYF meetings in tears, not wanting her son to be placed where social workers suggested. They never stuck to a plan for him, and he was constantly on the move, she says.

When he was 18, Baker lived rough on the streets of Hamilton and Auckland. Prostitutes gave him accommodation in return for finding them customers.

On January 16, 1999, still aged 18, Baker's life took a fateful turn. He and two female cousins, high on LSD and amphetamines, went to the Hamilton home of a 73-year-old woman and claimed to be looking for a lost child.

Baker claimed to be following the two young women, and that he didn't know a crime was to take place. They robbed the woman at knifepoint and left her tied to a bed with a scarf.

Boynton says her son was always a "follower", that it was others who led him to trouble. But the courts didn't buy it — he was sentenced to seven years' jail. The boy who had been a promising basketball player and dreamed of playing in the NBA was on his way to a lifetime in captivity.

AS GEORGE BAKER embarked on his life of crime, Lorraine Ashley gave birth in Auckland to her fourth child, Liam. Lorraine had come to New Zealand from Scotland with her parents when she was about 14.

She and her husband Ian had met at nightclub Shades in central Auckland when they were in their early 20s. Ian was on a boys' night out, Lorraine was out with the girls. She knew straight away he was the man she'd marry.

They wed in March 1982 and Ian moved into the car sales business. The family prospered on the back of Ian's success in the buoyant 1980s car market.

Liam was born on May 17, 1989, and it did not take Lorraine long, as an experienced mother, to notice there was something not right with him.

He didn't like being cuddled, his balance was off, he was loud, clumsy, impulsive and had a strangely high tolerance for pain — often banging his head against walls.

The term attention deficit hyperactivity disorder (ADHD) was not around and it would be several years before that diagnosis was given. But Lorraine discovered there was help from special education services for boys like Liam. She fought to get him teacher aides and went into class with Liam herself. He went to five different primary schools and the refrain was always the same: "We don't want him any more, we can't cope, please remove him."

He would be disruptive in class, frustrated at his inability to concentrate, so would play the clown. Liam was sent to Waimokoia school in Auckland for children with behavioural and learning difficulties. He was put on Ritalin for the first time and his behaviour improved. But it was a live-in school and Liam started to feel that his parents didn't love him as much as his brother and sisters and that they were sending him away.

Liam was tired of being different. He didn't want to have to take pills, he didn't want to have a teacher aide — none of the other kids did. He just wanted to be a normal boy.

DENISE BOYNTON lives in a flat on the second level of a three-storey Housing New Zealand block in an Onehunga cul-de-sac. There is a bad smell in the building's graffiti-covered stairwell. Boynton is embarrassed when visitors see peeling wallpaper in her living room, but she keeps the flat clean and tidy.

One day in February of last year, Boynton and a friend were at her flat when there was a knock at the door. "It's a fella called George," the friend said.

Boynton was shocked — her son had been in prison for seven years and she didn't know he was out.

One of his parole conditions was that he live with his mother, but no one had bothered to tell Boynton. She thought Baker must have escaped, and kept expecting to hear sirens.

Baker had another surprise — a girlfriend waiting downstairs. It eventually came out that she had been a prison guard at Paremoremo. Boynton was shocked, thinking it was part of some grand prison break.

She grilled the girlfriend, Te Awhina Nepia. "How?," she asked. "How can you fall in love with someone in prison?"

Nepia insisted there had been no physical contact inside, only letters. She said she fell for Baker the first time she saw him.

He was coming out for roll-call and was the tallest inmate by far. He hit his head on a bar and made a joke out of it, acting the clown.

Despite his problems, George had always had a way with people. They seemed to relax around him — he made them feel comfortable, his mother says.

Nepia, who had quit her job, moved in with Baker and his mother. But they were continually fighting, and Boynton did not approve of the relationship, feeling that her son had no experience of women and needed time to adjust.

Nepia slept with a man downstairs to try to make Baker jealous. Boynton asked her to leave. Later, Nepia would write to Boynton, apologising for causing so much disruption.

"Basically I have learned that I'm an emotionally driven person who acts without logic and on impulse."

Baker's years in prison had been tough, and he had spent a lot of time in a special needs unit because of his self-mutilation.

He once ended up in Auckland Hospital when he cut his penis and almost bled to death.

Baker had also stabbed another inmate with a pencil, set his bedding on fire and went on hunger strikes.

He told prison authorities he was a "hit man" for the gangs, and in an effort to draw attention to himself claimed he had raped, murdered and burned someone in south Auckland. That "confession" was investigated by police, and discounted.

Baker was diagnosed with a borderline personality disorder — it was considered he was faking the voices he claimed to hear — and put on Prozac and Epilim. It did nothing to improve his behaviour.

Psychologists warned that Baker was so immature, impulsive and unresponsive to treatment that if he continued on that path, he would eventually require complete institutionalisation.

And this stark warning to the Parole Board in 2004: "In consideration of Mr Baker's references to potentially competing with other criminals for notoriety, there is some possibility that he may resort to extreme violence in order to obtain fame. In this scenario, Mr Baker would . . . attempt to injure, wound or kill as many victims as possible."

Baker said in a letter to the board: "I had never dreamt of hurting innocent people or anyone in my life, but to say I did have a terrible upbringing. But that still gives me no right to do what I did!!!!"

Prison was not all bleak. He had improved his reading and writing skills, done carving, and won a certificate for his kapa haka. His relationship with his mother had also improved, and he had come to realise she had always been there for him, while his father had not.

When he was eventually released, having served his entire sentence, Baker spent most of his time at his mother's flat, afraid that if he ventured out, he would commit another crime. It wasn't long before he did, linking up with a cousin on the North Shore and robbing a youth at knifepoint.

Baker was soon back behind bars. And on a collision course with Liam Ashley.

PIRATE LIFE. That was the motto of Liam and his mates. At his funeral, his friends put on pirate voices and said, "You know, 'arrrrrr', and a bottle of rum," as if that explained it all.

Liam liked to be known as Crazy Liam, the Pirate King. In his last years of schooling, his parents sent him to Halswell Community College in Christchurch, the only school of its type for boys like Liam. He flourished academically, but was desperately unhappy so far away from his family.

In 2004, he returned to Auckland. Liam didn't want to take Ritalin, so his mother started slipping him pills in food. His father didn't like the way the pills made him drowsy and lose his character.

After so long away from the family, Liam wanted to take a year off. His father was for it, but his mother wanted him to find work.

Liam began stealing from the family — cash, electronic goods, even a couple of canoes. He hung out with a 25-year-old gang prospect nicknamed Ford, who got Liam to steal for him to fund his P-habit. Liam stole his brother's electric guitar and amplifier and Ford sold it at a second-hand store in Highbury on the North Shore.

The company Liam was keeping terrified Lorraine. Liam was sent to Wellington to stay with his sister Bailey, on the condition he find work or enrol on a course. She was studying criminology. When Liam showed no interest in getting work, Bailey put him on a plane back to Auckland.

As his stealing continued, Liam was placed by CYF in the custody of Earl Opetaia, who ran a home for troubled boys above a boxing gym in west Auckland.

His parents were convinced that Liam was at the age where he would grow out of his wild behaviour, if they could get him back on Ritalin. Liam agreed to try, but they couldn't get an appointment at North Shore mental health services, which was so overloaded they were taking only patients who were hearing voices.

Throughout June and July of last year, Liam appeared in North Shore District Court on a string of charges relating to crimes against his family. He was bailed, but on August 17 he stole his mother's car. When it was pulled over by police in Orewa, north of Auckland, Ford was driving.

Ford was bailed, but Ian and Lorraine asked Orewa police to keep Liam in the cells overnight to give him a shock. Liam was held in Mt Eden prison for the next few days.

The Ashley family held a family meeting on the evening of August 23 and decided on a strategy for Liam. Ian and Lorraine would, for the first time, stay away from court the next day, to send Liam a message. Bailey and Downee would go instead. They would not try to bail him.

The idea was if Liam spent a few days in custody, it would give the authorities time to prepare a supervision order for Liam's release that would include going on Ritalin and getting psychiatric help. In his parents' eyes, he was going on a 10-day holiday.

When Liam walked into the North Shore courtroom, he looked around for his parents, then caught Bailey's eye. His face erupted in a big grin, but back in the cells he began sobbing — he hadn't expected to see Bailey and Downee.

Baker was also in the cells, and he put his arm around Liam to console him.

Later he started teasing Liam, and at one point put him in a sleeper hold until he started to go red. The other inmates thought Baker, who had been "big noting" about his crimes, was just messing around.

Liam was in the dock for about five minutes. The next time his sisters saw him, he was on his death-bed.

DENISE BOYNTON went to visit Baker in Paremoremo prison after his arrest for murder. For 15 minutes neither spoke. Boynton couldn't even look at her son. Then she started crying. Baker cried too.

"It's all right, mum, I won't let anything happen to you."

Boynton asked: "Why did you do it?" Baker said: "He was a nark, mum."

Boynton: "If I saw someone on the street in trouble and I rang the police for help, would you come and kill me because I'm a nark?"

Baker: "It's not the same, mum."

Boynton: "Yes it is."

Baker said: "That boy was cheeky, mum, he had information on me. Forget it, mum, it's happened and I'm going to do time."

The third prisoner inside the van's compartment with Liam and Baker, David Olds, told police Liam had seemed scared of Baker, but was also "brave" in talking back to him. Liam had helped Baker try to escape, taking turns to kick the emergency door. Baker told Liam to fake a seizure, but Liam said he didn't want to.

Baker put him in a headlock, telling Liam to relax. He then snapped, wrenching Liam's neck from side to side trying to break it. "Be a man, die, be a man," Baker said, complaining that "this guy is taking ages to die". It took about 15 minutes for Liam to stop struggling. Olds was too scared to intervene and the guards in the cab never once looked around to check what was happening.

As the van pulled into the prison, Baker began kicking Liam in the head repeatedly until the door opened.

The pair should never have been put together — Liam was classified a vulnerable youth and should have been transported alone, and Baker was also supposed to be segregated and under 15-minute observations.

The Chubb officer who put the pair together had earlier shaken hands with Baker — he knew him well from Paremoremo. He had never seen Baker be violent to anyone but himself, and had seen Baker console Liam in the court earlier.

"Baker showed genuine concern when Liam came downstairs from court, and that just confirmed the fact that what I was deciding to do was the right thing," the officer told an inquiry into the killing.

Denise Boynton stayed in the background during her son's first court appearances. At sentencing — Baker got 18 years — she approached Lorraine Ashley and the pair hugged. Boynton describes Ashley as "amazing".

"I'm a mother too, I felt every pain she felt, and I know what that young boy suffered."

Lorraine Ashley also sympathises with Boynton.

"You can't help what your children do. You love them and stand by them no matter what and that's what she has to do for her boy. He's fallen through the cracks the same way Liam has."

CHAPTER TWENTY-THREE

Taking on the Crown

2009, *North & South*: Mike White investigates the conviction of daughter-killer Mark Lundy.

If you had to run a popularity contest for convicted murderers in New Zealand, Mark Lundy would come close to last. Of all the cases of wrongful conviction for a journalist to consider, his is among the least likely to win public sympathy. The big, fat, whoring drunk who bashed his own wife and daughter to death with an axe — and then slobbered unconvincingly at their funeral? Even if there was something wrong technically with the evidence against him, just take one look at him — he did it, surely?

All these thoughts and others no doubt went through *North & South* journalist Mike White's mind when he was approached by Lundy supporters, shortly after his conviction, with a request that he write an article about his case. For them, Mike was the court of last resort. Lundy had been found guilty in 2001 of murdering his wife Christine and daughter Amber at their Palmerston North home. There was little doubt in the minds of most New Zealanders that he was guilty. At first, White turned them down. But something rankled, and after a few months, and reading through the evidence they had presented him with while on holiday, he rang his editor and asked for a month to investigate. Then he rang back and asked for three.

The story that resulted is a powerful, compelling narrative. Piece by piece, White took apart the Crown case against Lundy. There is no better testament to the robustness of his inquiry than the fact that it was this story that convinced a London-based barrister, David Hislop, to take on the case *pro bono* to the Privy Council. By a strange coincidence — or perhaps a demonstration of the power of the media when it is on fate's side — the story was also read by Professor Helen Whitwell, a Home Office pathologist who happened to be holidaying in New Zealand. She became the expert witness at the Privy Council who helped overturn Lundy's conviction. All the doubts White raised about the Crown evidence were eventually upheld. At Lundy's second trial, the Crown case changed, and was based on different evidence.

For White, there was great satisfaction in seeing his journalism make that kind of difference. He is driven, he says, not only by the mystery element of wanting to find out what happened, but also by anger at injustice. In this case, the satisfaction was tinged with disappointment, because at Lundy's retrial he was again convicted and remains in prison. 'I have serious concerns about what happened at that trial. I still feel very uncomfortable about the conviction and I don't think we have heard the last of that story.'

White, M. (2016). Interview with author, J. Hollings.

What the jury didn't hear
North & South, February 2009

Big fat bastard. How could he? Axed his wife to death in her bed, made her face unrecognisable, then turned round and smashed in his little daughter's skull. Then he drove like a lunatic back to Wellington and hired a hooker to celebrate.

And remember him at the funeral? All that over-the-top distress and collapsing bullshit masked by dark glasses. All for an insurance payout.

Are there words that come close to describing Mark Lundy, how vile and despicable, human only in form?

When he insisted he was innocent, the Court of Appeal tossed it out and added three years to his sentence. Big fat filthy bastard.

That's pretty much what people remember about Lundy — the high-speed car trip, the prostitute, the funeral performance.

The case against him was circumstantial and scientific, the result of 24,000 police hours and thousands of interviews. Few argued with the verdict, virtually everyone abandoning him, repulsed by the mere thought they'd ever shaken the hand that hacked his wife and daughter to death. But new evidence including undisclosed police information and expert opinion significantly undermines the case against him — to the point where "How could he?" arguably becomes "How could he have been convicted?"

Mark and Christine Lundy owned a small business supplying kitchen sinks and benches which they ran from their Palmerston North home. They'd met through Scouting, been married 17 years and had one child, seven-year-old Amber.

On Tuesday, August 29, 2000, Mark Lundy, 41, headed to Wellington on one of his fortnightly sales trips to visit kitchen suppliers. Around 5pm he checked into his usual Petone motel. At 5.30 he received a call from Christine, 38, and Amber back in Palmerston North, saying Amber's Pippins (Guides) group had been cancelled and they were going to have McDonald's for tea.

And it's the next three hours that are crucial, where police argue the suburban dad, well known for his community work and who'd never been in trouble before, became a murderous monster.

Lundy says he drove to Petone's foreshore, read his book for a bit, went back to the motel and drank half a bottle of rum while watching TV. Just before 11.30pm he rang an escort agency, as he'd previously done on trips away, and spent the next hour with a prostitute at his motel.

But police say when Lundy spoke to Christine at 5.30pm he somehow convinced his wife to get herself and Amber into bed by 7pm, supposedly by saying he was coming home for sex.

He then drove 150km back to Palmerston North at high speeds, parked 500m from his home, ran to his house around 7pm, attacked his wife with a tomahawk, then, when Amber got out of bed to see what the disturbance was, he killed her also. Lundy then allegedly ran back to his car and sped back to Wellington, arriving just before 8.30pm.

The bodies were found by Christine's brother around nine the next morning.

A massive police investigation that stretched from Palmerston North's streets to a laboratory in Texas led to Lundy's arrest six months later. His six-week trial resulted in a guilty verdict which was upheld in the Court of Appeal and his life sentence increased from 17 to 20 years without parole.

The Crown suggested Lundy was in financial trouble over a vineyard venture and killing his wife was a way to get her life insurance payout. Killing Amber became necessary when she saw him attacking Christine.

While the case was complex and often complicated, it essentially came down to those critical three hours and whether Lundy could have done what he was accused of.

Time of death I

Pinpointing when Christine and Amber Lundy were murdered was pivotal to the case, with the alibis of all suspects, particularly Mark Lundy, dependent on the time of death.

Palmerston North pathologist James Pang of Medlab Central was advised of the murders soon after the bodies were found on the morning of Wednesday, August 30. However, he didn't visit the murder scene until seven hours later, staying just over half an hour. According to police, most of this time was spent talking about the scene and getting into protective clothing.

Pang merely observed the scene and made no tests, saying he didn't want to disturb the bodies while forensic examinations were being carried out. This meant he didn't conduct crucial early tests, including body temperature and stiffening, to help ascertain time of death.

However, Pang claims it's standard practice not to test bodies at a murder scene.

Amber's post-mortem examination was done on the evening of August 31 and Christine's on September 2.

Pang's most critical findings were that the stomachs of both victims were "full", with no observable food in the top of the small intestine, and that there was no "gastric smell" similar to vomit, which occurs when digestive juices are mixed with food.

Thus he estimated both died before digestion of their last meal began, within an hour of eating. In the stomach contents he identified potato chips and probable fragments of fish.

A receipt found in the Lundy home showed Christine and Amber had bought McDonald's takeaways at 5.43 on the Tuesday evening. The meal consisted of one chicken burger, one filet-o-fish burger, nine chicken McNuggets, one large fries, one medium fries and two apple pies. The wrappers for these and an empty ice cream sundae container were found in the McDonald's bag in the kitchen tidy.

The Lundys lived about 10 minutes' drive from McDonald's and it was assumed they would have started eating around 6pm.

At trial, Pang said the stomach findings led him to believe the time of death was approximately 7pm — perhaps 7.10pm or 7.15pm at the outside, adding "it is within my expertise to say that".

His view was supported by Professor Gilbert Barbezat from Otago University who, after reviewing Pang's autopsy findings, estimated time of death to be "between 30 and 60 minutes" after eating but he also said he could push that out to 7.15pm. Barbezat said Pang's evidence of no gastric smell was a "very striking finding" which reinforced the conclusion digestion hadn't started and death followed shortly after eating.

It was known early on that Christine Lundy had taken a short phone call at 6.56 that night so was alive at least until then. Hence, if Pang's and Barbezat's evidence is accepted, the murders must have occurred within the next 20 minutes.

At trial, no expert evidence was called to challenge these very precise estimates.

However, even a basic reading of relevant literature shows estimating time of death is a notoriously uncertain science and using stomach contents/digestion as a guide is the most unreliable tool a pathologist has. Because there are so many variables, such as the amount and type of meal and a person's physiology, most experts advocate giving a very broad window when estimating time of death — at the very least several hours.

At trial, Pang referred to perhaps the world's leading expert in this field, Bernard Knight, emeritus professor at the University of Wales, who has written numerous papers and texts on the issue, including *The Estimation of the Time Since Death in the Early Postmortem Period*, the only book in the English language devoted to this subject.

In 2008, Pang's evidence was sent to Knight, who has conducted more than 25,000 post-mortems. (While Pang routinely did post-mortems in Palmerston North, Barbezat accepted at trial he'd never performed one, though he'd witnessed more than 100.)

Knight replied that estimating time of death based on stomach contents is "so unreliable as to be of little value".

Regarding the supposedly crucial fact that Pang could detect no gastric smell when he opened the stomach and that this was a guide to the interval between the last meal and death, Knight states: "I consider this to be utterly without foundation. I am conversant with virtually all of the literature about estimation of time of death . . . and I have never heard of such a contention. I have asked several of my former colleagues about this and the suggestion was met with derision . . . His contention that absence of smell on gastric contents means less than an hour since death is little short of ludicrous."

North & South also referred the case to Professor Derrick Pounder, head of the Centre for Forensic and Legal Medicine at Dundee University in Scotland, another recognised international expert in this field.

"In my view there would be a general consensus amongst forensic pathologists that estimating time of death from stomach contents with an accuracy of within half an hour, as is suggested in this case, is simply impossible. My personal opinion is that estimating time of death to an accuracy of within half an hour based upon stomach contents amounts to little more than quackery.

"There is to my knowledge no scientific literature with respect to stomach contents' smell and time of death, and the comment on this matter is incomprehensible to me."

Pang didn't weigh, measure or preserve the stomach contents. He kept only samples from Christine's stomach, including pieces of chips, which were photographed and sent for toxicological testing and have now been destroyed. Thus we only have his description as to the stomachs being "full".

But this description, like the stomach itself, is elastic. We all consider our stomachs full after a normal meal. But when world eating champion Joey Chestnut devoured 93 hamburgers in eight minutes in September 2008 his stomach would no doubt have also been described as full.

The meal that Christine and Amber ate was sizeable (Christine weighed 112kg, Amber nearly 45kg) and there's no way of knowing what else they may have eaten or drunk that afternoon or evening. (Several snack food packets were also found in the kitchen tidy; a police officer records seeing a half-cut banana he thought was fresh on a kitchen board; and a batch of muffins appeared to have been made recently.)

Pang admitted he opened only the top part of the small intestine, the duodenum, and observed no digested food in it.

But gastroenterologist Dr Nicholas Diamant from Toronto Western Hospital, who has studied stomach functions for more than 45 years, told *North & South*: "The meal eaten normally empties into the duodenum in small amounts as liquid, with solid particles less than 2mm in size. This content is moved rapidly out of the duodenum and further down the small bowel. Therefore solid gastric content is in fact not seen in the duodenum during the time of digestion in the stomach. Solid food can be recognised in the stomach for up to 10 hours after it is eaten.

"The stomach accommodates to the size of its contents, which also includes gastric secretions and would look 'full' as long as content was present.

Furthermore, types of food markedly affect gastric emptying. For example, fat significantly delays emptying."

In 2007, Ontario's Court of Appeal quashed a murder conviction in a case with remarkable similarities to Lundy's.

Fourteen-year-old Stephen Truscott had been convicted of murdering 12-year-old Lynne Harper in June 1959. The charge rested on a pathologist's initial claim that Harper died between 7.15pm and 7.45pm based on her stomach contents — a period she was known to be with Truscott.

Sentenced to hang, Truscott eventually spent 10 years in prison and nearly 40 on parole before being acquitted.

At his 2007 appeal, numerous experts gave evidence that time of death based on stomach contents can't be pinpointed to such a specific timeframe. The appeal judges' decision was largely based on the fact the pathologist's estimate "had no scientific justification".

Pang acknowledged at trial that he didn't take notes during the post-mortem of everything he observed, relying on memory when making his full report later.

His initial post-mortem notes don't appear to refer to bladder contents but his final report records Christine's bladder having a "minimal amount" of urine and Amber's a "small amount" — suggestive perhaps that they'd only just gone to bed, as would fit with an unnaturally early hour of 7pm.

However, the officer in charge of Amber's body, Detective Constable Brett Calkin, who attended her post-mortem and made extensive notes throughout, recorded: "Mortuary attendant Matheson finds bladder is full of urine." This notebook was available to Lundy's lawyers but the jury never heard its contents. Would Amber's bladder have been full if she'd just gone to bed?

(Interestingly, Pang also suggested during the post-mortem that the victims had eaten McDonald's and told *North & South* this was because he recognised "shoestring" chips. Calkin's notebook records: "It definitely appears that the potatoes were potato chip/fries thicker than shoestring." Photographs of chips from Christine's stomach appear much larger than shoestring, measuring about 1cm in width. Whether she also ate other chips at some stage, for which there is no record, is unlikely ever to be known.)

Pang, however, stands by his evidence of time of death, repeating it was an "educated estimate" and up to the jury and others to decide how much weight to put on his statements.

But his reports and trial testimony are quite definite and leave little room for flexibility or jury interpretation — death was within an hour of eating, or around 7pm. At the very outside 7.15pm.

And when *North & South* asked whether, on reflection, a time of death of even 8pm or later could have been consistent with what he found, Pang stuck to his estimate, responding: "Probably not."

Crucially, 7pm was the exact midpoint of the less than three hour window Lundy had to commit the murders.

Time of death II

Professor Derrick Pounder, in a paper on the subject, says estimating time of death should be based on three sources: evidence from the body, evidence around the body and evidence from the deceased's common habits.

"All three sources of evidence should be explored and assessed before offering an opinion on when death or a fatal injury occurred."

In this case the pathologist and police relied on a single aspect of just one source, stomach contents at the post-mortem.

Other factors suggesting a later time of death were known and some raised at trial — but obviously not considered as important as Pang's stomach-contents evidence.

Witnesses, including Christine's mother, said Christine usually went to bed after 11pm and Amber around 8pm.

Others stated Christine told them that when Mark was away she got more done and often read till late.

Julie Burnett, who rang Christine at 6.56pm that Tuesday, inquired whether Mark would be at wine club the following week. At trial, she merely said Christine told her Mark was out. But in a previously undisclosed notebook from an interview with Burnett, Detective Melinda Rix writes: "CL tells JB ML out and will be back in town <u>Wed</u>" — not that she was expecting him home any moment.

Christine was found in bed, with the glasses she always wore put away in their case on the bedside cabinet. The TV in her bedroom was on standby, having been turned off with the remote control. Both these are as they would be if she'd gone to bed normally, much later than 7pm.

When switched on, the TV was on channel 4 — Prime.

Christine and Amber were *Shortland Street* fanatics. If Christine had been in bed at 7pm waiting for her husband to come home for a romantic evening, it's curious the TV wasn't set to TV2 for this.

Other witnesses described seeing lights on in the Lundy house after 11pm. The most specific was a next-door neighbour whose phone records show he was talking to his father between 10.59pm and 11.06pm. He described being outside at the time and clearly seeing lights on at the rear of the Lundy house. These were off the next morning.

The first three people on the scene the next morning — Christine's brother, a close friend and an ambulance officer — all said there were no lights on in the house when they arrived. So who switched them off if they were seen on after 7pm?

Trial judge Justice Tony Ellis realised how important time of death was when summing up to the jury.

"Plainly, for the prosecution to succeed the time of death of around 7pm is essential. If you are not satisfied on the evidence of this, or are left in a reasonable doubt about it, then it is fatal to the prosecution case."

The computer shutdown

Perhaps the clearest proof Christine and Amber were alive well after 7pm was that the family's main computer in the office showed it was shut down at 10.52pm.

At trial, however, the national manager of the police Electronic Crime Laboratory, Maarten Kleintjes, raised the scenario that Lundy had manipulated the computer's time so it appeared it was shut down at 10.52pm but had actually been done much earlier.

Most people can change the time on their computer in normal operating mode — but it leaves a trace. Supposedly Mark Lundy, who witnesses said had no great computer ability, used a much more complicated method of doing this.

Kleintjes' theory was that Lundy had copied another computer's time/date control panel onto a floppy disk, opened this on his family's computer, changed the computer's time to 10.52pm and shut it down. Then he restarted the computer but before it went into operating mode, he went into setup mode, changed the time back to normal again and then turned the computer off, leaving no trace of his actions or the second shutdown.

Kleintjes' evidence supporting this was that the computer's registry backup files, which hold essential computer data, were out of order. He said this showed the computer's clock had been altered up to five times in the past, presumably while someone practised the necessary manipulation.

Thus, police argued Lundy had gone into the office next door to where his wife was waiting for him at 7pm, altered the computer and closed it down so when it was restarted, it would show a shutdown of 10.52pm.

No evidence was ever produced that this actually happened, that anyone had taught Lundy how to do this technical procedure or where he copied the time/date control panel from.

Even at trial, Kleintjes was forced to admit the registry files would be out of order only if someone had practised changing the date — not the time. This raised the question why Lundy would have practised altering the date when that was never what he was likely to be trying to leave evidence of.

A copy of the computer's hard drive and Kleintjes' evidence was given to computer forensic expert and former police intelligence officer Allan Watt.

He utterly dismisses the police theory, saying it's "so far-fetched and beyond reality it can't be comprehended". Watt says few people would know how to manipulate a computer as Kleintjes suggested, let alone realise other methods would be traceable.

Now living in Australia, Watt has spent more than 400 hours examining the computer's files.

He quickly discovered it was infected with what's known as a KAK virus, commonly spread through emails and the internet, which affected, among other things, registry files. Another computer forensic expert, the late Alan Peacock, also easily found this virus.

Kleintjes says he didn't detect any viruses and had never heard of the KAK virus.

Watt removed the virus and ran the computer for several days, switching it on and off at various times.

The registry backup files immediately returned to normal.

Mark Lundy also had a laptop that he used for work and Christine used it to do accounting work for her brother, Glenn Weggery, who had his own business.

On Monday, August 28, Weggery left his chequebook with Christine for her to do his GST return, which was due at the end of the month. The next morning he called again, but Christine hadn't finished the return.

But by the morning of Wednesday, August 30, when Christine and Amber were found dead, the work was done, with Weggery's chequebook found on the kitchen table together with his completed GST return and an ACC invoice.

In police photos taken inside the office after the murders, the laptop can clearly be seen in its case, sitting on a chair in front of a desk with a clear area where it appears the laptop has been. Just as the police knew the family's main computer could contain crucial clues, they must have realised the laptop was also important.

Weggery had told them Christine did his GST returns on the laptop as it had the necessary computer program. And some time between Tuesday and Wednesday morning she'd done his GST return — quite possibly after 7 that evening, after Amber went to bed. If it could be identified what time she did it, surely that would be crucial.

What happened with the laptop is, at best, confusing. At trial, Kleintjes said he received the laptop. But afterwards police claimed the laptop had never even left the house.

The officer in charge of the case, Detective Sergeant Ross Grantham (now a detective inspector), acknowledges he asked for the laptop to be cloned.

But Kleintjes denies being asked to do this or even looking at it.

When asked why Kleintjes would seemingly ignore his request and why the laptop was never investigated, given the vital information it might hold and how detailed the rest of the investigation had been, Grantham simply shrugs and says he doesn't know.

Curiously — given the police claim the laptop was never looked at — a previously undisclosed notebook from police forensic accountant Reg Murphy has an entry from October 4 relating to a discussion with another officer.

"Advise thoughts on Marchris [the Lundys' company] and that unable to look at laptop until made available by Maarten Kleintjes." By this time the laptop had been returned to Lundy, so it raises questions whether Kleintjes in fact had some information from it, or even a clone.

In material obtained from Lundy's defence team, there is also a CD labelled "Lundy Computer & Laptop Emails".

Kleintjes says he can't explain this given they had never examined the laptop.

When the laptop was returned to Lundy it crashed when a new operating system was loaded, making retrieving meaningful data from it virtually impossible.

Margaret Dance's evidence

Despite his high-speed journey to and from Palmerston North and the bloody murders of his wife and daughter, police had no eyewitnesses who'd seen Mark Lundy.

Except Margaret Dance. Dance, 60, lived in Hillcrest Drive, 500m from Lundy's home. A week after the murders, she went to the police.

Only some of her first statement deals with a man she saw running near her house as she drove to her choir practice at 7.15pm. But over several days she added to this description as more "images" came to her.

At trial, Dance claimed she had psychic powers and a photographic memory.

Her account of the runner eventually evolved to be incredibly detailed, including a lengthy description of a tracksuit top that he wore over a business shirt and tie; the fact his tracksuit bottoms were slightly wrinkled around the ankles; that he was wearing a blonde curly wig that was slipping down over his forehead; and that he appeared to be trying to look like a woman.

She couldn't remember details of his face other than he had a "desperate, frantic look".

It was dark when Dance turned out of Hillcrest Drive into Rhodes Drive and the runner went past in the opposite direction, on her left. She admitted at the time there were one or two cars coming in the other direction and she was concentrating on making a right-hand turn into Karamea Cres just ahead.

However, as well as the detailed runner description, she was also able to describe seven people in and around the takeaway shop on the other side of the road, including, in some cases, their build, clothing, hair and ethnicity.

Dance claimed she didn't look closely at pictures or stories about the murders but when she saw Lundy on TV she immediately recognised him as the runner, based on "the shape of his face and upper body".

She had also described the person as "running fast". However, Mark Lundy, who weighed 130kg, wore an orthotic aid in one shoe after an accident that required ankle surgery and struggled to do anything vaguely athletic.

Nobody else, including the seven people Dance described around the takeaway shop, saw anyone running in the area that night, let alone a 130kg, 190.5cm (6'3") man trying to disguise himself as a woman with a blonde wig.

Dance suggested the runner's trackpants were light blue. Mark Lundy's were green. Her description of a two-tone tracksuit top is hard to reconcile with the maroon non-zip sweatshirt found in Lundy's car.

At trial, she said: "I saw the toes of the shoes and they definitely weren't running shoes. I just thought they were probably leather."

However, the Crown conveniently translated this into the runner wearing "dress shoes" — the only shoes Lundy had with him.

In June 2007, long after Mark Lundy was convicted, Dance wrote to the *Manawatu Standard* regarding treatment at Palmerston North Hospital's eye clinic.

She thanked them "from the bottom of my heart for the vision I have not had for over 60 years — in spite of now being able to see my wrinkles and cobwebs in the house!"

Ross Grantham says he has no reason to doubt what Dance had to say. "She gave very good evidence."

Dance refused to talk to *North & South*.

Dance's evidence was crucial in another area. She described seeing a car parked outside her house as she headed to choir practice that night, saying it was dark blue, new, streamlined and rounded.

Thus the police case was that it was Lundy's car, parked well away from the murder scene, and when he ran past her on Rhodes Drive he was returning after murdering Christine and Amber. It's worth mentioning that her first statement to police doesn't mention the car.

Her next-door neighbours were also interviewed by police and both clearly remembered a "dark-blue or black vehicle . . . just a little car, like a little Ford, something like a Laser from the early eighties", parked outside Dance's for several days around August 29. The jury never heard their evidence.

If it was Lundy's car outside Dance's property it was a strange place for an intending murderer to park, given it was virtually opposite a friend's house, near a streetlight and close to his brother's home.

Dance's estimate of the time she apparently saw Lundy is also open to challenge. She said she was preparing to go to her 7pm choir practice when two friends called by. They stayed just a few minutes and as Dance was about to leave she saw it was between 7.10pm and 7.15pm.

Her visitors told police they'd been to a nearby store, T-Market Fresh, around 6pm, spent about 20 minutes shopping there and then went to Dance's house, which was very close. They weren't wearing watches and the shop normally closed at 6pm. This suggests their visit to Dance was likely to have been well before 7pm.

North & South has seen security records from the T-Market Fresh store and it shows the owners, who usually spent some time in the shop after the last customers left, switched on their alarm at 6.37pm that day.

The owners were never contacted by police to help verify the times Dance gave in evidence.

The car-trip time

That crucial sighting by Margaret Dance fitted the police scenario of Lundy's movements that night: that he'd driven rapidly back from Wellington to Palmerston North after 5.30pm, murdered Christine and Amber about 7pm, rushed back to his car by 7.15pm and raced back to Petone, arriving there just before 8.30pm.

On top of driving 300km in this three-hour period, at a minimum Lundy also had to: run 500m to his house; manipulate the computer's clock; murder his wife and daughter in sustained attacks; take a large jewellery box from the bedroom to make it look like a burglary; remove the coveralls police believe he wore to commit the murders; fake a break-in via a rear window; and run 500m back to his car.

Since Dance said Lundy wasn't carrying anything when she saw him, we have to add in disposing of the murder weapon, the overalls, the jewellery box and possibly equipment he used to fake the break-in — all between his house and being seen by Dance. Despite extensive searches, none of the above has ever been found.

It's difficult to estimate how long all this may have taken — perhaps 20 minutes — but it needs to be subtracted from three hours when considering how fast Lundy would have had to drive to be back in Wellington at 8.29pm.

Cellphone records put Lundy at his motel at 5.30pm when he received a call from Christine's phone. The call lasted eight minutes. If he left immediately afterwards he had about 1 hour 20 minutes to get home — requiring an average speed of close to 117km/h.

His return trip had to be done in under 1 hour 15 minutes based on Dance's sighting, requiring an average speed of at least 120km/h.

There are numerous routes Lundy could have taken but the quickest is probably turning off SH1 near Levin, passing through Shannon and Opiki then turning onto what is known as the No. 1 Line that leads onto Tremaine Ave and Kelvin Grove on the north side of Palmerston North.

Whatever route is taken requires travelling through numerous built-up areas with 50km/h speed restrictions, many traffic lights, pedestrian crossings, stop signs and roundabouts.

Police tried to replicate Lundy's trip, using a similar car to his 1998 Ford Fairmont and driving at up to 140km/h.

Their best time travelling north was 1 hour 29 minutes, an average of just under 100km/h — but was done leaving Petone just before 9pm when the roads are relatively empty — not anything like Wellington's notorious rush-hour traffic when Lundy was supposedly driving.

Their job-sheets record the fastest trip south was 1 hour 33 minutes at an average speed of 91.4km/h. (However the police numbers don't add up. They claim the trip was 150.2km; if this is so, at 91.4km/h the trip would have actually taken nearly 1 hour 39 minutes.)

At trial, one of the officers involved said he believed he could have gone faster if he'd "thrown caution to the wind". Given their northward trip wasn't in rush hour and their average speed still wasn't even close to that supposedly done by Lundy, this has to be questioned. As must be their ability to do the trip much more quickly and not be noticed, as Lundy allegedly did.

The defence employed former police detective and reconstruction expert Paul Bass, who made three trips north from Petone to near Lundy's home at the same time Lundy would have been travelling, through rush hour. Bass's quickest time was 1 hour 56 minutes, with an average speed of 77km/h.

However, his evidence was challenged by Crown claims he didn't use an identical car to Lundy's — although his Nissan Skyline GTS is arguably quicker and more agile than Lundy's Fairmont.

... Nobody has been able to get close to the trip times Lundy was required to do.

In the Court of Appeal, the Crown could merely submit that the drive from Petone was "made with some urgency but the return drive was undertaken in extremis which no one could replicate".

Which poses the obvious question: If nobody could replicate it, was it possible in the first place?

. . .

The brain tissue

While everything detailed thus far may give grounds for doubt about Lundy's guilt, by far the most damning evidence against him were two minute specks of tissue found on one of his shirts.

This polo shirt was in an open suit carrier with other clothes and miscellaneous items on the back seat of his car when police intercepted him on Wednesday, August 30.

Nearly two months later, ESR scientist Björn Sutherland examinined it with a bright light and found two faint stains, one on the left sleeve near the shoulder seam and another on the left-hand chest pocket, which he suggested had blood in them.

He wet the sleeve stain and pressed it against a slide to make a sample. The two stains were then cut from the shirt and sent for DNA testing.

This involved rinsing the stains with water, and both tests showed high probability of Christine's DNA. This on its own couldn't prove anything — her DNA might have got there if she gave him a hug or put away his shirt.

The slide taken by Sutherland was shown to a number of doctors and several suggested it might contain a few cells found only in brain or spinal-cord tissue. However, because the material on the slide was "scanty" and "shrivelled up", as one expert put it, and "suboptimally preserved", as another described it, it wasn't definite it was brain tissue.

... Dr Rodney Miller, a partner at the private ProPath Laboratory in Dallas, Texas ... had supposedly helped pioneer a technique that allowed samples to be lifted from slides, such as the one the police had, and coincidentally had spoken at a Palmerston North conference just days before the Lundy murders.

Thus, in February 2001, Grantham went to Dallas with the polo shirt, the two samples cut from it that showed staining, and the ESR slide taken from the more distinct stain.

However, Miller never employed the new technique he'd suggested and didn't even open the ESR slide.

Instead, he conducted a standard scientific procedure called immuno-histochemistry (IHC) to see if there was any brain tissue on the shirt samples. IHC is commonly used as an adjunct test in cancer diagnosis, and in research laboratories, to help establish what cells are present.

What Miller did that was new was use IHC on a fabric sample and on tissue that hadn't been specifically prepared for IHC. However, he'd satisfied himself the process could work. The week before Grantham arrived, Miller had been preparing a chicken for dinner and smeared material from its neck and kidney on an old shirt, then tested it with apparent success.

. . .

His report concluded that there was brain or spinal-cord tissue present on the shirt. Together with the fact that the shirt samples tested positive for Christine's DNA, this was the killer blow for Lundy. How on earth could he explain Christine's brain tissue on one of his shirts unless he was the killer?

At trial, his defence suggested accidental contamination and even police planting but failed to provide strong evidence for this.

At this point, however, it's useful to step back from the science and logically consider, if it is indeed brain tissue, how it got on Lundy's shirt.

You'll remember Crown witness Margaret Dance was clear the man she saw running was wearing a business shirt and tie — not a purple and navy striped polo shirt.

The murders were incredibly vicious, with blood and tissue covering walls around the victims. There was so much blood that a "shadow" was formed on the curtains behind where Christine's attacker stood. Lundy's car, glasses, wedding ring, shoes and other clothes were all tested for blood or other tissue and absolutely nothing was found.

Police said Lundy wore coveralls that protected him from the blood, but remember, these were never found.

But if we accept Lundy was wearing coveralls, then how can a piece of brain tissue get inside them and onto the left sleeve of his shirt? Try it yourself with a jacket or something similar — unless the zip is undone close to halfway it seems impossible. Would the murderer have gone to the trouble of wearing coveralls only to leave them partially open? And if that was the case, would only two tiny flecks of tissue, 1–2mm across, and no other blood have got onto the shirt?

The other way brain tissue might have got on the shirt is if the killer perhaps brushed their hand or glove across their chest when removing their coveralls.

However, this would have had to be done almost instantly after the murders and still raises issues of how only two tiny stains, both with only brain tissue and no skin or blood, were found.

And if Lundy had been wearing the polo shirt, wouldn't he have disposed of it along with all other possibly incriminating evidence?

You might also expect the exertion of a 130kg man having to run 500m each way and carry out a frenzied murder with all the attendant stress during the high-speed drives may leave signs of perspiration. ESR noticed no obvious sign of sweat on the shirt.

But back to the science.

While immunohistochemistry is a potentially powerful tool, its limitations and fallibility mean it has to be used and interpreted with caution.

Numerous scientific papers outline its unreliability, and even the United States Food and Drug Administration repeatedly describes it as "subjective and variable".

For this reason very strict controls are necessary, particularly when the tissue being tested hasn't been prepared in anything like a laboratory or medical environment as normal IHC samples would be.

This supposed brain tissue had randomly flown or been smeared from Christine Lundy's skull onto a shirt; been discovered after 58 days by a scientist who wet it; been sent to another ESR lab which rinsed it with water to extract DNA; been taken by Ross Grantham and kept in his safe at Palmerston North's police station for two months; then, more than five months after it got on the shirt, it was finally preserved and tested.

Brain cells are perhaps the least robust in the body and start to break down immediately after death — within seconds. Therefore few expected the shirt to have any cells that could be identified after five months and non-laboratory care for much of that time.

That Miller was able to identify brain cells was little short of miraculous. His evidence at trial appeared convincing and was largely unchallenged, the defence's only witness on this issue not having even seen many crucial parts of the prosecution's case.

Miller, Pang and Dr Cynric Temple-Camp, another pathologist from Medlab Central, all explain this incredibly fortunate preservation of the brain tissue by saying it got onto the shirt almost immediately from Christine's body, was smeared very thinly, dried virtually instantly and was thus preserved.

Now, it's important to consider how unlikely or indeed remarkable this would have been.

There are several ways scientists preserve fresh brain tissue. It can be fixed immediately using a preservative such as formalin; snap-frozen in liquid nitrogen and kept in a freezer; or sometimes, when doctors take biopsies, it can be air-dried — the method essentially being suggested in the Lundy case.

But even Temple-Camp admitted at trial this last method is very imprecise because the cells begin breaking down so quickly. "It is very difficult to do. The air drying has to be done immediately after removal from the body . . . It is a difficult technique for surgeons, even trained surgeons, to do."

It tests credibility that this critical process, which is very difficult for even surgeons using slides in a hospital to get right, was achieved utterly by random on a shirt in the midst of a frantic murder.

Temple-Camp also said that if the shirt was wet, the vital instant drying that supposedly occurred would be even more difficult. Supposedly the 130kg Lundy wasn't sweating around his armpits during or after the murders.

North & South referred Dr Miller's report — including his photos, court testimony and a medical journal article he wrote (along with Grantham, Pang and Temple-Camp) — to two leading scientists at Otago University who deal with immunohistochemistry for comment.

Both find aspects of his procedures highly questionable and his findings concerning. Primary among them is the lack of adequate controls in Miller's testing.

Dr Philip Sheard from Otago Medical School's physiology department says because what Miller was attempting to do — testing tissue that had been on a shirt for more than five months rather than a normal, instantly preserved medical sample — it was impossible to know if the technique could still work and if the antibodies used could still reliably recognise the antigens.

"The tissue was treated in a way that was really so very, very far removed from the technique used reliably to treat tissue in my lab, for instance, I regarded the process as experimental.

"Somebody's life is on the line as a consequence of this so as I see it, it's important the process be done properly, and what's of interest to me in this case is the lack of scientific rigour in processing and judging of the tissue with regard to immunohistochemistry."

He describes most of Miller's controls — putting an unstained sample from the polo shirt through the IHC testing as well as another sample from an unassociated shirt — as virtually irrelevant.

Sheard doesn't question that routine aspects of the testing were done professionally, though he says final documentation of results and photography were poor. But what most concerns him was that Miller didn't use an appropriate positive control — fresh brain tissue smeared on a shirt and left for several months and treated in an identical way to the police sample before being tested by IHC. Only by doing this would it be possible to know whether IHC could even be used reliably in this situation.

Sheard says validating the findings by having stringent controls was doubly necessary because the tissue evident in Miller's report was poorly preserved, with no intact cells.

He says if cell contents aren't preserved in their normal form, the antigen proteins that the antibodies bind to can change their properties, easily giving false results — something he's frequently seen in the 20 years he's used IHC.

Sheard believes Miller's results are uninterpretable and if they'd been in a paper presented to him by a student he would have rejected it.

"If somebody came here and presented that as a seminar, the first thing anybody would say at question time is, 'Where are the controls?'"

Miller's findings were published in the *American Journal of Forensic Medicine and Pathology*, which means they were peer reviewed.

But Sheard points out this publication has a low rating in the scientific-journal ranking system and "just because it's published doesn't mean it's true", adding that scientific literature is littered with disproved or misinterpreted experiments.

When Dr Marilyn Duxson from Otago University's department of anatomy and structural biology was independently shown Miller's reports and evidence, she immediately echoed Sheard's concerns about lack of necessary controls.

Duxson, who has taught neuroanatomy for 25 years and done IHC for 16, also criticised the lack of serial photos (showing the same area of tissue tested in different ways, rather than random areas as Miller presents) — something she says is basic good science.

And she questions why all the tissue stained the same way when treated with IHC — normally each different antibody would stain in different patterns and in different areas as they attach to different parts of the tissue.

Moreover, she raises an issue noted by other experts who've viewed the photos: Why are there no blood cells evident?

She said it seemed "at the very limits of probability" that in such a gruesome murder the brain tissue would not have had any blood cells with it.

(James Pang, who gave evidence on the possibility of brain tissue being on the shirt, told *North & South* the brain doesn't have much blood in it — only in the scalp area — a suggestion met with incredulity by other doctors and scientists it was referred to.)

But above all Duxson finds it hard to believe any tissue could have been preserved on the polo shirt. "That really blows the minds of anybody who's experienced in this area that I've mentioned it to — we just can't believe he could get anything surviving, any real tissue surviving, after what that shirt went through."

Even if tissue had been preserved, she says the fact it was dried for a long time at room temperature means, in her experience, it became "sticky" and in IHC testing would bind with things it normally wouldn't if it was in good condition, thus giving totally unreliable results.

"It's something I tell my students to be very careful not to do. That kind of drying is the last way I'd preserve tissue for immunohistochemistry."

Further complicating the reliability of Miller's tests is that even if the brain tissue had been miraculously preserved initially on the shirt by sheer fluke, it was then wet again (twice, in the case of the more important sample) during ESR tests.

Pang argues once the tissue was dried on the polo shirt it was preserved forever and the cells wouldn't have been affected by being rehydrated.

Duxson's response: "Oh I completely disagree — utterly disagree. I don't think he's correct."

She says great lengths are gone to in laboratories when preparing IHC samples to prevent moisture getting on them before they're fixed with formalin or liquid nitrogen, as enzymes in the material will be reactivated, degrading the material.

Duxson says there's no way what Miller did would stand the scientific scrutiny necessary for a top scientific journal or one that routinely published about IHC.

"There are so many variables there — oh man, I wouldn't put a man in prison on that evidence. It's just a pity the defence didn't manage to get the right sort of expert witness who could stand up to [Miller] and say, 'But what about this — this isn't beyond doubt?'"

Miller, however, maintains his work is above question.

He rejects suggestions his controls were inadequate, insists the antibodies stained as expected and claims the tissue was well preserved.

"Those who are familiar with my work know that there are few immunohistochemists on the planet that go through the trouble that I do to ensure the accuracy of my results. That is one of the reasons I have been so successful as a consultant to other pathologists. For that reason I can say with 100 per cent certainty that the tissue on Mr Lundy's shirt was central nervous system tissue. Not 99.999 per cent certainty — 100 per cent . . . Any appropriately trained pathologist or other scientist who examined the evidence that I did and reviewed the immunostains that I performed would come to the same conclusion that I did. If they did not, they are either incompetent, hopelessly naive or unwilling to believe the truth."

None of this sways Sheard or Duxson, who describe Miller's responses to questions as "unbelievable", "astonishing" and showing a "worrying degree of over-confidence".

Sheard adds Miller's insistence on 100 per cent certainty "reflects a remarkable ignorance of the uncertainty inherent in all biological investigations".

When ESR scientist Björn Sutherland examined the polo shirt, he also found red particles that he said were so small it was difficult to conduct tests for blood. Only one red particle he tested returned a positive result, and Sutherland stressed it was "a probable indication that blood is present, however it is not conclusive".

Subsequent DNA testing strongly suggested Amber's DNA in the sample but Sutherland said other cellular material from Amber could have been found in the same area.

This microscopic particle of "blood dust" is the basis for the common claim that Amber's blood was found on Lundy's shirt. Lundy supporters say if it was blood dust, it was just as likely to have come from an old scabbed-over leg wound found at the post-mortem and could have got on Lundy's shirt as the two cuddled up on the couch watching TV, as they often did.

Meticulous or ridiculous?

Judges, including the one in the Lundy case, often instruct juries to use their common sense when deciding guilt.

So it's worthwhile standing back and looking at the Lundy case from that perspective.

According to police and the Crown, Lundy had been planning the murders for weeks, his plan was "meticulous" and he believed he'd committed the perfect crime.

If that's to be believed, Mark Lundy left an incredible amount to chance.

- If his alibi was to have been out of town, but then drive home and back so fast nobody would believe he could have done it, his whole plan relied on not one single person in rush-hour Wellington, on SH1, or on the streets of Palmerston North seeing him drive at arguably impossible speeds. It would have taken just one person to notice this lunatic drive, to have *555ed him, to have been run off the road by his wild passing manoeuvres, just one cop or traffic camera to have seen him — and he was toast.

- Lundy had no way of knowing Amber's Pippins group was going to be cancelled that night — he found out only when Christine and Amber rang him at 5.30pm — supposedly when he was about to set off to murder one or both of them. Until then, he would have expected them to be up when he stole home at 7pm. Wouldn't this have thrown his meticulous plan into disarray and caused him to reconsider or postpone the murders? Did he really instantly come up with the bizarre request for Christine and Amber to be in bed by 7pm because he was coming home for sex?

  Wouldn't the practical Christine have said, "Don't be silly, Mark, there's no way I can get Amber asleep by 7pm/you'll never make it home by 7pm in that traffic/why don't you wait till later this evening if you really want sex tonight/but you've already booked into your motel/couldn't it wait till tomorrow night/make it after *Shortland Street*?"

  Ross Grantham says, "It's plausible that Lundy convinced his wife that they should have a romantic evening and it's not uncommon for married couples." Really? At 7pm when your kid's normally up and about; when the husband's already checked into a motel for the night; when it requires a 300km round-trip?

  And did Lundy make Christine promise not to tell anyone she might talk to in the meantime — like Julie Burnett — that he was unexpectedly coming home? Because if she did, he was toast again.

- Why would Lundy have said a ludicrous time of 7pm? Why not 9pm or 10pm? What made him think he could actually make it home by 7pm anyway?

- If Amber had been put to bed so early, there was every chance she wouldn't be asleep at 7pm and would get up when she heard her dad come home. If so, you have to accept Lundy planned to kill her all along.

- Meticulous? Why would he park opposite a friend's place and later run 500m through suburbia and past shops trying to disguise himself with only a curly blonde women's wig? If speed was essential, why would he park so far from the main route back to Petone?

- Meticulous? How could he have been so dumb to keep the shirt he wore during the murders?

- Meticulous? If he wanted to avert suspicion he wasn't the loving spouse and father virtually everyone described him as, why would he have done the one thing that would have confirmed he was a heartless husband and hired a prostitute?

  If he wanted proof he was in Wellington around midnight, why wouldn't he have bought a burger, used an ATM, phoned for a pizza — anything that proved where he was without bringing suspicion and opprobrium?

- If he was such a lousy actor at the funeral and in the various times police construed his body language as false or unbelievable, why did the prostitute, the motel manager and his customers the next morning describe him as normal and cheerful? *North & South* has listened to the phone messages Lundy left for Christine on the Wednesday morning when he was trying to find a central Wellington address so he could chase up money owed to them. They sound so unlike a man who's murdered his wife and daughter hours earlier that he either truly doesn't know they're lying hacked to death or he's a superb actor.

- The suggested motive for the murders was an insurance payout. The Lundys were in the process of increasing their life cover (as part of a normal annual review of their policies and in light of a new vineyard venture) from $200,000 to $500,000 each, but this hadn't been completed.

Why then would Lundy murder his wife before the increased cover was in place?

If not Lundy then who?

Ross Grantham remains in no doubt police got the right man, despite Lundy's protestations, despite a small group of friends who still work to prove his innocence.

"I'm convinced that the evidence produced is irrefutable . . . I admire friends of Mark Lundy for sticking by him — that's admirable, but I think it's futile. I think because he has no remorse for what he did, because he's so dishonest, he appeals upon these people, and that's unfortunate."

Christine's brother, Glenn Weggery, also insists police got it right and says Lundy's supporters are very misguided and keep stirring up the case "so the rest of our family gets put through hell again".

Grantham says it's unfortunate that most of those who believe Lundy's innocent weren't present during the whole trial and didn't see all the evidence.

Campaigner Geoff Levick admits he wasn't at the trial but you'd struggle to find anyone who knows more about the case. He used to own a chemical-importing company and would visit clients in Petone and Palmerston North, near the Lundy home. He drove that route dozens of times and it always took him about two hours. When he heard of the times Lundy was supposed to have managed, he simply didn't believe it.

Now a horse-breeder in Auckland, Levick has devoted more than five years, 5000 hours and many rooms of his house to investigating the murders, amassing expert evidence challenging the police case and helping establish the website www.lundytruth.com. He never knew Lundy before the murders and insists he's interested only in evidence and not emotion.

Despite obtaining many undisclosed documents, he estimates there are several hundred more the defence never received, as well as more than 20 police notebooks.

So what might really have happened that night? It's difficult to go into detail because of court suppression orders among other things. But it's possible to say this much:

- For several months police believed there was more than one person involved, saying someone else helped clean up the scene afterwards.

- At trial, it was revealed there were four uneliminated suspects, not counting Lundy. Grantham says these people had one alibi for the time of death but not the two police required. However, all alibis revolved around a time of death of 7pm, which must now be questioned. The original suspect list had more than 30 names.

- During the investigation, police actually accused one of those people of being the murderer, but later said he wasn't involved.

- Grantham's notebook suggests he also offered immunity to a friend of Lundy if he admitted involvement. (Grantham now says he offered only the opportunity of immunity from prosecution, as only the Solicitor-General can grant immunity.)

- Seven unidentified fingerprints and a palm print were found around the house – a fact not revealed to the jury.

- Lundy was a suspect from day one. In the arrest interview, Detective Sergeant Steve Kelly told him: "If you want to know what we've been doing for six months, we've been working on you, all right, for six months, from day one. The number-one suspect on my spreadsheet is you all right.

  "Now that's the way it's been for all those man-hours, all of those going to work at six in the morning till nine at night, seven days a bloody week, with the cops thinking that you killed your wife and daughter."

  It's impossible to say whether this resulted in any tunnel vision, but it clearly suggests Lundy was the investigation's main focus from very early on.

More than 24,000 police hours were invested in convicting Mark Lundy. In attempting to defend him, his lawyers had to haggle to get legal-aid funding for a few hundred hours to investigate the case, question witnesses and counter police claims in what was often an extraordinarily complex case.

The jurors heard six weeks of evidence and deliberated for seven hours before finding Lundy guilty. Nobody should challenge their decision based on the evidence they heard.

However, the police and Crown's common cry that only those who sat through the trial have a right to comment on a person's guilt is spurious. If not all the relevant evidence was produced at trial, if compelling expert evidence challenging the Crown case was never presented, how can this claim be sustained?

A thorough sifting of trial transcripts and evidence; much more background research into complex areas than was ever presented to the jury (it was exposed to the case for only about 200 hours); and studied reflection on this, away from the heat of the courtroom with its theatrics and tactics — is that not arguably an acceptable basis on which to question a conviction?

If it is, and if the benchmark for justice in New Zealand is "beyond reasonable doubt", it seems only fair Mark Lundy's case be viewed again dispassionately and with all the available evidence.

$ %
3 4 5

W E R T

S D F G

X C V

Alt

CHAPTER TWENTY-FOUR

Data mining

2012, *OnPoint*: Keith Ng reveals a privacy bungle.

Much has been written about the inevitable death of print newspapers, due to the rise of the internet. But as some of the great mastheads of yore have cut or scaled back their investigative teams, a new breed of investigator has started to fill the gap. Independent, usually operating alone, publishing entirely online, and funded by donation, crowdsourcing or other jobs, they are the modern equivalent of the 'typewriter guerrillas' Tom Behrens profiled shortly after Watergate (Behrens, 1977).

Keith Ng is probably New Zealand's best-known and most effective example of the breed. He calls himself a blogger, but that title does not capture the depth, range and intelligence of what he does. Investigative blogger, or journalist, would be a more accurate description.

He lives in Wellington, where he trod a well-worn path to journalism, via Victoria University (where he honed his interest in politics) and its student magazine, *Salient*. It was at *Salient* that he developed the knack of getting stories, especially using his gift for quantitative research skills — what is now known as data journalism.

After a brief time working for government, in 'Helengrad' (the insiders' nickname for the fortress-like atmosphere in the Beehive during the last years of the Labour-led Helen Clark government), he branched out on his own as a freelance writer. He combines his interest in politics and policy with an aptitude for mining large amounts of data to ask the kinds of questions that many politicians would rather were not asked.

This story came from a tip-off. He had heard that the Ministry of Social Development — which channels billions of dollars in welfare payments to beneficiaries — had inadvertently left the sensitive personal files of many of those people unprotected on public kiosks. In other words, anyone could walk into a Ministry office, open a computer at a kiosk, and read the name and address of children being protected from domestic violence or sexual abuse, as well as those of hundreds of thousands of people accessing benefits.

Ng broke the story on his blog, *OnPoint*. Quickly picked up by mainstream media, it left officials very red-faced. The inevitable inquiry concluded that a number of people within the Ministry's IT function were aware of the 'kiosk' security weaknesses and the risk posed in relation to the access to information on the Ministry's corporate network, but that appropriate follow-up action had not been taken. It recommended the kiosks be kept closed until they could either be physically separated from the Ministry's network or have effective firewalls installed.

Although it's probably attracted the most attention of any story he's done, Ng says it's not his best work. 'In terms of the substance, and consequences, of the story, I'm much prouder of my tobacco pieces' (Ng, 2016).

Since this break, Ng has gone on to pioneer collaborative investigative data journalism in New Zealand. In a recent story, he worked with reporters at *The New Zealand Herald* to probe the taxpayer-funded allowances paid to Members of Parliament, using custom-built software to mine public data to generate important questions. Claimed at the time to be the biggest data journalism project undertaken in New Zealand, it trawled 7.2 million property records, which were combined with other data on cloudservers to make a searchable database. Ng says that he got the *Herald* involved because he found that National Party MPs were not responding to his enquiries. The story shows how a specialist in politics and data mining can combine skills with more traditional journalists to produce something that probably neither could have achieved on their own.

This excerpt, from his series about the leaky servers, showcases the blogger's style: casual, down-to-earth, self-deprecating and unashamedly personal, but with a serious core of fact that makes it impossible to ignore.

Behrens, J. C. (1977). *The typewriter guerrillas: Closeups of twenty top investigative reporters*. Chicago: Nelson-Hall.

Ng, K. (2016). Interview with author, J. Hollings.

MSD's Leaky Servers

OnPoint, 14 October 2012

My jeans were torn, my hoodie was pretty ragged, and I hadn't shaved for a week. It turned out that bloggers are remarkably good at disguising themselves as unemployed, without even trying.

Last week, I got tipped-off that the parts of the MSD network were completely exposed to the public. You could go into any WINZ office and use their self-service kiosks to access their corporate network.

These locked-down kiosks are provided so you could look for jobs online, send off CVs etc. They've had some basic features disabled, which supposedly meant that you couldn't just open up File Manager and poke around the machine. However, by just using the Open File dialogue in Microsoft Office, you could map any unsecured computer on the network, and then open up any accessible file.

This basically means you can grab any file that wasn't bolted down on the network, while standing in the middle of a WINZ office. And that's what I did.

So what wasn't bolted down? Let's start with the boring stuff. There were servers connected to their call centre systems, logging calls going in and out. They contained sound recordings which I couldn't open, but which I suspect (for various reasons) are NOT complete recording of calls. I guess I'll leave that for the Privacy Commissioner.

And then there were file server logs. Normally, they aren't that exciting. Except that WINZ name their files quite well. For example:

> s:\SharedData\wi_wites\Waikato\HAM\Fraud Investigations\
> [Name of investigator]\[Name of WINZ client] 23 Jun 2011 Case
> 640026-10.WMA

And so on. There were similar files for other "special" clients as well. There are probably a lot of personally identifying details in there, but I didn't spend much time going through them, because then I got tipped-off about the invoice server. It contains what appears to be all of MSD invoices for this year. Among all the invoices for milk and sausage rolls were invoices for:

Contractors — With full names, hours worked, pay rates and pay details for all of MSD's contract workers (Studylink/Call Centre staff, consultants, *coughmediatrainerscough*, temporary staff, etc).

Doctors/Radiology — With full names of candidates for adoptions, foster parents and Limited Services Volunteers (they have to get medical reports first). Others were for children in CYFS care, with their full names and their chief complaint; some of these were for x-rays after injuries.

Debt Collection — MSD's Collection Units uses Veda to keep track of people who owe them money. And Veda's invoices to MSD shows the full name of every person they helped MSD to locate. i.e. *The invoice is a list of people who owe MSD money*. MSD outsources debt collection to another vendor, whose invoices detail the full name of each person owing money, how much they've paid and how much they still owe to MSD.

Fraud Investigation — The Benefit Control Unit and Intelligence Unit (basically the fraud investigators) also used Veda to locate and get credit records for people they're investigating (with full names, of course). Conveniently, these are billed separately, under "Benefit Control Unit" and "Intelligence Unit", so it doesn't get mixed up with the Collection Units' invoices. Another set of invoices are for the servicing of court documents on behalf of MSD, some done by private investigators.

That's the light stuff. Now it start getting messy:

HCN — HCN stands for "High and Complex Needs". These are:

> ... short-term, intensive interventions aimed at addressing the severe
> and current needs of the most challenging children or young people

Note "the most". Because of its interagency nature, invoices come from other agencies to CYFS. These invoices contain the full names of kids in the HCN programme and the cities they live in. In a few cases, they also contain the date of birth and the name of the school which they attend.

Care & Protection — Care & Protection homes are:

> This is a safe and secure place where children and young people
> will go if they are in our care and can't live in the community for a
> while. They might stay at a residence if:
>
> • there are worries about the child or young person's safety
> • their actions are putting themselves at risk
> • or they are putting others around them at risk.

These invoices contain the first names, dates and costs of children living in CYFS Care & Protection homes. Other CYFS residential arrangements are also listed, containing the full name of children.

Phone bills — Bills from Telecom for CYFS Family Homes and Care & Protection facilities. Since the billing address is just MSD, it's often hard to tell which facility the phone bill is for. So Accounts has handwritten *the full address of each of these facilities* on each bill.

Along with the name of the facility and its address are the normal stuff contained in a phone bill: The phone number of each of these facilities, along with a complete log of all the toll calls made from that location.

Pharmacy — Bills from pharmacies to CYFS facilities, listing the children in that facility and the medication they are prescribed. These range from the antibiotics and scabies cream to cancer drugs, ADHD drugs, anti-depressants and anti-psychotics.

Legal bills — All of MSD's legal bills are in there, along with other legal bills paid for by MSD (e.g. Representation for foster parents). Most of these are invoices from Crown Law. They often mention the full names of parties and lawyers in the case, as well as the nature of the case. This can be very revealing information, for example, if the nature of the case is "Historical Claims", and the lawyers representing one side specialises in historical abuse and the other side is CYFS.

Some of these claims were settled out of court. The details of the settlements are not there, just the fact that a complaint was made and that it was settled.

In any event, all of these invoices are legally privileged.

Last one — One community group invoiced for providing support to a whanau after a suicide attempt (full name of that person included).

I sorted through 3500 invoices. This was about half of what I obtained, and what I obtained was about a quarter of what was accessible. There are probably more outrageous things still on that server, and there are probably other servers that I've completely missed. But I'm done for now.

This stuff was all a few clicks away at any WINZ kiosk, anywhere in the country. The privacy breach is massive, and the safety of vulnerable children was put at risk.

This should never have happened:

- Public kiosks should not have been connected to the corporate network.
- Servers that didn't need to be globally accessible should not have been globally accessible, even if they only contained innocuous data.
- Invoices, file logs and call logs, at a place like MSD, should not have been treated as innocuous data.

Aside from the files I got my hands on, I was also told that the configuration files for virtual machines were readily accessible in the same way. I've had no experience with setting up virtual machines, but here you go:

[Original blog contains three screenshots at this point.]

If someone knows how bad/not-bad this stuff is, please explain it to me in the comments section! And yes, the bits I blanked out were passwords in plaintext.

The Acting Privacy Commissioner was briefed on this today, and I'll be handing the files over to them tomorrow. This story took most of the week to do, so if you like it, some money would be greatly appreciated.

UPDATE: MSD has told me that they will be taking the kiosks offline until the problem is resolved.

CHAPTER TWENTY-FIVE

Stolen identity

2012, *The Press*: Martin van Beynen exposes the fraudster who helped build Christchurch's CTV building, which killed 115 people when it collapsed.

Just after midday on 22 February 2011, about 114 young, mostly Asian students were gathering on the third floor of the CTV building in Christchurch. They were preparing for the afternoon's English-language lessons. Meanwhile, on floors above and below them, hundreds of other people were going about the various activities housed in this typical central-city building: getting counselling from a relationship counselling service, receiving treatment from a medical centre, or preparing television bulletins for Canterbury Television, which was housed in the two floors below.

Then, at 12.51 p.m., the earth shifted, violently. It wasn't a particularly large earthquake, in terms of the amount of energy released, but, unfortunately for the occupants of the CTV building, it had unusually large vertical acceleration. This meant that buildings in Christchurch were effectively lifted several metres, then slammed back into the ground, with extraordinary force. Luckily, most buildings — including some very old ones — survived. But the CTV building, despite being one of the most modern, and built to the most modern earthquake-resistant guidelines, did not. Under the immense pressure of the seismic rupture, its six floors, already weakened by another large earthquake five months earlier, collapsed in seconds. Between the pancaking concrete floors, 115 people died, including 70 of the foreign students. Most would have died mercifully quickly, but some did not, either burnt alive in the subsequent fire or drowned as the fire was put out.

Across Christchurch that day, a total of 185 people were killed, in what was New Zealand's third-deadliest natural disaster. Two-thirds of them died in one relatively new building that was supposed to be state of the art. Even as the dust was settling that day, many people were asking what went wrong at CTV?

The subsequent official inquiry found that the CTV building had been poorly designed, by an engineer not qualified to design multi-storey buildings, who in turn was largely unsupervised. Christchurch City Council officials had been pressured into approving the design, and had also failed to declare it unsafe after the 2010 earthquake (Canterbury Earthquakes Royal Commission, 2011).

But that wasn't the full story. On 15 September 2012, readers of Christchurch's *Press* newspaper learned something perhaps even more shocking: the building's construction was 'supervised' by a fraudster — someone who claimed to be an engineer, but was not. The story raised disturbing questions not just about the construction of the building but also about the regulation of the engineering profession itself. Suddenly, it wasn't just a story of one incompetent engineer — it was a story of a profession, and a regulatory system, that had failed.

How could someone have faked not only his name but also an engineering degree, and been left in such a responsible position? How many other buildings were at risk from a profession that didn't seem to be able to regulate itself? And it wasn't just New Zealand's problem — after the story's publication, Australian authorities worriedly began checking all buildings that Gerald Shirtcliff had worked on.

The reporter who broke the story, Martin van Beynen, doesn't really consider himself an investigative journalist. After training as a lawyer he became fascinated by journalism, but not of the investigative kind; more the kind of 'gonzo' journalism of Tom Wolfe and Hunter S. Thompson. He says he still sees himself more as a writer than an investigator, but nonetheless he's racked up an impressive list of investigative stories during his time at *The Press* in Christchurch, often on corporate fraudsters. So when questions began to be raised about Shirtcliff's role in the CTV building's construction, he was given the job of getting answers (van Beynen, 2016).

While he didn't prove that the CTV building would have stayed up if Shirtcliff had done his job, he did show that Shirtcliff should never have been supervising its construction. 'He didn't have a lot to do with the building. If he had been more on the ball and been a proper engineer, maybe he would have seen the building wasn't being built right.

'He was working for a company that was pretty dodgy and spending most of his time on other sites and trying to hide the fact that he didn't know what he was doing. I can't show he was there on the day when they did the pour [of that beam that failed]. It's a pretty long bow to draw to say that had he [been more on the job] that the building might have stayed up.'

Nonetheless, a more qualified site engineer might have noticed one of the building's crucial flaws: that its walls were not connected to the floors properly. 'He might have spotted that if he had been there more often.'

Van Beynen is satisfied with the impact of the story, especially the fact that the engineering profession has changed its procedures to prevent fraudsters like Shirtcliff slipping through again. 'He was able to fool the universities, he was able to fool the industry, and nobody picked it up. It's certainly one of the stories people talk about. It has highlighted the ease with which someone like him can fool the authorities, so that's all been tightened up' (van Beynen, 2016).

He's also proud of the craft that went into the story. One of the most difficult aspects was proving that Shirtcliff had stolen another man's identity, rather than just changing his own name. The story required a lot of tracing of people and events from the pre-internet era. Not only did he have to find Shirtcliff, in Australia, but he also had to find people who had worked with Shirtcliff in South Africa, 30 years earlier. 'Dealing with overseas authorities was really tough. None of the universities would talk to us. I still think I have done better stories. But the results were just fantastic, because it was a long haul, and then everything just fell into place. Even at the last minute we were thinking "What if we are wrong?" We will be in so much trouble' (van Beynen, 2016).

For someone who has had so much success as an investigator, van Beynen remains very self-deprecating about his achievements. 'I don't see myself as an investigative journalist. I'm just a reporter that likes exposing people that [deserve being exposed].

'It's been a very rewarding career. I couldn't ask for more. I never thought I would get to the top of the game.'

Canterbury Earthquakes Royal Commission (CERC). (2011). *Final Report*, part 3, volume 6: Canterbury Television Building (CTV). Christchurch: CERC. Retrieved from http://canterbury.royalcommission. govt.nz/Final-Report-Volume-Six-Contents

van Beynen, M. (2016). Interview with author, J. Hollings.

A life of lies

The Press, 15 September 2012

His $200,000, 13 metre motor cruiser *Vagabond* bobs on the sunny water of beautiful Manly Boat Harbour, Brisbane.

His home, only a stroll from the picturesque Cleveland coastline, is spacious and comfortable. A late-model white Mercedes shares the double garage with his wife's Citroen.

He works for a multinational engineering firm and has his own office in the firm's impressive building near the Brisbane Botanic Gardens. He is a husband, father, grandfather and respected professional, still working in his mid-60s.

Not bad for someone who secretly has a serious fraud conviction and a stolen identity. But life is about to change dramatically for Wellington-born Gerald Shirtcliff. The past is about to catch up.

The event that begins the unravelling of Gerald Shirtcliff's lies came on February 22, 2011, when an earthquake ripped through Christchurch. It damaged a multitude of commercial buildings in the central city, but toppled only two. One was the six-storey Canterbury Television building at 249 Madras St.

Built in 1986–87, the building collapsed, killing 115 people and injuring scores of others. Some victims lost their limbs, others survived the initial collapse, but perished in a fire that broke out near the lift shaft and then spread.

It's not known if the collapse sent shivers down Gerald Shirtcliff's spine, but it should have. He was the construction manager for the company that built the CTV building. Earlier this year, he appeared, somewhat reluctantly, before the Royal Commission to explain his role in the construction.

It wasn't much of a role, he claimed. But whatever his culpability, and to be fair it might be little, being thrust in the limelight was the last thing Shirtcliff needed.

The tower of lies he had built his successful life on was starting its own collapse.

In Brisbane, only his family appear to know him as Gerald Shirtcliff.

To others he is Will Fisher, a university-educated engineer with a CV that would make any professional man blush with pride. Late last month, he was working as a contractor for WorleyParsons, an international engineering consulting firm based in Brisbane, which specialises in mining and infrastructure.

He was born Gerald Morton Shirtcliff in 1945, the third-born and first son of a respected family in Wellington. His father Morton, a business executive, would end his career as the South Island manager for Shell Oil.

Gerald, who was a choir boy, was bright but did not thrive academically at Rongotai College and left school to work in a Wellington bank and then for an insurance company. Associates of the time say he had a proclivity for telling lies. He joined the Territorial Army as a bandsman, playing the cornet or trumpet.

His early jobs did not work out and he left to train for his commercial pilot's licence at the then Wanganui Flying School. His father, thinking some overseas experience might straighten out his wayward son, organised a job for him at a South African firm of consulting engineers in which his friend Piet van Zyl was a partner.

Shirtcliff landed in Pretoria in 1968 to work for Van Niekerk, Klein and Edwards, now VKE and part of the multinational Smec group. According to his own version of events, he rose quickly through the ranks and was soon supervising construction projects and, with a new "airline transport" rating, flew staff to remote locations in the company aircraft.

An associate of the time, South African engineer Niek Diedericks, has a different recall. He says he and Shirtcliff were employed as technical assistants with no supervisory responsibilities.

Diedericks claims Shirtcliff told him he was escaping the Vietnam War draft in New Zealand (New Zealand did not have a draft for Vietnam) and he cannot remember Shirtcliff doing any flying. Although some partners had their own aircraft, the South African branch of the firm did not, he says.

The two also knocked around with young English engineer William Anthony Fisher, who had recently graduated from the University of Sheffield with a top Bachelor of Engineering. They went camping and drinking together and enjoyed the social life Pretoria had to offer. Fisher, speaking from England where he has retired from his career as a civil and structural engineer, told *The Press* Shirtcliff was good company but he was disturbed by the lies Shirtcliff told, apparently to escape an arranged marriage in New Zealand. "We flatted together for about eight months. He was good fun to be with. Lots of quips and jokes. He was very much his own man, doing what he wanted to do," Fisher says. Shirtcliff was "pretty bright". "He was always keen to learn how things were done."

Diedericks claims Shirtcliff left the firm under a cloud, due to an incident over Shirtcliff allegedly forging Piet van Zyl's signature on a cheque and cashing it.

Late in 1969, Shirtcliff left South Africa for Sydney, Australia, ready to start afresh. So fresh, in fact, he had a new name. It had a familiar ring. It was William Anthony Fisher. Later, he would claim he changed his name to disassociate himself from his family name, due to abuse by his father, but the change was more than a shift in moniker.

He also took the real Will Fisher's birthdate, birthplace and engineering qualification. In 1971, he used the real Fisher's Bachelor of Engineering to gain entry to the masters programme at the University of New South Wales in Sydney, and in 1972 to become a member of the Institute of Engineers in Australia.

For a man who wanted nothing to do with his family, especially his father, he was not averse to getting his father to help him with his masters project. Morton Shirtcliff, who was also a pilot and who taught Gerald to fly, was well versed in roading surfaces and bitumen from his stint as bitumen manager for Shell Oil in New Zealand.

In 1974, Gerald Shirtcliff was awarded a Masters of Engineering in highway engineering. In Sydney, Shirtcliff worked for a short time as a project manager, including on a 33-storey building in Kings Cross, and also as a fleet manager for Streets Ice Cream. He also worked as a qualified engineer for the firm MacDonald, Wagner Priddle which became Connell Wagner and then came under the Aurecon umbrella in 2009. He met his wife Julie at the firm.

By the mid 80s, he and his family were on the move again, this time landing in Christchurch. The move, he would say later, was an attempt at a family reconciliation, but sources close to the family say that is misleading.

In any event , the family reverted to the name Shirtcliff. One day at Christchurch Airport he met Murray Cresswell, a commercial pilot with ideas of setting up a regional airline.

Shirtcliff expressed immediate interest, maintaining he had money to invest from a stint as a nuclear engineer in South Africa, Cresswell claims. Shirtcliff, he says, also asserted he was a top pilot. Shirtcliff took a management role in the company, Goldfields Air, and convinced the other stakeholders his plans for the company, which operated a seven-seater Piper Navajo previously used by the Victorian state premier, would lead to success. The big plans seemed unrealistic to Cresswell and the two quickly fell out. Goldfields Air failed in 1986.

Cresswell wasn't impressed with Shirtcliff's ability as a pilot. He flew with him rarely but says on one occasion Shirtcliff was about to fly into a "reinforced cloud" before he corrected him. Cresswell claims the operation's chief pilot, Neil Abbott, told him after doing a run with him, he thought Shirtcliff was unteachable.

In 1986, Shirtcliff was employed by Williams Construction, the company contracted to build the CTV building.

Williams was a public company founded by Wellingtonian Arthur Williams (later knighted) and had a solid financial history, making it attractive to the many entrepreneurs out to make hay in the heady mid-80s. The company had expanded rapidly and managing director Michael Brooks was keen to add someone with structural engineering experience.

When Shirtcliff gave evidence to the Royal Commission on the Canterbury Earthquakes by video link from Brisbane last month, he claimed he visited the construction site in Madras St only about once a month because it was a straightforward job and he was needed on other more difficult Williams projects.

However, in earlier emails to the commission, he denied any involvement with the project. At the commission hearing, Brooks said he "wasn't up to the job" but was not asked to elaborate.

Tony Scott, a quantity [surveyor] for Williams, told *The Press* it was easy to scapegoat Shirtcliff, but if he had turned up regularly on the CTV site, he might have prevented some of the construction mistakes highlighted in evidence before the commission.

"If Gerry wasn't at the CTV site, what was he doing all that time?" Scott says.

Shirtcliff continued as construction manager for a new company (Union Construction) set up by Scott and Brooks. Union took over the CTV job and the building was finished towards the end of 1987.

After both Williams and Union failed, Scott and Shirtcliff set up their own construction company, with Shirtcliff looking after practical aspects on site and Scott "in charge of the office and finances".

Scott says the company did mainly design-and-build projects, including the huge Caxton Warehouse in Halswell and a five-storey apartment building in Park Tce. "I have to say Gerry was generally capable and conscientious," Scott says.

"He was a hard driver and sometimes I would have to tell him this wasn't South Africa. He wasn't well liked. Although things turned sour at the end, we had a good partnership and didn't interfere with each others' jobs. I kept a tight control on the financial side of things."

Scott saw the need for the new company to promote itself and encouraged Shirtcliff to put together a CV, which he kept for 25 years, and provided to the commission into the CTV collapse. In it Shirtcliff claims to have:
- A B.Eng from the University of Sheffield.
- Managed construction companies in New Zealand and overseas.

- Experience managing an international company.
- Four years corporate flying experience and management of "corporate flying division".

"He did try to pull a couple of swifties on me, but nothing I couldn't handle," says Scott, who also recalls some of Shirtcliff's interesting stories.

Shirtcliff, he claims, said his father was the legal representative for Shell in Britain and that was why he studied at the University of Sheffield.

Shirtcliff also claimed to be an old boy of Christ's College.

After Scott Shirtcliff Ltd foundered, Shirtcliff set out on another venture based on an idea the company had bought from an American entrepreneur in Rangiora.

"Gerry took the idea and came around boasting how much money he was going to make and how he had got one over on me. I didn't care. I had much more important things to worry about," said Scott.

The idea involved setting up hamburger outlets in service stations. Thus, in October 1992, Autoburger Ltd was born. Autoburger Ltd changed its name to Langford Services and went into liquidation in 1999.

During the 90s, Shirtcliff also worked for March Construction as its in-house engineer. Owner Edwin March told *The Press* Shirtcliff worked for the company for about eight months in the early 90s on a sewerage pipeline in Whanganui. March says by chance he found out Shirtcliff was not registered as an engineer in New Zealand and queried him.

"He told me [he] was registered in Australia under the Fisher name. He just did levels for us, things like that. There was no problem with his work. He did a good job for us." But this is not what March told the police in March 2003 as evidenced by a statement released by the police under the Official Information Act.

In the statement, March said Shirtcliff had been the "house" engineer for March in 1993–4 and again in 1998 when he was employed "on and off" as a consultant.

Shirtcliff, March told the police, had signed off an engineer's design certification on a sheet pile wall at the Peterborough apartments in Christchurch using the name Shirtcliff and giving a registration number.

Another engineering firm queried the certification. When confronted, Shirtcliff said he used his Australian registration, which was under the name William Fisher.

"He told me the reason for using another name was because his father had hated him so he was brought up by his aunts in London and renamed," the statement says.

Shirtcliff's next business venture was a Nationwide Service Centre franchise, in St Asaph St. The business was busy but not profitable and by 1997 Shirtcliff was wanting out. But how to sell a failing business?

Successful Queenstown business couple Eric and Kay Zust had their children in boarding school in Christchurch and wanted to move closer. They had run a thriving souvenir business but knew nothing about the automotive trade.

The initial negotiations stalled over the franchise agreement, but Shirtcliff contacted the couple again about a year later saying the business had experienced phenomenal growth and produced the GST figures to prove it.

Zust thought he was on to a winner.

Shirtcliff stayed on for two weeks to show Zust the ropes and then left quickly for Australia, taking all the vehicle records with him.

Zust smelled a rat, checked the previous GST returns actually provided to IRD and found they were nothing like the ones provided by Shirtcliff.

"I realised immediately the business would fail, but I didn't know how to get out of it."

Zust, originally from Switzerland, hung on for a year, paid all the business creditors and virtually gave the business to its employees. He also pursued Shirtcliff and, in December 2000, the High Court awarded the Zusts $640,000 in damages and costs. The Zusts also pressed the New Zealand police to act and wrote to MPs and the prime minister.

Shirtcliff was arrested in Brisbane in 2003 and was adamant he was not Gerald Shirtcliff, despite a car in his driveway registered in the name of his daughter Kate Shirtcliff.

After many twists and turns, Shirtcliff agreed to return to Christchurch to face charges. In 2005, he was found guilty of fraud and jailed for 20 months by Christchurch District Court Judge Murray Abbott, who said Shirtcliff was "grossly dishonest" and his actions displayed "patent criminality".

Zust's victim impact statement said Shirtcliff had made a mockery of the New Zealand justice system.

"I believe in his vocabulary the words honesty and compassion have the meaning of stupidity. He is intelligent but also devious, calculating and cunning. I and my family will never recover what we lost or heal the emotional damage he has done to us."

Shirtcliff was in jail for only two weeks before his lawyer got his sentence changed to home detention. Phil Stanley and Sue Lyons, who knew him from being fellow franchisees in the failed Nationwide network, agreed to take him in.

"None of his family wanted him and we felt sorry for the poor old bugger," says Stanley.

At the time, Stanley owned another autoservice business in Sydenham and Shirtcliff helped out with the paperwork to pay his way.

"He convinced us he was innocent. He had a lovely smile and came across as a kind grandfatherly type of guy. We could see he was a pretty sharp character but we sort of admired him," Stanley says.

The couple treated Shirtcliff like one of the family and Lyons cooked and cleaned for him. Stanley, who has worked with alternative fuel systems for most his life, had developed over the past 10 years a dual-fuel injection system for diesel engines. He had a diesel generator set that could run on ethanol, methanol, LPG or diesel, running on a test bed in his workshop.

Normally he made interested parties sign a confidentiality agreement, but he trusted his friend Shirtcliff and spent a lot of time explaining the invention.

Lyons says Shirtcliff often talked about shouting them a holiday for being so kind to him.

"He would say, 'as soon as I get out of here you guys are coming over. I'm shouting you a holiday. We will go out on the boat'.

"As soon as the bracelet was off, Julie [Shirtcliff's wife] was on the plane and boof [Shirtcliff was] off to the airport. No goodbye. No nothing."

Shirtcliff resumed his life as Will Fisher in Brisbane and told some wealthy investors he had an idea for a dual-fuel system. Brisbane contractor Wayne Smith paid him $1000 a week to develop the idea and get it working. Only eight months after Shirtcliff left Christchurch, a company called DGC Industries, of which Shirtcliff's wife Julie Rook was a director and shareholder, filed a patent for a dual-fuel system for diesel engines.

The inventor on the document: Will Fisher.

Stanley did not know about the patent application until informed by *The Press* a few weeks ago. His initial reaction is not printable.

"He is a lifetime cheat," Stanley says in a calmer moment. "He's done it to everybody. He has no compunction." The patent documents filed by Shirtcliff had changed the invention slightly but not much, Stanley says.

Through his lawyer, Shirtcliff has denied all negative assertions contained in this story. He says he is a qualified engineer and has not done anything wrong. Although he refused to answer specific questions, he says he has worked hard and all he wants is to be left in peace to get on with his life.

With his lifetime of dishonesty now exposed, that seems unlikely as a number of organisations begin inquiries.

The Press has provided information to Engineers Australia and the University of New South Wales. The Royal Commission into the Canterbury Earthquakes is also aware about Shirtcliff's past. His present employer has sacked him.

There is no certainty this will prompt any new action against Shirtcliff, but his past has finally caught up with him.

None of it was necessary, says a close associate, who asked not to be named.

"He was bright enough and hard-working enough to have achieved it all honestly. It's such a waste and he has done so much damage to his family, to others and to himself."

CHAPTER TWENTY-SIX

Did the police bungle this murder case?

2013, *The New Zealand Herald*: Phil Taylor campaigns to free Teina Pora, wrongly jailed for the murder of Susan Burdett.

As a boy growing up in the working-class Christchurch suburb of Linwood, Phil Taylor remembers being taken by his mother on a search for a missing uncle. The uncle was intellectually disabled and had fallen on hard times. The search led to a doss-house; not one of the more reputable ones. Like Taylor's uncle, many of the residents were people who had little and needed help.

As Taylor and his mother were leaving, with the long-lost uncle, some of those left behind were crying, and begging to be taken away. Taylor says it's a scene that has stayed with him. 'It was pretty clear that it was a place that made money out of the people living there. What I took away was the sense of the powerlessness of those people' (Taylor, 2015).

Another thing Taylor took with him from that rescue was an interest in giving the powerless a voice; his work as a journalist has often involved a search and rescue of those beaten down by circumstance or just plain wrongdoing. His desire to help people took him first to law school, at the University of Canterbury. But he soon switched to journalism. 'I came to realise that I was a story teller. I was a rep cyclist, and the law library scared me, because [to do a law degree you had to] spend so much time in there' (Taylor, 2015).

Since graduating with a BA and, in 1981, a journalism diploma, Taylor has slowly built up a reputation as one of the doyens of New Zealand investigative reporting. He has won most of the awards going — Reporter of the Year, Feature Writer of the Year and Sports Reporter of the Year — and has been awarded journalism fellowships to Green College, at Oxford, and Wolfson College, at Cambridge.

But awards, nice as they are, don't tell you the full story. It's his stories that show his range, his persistence and his dogged determination to do journalism that goes beyond the routine. Since the early 1990s, when he showed that a death the police were treating as a suicide was most likely a murder, his scrapbook is a roll-call of holding power to account. His passion for cycling led him to Stephen Swart, who was the source for a world exclusive: the first English-language exposé of Lance Armstrong's drug cheating. Taylor exposed what appeared to be insider trading by bankrupted Blue Chip boss Mark Bryers, and has continued to track his business activities in Australia because he feels that Australians deserve protection. He's exposed a paedophile principal, shown that a stockmarket darling was, despite its PR, involved in the arms trade, and helped put a corrupt detective in jail for attempting to pervert the course of justice. But in recent years, the story he's most proud of was helping rescue someone who did not have the capacity to help himself: Teina Pora.

If anyone needed a hand, it was Pora. His story is a tragic tale of justice gone wrong. He was jailed, at the age of 17, in 1994 after 'confessing' to the murder of 39-year-old Aucklander Susan Burdett. It later emerged that Pora suffers from foetal alcohol syndrome, which makes him especially susceptible to suggestion. There was never any physical evidence to show that he was at the scene.

Like many, Taylor did not pay Pora's conviction much attention at first. But after attending the trial of serial rapist Malcolm Rewa, Pora's case started to niggle. Unlike other supposed miscarriage-of-justice cases, where it was a case of 'If not him, then who?', here there clearly was a 'who': the serial rapist Malcolm Rewa, whose semen had been found at the scene of Burdett's murder. Yet somehow, Pora had ended up going to jail.

Pora's eventual freeing was the work of many people. But Taylor's early stories questioning the evidence against Pora were undoubtedly crucial. They came to the notice of Pora's defence team, and helped build the case for his successful appeal to the Privy Council. But Taylor says he had to push the paper to run the first story. '[The attitude was:] Who cares about a brown car thief? He's not going to get many clicks on the website. I realised I needed to get some big hit, to attract attention' (Taylor, 2015).

The big hit was Dave Henwood, the police officer whose evidence had been crucial to Rewa's conviction. Taylor located him and persuaded him to go on the record with his misgivings about Pora's conviction.

One of Pora's team, former police officer and now investigator Tim McKinnel, says that story made an enormous difference. McKinnel had known of Henwood's doubts, but until then Henwood had resisted becoming publicly involved. 'His first article [about Henwood], in many ways, and certainly in the public eye, changed everything. That was a watershed moment for us. Certainly in the public consciousness' (McKinnel, 2015).

Taylor also took the unusual step of joining forces with television. He contacted Eugene Bingham and Paula Penfold, at TV3, to help spread awareness of what he considered was a miscarriage of justice. As in the Louise Nicholas story, the power of television brought forth more witnesses and built public momentum.

The excerpt below is not the first story Taylor wrote about the case. But it pulled all the strands together and told the story as it had not been told before. Pora's case went to the Privy Council, in London. It recommended that the conviction be quashed. In 2015, Teina Pora was released from prison. Malcolm Rewa, the man many believe knows most about Susan Burdett's death, remains in prison.

After nearly 40 years in journalism, Taylor still believes it can make a difference. '[I like] the idea of standing against what's wrong. And trying to sprinkle a little water on the good. Mostly in journalism you can't do anything about anything, but occasionally you can. By being part of this process of holding power to account, I can help expose what's wrong, and shed a little light.

'Somewhere in there's a big strand, an ideal of justice and wanting to expose unfairness and help put right what might be wrong. That still motivates me.'

McKinnel, T. (2015, August 25). Interview with author, J. Hollings.

Taylor, P. (2015, August 19). Interview with author, J. Hollings.

The case that won't go away
Weekend Herald, 18 April 2013

Had the police known the semen in Susan Burdett's body belonged to an infamous solo stalker rapist when Teina Pora began to tell his stilted, vague, contradictory stories about a gang home invasion, he would likely have been charged with wasting police time rather than rape and murder.

There is no doubt Pora was a fool who played a dangerous game by implying he knew who was responsible for one of the most shocking murders of its time. Susan Burdett was a 39-year-old accounts clerk and an avid ten pin bowler who lived alone. She returned late from club night at the Manukau Superstrike on Monday, March 23, 1992, and after showering, was raped and battered to death. Her killer posed her body, crossing her legs, which were positioned off the bed. Lying on the bed beside her was the softball bat she kept for protection.

Pora was convicted of her rape and murder in 1994 and was again found guilty at a retrial in 2000, ordered after the semen in Burdett's body was found to belong to Malcolm Rewa, the country's second-most prolific rapist and someone who otherwise always attacked alone. Rewa was eventually convicted of Burdett's rape, but two juries couldn't decide about murder.

Many people have had trouble with the case, including chief justice Dame Sian Elias, who sent the case back to court commenting that the Crown had been "selective" in saying Pora told a pack of lies about almost everything except his involvement.

Pora's motives for lying lay in the situation he found himself in, says Tim McKinnel, the former policeman who, as a private investigator, has taken up Pora's cause.

Pora was a prolific car thief and had been arrested on a bench warrant for failing to attend court. Though relatively minor, jail was possible because of his long rap sheet for such crimes. He was a kid without a mother, father or job and, already a parent himself; his habit was to try to ingratiate himself to police when in trouble.

Since being charged with the rape and murder of Burdett, Pora has maintained he had no part in it, even though that stance has made it difficult for him to be granted parole. Senior detectives who worked on the case are among those who share that view, and new evidence collected during the past year supports it. The central plank of the case against Pora was his own varying admissions, which the world's leading authority on false confessions has recently described as "fundamentally flawed and unsafe".

In a second piece of new evidence collected by McKinnel and barrister Jonathan Krebs, who are working to have the case reviewed, a British criminal profiling expert has concluded Rewa was "highly unlikely" to have worked with any co-offenders, let alone Pora, a juvenile associate of an enemy gang.

It began for Pora on March 18, 1993 when he was arrested on the court warrants. He was 17, the son of a teenage mother who died when he was 4 and a father who was never around; he had a baby daughter to look after, was in a bitter dispute with senior Mongrel Mob members, having pinched back a car they had taken from him. Mobsters had turned up looking for him with a gun. He knew the gang was after him and he was in trouble with the police too.

It has never been explained how Pora went from being processed on the warrants at the Gordon Rd police station to . . . being quizzed about the Burdett rape and murder. He had provided his DNA and been excluded as a suspect the year before. In the normal course of events he would have been escorted to court on the warrant matters that day. Instead, Pora was held in custody for four days, during which he was questioned about the Burdett case for 14 hours, without a lawyer.

What is known about that morning is that Pora was brought in at 7.45am. According to a police job sheet, the head of the Burdett homicide inquiry, Detective Inspector Steve Rutherford, received an anonymous phone call 40 minutes later from a female who named a prominent Mongrel Mobster as responsible for the killing. The woman cautioned that her information was hearsay, refused to give her name or number and hung up.

Serendipitous? Sitting in an interview room having been dealt with on the warrants was Pora, a young Mongrel Mob associate.

Whether or not at the instigation of the anonymous call, within 30 minutes Detective Sergeant Mark Williams went to speak to Pora and the Burdett case was raised. Williams recorded in a job sheet that Pora asked whether police had anyone for it yet.

"No, but if you know something about it, tell me."

"I know who did it."

"Tell me about it."

"They'll get me."

"Who?"

"Mobsters."

"Did you do it?"

"Nah, nah but I know who did. I'm just shit-scared of them. They'll get my missus and my baby."

"Did you know there's a reward?"

Pora was told the reward was $20,000 and there was an indemnity against prosecution for non-principal offenders. Williams fetched the indemnity form and when Pora told him he couldn't read, explained it and read Pora his rights.

Over the next four days, Pora's story evolved from claiming he'd driven two Mongrel Mobsters to Burdett's house, to having kept lookout, to having witnessed the attack, to having helped hold her down on her bed with one mobster while another raped her. Pora didn't volunteer names but when police put names to him — including the one nominated by the anonymous caller — Pora went along with it.

IT WAS a significant development for a police inquiry that was going nowhere. A year had passed and despite an enormous effort, they were struggling. Several hundred people had volunteered DNA and been eliminated as having deposited the semen found in Burdett's body, including Pora. The homicide inquiry team had been halved.

On the fourth day, exactly a year after her death, Pora was charged with the sexual violation and murder of Susan Burdett and burglary of her house. "Will my baby get the [reward] money?" were the first words a weeping Pora said to a lawyer after he was charged.

The charges were laid despite Pora's story being shot through with holes. He couldn't find the street Burdett lived in, couldn't point out her house when police stood him in front of it, described her as fair and fat when she was dark and slim, didn't know the bed he claimed three assailants and the victim were on was a waterbed. He couldn't describe the house layout, claimed to have taken a ten pin bowling trophy when none was missing, didn't know the position her body was left in, said she screamed and yelled when her closest neighbour heard only a series of dull thuds. And those he claimed had raped her were all cleared by DNA.

There was no physical evidence to show Pora was ever there. Critics say police sought to build a case on his words rather than test whether he knew anything about the crime at all. Otherwise, says McKinnel, a neighbouring house could have been pointed out and Pora asked whether that was the one. The scene of a brutal murder is not easily forgotten. Had police done that, says the investigator, it would have been obvious Pora didn't know what he was talking about.

Instead Rutherford, a celebrated detective whose successes include solving a cold case botched by the original murder inquiry team, stood Pora in front of Burdett's house and asked, "would it help if I showed you the house?" In explanation for not recognising it, Pora said that the hedge had grown. In fact it had been trimmed to about half the 3.5m it was at the time of the murder.

McKINNEL WAS a junior detective working in Manukau at the time of Pora's retrial. He recalls being an observer during many "vigorous debates" in the police bar about whether Pora was innocent. "If you wanted to start a verbal altercation, that was the case to mention." After Pora was again convicted, a cop expressed his disbelief to McKinnel, calling it an outrage. "I was a young cop and I thought that was an absurd thing to say. It stuck with me over the years."

McKinnel completed a degree in criminology, travelled overseas and on his return set up a private investigation business. An Innocence Project conference looking at possible cases of wrongful convictions prompted him to act on the unease he felt. He visited Pora in prison and got his permission to make some inquiries.

He read the transcript of the confessions.

"The question I had then was what parts of the confessions are they accepting and how have they selected those? He has no reason to lie because he is trying to convince them that he was there." An eye-opener was seeing the video interviews, the body language, the prompting.

McKinnel sought the opinion of Gisli Gudjonsson, professor of forensic psychology at the Institute of Psychiatry, King's College, London, who pioneered the study of false confessions. Gudjonsson assessed Pora, reviewed the video interviews and in an 80-page report concluded Pora had caught himself up in a web of lies due to low intellect, psychological vulnerabilities and the incentive of the reward. Gudjonsson's impression was Pora didn't know the crime scene and was trying to pretend he did.

He was repeatedly caught lying but could not tell the truth if he was to maintain the story he hoped would gain him the reward, the professor says. "The longer he lied, the harder it became to own up to having no useful knowledge about the crime whatsoever and to having completely wasted the time of the officers who had been kind to him." The flaws in Pora's story should, Gudjonsson says, have "alerted the police, prosecution, defence and trial judges to their apparent inherent unreliability".

It wasn't just Pora who was unreliable. Statements in the weeks after the murder by some of his family were so flawed the police dismissed them as a conspiracy. An aunt, Terry McLoughlin, told police a few days after the murder that Pora had talked about a softball bat in a drain and said she believed he was involved. From then on she promoted that view and began meddling. "I did a dirty," she says in a police statement. "I told [her daughter] to phone [one of Pora's sisters] and tell her I knew it was Teina. I didn't really know. I was trying to get her to talk about it. I had a funny feeling she knew something."

The sister implicated Pora when interviewed by police later the same day but in a subsequent statement admitted lying because she didn't like her brother and her aunts thought it was best he was in jail. Pora denied involvement and provided a blood sample. On 10 June, 1992, 10 weeks after the murder, Pora was dismissed as a suspect. In his file note, detective sergeant Karl Wright-St Clair (now Inspector) cited "false evidence and conspiracy". "The motive for this was that neither aunt approves of Teina's criminal behaviour and they all wanted him placed in prison and out of the way. I suggest that no further action be taken in relation to Teina Pora as a suspect . . . There has already been enough police resources wasted in relation to this matter."

Wright-St Clair's advice was followed until nine months later when Pora was arrested on the warrants. Eventually Aunty Terry testified and claimed Pora had admitted it. The police have declined the *Herald*'s Official Information Act request for information about payments made to witnesses in the Burdett court cases but court documents show the aunt was paid $5000 after giving evidence at Pora's first trial. She is one of three witnesses in trials associated with the murder known to have been paid.

This week she told the *Herald*: "He may not have done the rape or the murder but, as far as I am concerned, he was there. He knew too much." She said she was "embarrassed" that Pora named people who were not there. But she seemed unaware that Burdett's softball bat found by her body and not the bat in the drain was regarded as the murder weapon (at least until Pora was charged). Asked whether Pora might have invented a story to try to avoid jail and gain a financial reward, she said she hadn't thought of that.

The matching in May 1996 of Rewa's DNA to the semen from Burdett's body two years after Pora was convicted presented a dilemma for two reasons. As such a prolific rapist, Rewa's modus operandi was well established. Rewa attacked 26 women from 1975 to 1996. Twenty-five survived to tell that Rewa was alone. Nothing was found at Susan Burdett's house to show Rewa had accomplices.

The second reason was the care Rewa took to avoid detection. After he was caught by a palm print he left at his first known sex attack, an attempted rape in 1975, Rewa never again left a print, and it was four years and 15 known victims after Burdett before his DNA showed up again — a tiny semen spot on a dressing gown. To take along anyone, let alone a juvenile associate of an enemy gang, would have been quite a departure.

The identification of Rewa's semen left police with a choice. They could raise at an official level the kind of alarm that was being expressed privately in police bars about the safety of Pora's conviction. Or, they could try to link the 39-year-old Highway 61 enforcer with the 16-year-old Mongrel Mob bum boy (or "associate" in police speak). They chose the second option.

In a to-do list jotted in his notebook, Williams, the detective who first interviewed Pora about the Burdett homicide, wrote: "Who should we see to show an association between Hama [Rewa's nickname] and Teina?" The phrasing, McKinnel says, suggests a mindset.

Aunty Terry was brought back into the frame. Shown three photos of Rewa (when normal police practice requires a photoboard of at least six different people) the aunt claimed she recognised him.

A witness paid $3000, another paid $7000 and a jailhouse informant testified in court cases to the effect that Pora and Rewa knew each other. All were granted name suppression.

WHETHER OR not Pora is a sympathetic character is irrelevant to the question of whether a miscarriage of justice occurred, but his is a mean story. After his mother died he lived with grandparents and other family members, interspersed with stints in boys' homes, from which he would periodically abscond. He once went to Aunty Terry's to ask why no one had visited him. After another breakout he was found at hospital with his pregnant girlfriend. That was the baby for whom Pora tried to get the reward money. Her name is Chanelle and she is 22, a mother to Benson — Pora's 3-year-old grandson.

Last month Pora clocked up 20 years in prison and last week made his 11th appearance before the Parole Board. Its decision is pending.

CHAPTER TWENTY-SEVEN

A failure of moral courage

2013: Rebecca Macfie tells the story of the corporate carelessness that led to the deaths of 29 miners at Pike River.

Two separate disasters hit New Zealand in the space of three months in 2010 and 2011, taking the lives of 214 people. One, the Christchurch earthquake of February 2011, was caused by the forces of nature — even if much of the loss of life was the result of two poorly designed buildings. But the other, at Pike River Mine on 29 November 2010, was entirely man-made. All 29 lives were lost as a direct result of a cascade of incompetence, carelessness and reckless disregard for the safety of the miners on the site. It was the country's worst non-natural disaster since the crash of an Air New Zealand DC10 in Antarctica, in 1979.

Pike River Mine was supposed to have been a showpiece of green mining. Built in a remote, beautiful wilderness, it was carefully sited and designed to cause almost no damage to the environment. But behind the Potemkin-like charade of greenwashing, the mine was a catastrophe. Built without a proper ground survey, it ran into problems. Without adequate capitalisation, the pressure to produce coal quickly to meet spiralling costs meant that safety practices were ignored. The recklessness of Pike River's managers is, in retrospect, breathtaking — they didn't just gamble with their employees' lives; they arguably signed their death warrants.

A Royal Commission of Inquiry into the disaster found, apart from a litany of failures by mine management, that the Labour Department's regulation and inspection of mining had failed to prevent the event. As the Royal Commission's report stated, 'The Department of Labour did not have the focus, capacity or strategies to ensure that Pike River was meeting its legal responsibilities under health and safety laws . . . The department should have prohibited Pike River from operating the mine until its health and safety systems were adequate' (Royal Commission on the Pike River Mine Tragedy, 2012).

The day that report came out, the Minister of Labour, Kate Wilkinson, resigned. However, attempts to sheet home blame against Pike River management were less successful. Charges brought against chief executive Peter Whittall were later dropped, with the prosecution saying that many witnesses were overseas and unavailable, and the cost would outweigh the benefit. Pike River Coal Ltd was convicted and fined $760,000, and ordered to pay $110,000 to each of the victims' families. However, by then it was in receivership and paid only $5000 to each family. Another company, VLI Drilling Pty Ltd, was fined $46,800 (Bayer, 2013). Fortunately for New Zealanders dismayed by the unwillingness of their official bodies to probe further, journalism has provided a kind of court of last resort.

This investigation, by Christchurch-based journalist Rebecca Macfie, is unusual in that it was commissioned by an independent publisher. Macfie was at her home in Christchurch when she had a call from Awa Press owner Mary Varnham. 'While I was on the phone with Mary in that initial call, the Feb 22 earthquake occurred. We had to abandon our house that day for the next nine months before returning to it in a patch-up shape' (Macfie, 2016).

Initially, she resisted Varnham's suggestion that she write a book about the disaster. She was still dealing with the aftermath of the Christchurch earthquakes, and her own feelings about the Pike disaster. 'I had so much rage about it, from the first weekend. For weeks and weeks I could not believe that this country could have done this. I was shocked. I still can cry about it now. I would get up and get in the shower and just cry. I was just so . . . ashamed about it.

'Eventually, I realised I couldn't say no and I just had to man up. I told myself, if I was worth anything, I was going to do it' (Macfie, 2016).

Macfie was a good choice; she had over 25 years of experience as a journalist, together with a good knowledge of the area and an understanding of financial journalism. This enabled her to get to the gist of how the inadequate financing of Pike River happened, and how the corporate structure of Pike River contributed to the tragedy. 'I said right from the beginning this wasn't an accident. This wasn't some worker who did some terrible thing. You had a series of failings that have occurred to make this happen' (Macfie, 2016).

But the story of Pike River is not just a moral fable about a company that put profit ahead of human life. It is the story of a failure of moral courage by those whose job it was to regulate workplace safety, to speak out not just when they were sure that people's lives were in danger but also when they could not be sure they were not.

As this chapter from Macfie's investigation shows, the roots of the tragedy went right down into the subsoil of New Zealand government, and were due in part to the cult of management that took over New Zealand in the 1990s. This cult held that unions had little or no place in the workplace; a view entrenched by memories of the irresponsible behaviour of some unions in the 1970s and

'80s. Worse, it said that the market would be able to regulate workplace safety; that given the right incentives, companies and workers would somehow find a magic balance between the pressures to meet shareholder expectations and the need for workplace safety. The events at Pike River Mine were the tragic rebuttal of that argument.

Macfie admits that she could have taken the investigation one step further, into the realm of government responsibility, but argues that it was not the main focus. 'It was just one chunk of work I didn't have time for. I have never picked up the phone and called [Former Minister of Labour] Max Bradford. It would have been a more complete book, but . . . right from the beginning I have seen it as a corporate story.

'There was a failure of regulation, and an effective regulator could have stopped it happening, but I don't think that was enough. Pike could have gone bankrupt. One of the tragedies was that it blew up before it went bankrupt.

'I think the Pike story is always the story of a financial balls-up with the worst possible outcome. There was enough regulation in place to shut the mine down, but basically the inspectorate was so run down. To focus on the law lets the company's leaders off the hook. They had active duties as directors' (Macfie, 2016).

For Macfie, there is some satisfaction in knowing that the lessons she has drawn out have resonated in boardrooms; she has been asked to talk to several large companies and groups of business leaders about her book. 'I was motivated by two goals: that anybody ought to be able to read the story and understand it, and that the boardroom got the message that this was about them' (Macfie, 2016).

She is gratified, and surprised, by the thanks she received from family members of those who died. But she is realistic about how much even such a thorough inquiry as hers can achieve. 'It hasn't got them anything more than a lot more understanding. It didn't make a difference to the dropping of charges. I haven't been able to achieve accountability for them.

'[But] I don't think it works that way . . . I tend to think what we [journalists] do is change perceptions . . . Having said that, I will never be able to accept that no one has been held accountable for this tragedy. It would have been nice to have seen some people held to account.'

Bayer, K. (2013, December 12). Charges dropped against ex-Pike River boss Peter Whittall. *New Zealand Herald*. Retrieved 2014, July 24 from http://www.nzherald.co.nz/nz/news/article.cfm?c_id=1&objectid=11171336

Macfie, R. (2016, September 1). Interview with author, J. Hollings.

Royal Commission on the Pike River Coal Mine Tragedy (2012). *Final report*, vol. 1. Wellington: New Zealand Government. Retrieved from http://pikeriver.royalcommission.govt.nz/vwluResources/Final-Report-Volume-One/$file/ReportVol1-whole.pdf

Who will say stop?

Tragedy at Pike River Mine: How and why 29 men died, by Rebecca Macfie, published by Awa Press, 2013.

It was almost two decades since Harry Bell, then chief inspector of coal mines, had brought his regulatory authority to bear at the Huntly West underground mine. In September 1992 he had ordered the place shut, thus saving the lives of dozens of workers when it exploded three days later.

In the intervening period, the skilled and robust inspectorate that Bell had served for 15 years and led for two had been all but destroyed. By November 2010, underground coal mines such as Pike River were effectively left to run their operations however they chose, provided they were seen to work within the vague and elastic framework of rules that had emerged from a tsunami of deregulation in the early 1990s.

As a young regional inspector overseeing the underground mines of the West Coast in the 1970s and 1980s, Bell had been under an obligation to visit large gassy underground coal mines weekly and smaller mines monthly. His job was to ensure compliance with the 1979 Coal Mines Act, a prescriptive and detailed rulebook written in the blood of miners killed at Strongman, Dobson, Brunner and other miners' graveyards over a century of coal mining in New Zealand.

At every inspection Bell would first look at the gas book, in which mine officials were obliged to record every instance of methane detected. . . . Bell would then walk through the mine and talk to the workers, the workmen's safety inspector and the mine manager. He'd take his own gas readings, inspect stoppings, and assess ventilation. If a mine was struggling with a problem, he would suggest solutions based on his decades of experience as a miner, manager and regulator.

If an application to develop a new coal mine in his district was lodged, the document would be sent to him for detailed review. As well as checking the technical viability of the application — the proposed ventilation system, the method of extraction, and so on — he would look into the developer's financial credibility. It was well understood that if a company attempted to mine on the basis of inadequate exploration or flawed methodology, or ran short of money and took safety shortcuts to win coal, there was a high chance things would go tragically wrong.

But by the time New Zealand Oil & Gas applied for a licence to develop an underground coal mine at Pike River in 1996, the mining inspectorate was in the process of being dismembered. It had no say at all in whether NZOG's scanty 28-page application ought to be granted. That role had become the sole preserve of a unit of government called Crown Minerals. And Crown Minerals had no interest in whether Pike's proposal was technically sound, financially viable or safe; it called for no information on its capital requirements or expected profitability.

Had NZOG's application for a permit to mine at Pike River come across

Bell's desk when he was an inspector, he'd have recommended it be declined on the basis that there wasn't enough information to properly assess whether it could be developed according to good mining practice. As it happened, Crown Minerals served simply as a permitting factory. In 1997 it gave NZOG the licence.

By the time Pike River Coal Ltd was tunnelling towards the coal seam ten years later, it had crafted a highly polished corporate profile as a modern resources company that would extract high-value coal from the pristine wilderness with surgical precision and safety. It promised to be an industry leader that would set new standards of excellence in an industry hidebound by tradition.

The inspector responsible for checking on Pike's health and safety during the early phase of the project was Michael Firmin. At the time, Firmin was the sole mining inspector in New Zealand, responsible not only for underground coal mines but also quarries, tunnels and opencast mines — about a thousand workplaces in all. His superiors in the Department of Labour had no knowledge of underground coal mining, and the post of chief inspector of coal mines, once filled by Harry Bell, had been abolished.

Gone, too, was the obligation to inspect underground coal mines frequently. Firmin's task was to make three-monthly visits, which were generally prearranged with the mining company. If he wished to inspect a mine more often than that, his bosses were inclined to ask: 'Why do you need to go to these places this often?'

Firmin made his first inspection of the Pike site in 2007, when the McConnell Dowell crew were still slowly boring the tunnel through crumbly rock. He was shown a PowerPoint presentation of the project by Peter Whittall, who mentioned that the company intended to put its main ventilation fan underground. By then, the detailed coal mining legislation that had guided the inspectors of Bell's generation had been thrown out, replaced with the Health and Safety in Employment Act and its supporting Mining Underground Regulations 1999.

Firmin consulted the regulations and concluded there was nothing to prevent Pike putting the main fan underground. Whittall, too, assured him there was 'nothing that would stop Pike River doing this'.

Pike's public relations efforts over the previous few years had won over not only investors, financial analysts and politicians. They had also helped convince Firmin that Pike was a company with well-developed health and safety practices. 'They were willing to comply, wanting to perform, wanting to be involved with best practice.'

Pike was always responsive to his queries, and seemed committed to safety. It was thus the sort of employer to whom the Department of Labour was reluctant to apply a heavy regulatory hand. Rather than use its legal powers of enforcement to stop unsafe work, or prosecute for poor health and safety practices, the department preferred to negotiate solutions.

Firmin was reassured about the proposal to locate the main fan underground because Whittall told him there would be a back-up fan on the surface that would kick in whenever the main fan stopped. And the underground fan would be positioned in such a way as to protect it from the path of an explosion, should such an unlikely event occur. He therefore mounted no challenge to Pike's unconventional plan.

In April 2008 the size of the mining inspectorate doubled: Firmin was joined by a trainee inspector, Kevin Poynter, who took over responsibility for policing safety at Pike. Poynter was an experienced mine manager, but in line with the department's policy he, too, took a light-handed approach with Pike. It continued to be seen as a 'reasonably compliant employer' and a company striving for 'best practice'.

Poynter was not dissuaded from this view despite a succession of incidents and accidents at the mine during the 28 months he monitored the site. In November 2008 there were the ten gas ignitions that had terrified the workers. Under the regulations, Pike was obliged to notify the inspector of each one, but it let Poynter know of only four of the incidents. He found out about the rest only because Harry Bell blew the whistle.

Then there was the collapse of the ventilation shaft in early 2009. This might have prompted a more sceptical view of Pike's competence to manage the geological risks of its ambitious project, but appears not to have damaged Pike's brand as an exemplary outfit. And in early 2010 Poynter was called to investigate a serious accident at the mine in which a worker's foot was severely crushed and partially degloved, the skin and subcutaneous tissue torn off. In the course of the investigation it was found that a safety mechanism on a machine had been deliberately bypassed.

None of these incidents prompted Poynter to revise his view of Pike. His attitude may perhaps have been different had he not been so overburdened by the scale of his job and so poorly supported by his employer, the Department of Labour. Without fail, Poynter issued a monthly cry for help on his report to his superiors, writing under 'Issues and Risks': 'With only two warranted inspectors covering the country, resources are extremely stretched. In addition there is a lack of knowledge or inspections of high-risk extraction sites throughout the lower half of the North Island.' He made repeated pleas for a third inspector, for the reinstatement of a chief inspector of mines who understood the industry, and for proper training.

At one meeting of the Mining Steering Group — a ragbag group of officials formed to lend support to the lonely mining inspectors — Poynter noted that the chief inspector of mines in Tasmania had told his masters just before the 2006 Beaconsfield gold mine disaster, in which one man was killed and two trapped underground for two weeks, that he was 'not in a position to provide an adequate inspection service with the resources at his disposal'. Poynter's implication was plain: an inadequately resourced inspectorate could open the way for a similar tragedy in New Zealand.

The steering group attempted to get the message across to those higher up the departmental hierarchy. 'Should there be deaths or catastrophic failure, as can occur in mining, questions of our current staffing and regime will be asked. We need to be comfortable with the investment decisions made,' the group advised in a February 2010 request for a third inspector. The request was rejected, although departmental officials made a file note that the organisation would look bad if the worst happened.

In March 2010 the following item was lodged in the department's risk register: 'Limited mining resource. May have service failure, certainly very constrained service. Reputational risk in an event.'

Despite his formidable workload, Poynter was saddled with additional tasks, including accompanying the minister of labour, Kate Wilkinson, on an underground visit to Pike in mid 2009. A few months later the company's annual review sported a photo of a smiling Wilkinson kitted out in protective clothing in readiness for a trip underground with Peter Whittall and other members of Pike's management team, an image that helped maintain the company's brand as a standard-setting modern miner.

On November 2, 2010 Poynter made his fourth inspection of Pike River Mine that year. No one told him, and he didn't ask, about the recurring problem of methane spikes virtually every time the hydro monitor started cutting coal. He didn't see, and wasn't shown, the readings from the one functioning methane sensor measuring the contaminated air leaving the mine, which indicated that gas levels had risen frequently into the explosive range over previous weeks. Pike was obliged under the underground mining regulations to report to him every instance of uncontrolled methane accumulations. It had not done so.

Poynter similarly had no idea that the mine's gas sensors were not being calibrated regularly, nor that electrical machinery was often tripping out because of high methane levels. He wasn't told of incidents where cigarette butts, lighters and aluminium drink cans — all prohibited items that could provide a spark sufficient to ignite explosive methane — had been found underground. Nor was he told of further instances where safety devices on machinery had been overridden by workers. He didn't read the incident book, which was littered with workers' reports on safety issues.

The information was all there, buried in the organisational dead ends of a failing organisation, but it wasn't readily apparent to a time-poor and underpowered inspector. And where problems such as the mine's continued failure to construct a proper emergency exit were obvious, Pike's profile as a cooperative and well-intentioned employer guaranteed a muted regulatory response.

Poynter was well aware that the ladder up the ventilation shaft was the only way workers could get out of the mine if the main tunnel were blocked by fire or rock fall, and he knew it was unsatisfactory. In April 2010 he had asked the company to provide a plan for the development of a proper walk-out exit. Pike management assured him the matter was a priority, but it was six months before the plan was produced. Drawn up by Greg Borichevsky, it pinpointed the location of the proposed exit, outlined the roadway development needed to reach that part of the mine, and estimated it could take a year or more to complete it.

Meantime Pike was pulling out all stops to ramp up the hydro-mining system. Getting coal out was more important than building a usable emergency exit for the workers.

Poynter contemplated using his powers of enforcement over the issue, but thought such a move would be difficult. The law was vague. The regulations stated that mine employers had to 'take all practicable steps to ensure that every mine . . . has suitable and sufficient outlets, providing means of entry and exit for every employee in the mine.' But what on earth did that mean? He thought that even though it was unsuitable the ladder probably met 'minimum requirements' — but told Pike a new egress needed to be established as soon as possible.

Even if he did issue a prohibition notice against Pike, forcing mining to stop until the second exit was constructed, Poynter thought the company would challenge the Department of Labour in court. After all, it was humanly possible to climb the ventilation shaft and he had been assured that people had done it. In any event, Poynter thought it most unlikely that his superiors would support his flexing his legal powers to shut down the mine. 'With the profile that Pike River had, I did have concern that I wouldn't have got the support.'

By November 19, 2010, neither Poynter nor Firmin had raised a single regulatory stick against Pike, and the mine's march towards catastrophe was uninterrupted.

Pike's six-man board of directors held its monthly meeting at the mine site on November 15, 2010, just before shareholders were due to assemble for the annual general meeting. Only three of the six directors were physically present. Tony Radford dialled in by phone from Sydney, and Arun Jagatramka and Dipak Agarwalla sent their apologies. There was nothing unusual about the poor turn-out. Radford usually attended by teleconference and seldom made it to meetings at the mine site.

However, the level of board participation by the Indian directors was of particular concern to the Pike chair, John Dow. The board had gone to some lengths to accommodate the geographical spread of directors: meetings were an equal mix of in-person and telephone conferencing. In 2010, meetings had so far been held in Sydney, in Wellington and at Gujarat's mine site in Wollongong, New South Wales. Dow had also encouraged the Indians to appoint alternate representatives, which they did. But by October 2010 he still harboured concerns.

The first item of business was, as usual, finance. The company was about to start its fourth capital-raising since the IPO, this time for $70 million, and had reputable finance house UBS on its side.

Dow thought it was also 'timely' for the board to focus on health, safety and environmental matters at the meeting, and asked Doug White in for a briefing. It was the first time the board had ever called on White to answer questions about topics such as gas, ventilation and risk management. He delivered a reassuring overview. The mine, White said, was following the stringent Queensland recommendations for dealing with gas emissions, and the new underground ventilation fan — which had been running smoothly for only a few days — had greatly increased the amount of air moving through the mine. Methane in the gassier part of the mine was being drained away, and with 'adequate ventilation' it was 'more a nuisance' than a barrier to operations.

White advised that procedures existed for evacuating workers in the event of ventilation failure, and said a second fan and emergency exit were to be installed the following year. In the meantime the ventilation shaft 'provided a means of emergency egress' and there were plans to increase the size of the underground refuge station. Nothing in White's reported comments revealed the extent of his disenchantment with Whittall, whom he referred to the next day, in an email to a friend in Australia, as a 'dodgy git'. He found it very hard, he wrote to his friend, 'to work for someone who has made or overseen so many stuff ups and blames everyone else'.

The board didn't ask for, and wasn't given, the information that would have flashed warning lights about the mine's safety management systems failing. Members took White at his word that methane levels and ventilation were under control; they had no system for independently verifying that the mine's most significant danger was being properly managed. Aside from White's verbal assurances, their primary source of information on safety at the mine was statistics that set out the number of accidents that had required workers to seek medical treatment — sprained ankles, chipped teeth, cut fingers and the like. They had no way of knowing how often the atmosphere in the mine was in a potentially explosive state.

The board had a subcommittee dedicated to health, safety and environmental issues. It was chaired by Dow. It hadn't met for 13 months. There were plans for third-party audits to help the board assure itself that Pike's safety and risk management systems were up to scratch. This was an excellent idea, particularly as, with the exception of Jagatramka, none of the directors had any experience in the underground coal mining industry. Jagatramka's company Gujarat NRE had two underground coal mines in New South Wales, and Jagatramka had been touted as a visionary of rare distinction who had led the growth of Gujarat NRE into Australia. Unfortunately, he was frequently absent from Pike's board meetings.

By November 2010 the board had still not undertaken any third-party audits. Dow was in favour of such measures, but management had argued that outside audits would be more useful after the company's entire safety management system was fully implemented and in operation. In the meantime, the board appeared to have reasonable grounds for assuming the safety of the workforce was uppermost in the minds of the company's management. Peter Whittall had just a few months earlier taken a leading role in the establishment of a high profile organisation aimed at improving workplace health and safety throughout New Zealand. The Business Leaders Health and Safety Forum, of which he was a steering group member, had been launched by Prime Minister John Key in July

2010, and celebrated as the first of its kind in the world.

There was also the reassuring presence of Neville Rockhouse on Pike's management team. Rockhouse had been the mine's safety and training manager since 2006. He was a qualified health and safety professional with many years' experience. And while he had never worked at a gassy mine such as Pike before, nor developed a health and safety system for an underground mine from scratch, he shared the dream of making Pike the best new mine in the country. Two of his three sons worked underground in the mine.

The board failed to detect that Rockhouse was struggling to implement the safety rules and procedures he was tasked with designing, and was so underresourced he barely had time to go underground to check out things for himself. A colleague, Michelle Gillman, feared he would have a heart attack or breakdown because of the stress he was under.

Rockhouse asked often for more staff and resources to help develop the mine's health and safety systems, mostly without success. His relationship with Whittall was tense. On one occasion the Pike boss humiliated him in front of his peers while he was giving a presentation on hazard identification. Whittall had objected to a couple of typographical mistakes, and when Rockhouse couldn't see them Whittall rose to his feet and began yelling and slapping at the wall to indicate the location of the errors on the screen. Rockhouse was so shocked he tried to resign — not for the first time — but was dissuaded by his management colleagues.

By October 2010 Neville Rockhouse had overseen the creation of 386 documents setting out a wide range of safety-related procedures — among them how to operate machines safely, standard responses to serious incidents, risk assessments and management plans. It was up to the manager of each specialist department — engineering, technical services, environmental and production — to sign off documents related to their sphere of influence. Less than a third had been signed and finalised. Rockhouse tried to help managers develop their safety documentation but Whittall rebuked him, saying on one occasion, 'Keep your bloody nose out of it.'

The board was unlikely to have known of such strains: the operational information it received from the mine was channelled through Whittall. Indeed, Rockhouse had been told by Whittall not to send emails directly to board chair John Dow.

Nevertheless, it was the task of the directors to set the company's direction and ensure the risks were being properly managed by the executives they appointed. And while they might struggle from the outside to discern interpersonal friction, such as that between Whittall and Rockhouse, there were other portents flashing under their collective noses. The enormous turnover of senior managers — including men such as Kobus Louw, who left after a short time despite having gone through the stressful business of relocating his young family from the other side of the world — pointed to a deep malaise. In four years the project had burned through four technical services managers — the fourth, Pieter van Rooyen, quit early in November 2010 — and was on to its third engineering manager. And in the two short years since the project had reached the coal seam, the critical position of statutory mine manager had changed hands six times.

None of this appeared to provoke alarm around the board table. It was simply assumed that the rapid churn was a result of the Australian mining boom and the tough competition for skilled mining personnel.

Nor did alarm bells ring about the extraordinary step taken by Pike's former project manager, Les McCracken, when he warned John Dow in August 2009 that the mine had serious problems with morale and leadership. Dow had told Whittall and Gordon Ward about his conversation with McCracken, and suggested they bring in experienced mining consultant Dave Stewart to help out, but he then had no further involvement in the matter. He considered the issues raised by McCracken to be 'routine' and not something the board needed to get involved in. So he didn't ask for, and wasn't given, the detailed reports from the coalface that Stewart completed at Pike in early 2010.

Had the directors read Stewart's work they may have been dissuaded from the assumption that all was well at the mine. Stewart's reports documented inadequacies with Pike's gas detection and ventilation systems, pointed out that the ventilation shaft was not a suitable emergency exit, and warned that workers felt their reports on safety incidents were being ignored by management.

Nor did the board ask for the results of a comprehensive risk survey done in mid 2010 on behalf of Pike's insurer by Hawcroft Consulting. Dow knew the work was being done but thought that this, too, was the preserve of management. Had the board been sufficiently curious to read the report it might have been moved to undertake more rigorous surveillance of risk management at the mine.

Hawcroft assessed the management of methane at Pike to be of a low standard and said general housekeeping was poor, with 'equipment, parts and rubbish evident'. It noted there were unknown risks associated with hydro mining — in particular the chance of a roof cave-in. And it judged Pike's general risk management to be below average.

Pike's directors didn't receive the Hawcroft report. Dow considered it dealt with matters that were 'operational' and therefore the domain of the company's managers. He thought directors needed to be careful not to dabble in the operational side of the business; the board's job was governance, not management. He likened the relationship between the board and managers to that of 'church and state'.

And so by November 2010 Pike River Coal's board of directors continued to believe, despite so many signs to the contrary, that everything was under control at the mine.

Pike River Mine was awash with information foretelling catastrophe, but all those who had the power to act on the warning signs were deaf and blind to them. Vital information lay fallow on desks and in files, and pleas from men at the coalface for action and improvements went unheard and unanswered. Even Doug White, Queensland's former deputy chief inspector of coal mines and a man admired by his staff for his efforts to improve safety at Pike, couldn't see the dangers that were keeping [miner] Willie Joynson awake at night.

After Peter Whittall moved to Wellington in early 2010, White was the most senior manager at the mine site. As operations manager he had overall responsibility for production, engineering, health and safety, and coal processing. He also absorbed the position of statutory mine manager in June 2010, a role that carried the legal duty to personally supervise the health and safety aspects of the operation.

Yet White had an incomplete picture of what was really going on. He didn't know the fixed sensors in the mine's return roadways that were supposed to transmit accurate and continuous methane readings to the control room were either not working, had been disconnected from the control room, or were inaccurate. He assumed the sensors were being regularly calibrated and maintained, but they were not.

After Steve Ellis arrived at Pike to take up the job of production manager at the start of October 2010, White effectively handed over his duties as mine manager to the new man, even though Ellis did not have the right qualifications to hold the job. Until that time White had been seeing regular updates on methane trends in the mine because Greg Borichevsky, the technical services coordinator, brought the information to daily production meetings. White assumed that this flow of information carried on when Ellis took command of those meetings, but it did not.

White was conscious of the need for better training at Pike, and engaged Harry Bell to provide refresher courses on self-rescue techniques. The first course was held on a Friday afternoon in early October 2010, but the following week only three men could be spared from production to attend. After that the sessions were put on hold.

White also knew that the lack of a proper emergency exit from the mine was a matter of ongoing anxiety for the men underground, and that the issue came up repeatedly at meetings of the company's health and safety committee. The committee — a poorly attended group where there were sometimes more managers than workers in attendance — had escalated its concern about the lack of a proper second egress in September 2010, writing a formal letter to Pike management. Yet White told the board on November 15 that the ventilation shaft provided an escapeway until a second egress could be built the following year.

White was justly proud of the improvements he had made at Pike — in particular bringing in the ABM20, which had begun to turn around the mine's chronic inability to produce coal. He considered the establishment of a second exit to be a priority. But despite his determination that Pike should be run according to the stringent mining standards applicable in Queensland — where two exits in fresh air are mandatory — he oversaw the push into hydro mining instead of suspending operations until a second escape route for the workers had been built. He knew that a mine of Pike's design 'would not have existed in Queensland'.

By November 19, 2010, the absence of an emergency exit from the mine was, on its own, sufficient cause to shut down production and address the safety deficit. Doug White did not take that step.

The union representing mine workers, Engineering, Printing and Manufacturing Union (EPMU), could have brought the mine to a halt, at least temporarily, by encouraging strikes, pickets or bans over safety. But it caused no disruption to Pike's path to calamity. It had a limp presence at the mine, in part because it wasn't welcome.

There was only ever one walk-out over safety, when mine deputy Dan Herk threw down the gauntlet about the lack of mine vehicles available to quickly evacuate workers in the event of an emergency. Herk called the local EPMU representative, Matt Winter, and said he was concerned for the men's safety; Winter advised he should, therefore, walk out. Herk led the men out of the mine. Shortly afterwards Winter received an angry call from Pike's human resources manager Dick Knapp, advising him to tell the men to go back to work; when Winter refused, Knapp threatened to sue the union. The issue the men were protesting about was attended to within a matter of hours, with the prompt repair of a broken-down vehicle that had been out of action for three weeks.

Winter was aware of workers' concerns about the lack of a proper emergency exit, and he had heard about the series of methane ignitions in late 2008. He was also worried about the high number of cleanskins — workers new to mining — at Pike. He understood that it was desirable in underground coal mining to have a ratio of experienced to inexperienced workers of about four to one. Pike had a much larger proportion of inexperienced men than other site he looked after.

It wasn't easy to enlist Pike workers into the union. Some told Winter they didn't want to upset management by signing up. And he got the impression Pike management wasn't interested in forming any sort of relationship with EPMU. Pike had an internal health and safety committee but the union had no representation on it. Winter found Pike management 'arrogant and unwilling to listen. They were prepared to tolerate the presence of the union in line with their legislative obligations, but they were not at all interested in developing a good relationship.' He left his job in early 2010 and handed over to a new man, Garth Elliot.

Others at the site also had the impression that the company preferred not to have a strong union presence. In 2009, when health and safety manager Neville Rockhouse sought to have the union involved in a training exercise, Peter Whittall told him in an email: 'Please do not use the union in the same sentence as anything at Pike. Our relationship and the way we communicate is between us and our employees.'

And so men like Willie Joynson, who went underground every day to earn a living, and who were entitled to the protection of robust safety systems and equipment that left a fat margin for error, were working on the edge. Pike River Mine, which needed to have the best of everything to succeed in its tough environment — the best geological knowledge, the best equipment, the most rigorous safety regime — had the worst of everything. Joynson and his workmates were exposed on all sides by those whose job it was to protect them: a regulator that was submissive and unwilling to use the powers at its disposal; a board that was incurious, bereft of knowledge and experience of underground coal mining, and unable to see the symptoms of failure; management that was unstable, ill-equipped for the environment, and incapable of pulling together all the pieces of its own frightening picture; and a union that was marginalised and irrelevant.

CHAPTER TWENTY-EIGHT

The forgotten

2013, *Sunday Star-Times*: Kirsty Johnston investigates the abuse of the disabled in private care homes.

It's one of New Zealand's darker secrets: the network of psychiatric hospitals that once threaded the country. Built with good intentions, to house the mentally ill, they became, over the course of the past century, a dumping ground not just for the mentally ill but for anyone who didn't fit in: the intellectually handicapped, the disabled, the behaviourally disturbed. They were a way to keep those that didn't fit New Zealand's image of itself as a bright, muscular young nation out of sight and out of mind. Often sited in the country, the bleak, cold wooden dormitories were this country's version of the Soviet gulags; our own gulag archipelago.

A mass deinstitutionalisation programme began in the 1990s, and most of the asylums were closed. The residents were moved to the cities, where an attempt, sometimes botched but again well-meaning, was made to place them in houses in normal communities, where they could take a part in normal life. For many, this meant a chance of a better life, and so it has proved. But for some, placed in residential units without proper scrutiny, it has not.

The great Australian journalist Philip Knightley, writing about the exposure of the thalidomide scandal in *The Sunday Times* of London, in the 1970s, noted how what has been held up as a shining example of investigative journalism was in fact, anything but. 'It has taken me twenty years to face up to the fact that *The Sunday Times*' thalidomide campaign was not the great success it was made out to be and that the full story is as much about the failures of journalism as its triumphs' (Knightley, 2004).

What Knightley meant was that the *Times*, like most of the British news media, had ignored the plight of the thalidomide victims for years. The story could have been done much earlier, and compensation gained that would have made their lives much easier, had anyone bothered to listen. Instead, families of thalidomide children born in the early 1960s had to wait 15 to 20 years for any meaningful financial help — more than a decade of carrying, lifting, feeding, washing and clothing severely disabled children, at a time when they most needed help.

The same could be said of Kirsty Johnston's investigation into residential care facilities in New Zealand. One of the main sources for her series was disability advocate Colin Burgering. It is a black mark on New Zealand journalism that Burgering had been trying to get a journalist to listen for 10 years before Johnston took notice. 'No one had listened to him. What he was saying [sounded so] crazy, and when I met with him I said I needed some documents to back up what you are saying. When we OIA'd it [made a request under the Official Information Act for a copy of the information], it backed up what he had been saying.

'These were the exact kind of people that we should be going into bat for. They don't have a voice. Even after we started listening to him, it took Colin a year to convince us to do something. It makes me feel embarrassed that we didn't pay attention to him straight away' (Johnston, 2015).

One of the unknown heroes of New Zealand's welfare sector, Burgering is a member of the Justice Action Group, which tries to advocate for the intellectually and physically disabled living in residential care homes. Unlike the slick non-governmental organisations or corporate welfare branding exercises, it doesn't have a staff of spin doctors peddling public sympathy. 'He's a one-man band and a lot of the people that he helps aren't friendly people. They are really fringe people. They don't make for attractive people that the public are going to get behind' (Johnston, 2015).

Johnston says her interest in writing about those who cannot help themselves developed slowly. She grew up around the Waikato, in a family that was not particularly interested in politics. During university holidays, at home in Gisborne, her interest in writing led her to a job on the local newspaper. While there, she found that there was more to journalism than just writing. 'I found myself quite attracted to the kind of social justice side of it' (Johnston, 2015).

That interest in social justice led her to study journalism at Massey University, in Wellington, and then to a job with Fairfax. She's shown that she is prepared to dig hard on stories that need it. The story here was the culmination of a six-month investigation (Johnston, 2013). It won her a Canon Award for best investigation, in 2014. Although proud of the award, she says that's not her main motivation. 'I try to focus on stories that make a difference rather than ones that will get my name in lights.'

Did this story make a difference?

'I think it did in that it kind of sent a message to health officials that they couldn't just close places up that had massive problems without telling the public.

'But no one was held to account criminally. No one was arrested or charged. I would like to see those people locked up, but [many of the victims] are unreliable witnesses so they are not going to be called in a trial. Even children can be called for evidence, but these guys won't be.'

Johnston, K. (2013, November 10). Two Chch residential care homes closed down. *Sunday Star-Times*. Retrieved from http://www.stuff.co.nz/national/health/9379405/the-shame-of-silence

Johnston, K. (2015, August 25). Interview with author, J. Hollings.

Knightley, P. (2004). The thalidomide scandal: Where we went wrong. In J. Pilger (Ed.), *Tell me no lies: Investigative journalism and its triumphs* (p. 359). London: Jonathan Cape.

The shame of silence

Sunday Star-Times, 10 November 2013

Terrified, the girl sits alone in the tiny room. She can hear the laughter of her tormentors through the wall but she is unable to move or talk. It is the second time that day she has been taken into the toilet and left there. The first was for almost two hours while her caregiver had a sleep, and now after dinner the staff have placed her there again, knowing she cannot move until they come to her rescue.

The girl is 17. She is intellectually and physically disabled. Placed into the care of Te Runanga O Toa Rangatira, a residential facility near Wellington in 2010, she turned from a happy teenager into an anxious wreck who was "petrified" of returning to the home and who cried every day at school. She was made to wear nappies and a bib, was underfed, and possibly hit and kicked and called a "bitch" by her carers, who also left her in soiled clothes and refused to let her use the phone to talk to her parents at night.

Staff at the service were later called for a meeting and reminded of best practice. The Ministry kept an eye on the organisation to ensure services improved. The family were apologised to. When approached this week, Te Runanga O Toa confirmed the client had been at their facility and said the service had improved had substantially since 2010.

The girl's story is just one of dozens of abuse cases uncovered this week by a *Sunday Star-Times* investigation into government-funded residential homes for the intellectually disabled.

The six-month investigation began earlier this year after it was discovered a home in Auckland had closed due to systemic maltreatment of clients, including one instance when a boy was left to eat grass in a paddock.

After revelations about two more organisations, including serious abuse at the country's biggest kaupapa Maori provider, Te Roopu Taurima o Manukau Trust, in Otahuhu, Auckland, the *Star-Times* requested information about abuses in the past five years. Documents provided catalogue clients being hurt, choked, neglected, sworn at, bullied and wrongly restrained, physically and with drugs. There were staff-on-client assaults and client-on-client assaults, including a frail resident raped by another person living in the home when staff left them together unattended.

Figures showed that only a small number of the complaints made to the Ministry of Health were able to be substantiated. Experts say it is extremely difficult to get the intellectually disabled to understand what has happened to them or to find the courage to report it, so it is likely there are hundreds more cases where complaints were not laid, let alone stood up. In fact, the case where the girl was left on the toilet was one of just nine incidents proven to have occurred out of more than 150 complaints received in the past five years.

Of the people caught abusing residents, only one was prosecuted by police — most were given more training or disciplined internally. Investigation reports and audits into the abuse were not made public. Even in cases where homes have been closed down, the ministry didn't put notices on its website or send press releases to media.

Disability advocate Colin Burgering, from the Justice Action Group, blew the whistle on Parklands, an Auckland disabled home where a boy was left alone to eat grass. He says figures prove what he has been trying to get across for 20 years. "It is very difficult to investigate abuse because there are usually never any independent witnesses. Staff won't talk about other staff. Management don't want to hear about anything. The ministry don't want to know," he says. "The whole system is designed to stop stories of abuse coming out."

Burgering and other sector advocates say the information released — alongside a soon-to-be released review into the residences commissioned by Health Minister Tony Ryall — should prompt a full overhaul.

"The residential system works but it doesn't work well," he says. "Even when there's a nice-looking house and the staff are nicely dressed there's still always that undercurrent of control and of danger, because in a small residence all you need is one bad staff member and the whole system is gone. They're very delicate places. There urgently needs to be better oversight and expertise."

. . .

Residential homes were created after the large health institutions of the 1950s were disestablished. Rather than living in cramped dormitories and on drugs, it was hoped the disabled could live in the community and make choices for themselves.

At first, providers like IHC ran the homes, some on a volunteer basis. Now they are funded through the government and clients are placed with them by a Needs Assessment Co-ordination Agency (NASC), which also monitors the funding provided by the ministry and is responsible for ensuring client welfare. The provider's contracts are with the ministry, which can audit it at any time and order changes.

In severe cases, the ministry can send in temporary managers. Closing them down is a last resort.

. . .

In the past five years, three homes have closed. Aside from Parklands, Mary Moodie in Christchurch was closed down after a resident was abused and left with carpet burns. Martos Ltd, also in Christchurch, was closed down due to financial issues and was potentially mismanaging clients' personal funds.

Temporary managers were sent into six homes in that same period. Many of the issues they faced were a hangover from the past — such as using chemical injections for restraint, taking a "do-as-I-say" approach and treating clients as if they were children. Complainants often took issue with that approach, including the school staff member who wrote about the use of bibs and nappies, saying "I find this way of dealing with people in a residential setting almost Dickensian".

The use of medicine was particularly concerning to experts. Long-time disability worker and former temporary manager Robyn Klos wrote in her audit report about the Hamilton Residential Trust in 2010 that she was disturbed to find many of the conversations about residents there were about "what was wrong with them. I thought that the sector had long moved on from that at least 15 years ago," she said.

Klos said while conditions were better in the residential homes than the institutions, they bred their own problems. "People are living in small homes and are isolated from each other. There's just one or two staff with five or six residents. It's very difficult to monitor."

While clients were supposed to make their own choices about things like when they got up, what they ate, and when friends visited, Klos said it came down to the intentions of staff as to whether that happened. Competent staff were difficult to find and while training was available, some of the skills needed — particularly for crisis intervention — required a high level of competency which many staff did not possess.

Often, because staff were not trained or not able to use their training, situations escalated quickly, she said. Staff instead used physical techniques to control residents. For example, at a Richmond residence in Christchurch in 2010, a former gang member was employed and was supposed to receive training, but it never happened. He went on to choke a resident and eventually left the service. There were many other instances where staff used incorrect holds, some resulting in bruising and carpet burns.

Clare Teague, head of the provider body New Zealand Disability Support Network, said poor pay due to a lack of funding stopped new staff entering the sector. She did not believe abuse was systemic, but admitted there were issues that needed to be addressed — and getting highly skilled staff was key. "Investment by the funding agencies is also necessary to ensure capable boards and managers are attracted to these demanding roles," she said.

Klos said it was up to the sector to provide better training and to get the right people on boards — and it wasn't always about money. She said the NASC needed to take some responsibility for ensuring there was a positive culture at the homes.

"In some ways, Parklands was an aberration, but the NASC should have picked up on it," she said. To the trained eye, it should be very easy to pick up on problems, particularly where there is a lot of assault, Klos said. "When you walk into a place, you know there's something wrong in an organisation. You can just feel it. But with Parklands, because it looked nice, kind of like the old institutions, people couldn't see it. Even when we went there people were saying, 'isn't this nice', there's a cherry tree and fish pond."

It was Klos who eventually recommended that Parklands close last year.

. . .

In 2008, the Social Services Select Committee held an inquiry into the quality of care and service provision for disabled people after concerns were raised in the media about two major residential service providers. Among its recommendations it noted there needed to be better leadership, advocacy, a better complaints process, better monitoring and a sector workforce strategy. The report said that if in six years the situation was no better, the government should consider removing the Ministry of Health as the lead agency and making a service solely for disability.

"It's coming up six years now," says the Human Rights Commission's disability commissioner Paul Gibson. "And there does need to be a different model. There needs to be someone in the system who can act quickly and with authority when there is a problem, to keep people safe. Disabled people have the right to feel safe in their homes."

Gibson believes the NASC role is crucial but it's not working as the safeguards aren't there and the power is solely in the hands of staff. "Power, choice and control should reside with the disabled people themselves and their families. That is not happening enough. There is more rhetoric around it than reality and practice."

The complaints and advocacy process also needs examining, Gibson says.

The Health and Disability Commission is supposed to be responsible for complaints about residential care. It received 66 complaints in the past five years. Only two were investigated. The rest were either deemed outside the commission's jurisdiction, were referred to the ministry or to the provider or had no action taken.

Gibson's call for better advocacy was echoed by the head of the country's largest NASC, Sonia Hawea. Her staff were responsible for both Parklands and Te Roopu Taurima. None faced disciplinary action over their failure to pick up on the abuse.

Hawea said while there had been changes since the select committee report, there were definitely issues where agencies overlapped. The sector included health, mental health, social development and ACC and could be confusing. Advocates — like Burgering — would help to pull together some of that fragmentation, she said.

"It would also help to ensure the NASC and the provider aren't making decisions for these people. It would give them a voice."

Burgering's Justice Action Group is the only one of its kind in the country. It strives to help clients through difficult situations and to make public the wrongs that happen to them. He believes the system has been corrupted by the focus on money. Providers do not report incidents because they do not want to lose their contracts, he says. The ministry doesn't want to tell the public because it will lose face, he says.

Two cases uncovered by our investigation gave examples of a lack of openness. In 2009, an aggressive and violent client was left alone with a frail woman at a disability service in the Nelson-Marlborough region. Staff came back to find him raping her but did not report it to the ministry. Ministry staff found out only when the NASC told them. The service said it didn't report it because it thought the sex was consensual. The ministry ruled it assault and the service was warned about reporting serious events in the future. Nelson-Marlborough District Health Board said police had been unable to substantiate the alleged rape. They said those at the house were semi-independent and there was no requirement for close supervision at the time. The man was relocated to another house with more support.

In 2010, a temporary manager (Klos) was appointed to the Hamilton Residential Trust after complaints of punishment, bullying, medication mismanagement, lack of training and lack of privacy. There was also evidence of chemical restraint despite a non-restraint policy. Klos found there were systemic issues at the service and recommended it would be easier to close it down. The ministry instead worked with the service to improve it and agreed not to make the damning audit report public. It was later released via the OIA and given to the *Star-Times* anonymously.

The ministry refused to discuss the reasons for keeping the audit secret. "And that is why abuse goes on," says Burgering. "We try to shine a light in dark corners but it's not just dark corners — it's huge places of shadow."

In Lo

JOH

26th March

L

VANESS

FIONA

Loving Gr

CHAPTER TWENTY-NINE

Culture of omertà

2013, *Pacific Journalism Review*: James Hollings details another unfortunate experiment: 25 years of censorship in suicide reporting.

New Zealand promotes an image of itself as an open, transparent society, an image neatly encapsulated in the '100% Pure' brand. It ranks near the top of measures of media freedom, and transparency. But for journalists working in New Zealand, the reality is very different. While there are many areas of New Zealand society that are open, and while much has been done by governments in recent years to make official work more transparent, New Zealand is, compared with many comparable democracies, still a very difficult place for journalists to get some kinds of information; in fact, New Zealand seems to specialise in saying one thing to overseas audiences when the reality is quite different. Recent research has shown how the Official Information Act, introduced in 1982 to free up access to official information and touted by New Zealand officials overseas as a model for others to follow, has virtually ground to a halt, at least as far as journalists are concerned, because of growing manipulation by politicised officials nervous of offending their masters, and a lack of teeth for those meant to enforce it.

But there are many other examples: vital parts of the government machinery are off-limits to journalists seeking information. Unlike the US, where journalists can usually gain access to court records as of right, here journalists have to apply through a judge and are often refused. The secrecy of the courts process in New Zealand is one of the great undiscussed travesties of this country, but the culture of official omertà does not stop there. The body that investigates complaints against police, the Police Complaints Authority (PCA), is also not subject to the Official Information Act and is therefore immune to journalists' requests for information. Thus anyone seeking to challenge the official inquiry into a police shooting, for example, has no right of access to the official records of the incident; they can see only what the PCA chooses to let them see.

Unsurprisingly, this culture of omertà has led to a climate of suspicion, often unjustified, around some of these public bodies. Most bizarre of all, perhaps, is the fact that Parliament, the body that is supposed to represent the public, is itself closed to public scrutiny because its administering body, Parliamentary Services, is not subject to the Official Information Act. This means that release of information such as politicians' financial affairs are subject to parliamentary whim rather than available as of right. So while politicians do have to disclose their assets, they do not have to disclose the amount of those assets or details of exactly what they are, and no one can make them do so.

New Zealanders seem strangely unconcerned by this culture of secrecy. But there is one area in which the censorship has been so unusual, and so unfair to some of those affected, that it has, finally, been challenged. That area is the media reporting of suicide. Since 1988, New Zealand has been virtually the only country in the world (Norway flirted with the idea briefly) to censor news media reporting of suicides. This law, sparked by understandable concern that suicide reporting would cause copycat suicides, remained in place until 2016. It was a law that in my view, and in that of many others, was based on an erroneous interpretation of research.

The effect of the law was to virtually eliminate news reporting about individual suicides and their possible causes. Sadly, besides having no apparent effect on New Zealand's high youth suicide rates, this law had the effect of making many bereaved parents and relatives of suicides feel isolated and ashamed. It also had a chilling effect on the news media's ability to probe the systemic causes of suicides, such as failures of mental health care.

As a health reporter at *The Evening Post*, I had grappled with this issue and been frustrated by the inability to report on what parents told me were issues of public interest. But I had accepted the view promulgated by some health officials, that reporting could be dangerous. It was only some 15 years later, as an academic, that I gained the research skills to question these assertions. The following article is based on an investigation that combined both traditional investigative journalism techniques and academic research methods. It formed the basis of a submission to a review of the suicide censorship law undertaken by the Law Commission in 2012 and 2013.

After hearing submissions from a wide range of people, the Commission recommended ending most of the censorship. Those recommendations were largely accepted by Parliament, which amended the Coroners Act. So, in 2016, for the first time in nearly 30 years, journalists no longer had to use the phrase 'no suspicious circumstances' when reporting a suspected suicide. They could call it what it was, a suspected suicide, without risking a criminal conviction.

Reporting suicide in New Zealand: Time to end censorship
Pacific Journalism Review, October 2013

Some kinds of news media reporting of suicide have been shown to be associated with higher suicide rates (Niederkrotenthaler et al., 2012; Pirkis, Burgess, Francis, Blood & Jolley, 2006). While no cause and effect relationship has been established (and it is unlikely an ethical experiment could be designed which would show one), the evidence that certain types of reporting can produce an imitative effect is now widely accepted by the suicide research community (Sisask & Värnik, 2012). The body of evidence that has emerged since the first studies in the 1970s has supported a push in many countries for moderation of news media reporting of suicides, to minimise the risk of "copycat" events. Several countries, mainly in Europe, have persuaded the news media to introduce voluntary guidelines in an effort to reduce the kinds of sensationalist reporting most associated with the risk of imitative suicides (Skehan, 2006).

New Zealand and Norway took a stronger line, adopting statutory provisions regulating what could be reported about suicide and when. Norway abandoned this approach in favour of voluntary guidelines some years ago (UKPC, 2008). New Zealand, on the other hand, has maintained and strengthened statutory restrictions on suicide reporting, despite periodic protests from news media, some coroners, and some members of the public, and is now thought to have the most restrictive laws on media reporting of suicide in the world (Pirkis, 2010).

. . .

New Zealand's restrictions on suicide reporting had their origins in the 1951 Coroners Act. Section 21 allowed the Coroner, at the commencement of inquests into deaths that may have been self-inflicted, to direct no reports of the proceedings be published until after the hearings. Introducing the Coroners Bill, Attorney-General Sir Clifton Webb told Parliament that the restrictions embodied a principle laid down in 1821 by the High Court that "in the interests of justice, decency, order, or even from a consideration of what is due to the family of a deceased, a Coroner may hold the whole or a part of the hearing in private". He added that this power was very rarely exercised.

While the legal rationale for this section appears to have been largely driven by privacy reasons, there was some discussion in the House about the public safety rationale for it. Sir Clifton advised the House that as early as 1936 the Wright departmental committee on coroners had heard evidence from chief constables, a Dr Roche Lynch, and the Trades Union Congress that publication of details of a suicide was harmful and could lead to imitative cases (Hansard, 1951).

While Sir Clifton may have envisaged this power being rarely exercised, by the 1980s this view had clearly changed. A new Coroners Act was passed in 1988, which effectively introduced censorship of news media reporting of suicide. Although the Act did not use the term censorship, it effectively did just that. A censor has been defined as "an official who examines material that is to be published and suppresses parts considered offensive or a threat to security" (Soanes, Stevenson, & Pearsall, 2004). Section 29 (an update of section 21) of the Act banned reporting any particular relating to the manner of death where there was "reasonable cause to believe that a death . . . was self-inflicted", even *before* the Coroner had commenced an inquest (Parliament, 1988). According to the influential media law text *Media Law in New Zealand* (Burrows, 1990), the Act effectively banned reporting of suicides as suicides, even before the Coroner had ruled, and afterwards only as far as permitted by the Coroner. Burrows advised that any breach of the Act would amount to contempt of court, which he defined as effectively a criminal offence (Burrows & Cheer, 2010). In line with Burrows' interpretation, the Act was generally given a conservative interpretation by the news media. As a result, reports of suicides, before inquests had been held, virtually disappeared from newspapers, to be usually replaced by brief items. A common strategy was using euphemisms such as "There are no suspicious circumstances and the death has been referred to the Coroner". News media were free to report on inquests, however, unless the Coroner suppressed details, and generally few coroners did.

The Act coincided with an increase in research on suicide prevention overseas and in New Zealand, particularly through the formation of the Canterbury Suicide Prevention Project, and a heightened awareness in the international medical and general community of the risks of media reporting of suicide. From the 1990s onwards, many countries introduced voluntary guidelines for media reporting of suicide, which reflected research suggesting that sensationalist media reporting (use of large headlines, page one display, graphic photos and description of methods, excessive repetition, glorification) were all risk factors (Etzersdorfer & Sonneck, 1998). Austria introduced guidelines in the 1990s, with considerable success in moderating media sensationalism (Niederkrotenthaler et al., 2010), and many other European countries followed, as did Australia (Mindframe, 2009). These guidelines generally promote restrained presentation of suicide stories, avoidance of glamorisation, and urge journalists to seek context. The Australian guidelines have also had a good uptake from the news media (Skehan, 2006). New Zealand was one of the early adopters of this voluntary guideline approach: in 1999 the Ministry attempted to promulgate modifications to reporting on suicide through the use of voluntary guidelines. These guidelines sat alongside the legislative restrictions in the Coroners Act 1988, and unsurprisingly, given the level of legislative restriction already in place, were not widely used by the news media, who also felt they had not been properly consulted on their content (Tully & Elsaka, 2004). One study found that their uptake was hampered by the fact that journalists tended to conflate the guidelines and the legislative reporting restrictions (Pirkis, 2010).

In 2006 New Zealand moved to tighten its legislative restrictions on media reporting of suicide still further. It passed a new Coroners Act, with a new provision that the only ground on which coroners could authorise the release of details of a suicide was if they were sure public safety was not at risk. It also changed the wording of the relevant section on reporting, from a ban on reporting anything on the "manner" of death, to a ban on reporting the "particulars". The intention, as subsequently interpreted by the Chief Coroner, was to make it explicit that any report that a death was a suspected suicide was forbidden until the inquest had been held, and afterwards only if the Coroner specifically allowed it. The Chief Coroner made it clear that "particulars" included the name, manner of death, and even the fact that a suicide was suspected (Roundtable, 2011).

The Act also ensured that the prohibition on news media coverage extended to family members. It made it an offence, subject to a $1000 fine, for anyone to make public the details of a suicide without the Coroner's permission.

The Select Committee considering the 2006 Bill received a number of submissions. News media, long unhappy with the 1988 Act, took the opportunity of the first look at the law on suicide reporting since then to try to get the ban lifted. It argued that the ban was against current international practice, an unreasonable inhibition on free speech, and that the evidence of the risks did not justify such restrictions. One coroner, Garry Evans, of Wellington, made a similar submission, arguing for the importance of openness in reporting suicide: "Concealment of evidence from the community disempowers it in dealing with the problem."(Evans, 2006). (NZLR, 1986; Tesoriero, 2006)

The committee also heard submissions supporting the ban. Dr Annette Beautrais, of the Canterbury Suicide Project, argued that there was an increasing body of evidence that suggested that media portrayal of suicide should be in accordance with guidelines recommending muted and cautious coverage, to minimise the risk of suicidal behaviour in vulnerable individuals. She summarised evidence that unrestricted reporting of suicides produced a "copycat" or imitative effect, and that restrictions on, or "muting" of, media reporting could reduce or eliminate this effect. Further, the impact on bereaved families was such that whenever possible, reporting should be limited to the name, address, and occupation of the deceased and the fact that the death was self-inflicted (Beautrais, 2005).

In summarising these submissions, the Ministry of Justice considered concerns about whether the prior restraint on publication was justifiable under the Bill of Rights Act, 1990, given the importance of the principle of open justice. It said Crown Law Office advice was that prior restraint was justified in some cases, especially where there may be "an identifiable risk of harm — the reporting of self-inflicted death is a special case" (Tesoriero, 2006). It based its consideration as to whether there was a risk of harm on a summary of the research evidence in *Suicide and the Media: Pitfalls and Prevention* (Crane, Hawton, Simkin, & Coulter, 2005). Here is the Ministry's summary in full (with original bolding and underlining):

> *i. Media reporting or portrayal of suicides **can** influence suicidal behaviour, leading to: increase in the overall number of suicides, and increases in the use of particular methods of suicide.*

> *The degree of influence is still being measured, although the report noted that in 21 of 30 studies which examined reporting of suicide in newspapers there was evidence of an increase in suicides after the reports (with 10 studies finding a causal link).*
>
> *ii. In contrast, there is no published evidence to suggest that reporting of suicide reduces suicidal behaviour by others below baseline levels or 'puts people off' attempting suicide.*
>
> *iii. However, modifications of reporting are possible and can lead to significant reduction in imitative suicidal behaviour.*

This summary of the research, while true in broad terms, ignored important nuances. These are discussed further below. It seems the Ministry was either unaware or chose to ignore these, because it concluded:

> *The Ministry considers that clause 61 [this became S71 in the Act] [be] retained in its current form until such time as there is conclusive evidence about whether media reporting on suicide has a positive, negative, or null impact on imitative suicide. (Tesoriero, 2006, p. 18)*

It added, in a further report to the Select Committee:

> *The present presumption . . . helps to prevent suicide and to protect the family's privacy. Prior restraint [of reporting before the coroner rules] . . . is consistent with MoH suicide prevention strategies of promoting careful, prudent and muted reporting of suicide issues in the media. (James, 2006, p. 2)*

As a mitigating factor in the restraint on free speech, it noted that coroners were required to consider the Bill of Rights implications for freedom of expression in each case, and that any coroner's decision not to make public details could be reviewed by a High Court judge.

The 2006 Act did not resolve the on-going concern in New Zealand about media reporting. If anything, it inflamed it. Some coroners, including the chief coroner, have since called for more openness in reporting of suicide (Fairfax, 2012a). This has been criticised by some suicide researchers, who say it risks causing copycat suicides (Beautrais & Fergusson, D.M., 2012). In 2010, the Ministry of Health made another attempt to introduce voluntary media reporting guidelines. This time it did consult the news media, and voluntary guidelines were agreed in 2011. But while the new guidelines now have the backing of the news media, they have been criticised in turn by several New Zealand and international suicide researchers for this time not consulting suicide academics adequately, and misrepresenting and marginalising research evidence on the risks of suicide reporting. One prominent New Zealand researcher, Professor David Fergusson, believes the Ministry of Health has mismanaged the whole introduction of guidelines (Fergusson, 2013). There is some evidence that the new guidelines have had some effect, as stories about suicide, where it can be reported, with permission from the coroner, now often display messages about where vulnerable individuals can get help (e.g. Hollingsworth, 2012).

In 2012, the Minister for Courts, Chester Borrows, announced a review of the Coroners Act. This was mainly on procedural issues, but he agreed to accept submissions on the issue of media reporting of suicide. In 2013, it was announced that the Law Commission would be asked to review the issue of media reporting of suicide, with a brief to report by March 2014.

Arguments for and against the removal of the current legislative restrictions.

New Zealand's suicide rate has followed a general trend downwards in most OECD countries since 1995. The overall rate in 2010 was 11.5/100,000 (OECD, 2011). While this crept up to 12/100,000 in 2012, it was still close to the 2010 OECD average of 11.3/100,000. This figure is higher than countries with a traditionally low rate (e.g. UK at 6.2/100,000, Australia 7.8/100,000) but about the same as Ireland, and lower than France (13.8), Switzerland (14.3) and Japan (19.7) (OECD, 2011). However, within this broad picture, there are areas of considerable concern. New Zealand's female youth suicide rate is the highest in the OECD, and the male youth rate the third highest (Health, 2012).

There is a growing body of evidence suggesting that certain kinds of media portrayal of suicide may provoke an imitative effect among vulnerable individuals. A recent summary of 72 known studies concluded:

> The vast majority of these studies provide support for the above
> hypothesis [that media reporting of suicide can lead to copycat
> behaviours] suggesting that reporting of suicide can result in
> imitation acts, particularly if the story is prominent, involves
> explicit descriptions of the suicide method, and it is framed in a
> way that glorifies the death. (Pirkis, 2010)

On the face of it, this would appear to justify New Zealand's current legislative regime around reporting of suicide. However, there are important methodological factors which need to be taken into consideration. These include the size of the risk, the type of reporting, and the occluding effect of censorship on the public discourse around suicide. Taking each of these in turn:

1. The size of the risk

While there appears to be strong evidence of a correlative effect, the size of the effect is small compared to other psycho-social factors (Niederkrotenthaler et al., 2010). A common estimate is that the risk is around 5 per cent of the total risk factors (Hollings, 2012). Thus censorship should not be seen as a silver bullet; any impact of it on suicide rates is likely to be small. All OECD countries that have achieved substantial reductions in suicide rates (e.g. Australia, UK) in recent years have done this without censorship. It can only reasonably be concluded that censorship is not a prerequisite of suicide rate reduction.

Of course, it could be argued that introducing censorship would have resulted in even steeper rate reductions in these countries, and that without censorship, New Zealand's rate would be higher. And it does not mean censorship may not be justified, as even a small effect may save lives. One estimate of the impact of media reporting of celebrity suicide in New Zealand, based on recent effect size estimates and the population here, is that unrestricted reporting of a celebrity suicide would lead to around 10 more suicides per annum, and possibly up to 23 more, if the celebrity was also an entertainer (Niederkrotenthaler, 2013). This is based on the premise that such reporting is likely to be more sensationalist. Presumably this figure would be less if the reporting was moderated by guidelines.

2. The type of reporting

Most of the studies showing a significant effect of suicide reporting on rates have been in countries with a highly sensationalist tabloid media, but few studies have distinguished between types of media reporting. Those studies which have tried to differentiate between types of reporting suggest it is the treatment, not the content, that may be the problem. In one study in Switzerland, tabloid editors were persuaded to eliminate the more lurid aspects of their coverage, such as dramatic page-one headlines, graphic pictures of the suicide method and dramatic accounts of circumstances of death. They kept much content that would be banned in New Zealand, such as the fact it was a suspected suicide, the name, and the manner of death. Although the number of stories on suicide increased four-fold, the study coincided with a slight reduction in the national suicide rate, from 20.7/100,000 in 1991 to 19.6/100,000 in 1994. The authors concluded: "This may indicate that it is not the number of articles that matters, but the quality of reporting" (Michel, Wyss, Frey, & Valach, 2000). A recent study in Austria found that over 70 per cent of media reports of completed suicides were not associated with an increase in suicide rates (Niederkrotenthaler et al., 2009). In other words, responsible reporting of suicides is possible without the risk of harm to more than two-thirds of vulnerable individuals. The importance of differentiating between types of reporting is implicit in all media guidelines that have been endorsed by suicide researchers. Invariably, these emphasise the importance of avoiding sensationalism, such as page-one placement, large headlines, graphic photos and descriptions of method, and repetition, especially in the few days following the death. However, a recent large-scale study in Australia, which did attempt to measure item quality, found it had no relationship with suicides. The authors noted it could have been due to a small sample in the quality analysis, and added: "It is counter-intuitive to dismiss the hypothesis that item quality would be likely to have an impact upon the likelihood of a given media item influencing imitation acts" (Pirkis et al., 2006, p. 2884). In fact, at least some respected suicide researchers believe some kinds of media reporting of suicide is desirable if it can be done in a restrained way (Niederkrotenthaler, 2013; Pirkis, 2013). In particular, reporting that challenges the idea that suicide is a valid response to crisis may be helpful; a recent study found that some kinds of reporting (of cases where people had contemplated but decided against a suicide) may reduce the suicide rate (Niederkrotenthaler et al., 2010).

The distinction that should be drawn about the quality of reporting is particularly relevant to the New Zealand context. While concerns have been expressed that the New Zealand news media is becoming more sensationalist (Hollings, Samson, Tilley, & Lealand, 2007) it is questionable as to whether this is actually true; some early newspaper reporting in *The Truth* newspaper, for example, was highly-coloured (Yska, 2010). A recent study found that the mainstream media in its reporting of suicide is mostly of a more conservative type, and avoids lurid headlines, pictures of method, and romanticised portrayals of content — the kinds of reporting that studies have associated with increased suicide rates — in favour of a more objective style of reporting that concentrates on the basic facts (Collings & Kemp, 2010).

These nuances in the research are not reflected in New Zealand Ministry of Health summaries of suicide reporting risks, which tend to emphasise the risks of news media reports, with little or no qualification with regard to the kind of reporting most associated with imitative effects. This has tended to skew the discourse in New Zealand, creating a kind of "moral panic" around the risks of media reporting. For example, Goal 5: the Ministry of Health's Suicide Prevention Action Plan:

> A large body of international evidence suggests that the way suicide is reported and portrayed in the media may increase rates of suicidal behaviour (e.g., Gould 2001; Hawton & Williams 2001, 2005; Institute of Medicine 2002; Pirkis & Blood 2001; Schmidtke & Schaller 2000; Stack 2005; Sudak & Sudak 2005). This evidence suggests that media depictions may influence suicidal behaviour in the following three ways.
>
> 1. Imitation: Reporting a method of suicide may lead to imitative or "copycat" suicide attempts using that method. This result is especially likely if media coverage is repetitive, gives details of

methods or highlights the suicide of a celebrity or well-known person. These findings have been produced across different times, places, contexts and cultures (e.g., Hawton & Williams 2005; Liu, et al 2007; Phillips 1974; Sonneck, et al 1994; Yip, et al 2006).

2. Contagion: Media depiction may facilitate contagious behaviour. Specifically, the way in which suicides are reported may encourage further suicides within a population of individuals who are interlinked or interrelated. In turn, contagion may lead to the formation of clusters of suicides or suicide attempts. Many case studies and reviews of suicide clusters report exposure to media influences in those who have died by suicide or made suicide attempts (e.g., Davidson 1989; Gould 1990; Gould, et al 1989; Hazell 1993; Tousignant, et al 2005; Wilkie, et al 1998). Young people, people in institutional settings and indigenous communities are overrepresented in suicide clusters (Earls, et al 1990; Gould, et al 1990; Hazell 1993).

3. Normalisation: Frequent or repetitive reporting of suicide may encourage the public perception that suicide is a reasonable, understandable and common approach to solving life difficulties (Beautrais, et al 2004).

All the above evidence clearly suggests the potential for some ways of reporting and portraying suicidal behaviours to influence vulnerable people to make suicide attempts. There is little evidence to suggest that media reports of suicide will reduce population rates of suicidal behaviour or deter people from suicidal behaviours (Crane, et al 2005; Hawton & Williams 2001). There is no evidence to suggest that increases in suicide rates or in the use of a particular method following the report of a suicide in the media simply represent suicides that would have occurred later anyway but that have been brought forward in time (Crane, et al 2005). (Health 2008)

While the above summary is true in itself, it gives an unbalanced impression as to the risks of media reporting of suicide. It gives the impression that it is the reporting itself, rather than the presentation of it, that is the main risk. It does not mention that some kinds of reporting may incur little risk. Nor does it mention that New Zealand has very little, if any, of the kind of tabloid sensationalism captured in most overseas studies. As discussed above, where research has differentiated between sensationalist and non-sensationalist reporting, the picture is different. It does not point out that the effect size is small, and that many comparable countries allow it and have still managed to reduce suicide rates. Its claim that there is "little evidence" on positive effects of media reporting on suicide is misleading; there may not have been any in the suicide field, but that is because no one has looked for it in ways which draw on the substantial evidence in the wider media effects literature on potential positive media effects. These are discussed further below.

3. Wider consideration of media effects

Another problem with the current research is that it takes little account of the risks of non-reporting. Suicide researchers have rightly pointed out that there is no evidence that reporting of suicide risk factors has a beneficial effect on vulnerable individuals, and that in fact may even be harmful (Beautrais, & Fergusson, D.M., 2012).

However, media suicide research has so far appeared to ignore the potential beneficial effect of publicity about the issue on the wider community, and particularly policy makers. In fact the entire debate around media reporting of suicide appears to have been conducted within a paradigm akin to the earlier hypodermic and magic-bullet models of media communication. Working with a largely passive conception of media audiences, these models argued that media effects could be targeted at a precisely defined audience, and exaggerated the capacity of mass media messages to have all-determining effects on social behaviour (Rosenberry & Vicker, 2009). More recent and sophisticated theories of mass communication, such as agenda-setting, priming, and framing, have shown the effect of media intervention on the wider community, by setting the agenda of which issues are considered important, and even how they should be thought about (Scheufele, 2000; Scheufele & Tewksbury, 2007; Sniderman, 2004). It is argued here that any discussion of the effects of media intervention (such as censorship) needs to consider the wider effects on the entire community. No such effects were considered by the Select Committee considering the 2006 Coroners Bill. It is worth considering what some of the wider media effects of censorship are (what might be termed the costs of censorship), so they can be balanced against the undoubtedly life-preserving benefits which have so far dominated the discourse. What are some of these effects?

a. Censorship inhibits responsible reporting

The current restrictions effectively eliminate the opportunity for restrained, responsible reporting that may promote discussion of the systemic causes of suicide. Several countries have introduced guidelines for media reporting (e.g. Australia, the UK). These typically arise through consultation with media representatives, and encourage news media to avoid the sensationalist elements described above. Reporting of a suspected suicide as such before an inquest is still allowed, as is moderate reporting of the facts, such as the name and circumstances. Journalists are encouraged to provide a balanced report, avoiding, for example, attribution to a single cause (e.g. a relationship problem) and encouraging them to seek comment from relevant experts. Such guidelines were introduced in Australia around 2000, and their dissemination funded nationally since 2002. According to one recent study, their uptake by Australian media has been considerable (Skehan, 2006). Two international suicide researchers, Jane Pirkis (2013), and Dr Thomas Niederkrotenthaler (2013), both believe that a voluntary, guideline-based approach to reporting is preferable to New Zealand's legislative approach.

Because the current restrictions in New Zealand effectively ban any reporting of a suspected suicide before an inquest, they effectively mean that nothing is reported until months after the event. Typically inquests in New Zealand are weeks, but more usually months or even years, after the event. By this time, the news value of the event has reduced, and reports of inquests are usually run in the back pages of a newspaper. This reduces the opportunity for any witnesses to the event with relevant information to come forward in a timely manner. The news media plays an important role in helping police source witnesses and gather information. In some cases, where police suspect a suicide, they themselves may not be aware that there may be another explanation. A recent case in Australia, where a family contested the police assumption of the suicide of a family member, illustrates this point (Fairfax, 2012b). Under New Zealand law, the family could presumably be prosecuted for discussing the case in public, and face a fine of $1000, even though they have legitimate concerns that the death was not accidental.

It could be argued that potential witnesses could simply contact the coroner and give evidence at an inquest. However, often witnesses may not be aware that some small piece of information may be relevant. The effect of seeing an issue highlighted in the news media often has the effect of jogging people's memories and encouraging them to contribute to the public discourse. Reporters can also go places and gain evidence that the police cannot — particularly in talking to witnesses who may be reluctant to talk to the police. The police have long been aware of this media role and use it to good effect.

b. Censorship distorts the issues agenda

Another side-effect of censorship, as might be predicted by agenda-setting theory, is that the topic of suicide censorship itself has dominated the discourse, rather than the more significant drivers of suicide themselves. Many studies on agenda-setting have shown that issue salience, usually operationalised as perceived public importance, determines which issues dominate the public agenda (McCombs & Shaw, 1993). Priming theory — sometimes called second-stage agenda-setting — argues that the portrayal of an issue can guide how those issues are talked about (Scheufele, 2000). Framing theory, and more recently, studies in priming theory, suggests that audience responses to those issues can be guided by negative or positive portrayal of the issues (Sheafer, 2007; Sniderman, 2004). With censorship dominating the discourse in New Zealand, a noticeable side-effect has been the lack of discussion of perhaps more significant issues. One suicide researcher put this neatly, albeit unintentionally, in a recent email exchange on the censorship debate:

> *Media effects on suicide are small and even the best guidelines in the world would only have a small impact on the overall suicide rate. However . . . this relatively minor policy issue has taken a disproportionate amount of time to be resolved. We would be far better investing in policy debates about how to reduce rates of depression; how to manage those who arrive in hospital after a suicide attempt; how best to regulate access to methods; etc. rather than continuing to debate how best the media can report suicide.(Fergusson, 2013)*

It should be pointed out, however, that Fergusson believes that legislation should remain until adequate reporting guidelines are agreed with the news media (Fergusson, 2013).

There is evidence that the public would see the kinds of public safety concerns raised by individual suicides as high-salience issues, and therefore give them a higher priority as issues worthy of action, if we look at the debate on four other current issues: the road toll, fire safety, child abuse, and infectious disease. Undoubtedly the most coverage around these are generated about specific events. Publicity about a series of crashes at known black spots helps focus community awareness that there is a common factor, and has highlighted the need for action, while repeated mention of drink or speed or lack of safety belts as factors in crashes has helped build public awareness of these as important factors in road safety. Firefighters miss few opportunities to mention the protective role of smoke alarms after fatal house fires. Tragically, the extensive coverage of the killing of the Kahui baby twins has raised awareness in the wider community of the circumstances which can lead to such deaths, and the part we can all play in avoiding them. Likewise, widespread coverage of the recent meningococcal epidemic in New Zealand (Health, 2013) has helped raise awareness in the general public of risk factors and the need to get immediate treatment. However, and this is a difficult point for some to accept, the salience of these issues rises when the issue is seen as topical, and relevant, and when people can identify with the subject of the story, through what are known as "human interest stories". Undoubtedly, the most influential coverage has been around the tragic deaths of specific individuals, such as that of 12-year-old schoolgirl Amanda Crook-Barker from meningococcal disease (Boyer, 2012). While some suicide researchers may understandably see the media demand for topicality and subjectivity as an unnecessary risk to vulnerable individuals, given research which suggests risk is higher in the days immediately following a suicide (Crane et al., 2005), it is precisely these factors which are likely to increase the salience of the underlying issues in each suicide in terms of the public discourse. By eliminating the ability to report topically (i.e. on recent suicides) and largely eliminating the ability to provide human-interest stories, censorship has occluded a potentially powerful agenda-setting and priming effect. Of course, these points are conjectural, and must be balanced against the known risks of these kinds of stories.

While there is no research in the New Zealand context that provides a framework to balance these risks, there is anecdotal evidence of the cost of censorship. Recently, the parents of a suicide expressed regret they were not made more aware of the risks of helium (Francis, 2011). Coroners have also highlighted concerns with the way health professionals have interpreted the Privacy Act, as factors in suicides (Hollingsworth, 2012). However, preventable risk factors such as these get little publicity because the censorship regime ensures that media reporting of the suicides to which they are believed to have contributed is delayed and minimal. This is unfortunate in terms of the public policy debate, as these kinds of high-salience issues, often reported in a negative tone, are likely to have a strong effect in terms of framing and priming the public issues agenda (Sheafer, 2007).

c. Censorship does not equate to privacy

The Select Committee considering the 2006 Bill stated that a key rationale for keeping the current restrictions was to protect bereaved families from media intrusion. There are good reasons for this; families of suicides can be more vulnerable to suicide themselves. However, the current restrictions do not effectively promote family privacy. This is because despite the restrictions, news media can and do still approach families. Proscribing the publication of certain details undoubtedly has made it less likely that the news media will take an interest, and thus less likely that many families will be approached. However, in those cases in which they do take an interest, they are just as free to approach the family, and publish a story about the death, albeit with certain details omitted. The recent death, in 2012, of the high-profile Wellington lawyer Greg King was one example. King was found dead beside his car, only a couple of weeks after a successful defence of the murder accused in a very high-profile murder case. He left a wife and two young children. His death was front-page news, but was subject to a Coroner's order that "in the interests of decency and personal privacy nothing at all may be reported other than the fact that Mr King is dead and his death has been reported to the Coroner. This does not prevent personal tributes being published" (Bain, 2012). There was a small comment from the family, through a spokesperson, but mostly the media respected their privacy and most of the coverage consisted of tributes to King's character and career. Due to the Coroner's order, this article is unable to report anything further, although online media not based in New Zealand is unrestricted.

There are no similar restrictions on approaching families who have experienced other kinds of illness or injury-related deaths, such as deaths from disease, car accidents, or crime. Why should families of suicides enjoy a special protection? On the surface this exception may seem kind, but could it not also stigmatise such deaths, resulting in effectively more trauma for the family? Some bereaved families have argued that the lack of publicity contributes to a sense of shame (Carville, 2013). Why should a death due at least in part to mental illness be more deserving of privacy than one due to meningococcal disease, drowning, a road accident, fire, or child abuse? In those cases where families genuinely do not wish to speak to the news media, they are able to refuse, and if they are harassed, may seek redress under the current laws on harassment (Burrows & Cheer, 2010). This approach has worked reasonably well for all for other kinds of death.

While it is laudable to protect bereaved families from unnecessary trauma resulting from media intrusion, why should bereaved individuals with legitimate concerns be effectively retraumatised and disempowered by the legislative prohibitions on their speaking out? There is anecdotal evidence that a number of bereaved would like to voice concerns but feel unable to do so (Hollingsworth, 2013). While many families understandably want privacy at such times, there are also many families, who if approached with sensitivity, welcome the opportunity to salvage something from a tragedy by warning others.

4. Conclusion: a way forward

The summary above shows there are good arguments for ending the legislative restrictions on suicide reporting in New Zealand, and replacing them with voluntary restraint. The question is: What kind of voluntary restraint?

New Zealand already has voluntary reporting guidelines, but they are of questionable benefit when so little reporting can be done, and when they do not have the support of suicide researchers here. A better starting point would be the Australian news media guidelines, promoted by the Hunter Institute, *in conjunction with* the repeal of the current legislative restrictions on reporting. The Australian guidelines have gained good acceptance from news media there, without unduly inhibiting news media reporting of suicide, and have been shown to be not incompatible with a decreasing suicide rate. Similar guidelines in New Zealand would still allow reporting of facts, and meet the goals of allowing public debate about issues raised by individual cases, while minimising the risks of an imitative effect. They would also gain the support of at least some suicide researchers here. Even some of those suicide researchers here who support the current legislative approach do so only until a satisfactory voluntary approach can be agreed on.

Whatever the final form of such voluntary guidelines, it is vital that some form is found that gains the support of news media AND at least some suicide researchers. This is not just to conform to some altruistic notion of consensus. If there is to be more reporting about suicides, journalists will inevitably be approaching suicide researchers for comment and information, and it is important that the latter have confidence that they can participate in a valuable public debate in a way which minimises the risk of harm. Equally, it is important that members of the public and journalists are able to raise issues of legitimate public concern without threat of criminal prosecution.

On the other hand, this has to be balanced against the likelihood that some relaxation of the current legislation may risk an increase in suicides, particularly in the event of a celebrity entertainer suicide. Ultimately, however, this is a risk other countries are willing to take, in the interests of a wider and fuller debate about suicide. While the benefits of such a debate have not been quantified in numerical terms of the impact on suicide rates (and are probably unquantifiable), there are good theoretical and practical arguments, and plenty of anecdotal evidence, that such a debate is worth having in and of itself.

Taking all the above into consideration, it seems more prudent to err on the side of overseas experience and allow modest, guideline-based reporting, rather than conduct what is effectively an uncontrolled experiment on the benefits of near-total censorship.

Minute of Coroner Wallace Bain: In the matter of an inquiry into the death of Gregory James King (Coroners 2012).

Beautrais, A. (2005). Submission to the Select Committee on the Coroners Bill. Christchurch: Canterbury Suicide Project.

Beautrais, A., & Fergusson, D. M. (2012). Media reporting of suicide in New Zealand: "More matter with less art". New Zealand Medical Journal, 125 (1362).

Boyer, S., & O'Callaghan, J. (2012). From rash to death in two hours. Stuff. Retrieved August 21, 2013, from http://www.stuff.co.nz/dominion-post/news/7613375/From-rash-to-death-in-two-hours

Burrows, J., & Cheer, U. (2010). Media law in New Zealand. Wellington: LexisNexis.

Carville, O. (2013). Teens' mothers united in grief. Timaru Herald. Retrieved August 21, 2013, from http://www.stuff.co.nz/timaru-herald/news/9094497/Teens-mothers-united-in-grief

Collings, S. C., & Kemp, C. G. (2010). Death knocks, professional practice, and the public good: The media experience of suicide reporting in New Zealand. Social Science & Medicine, 71 (2), 244–248.

Crane, C., Hawton, K., Simkin, S., & Coulter, P. (2005). Suicide and the media: Pitfalls and prevention. Crisis: The Journal of Crisis Intervention and Suicide Prevention, 26 (1), 42–47.

Etzersdorfer, E., & Sonneck, G. (1998). Preventing suicide by influencing mass-media reporting: The Viennese experience 1980–1996. Archives of Suicide Research, 4 (1), 67–74.

Evans, G. (2006). Submission to the Justice and Electoral Committee on the Coroners Bill. Welllington: Ministry of Justice.

Fairfax. (2012a). Coroner calls for more openness of suicide. Timaru Herald. Retrieved August 21, 2013, from http://www.stuff.co.nz/timaru-herald/suicide-time-to-talk/7111617/Coroner-calls-for-more-openness-of-suicide

Fairfax. (2012b). Family investigation calls suicide into question. Stuff. Retrieved August 21, 2013, from http://www.stuff.co.nz/world/australia/7941749/Family-investigation-calls-suicide-into-question

Fergusson, D. (2013). [Email to author].

Francis, C. (2011). Helium suicide sparks call for review. Stuff. Retrieved July 2, 2013, from http://www.stuff.co.nz/national/5484448/Helium-suicide-sparks-call-for-review

Hansard. (1951). *Coroners Bill 1951*. Wellington: NZ Parliament.

Health. (2008). NZ suicide prevention action plan 2008–2012: The evidence for action. Retrieved August 21, 2013, from http://www.spinz.org.nz/file/downloads/pdf/file_48.pdf

Health. (2012). Suicide facts: Deaths and intentional self-harm hospitalisations 2010. Retrieved August 21, 2013, from Ministry of Health http://www.health.govt.nz/publication/suicide-facts-deaths-and-intentional-self-harm-hospitalisations-2010

Health. (2013). Meningococcal [Disease]. Retrieved August 21, 2013, from Ministry of Health http://www.health.govt.nz/our-work/diseases-and-conditions/meningococcal

Hollings, J. (2012, November 2012). *Reasonable restriction or moral panic? The evidence for and against restrictions on media reporting of suicide in New Zealand.* Paper presented at the School of Communication, Journalism and Marketing Seminar Series Massey University, Wellington.

Hollings, J., Samson, A., Tilley, E., & Lealand, G. (2007). The big NZ journalism survey: Underpaid, under-trained, under-resourced, unsure about the future — but still idealistic. *Pacific Journalism Review, 13* (2), 175-197.

Hollingsworth, J. (2012). Privacy versus patient health under the spotlight. *Stuff*. Retrieved August 21, 2013, from http://www.stuff.co.nz/timaru-herald/suicide-time-to-talk/7918131/Privacy-versus-patient-health-under-spotlight

James, P. (2006). *Coroners Bill: Additional matters raised during consideration of the Coroners Bill Departmental Report.* Wellington.

McCombs, M. E., & Shaw, D. L. (1993). The evolution of agenda-setting research: Twenty-five years in the marketplace of ideas. *Journal of Communication, 43* (2), 58–67.

Michel, K., Wyss, K., Frey, C., & Valach, L. (2000). An exercise in improving suicide reporting in print media. *Crisis: The Journal of Crisis Intervention and Suicide Prevention, 21* (2), 71.

Mindframe. (2009). Reporting suicide and mental illness. A resource for media professionals. Retrieved August 21, 2013, from Hunter Institute http://www.mindframe-media.info/__data/assets/pdf_file/0018/5139/Media-Book-col.pdf

Niederkrotenthaler, T. (2013). [Interview with author].

Niederkrotenthaler, T., King-Wa, F., Yip, P. S. F., Fong, D. Y. T., Stack, S., Qijin, C., & Pirkis, J. (2012). Changes in suicide rates following media reports on celebrity suicide: A meta-analysis. *Journal of Epidemiology & Community Health, 66* (11), 1037–1042.

Niederkrotenthaler, T., Till, B., Kapusta, N. D., Voracek, M., Dervic, K., & Sonneck, G. (2009). Copycat effects after media reports on suicide: A population-based ecologic study. *Social Science & Medicine, 69* (7), 1085-1090.

Niederkrotenthaler, T., Voracek, M., Herberth, A., Till, B., Strauss, M., Etzersdorfer, E., . . . Sonneck, G. (2010). Role of media reports in completed and prevented suicide: Werther v. Papageno effects. *The British Journal Of Psychiatry: The Journal Of Mental Science, 197* (3), 234-243.

OECD. (2011). Health at a glance 2011. Retrieved August 21, 2013, from OECD Publishing http://dx.doi.org/10.1787/health_glance-2011-en

Parliament. (1988). Coroners Act 1988. Retrieved 21 August, 2013, from Parliamentary Counsel Office http://www.legislation.govt.nz/act/public/1988/0111/latest/DLM134197.html

Pirkis, J. (2010). Contribution to knowledge about media professionals' experiences with reporting suicide. A commentary on Collings and Kemp. *Social Science & Medicine (1982), 71* (2), 249-250.

Pirkis, J. (2013). [Interview with author].

Pirkis, J., Burgess, P., Francis, C., Blood, W., & Jolley, D. (2006). The relationship between media reporting of suicide and actual suicide in Australia. *Social Science & Medicine, 62* (11), 2874-2886.

Rosenberry, J., & Vicker, L. (2009). *Applied mass communication theory: A guide for media practitioners.* Boston: Pearson.

Roundtable. (2011). Reporting suicide: A resource for the media. Developed by the Media Roundtable and adopted by the Media Freedom Committee and the Newspaper Publishers' Association. Retrieved August 15, 2013, from Ministry of Health http://www.health.govt.nz/publication/reporting-suicide-resource-media

Scheufele, D. A. (2000). Agenda-setting, priming, and framing revisited: Another look at cognitive effects of political communication. *Mass Communication and Society, 3* (2–3), 297–316.

Scheufele, D. A., & Tewksbury, D. (2007). Framing, agenda setting, and priming: The evolution of three media effects models. *Journal of Communication, 57* (1), 9–20.

Sheafer, T. (2007). How to evaluate it: The role of story-evaluative tone in agenda setting and priming. *Journal of Communication, 57* (1), 21-39.

Sisask, M., & Värnik, A. (2012). Media roles in suicide prevention: A systematic review. *International Journal Of Environmental Research And Public Health, 9* (1), 123-138.

Skehan, J., Greenhalgh, S., Hazell, T., & Pirkis, J. (2006). Reach, awareness and uptake of media guidelines for reporting suicide and mental illness: An Australian perspective. *International Journal of Mental Health Promotion, 8* (4), 28-34.

Sniderman, P. M., & Theriault, S. M. (2004). The structure of political argument and the logic of issue framing. In W. E. Saris, & Sniderman P. M. (Ed.), *Studies in public opinion* (pp. 133–165). NJ: Princeton.

Soanes, C., Stevenson, A., & Pearsall, J. (2004). *Concise Oxford English dictionary* (11th ed.). Oxford: Oxford University Press.

Tesoriero, P. (2006). *Coroners Bill: Departmental report.* (Cor/Moj/4). Wellington.

Tully, J., & Elsaka, N. (2004). Suicide and the media: A study of the media response to 'Suicide and the Media: The Reporting and Portrayal of Suicide in the Media — A Resource'. Christchurch: School of Political Science and Communication, University of Canterbury.

UKPC. (2008). Reporting suicide in the media. Retrieved 21 August 2013, from UK Press Complaints Commission http://www.pcc.org.uk/events/pastevents/suicide/index.html

Yska, R. (2010). *The rise and fall of the people's paper.* Nelson: Craig Potton.

CHAPTER THIRTY

Dirty tricks campaign

2014: Nicky Hager shows that government security information was used to discredit political opponents.

Nicky Hager believes that *The Hollow Men* is his best work, and it is the book of which he is most proud. But in my view, his best reporting came later. That it was again about dirty political tricks shows that he is, as well as an investigative reporter, now also working like a very good beat reporter, on the political beat.

Dirty Politics (Hager, 2014) was published just a few weeks before the 2014 election. It was, by any measure, a bombshell. It quickly sold out its print run, and the revelations it contained dominated news coverage in the run-up to the election. It detailed a campaign of dirty tricks by National Party members, using a sympathetic blogger, Cameron Slater (who called himself Whale Oil), to leak damaging information about political opponents. The revelations were backed by a cache of emails to and from Slater that Hager had obtained. Some of the revelations concerned then Justice Minister Judith Collins, who soon resigned.

But perhaps the most disturbing were those about the behaviour of the Prime Minister's Office. In the following excerpt from *Dirty Politics*, Hager details how the PM's office helped Slater get exclusive access to information from the Security Intelligence Service which he then used to attack the Leader of the Opposition, Phil Goff. These revelations resulted in an inquiry by the Inspector General of Intelligence and Security, Cheryl Gwyn. She upheld the gist of Hager's claims, finding that a member of the Prime Minister's Office did disclose SIS information to Slater for political purposes. She also found that the SIS did breach the Official Information Act by refusing requests from other journalists for the information which it gave to Slater exclusively, but said there was no evidence the SIS was deliberately trying to smear Goff (Gwyn, 2014).

The case has parallels with the Watergate scandal, where a political leader's office attempted to manipulate covert agencies to discredit political opponents. Yet, bizarrely, no one has been charged with any offence over this misuse of official information, and even the Opposition appears content to let it drop. The only person who suffered any fallout was Hager, whose home was searched by police trying to find the source of the leaked emails. Hager took the police to court and won a judgment declaring the search illegal.

'What we were seeing in politics was that all the opposition parties were repeatedly finding themselves tipped up and discredited and smeared, and it was seemingly coming from nowhere. Out of all the books it has had as large and positive a reaction as you could expect from one piece of work.

'I really can't complain about how hard the media chased John Key, but the lasting disappointment, or outrageous thing about it, is that the Prime Minister could be caught out with a dirty tricks campaign, and he never answered the question, and he sort of got away with it' (Hager, 2016).

The question?

'"Did you have a dirty tricks campaign running from your office and did you do it?" He's never answered that. Somehow we don't have enough strength in the public sphere in New Zealand [to get that answer].

'We had to have civic institutions to follow it up, and we didn't have that. Why wasn't it like Watergate? We have a winner-takes-all, one-chamber system and once the government wins, they can stop an inquiry.'

Gwyn, C. (2014, November 25). *Report into the release of information by the New Zealand Security Intelligence Service in July and August 2011.* Wellington: Office of the Inspector-General of Intelligence and Security. Retrieved from http://www.igis.govt.nz/media-releases/archived-media-releases/new-news-pageinspector-general-publishes-report-on-inquiry-into-release-of-nzsis-information-to-cameron-slater/

Hager, N. (2014). *Dirty politics: How attack politics is poisoning New Zealand's political environment.* Nelson: Craig Potton.

Hager, N. (2016). Interview with author, J. Hollings.

Straight from the Beehive

Dirty Politics: How attack politics is poisoning New Zealand's political environment, by Nicky Hager, published by Craig Potton Publishing, 2014.

Slater's next attack that year began in July 2011, only four months before the general election, when John Key mishandled two foreign policy matters and embarrassed himself during a much-vaunted trip to visit US president Barack Obama. Although he was by now a capable politician, Key was neither very interested nor experienced in foreign policy. In the first case, he repeatedly refused to answer questions on news reports about suspicions of spying by a group of Israeli backpackers, who had hurriedly left the country after one died in the February 2011 Christchurch earthquake. His attitude merely inflamed the situation and he had to back down a few hours later. He was widely thought to have mishandled the issue.[1]

Then, while he was meeting Obama, news arrived of the mass killing of young Norwegian Labour Party members by a far-right racist at a summer camp outside Oslo. When Obama and Key spoke to the press after their meeting, the latter suggested that Islamic terrorists were responsible and tried to use the tragedy to score a political point. 'If it is an act of global terrorism,' he said, 'I think what it shows is no country large or small is immune from that risk and that's why New Zealand's played its part in Afghanistan.'[2]

He looked foolish. The media talked about it being two gaffes in a row. Labour Party leader Phil Goff jumped on Key's mistakes: 'the prime minister has to understand the responsibilities of his office. He cannot mouth off without checking his facts first, which he's now done . . . on a number of occasions in the past few days.'[3] National was looking for a way to recover and an opportunity appeared to turn the attacks against Goff.

While defending his actions concerning the Israeli backpackers, Key said that Goff had also been briefed by the Security Intelligence Service (SIS) director on the case, but Goff denied this. However, he had remembered wrongly and, after a conversation with the SIS director, admitted he had indeed been told about the affair. The SIS director 'said he flicked the issue past me and said there wasn't much to it,' Goff said. 'If there had been anything of substance said to me, I'm sure I would recollect it.'[4]

This presented a golden opportunity for the National government to embarrass Goff and draw out the matter by publicising the official records of the briefing. It would, however, have looked bad for the prime minister, who is minister in charge of the SIS, to release details of a secret intelligence briefing in order to embarrass his political opponent. The motives would have been obvious. So someone else was chosen to make the attack and that person was [Cameron] Slater.

Slater would later claim that he pursued the subject, using the Official Information Act (OIA), entirely on his own initiative. John Key would likewise claim no involvement. However, Slater's communications with his political friends show what actually happened. While Goff in part brought the trouble on himself, it is a textbook example of the prime minister's office using Slater to carry out their plans.

The story begins on the day Goff admitted his mistake. Slater published a blog post headed 'Goff needs to go': 'All somebody has to do now is ask [SIS director] Warren Tucker to produce the briefing notes and Goff is a goner.'[5] The following day he sent a carefully worded information request to Tucker asking for copies of the briefing notes and 'details of any acknowledgment' that Goff had read them.[6]

Just two days after that, on 28 July 2011, Slater boasted to Peter Smith via Facebook about what he had coming. Smith said it looked like Goff would last as Labour leader until the election date. 'No he won't,' Slater replied. 'I'll finish him off in the next couple of days.' 'More dirt?' Smith asked. 'Can't say right now,' Slater said. 'I'm sworn to secrecy. But it will be catastrophic.'[7]

They continued the discussion the next day. Smith asked if Slater's latest post, a joke text from Goff to Helen Clark about being in trouble, was 'the beginning of the end for Goff?'

> *Cameron Slater: yep*
> *Peter Smith: more to come? over the weekend?*
> *Cameron Slater: yep*
> *Peter Smith: misbehavior/lies/corruption? when will your post be?*
> *Cameron Slater: can't say, have to be patient.*[8]

On 1 August Smith asked again, 'getting close to a release of your Goff tease?' Slater said he was 'waiting on documents, then pow . . . it will happen this week . . . it should take him down'.[9]

Any regular user of the OIA knows that you almost never get a reply before the statutory 20 working days and that, with a sensitive subject, it usually takes considerably longer. But it seems someone had told Slater that his request would be processed, signed off and sent to him in just a few days. It also seems that Slater had some advance knowledge of what the information said.

At 9 p.m. the next day, 2 August, Slater was chatting via Facebook with Aaron Bhatnagar. 'Should be a big day tomorrow,' he said, 'if my PO Box has a nice brown envelope with OHMS [On Her Majesty's Service] on it.' Bhatnagar said, 'Oh, what's that about?' Slater said he had 'OIAd the briefing minutes and notes for Goff's SIS briefing . . . it has been expedited, in the public interest. It is devastating for Goff I am told.'[10] By the next afternoon, only six working days since making the request, Slater was feeling impatient. Bhatnagar asked him if the package had arrived. 'Nope,' Slater replied, 'getting really annoyed.'[11] It arrived soon after and Slater launched his attack on 4 August.

The SIS papers noted that Goff and Tucker had discussed 'Investigation into Israeli Nationals in Christchurch' and a briefing paper on the subject had been 'read by/discussed with Mr Goff'. This sounds like more than 'flicked by'. Slater wrote extravagant posts repeatedly calling Goff a liar, saying he had a 'history of lying'[12] and claiming that he had accused the SIS director of lying. Goff made it worse for himself by getting annoyed that his credibility had been questioned. The messy news coverage that followed did Goff no good. Key then joined in, saying on Radio New Zealand that someone was not telling the truth and that he did not believe Tucker would mislead the public.[13]

When Bhatnagar wrote to Slater a few hours after the news began, he said, 'Bet you have a shit eating grin right now.' Slater replied, 'Meanwhile Goff is dying by inches, it's on every channel and [media] outlet.' Bhatnagar said that David Farrar had chimed in attacking Goff as well, and Slater added that Larry Williams of Newstalk ZB private radio was also 'going large on it'.[14] Other commentators such as PR man Matthew Hooton joined in too.[15] That night, Smith wrote to ask if he was having a good day. 'Yep,' Slater replied, 'fucked him hard.'[16] It was the second big hit in a row, coming only weeks after the Labour Party data leaks.

Slater wrote that Goff's actions alone had 'led to a non issue being turned into three weeks worth of bad headlines', but this was disingenuous.[17] Slater knew his own actions had led to the bad headlines and was proud of it. The attack had successfully distracted attention from Key's gaffes.

Whether Goff deserved this or not, the point here is the nature of the attack politics. Goff is a conservative on foreign policy and intelligence issues who would not naturally question or criticise the intelligence services. The aim from the start was to cause him political trouble, not to reveal or debate anything about his beliefs or policies. Documents like the SIS briefing notes are not usually released to the public, under the official information law or otherwise. Someone had overruled the usual practice and then fast-tracked the release. The released documents were stamped as being declassified on 26 July 2011, the same day that Slater sent off his request. Where was the time for decision-making and consultations?

Slater had been 'sworn to secrecy'; he knew from the start that his information request had 'been expedited' and that the documents were 'devastating' for Goff. He was working clandestinely with insiders who knew what the briefing paper said and were involved in its release to him under the OIA. Those insiders can only have been in the SIS or Key's office, and the SIS, and especially Tucker, would surely never have done something so unusual, so political and so public without their minister's knowledge and approval. If Tucker had wanted to release the documents on his own initiative, he would normally have done so to the media first. Why would public servants expedite release to such an obviously partisan person?

In other words, it was not the SIS that tipped off Slater and arranged for him to run the attack. It was the prime minister's staff. Given that it was highly political SIS business, there seems no doubt that John Key knew what was happening, approved it and had his staff liaise with Slater about the release.

The Labour Party questioned whether the document release had been a political set-up, but Slater insisted it was all his own idea. 'The Official Information Act is designed so that the powerful can be held to account,' he wrote. 'While it is common for the Official Information Act to be utilised by journalists and others in the "media", it is a law designed to enable citizens to hold their government machinery to account. That . . . is all "Citizen" Slater did. That he was first off the mark, and cannily couched his request in deliberately limited terms that seemed likely to get a quick result . . . just make him an effective inquirer.'[18]

A spokesperson for Key said 'he had not contacted Slater about the matter'.[19] Another report said, 'Prime Minister John Key has denied his office had any contact with a right-wing blogger about requesting the release of the SIS papers that suggested Mr Goff had been briefed on the matter.'[20] It is worth stepping back and considering what had happened. Goff's memory lapse was minor but there were serious issues involved. The prime minister had abused his position as minister in charge of the SIS to embarrass another politician only months before an election.

The obvious guess for who liaised with Slater over the SIS papers is Jason Ede. It is exactly what he would do the following year when he quietly tipped off Slater to make another hurried official information request.

That case concerned the embarrassing discovery of a major computer vulnerability in the Ministry of Social Development's computers. In October 2012 an IT technician named Ira Bailey found a similar sort of fault to the one revealed the previous year in the Labour Party's computers, where people could access large quantities of unsecured data. But rather than publicising the private information as Slater and Ede had done, Bailey contacted the ministry and asked if, like many organisations, they paid for information about security faults. When they declined he gave the story to a journalist. Widespread publicity followed and Minister of Social Development Paula Bennett faced damaging questioning in Parliament about whether she had leaked Bailey's name to the media.

The Green Party requested copies of Bennett's communications and, apparently fearing more bad publicity, someone in the government decided it would be better if the news came out through the Whale Oil blog instead. Ede contacted Slater about the impending information release to the Greens, writing from one of his non-parliamentary e-mail addresses, to suggest that the blogger request the information as well. He had 'heard the Greens are getting it tonight — if you fire in an email you may be well served.'[21]

Ede recommended the wording that Slater use in his official information request: 'Written and email communications within, to and from, Paula Bennett's Ministerial office and its staff in relation to Ira Bailey from the beginning of last week til today'[22] and Slater sent the request that day, using exactly the same words, apart from inserting a bracketed date, 'Mon 8 October 2012', after 'last week'.[23] Slater received the information from Bennett by the following day and was able to publicise it with a government-friendly spin — 'Bennett's office in the clear' — less than two days after Ede wrote to him.[24] Slater used the occasion as an excuse for gratuitous criticism of the people who had embarrassed the government: Bailey and journalist Keith Ng.[25]

Slater finished his account of the incident by justifying the unnatural speed with which his information request had been answered, much as he had justified the rapid release of the SIS briefing. 'Normally government departments and politicians use 20 days as a target timeframe despite information being to hand,' he said. 'In this case it is apparent that the information was to hand, and because I confined the request to a small timeframe and specific details [it] was able to be provided in a timely manner. I think Paula Bennett's office are to be commended for that.'[26]

Journalists have reported that this has become a regular trick in various ministers' offices. One described how he would request information, wait the usual 20 working days or longer and then, when it was close to being released Slater would be tipped off to request the same information. The information would then be e-mailed to Slater at the same time as it was put in the post to the journalist. Slater could scoop the story on his blog, with his pro government spin, before the letter reached the journalist; he was undermining the media's work and helping the government's public relations work at the same time.[27]

A pattern emerges: when the National government had a sticky issue, Ede and Slater worked together to attack its opponents. Earlier in 2012, for instance, the government was facing a barrage of criticism and leaks over its plans to restructure the Ministry of Foreign Affairs and Trade (MFAT). Ede wrote to Slater proposing he seek information under the OIA in order to hit back at the diplomats about how well they were paid. 'The OIA would be to the department,' he wrote, seeking 'salary bands' and 'total remuneration packages for MFAT staffers based overseas. Needs to include a request for a list of all staff allowances.'[28] Slater was being used to show up the people who were challenging the government's actions. Later that month Slater wrote a scathing attack on 'fat cat' diplomats and how much they were paid in allowances while posted overseas. He headed the post 'There is someone paid more than wharfies for doing less . . . Kiwi MFAT troughers are living it large at the taxpayer expense.'[29]

There are numerous mentions throughout Slater's communications of contacts and meetings with Ede: 'spoken to Ede this morning', 'I told Ede that yesterday', 'should I call Ede and ask . . .', 'Ede needs to get the PM onto it', 'I've got good info from the PM's office, 'Jason is a good c**t' and so on.[30] Ede became Slater's point of contact on many matters concerning the government. During the 2011 election, for instance, Slater helped to identify people who had been putting stickers on National Party billboards. The first person to whom he e-mailed the information, before leading an attack against them, was Ede.[31] Ten days later, worried that a National candidate might be caught breaking the electoral rules, Slater contacted Ede.[32]

Other ministers' offices also began feeding information to Slater, such as Gillon Carruthers, press secretary for Education Minister Anne Tolley. 'I got those stats out of Tolley's office, seems Gillon has worked out that feeding the whale might help,' Slater wrote in early 2011. 'Yes they should have all worked it out now,' Lusk replied.[33] [Correspondence between Slater and political strategist Simon Lusk implicates the latter in the Whale Oil episode.]

The prime minister's office used the bloggers to launch attacks on anyone they saw as a political challenge. Each example is not earth shattering on its own but the cumulative effect is intended to wear down their opponents. This is reminiscent of the politics associated with US president Richard Nixon. His staff were instructed to use the resources of government to cause trouble for his political enemies. A 1971 White House document said, 'This memorandum addresses the matter of how we can maximize the fact of our incumbency in dealing with persons known to be active in their opposition to our Administration; stated a bit more bluntly — how we can use the available federal machinery to screw our political enemies.'[34]

Jason Ede was also in continuous contact with David Farrar and, as seen in Chapter 9, got National research unit staff to prepare material for Kiwiblog.[35] . . .

There is a constant stream of posts on Kiwiblog that look as though they have been supplied by the National Party. When political writer Jane Clifton gave the keynote speech at a 10th birthday celebration event for Farrar's Kiwiblog in August 2013, she said, 'I must say I still get quite a giggle when I hear various people around the traps saying, "It's disgraceful, Kiwiblog and Whale Oil get a feed straight from the National Party, straight from the Beehive." It's like, well yeah, why wouldn't National Party people feed to pro-National Party blogs?'[36] But Farrar and Slater both chose to deny this to their readers and the public, year after year, to preserve the illusion that their blogs were separate from the party.

1. Tracy Watkins, 'PM John Key finds himself on shaky ground', *Dominion Post*, 21 July 2011.

2. Danya Levy, 'P.M. regrets first comment on Israelis', *Dominion Post*, 25 July 2011.

3. Ibid.

4. 'SIS did tell Goff about spy inquiry', Fairfax NZ News, 26 July 2011.

5. Cameron Slater, 'Goff needs to go', Whale Oil blog post, 25 July 2011.

6. Cameron Slater, 'Official Information Act Request', letter to Warren Tucker, 26 July 2011.

7. Cameron Slater, Facebook messaging to Peter Smith, 28 July 2011.

8. Cameron Slater, Facebook messaging to Peter Smith, 29 July 2011.

9. Cameron Slater, Facebook messaging to Peter Smith, 1 August 2011.

10. Cameron Slater, Facebook messaging to Aaron Bhatnagar, 2 August 2011.

11. Cameron Slater, Facebook messaging to Aaron Bhatnagar, 3 August 2011.

12. Cameron Slater, 'Questions for Phil Goff', Whale Oil blog post, 4 August 2011.

13. 'P.M. says someone is not telling the truth', Radio New Zealand Newswire, 5 August 2011.

14. Cameron Slater, Facebook messaging to Aaron Bhatnagar, 4 August 2011.

15. Matthew Hooton, quoted in Cameron Slater, 'Why Goff can't be believed', Whale Oil blog post, 4 August 2011.

16. Cameron Slater, Facebook messaging to Peter Smith, 4 August 2011.

17. Cameron Slater, 'Goff continues to lie', Whale Oil blog post, 9 August 2011.

18. Cameron Slater, 'I wrote an email', Whale Oil blog post, 6 August 2011.

19. Audrey Young, 'Goff airs suspicions about spy briefing', 6 August 2011.

20. 'Today in Politics', *Dominion Post*, 9 August 2011.

21. Jason Ede, political.animal101@gmail.com, 'Useful questions', e-mail to Cameron Slater, 18 October 2012.

22. Ibid.

23. Cameron Slater, e-mail to Paula Bennett, 18 October 2012.

24. Cameron Slater, 'Bennett's office in the clear', Whale Oil blog post, 8.30 a.m. 20 October 2012.

25. Ibid.

26. Ibid.

27. Private source.

28. Jason Ede, politicalanimal101@gmail.com, 'Mfat', e-mail to Cameron Slater, 6 March 2012.

29. Cameron Slater, 'There is someone paid more than wharfies for doing less', Whale Oil blog post, 27 March 2012. This post was based on a leak to journalists and it was not clear if it was related to a Slater information request.

30. Cameron Slater, Facebook messaging to Jordan Williams, 7 May 2013; Cameron Slater, Facebook messaging to Aaron Bhatnagar, 24 November 2011; Cameron Slater, Facebook messaging to Jordan Williams, 26 August 2013; Cameron Slater, Facebook messaging to Simon Lusk, 20 February 2011; Cameron Slater, Facebook messaging to Aaron Bhatnagar, 30 September 2011; and Cameron Slater, Facebook messaging to Simon Lusk, 4 March 2011.

31. Cameron Slater, 'Whale Oil tips submission', e-mail to Jason Ede, 14 November 2011.

32. Cameron Slater, Facebook messaging to Aaron Bhatnagar, 24 November 2011.

33. Cameron Slater, Facebook messaging to and from Simon Lusk, 21 February 2011.

34. John Dean, 'Dealing with our Political Enemies', White House Counsel's Office, 16 August 1971.

35. Cathy Odgers, quoted in Peter Aranyi, 'In one swift blow, Kate knocked the wind out of the duplicitous toady', The Paepae blog, 18 May 2011.

36. Jane Clifton, keynote speech at Kiwiblog 10th birthday event, 26 August 2013.

CHAPTER THIRTY-ONE

A perfect storm of child neglect

2015, *The New Zealand Herald*: Jared Savage investigates how government welfare agencies let down a boy who murdered a shopkeeper.

The suburb of Henderson, in West Auckland, is mostly working-class, with schools that education bureaucrats would call decile one — the lowest socioeconomic category. It has more than its share, probably, of petty crime. But it's not the roughest in Auckland. So when local dairy owner Arun Kumar was stabbed to death in a bungled hold-up, it made the news. Not just because that sort of thing wasn't supposed to happen in West Auckland, but because the killer was a 13-year-old boy, and because he was convicted of manslaughter for what seemed a cold-blooded killing. (The boy cannot be named, as New Zealand law prohibits naming youth offenders in most circumstances.)

One of those reading the stories from the court hearings, with a slightly jaundiced eye, was *New Zealand Herald* assistant editor Jared Savage. As someone with plenty of experience with the court system, he is used to the way in which the public can get a distorted idea of a crime from newspaper reports, which tend to be dominated by prosecution evidence.

So when, in an editorial meeting in which the *Herald* team had been discussing the public reaction to the apparently lenient conviction of Kumar's killer, it was suggested that the story was worth telling in more detail, Savage says he was sceptical. 'I thought this is obviously just another sob story, without merit. A clever defence lawyer has painted a picture and confused the jury' (Savage, 2016).

But at the *Herald,* even the top reporters get to do 'on-diary' stories — stories they are assigned because someone has to do them. He guessed it wouldn't be a particularly difficult story — he just had to go through the routines of getting the court records and interviewing the various people involved. As he got into the story, however, he realised he'd been wrong. 'It was a lot different to what I initially thought . . . The reality is [that boy] never did have a chance. He was let down first by his family, then by the state, in a whole raft of ways that are quite horrific to think about' (Savage, 2016).

As this story makes painfully apparent, the boy was a victim not only of his family but also of state carers that failed to protect him. It is a compelling and powerful narrative of a kind of perfect storm of child neglect, and the result. What drew me to it was not only the quality of the reporting and the importance of the issues it raises, but also the essential compassion that Savage brings to the story. It is not sentimental, or sanctimonious. He shows, through the efforts he went to to find out what really happened to this boy, that he cared enough to tell the story of a boy who has had no one to tell it for him.

Savage grew up in Tauranga, and hadn't planned to be a journalist. It was only when he had to take a journalism subject, with a teacher who was reviving the school newspaper, that he realised he enjoyed meeting people and writing about them. From there, he's been on a fast track: graduating from Auckland University of Technology's journalism programme in 2004, within 12 years he was assistant editor at *The New Zealand Herald*, leading what is currently probably the country's best investigative team. He credits an apprenticeship at the *Herald on Sunday*, competing against top reporters from other papers, with honing his interest in off-diary, more complex stories. Combine that with a knack for cultivating contacts in the prickly crime and justice beat, and he's been able to crack a series of award-winning stories.

Savage has led reporting on the sleaze and corruption that has come with the New Zealand government's courting of wealthy immigrants. A series on the dealings of the Minister of Building and Construction, Maurice Williamson, with a Chinese businessman, Donghua Liu, forced Williamson to resign after Savage showed that he had lobbied to get Liu New Zealand citizenship, conferred the citizenship on Liu at a private ceremony at his electorate office, used his house and did work on it, and even phoned a senior police officer about criminal charges Liu was facing. That story was dug out by assiduous use of the Official Information Act.

A similar story was the inquiry into the dealings of alleged money-launderer William Yan, who also courted members of parliament. Another high-profile business story was his investigation into Mike Vukcevic, the chief executive of Auckland law firm Baldwins. Vukcevic stepped down after it was revealed that he did not have the law degree he claimed to have.

'I'm fascinated by cops and criminals and the legal system. Organised crime is quite fascinating in New Zealand. We do have an underbelly there,' he says (Savage, 2016). But it's a hallmark of a good reporter that they can turn their investigative skills to more than just one kind of issue. It shows that the journalist is not just reliant on one good set of contacts in the police, or the legal profession. It is also a test of their professionalism, of whether they can turn over the rocks on unfamiliar ground.

'It was a good reminder to not have a predetermined outcome. When you start looking at something it's a reminder that as a journalist you are not here to build a case. We are here to tell a story' (Savage, 2016).

And that Savage tells the story well can be shown, down to the last second. The story had an average read-time online of four minutes. That's unusually long, and shows that people are getting right to the end of a long, complex story (Savage, 2016).

Why? It's not a story that has had an obvious outcome, such as a law change or a resignation. It's not about a business high-flier, or a politician. It's about people at the other end of the economic ladder. But it undoubtedly has had an impact on the public consciousness. Along with the *Faces of Innocents* series by rival Fairfax journalists it has helped build momentum for a new way of helping vulnerable children. Ultimately, it's hit home because it's about something we all care about.

Savage, J. (2016, September). Interview with author, J. Hollings.

How we raised a killer
Weekend Herald, 29 August 2015

One piece of evidence seems to sum up the disturbing childhood of the boy who killed Arun Kumar.

The 13-year-old stabbed the West Auckland dairy owner with a knife — once, twice, the third time fatally in the neck — during a robbery attempt with his 12-year-old friend that went badly wrong.

Charged with murder and manslaughter respectively, the pair sat quietly and coloured in pictures as their trial in the High Court at Auckland started.

Representing the slightly older boy, defence lawyer Maria Pecotic called his brother as a witness to give the jury an insight into their lives growing up. Their mother was selling synthetic cannabis from her home on Great North Rd, where her son lived and his friends often stayed the night to get stoned. Addicted to synthetic cannabis, the boy was often a "zombie" according to his brother.

Pecotic: Did anybody do anything to help [him] with his addiction?

Brother: My mum done something to help him with his addiction.

Pecotic: What was that?

Brother: She was giving him marijuana.

The point was not lost on the trial judge, Justice Graham Lang, who specifically referred to the exchange in sentencing the boy on his manslaughter conviction.

The judge said his early childhood was "turbulent in the extreme" and helped explain why he was acquitted of murder, but found guilty of the lesser charge.

The jury were not convinced beyond reasonable doubt that the teenager intended to cause "really serious bodily harm" to Mr Kumar. "I am satisfied that you reacted in an impulsive and instinctive way with little or no thought for the consequences of what you were about to do," Justice Lang said.

The verdict and sentence of six years in prison outraged the victim's family. They believe the justice system failed Mr Kumar, left to die on the floor of his own shop.

But there are others who believe the boy was failed by his family and the system, even before he was born in January 2001. His mother drank alcohol and consumed drugs heavily during her pregnancy with him, her sixth child. He was raised in a home of fear, with 10 notifications to CYF of violence between his parents between 1999 and 2004.

That's if his parents were home. A neighbour alerted CYF that the boy, just 3, and a younger sibling were left in the care of their sisters, aged 12 and 13. The older children, who were not enrolled in school, then left the pre-schoolers home alone. "Parents rarely seen," according to the CYF file, and the situation for the children was "dangerous".

In 2005, the mother left all the children with a relative and disappeared, failing to return within three weeks. CYF were told she was using P and heroin daily, "shooting up" in front of the children, and that gang members raided the family home.

At a meeting, CYF established that the boy and his siblings needed care and protection, but the children were returned to their mother because she promised to engage with community groups.

The older brother told the jury he could remember living in 10 different houses. He said the children were not allowed to go to the doctor unless "we were dying" and their sister — who was just a few years older — took care of them because their parents were always "doing drugs and stuff".

"Drugs was there when we woke up, it was there when we were having breakfast, it was there, like before lunch, during lunch, after lunch and dinner."

By the count of Dr Valerie McGinn, a neuropsychologist who works with young people with learning and behaviour problems at Auckland City Hospital, there were about 20 notifications to CYF. "They painted a picture of a life of neglect and a lot of disruptions," she told the jury during the murder trial.

A Family Group Conference in May identified the teen as an "at-risk" child who should be removed from the home. But his social worker was unable to find him and his file was shifted between CYF branches. A month later, Mr Kumar was dead.

A spokeswoman for CYF declined to answer questions but confirmed the Office of the Chief Social Worker was conducting a review expected to take several months. "While neither of the boys [standing trial] was ever in Child, Youth and Family care we need to understand if there was more that we and other agencies could have done."

Considered an expert in her field, Dr McGinn previously gave evidence at the Privy Council in London about how Teina Pora's mental development was impaired by Foetal Alcohol Spectrum Disorder.

She spent time with the boy and interviewed his mother, conducted tests, and reviewed his "quite extensive" history with CYF, as well as education and medical records.

One piece of information, recorded on April 12, 2009, immediately caught her attention. The 8-year-old boy was struck by a car on a pedestrian crossing and flung 4m in the air. He was knocked out, suffered a seizure, fractured skull and a brain-bleed. Four days later, the youngster was discharged from Starship Hospital. An occupational therapist established he suffered a "traumatic" brain injury and wrote a referral letter to ACC for rehabilitation.

Despite this, the boy never received treatment.

"There were no further records, which either means rehabilitation wasn't offered — which I find hard to believe — or else for some reason, he was not provided with medical follow-up because perhaps the family didn't attend the appointments," Dr McGinn said.

An ACC spokeswoman said if there were insufficient telephone contact details on the referral, ACC would write a letter to ask the patient's family to contact ACC directly to arrange necessary treatment and support.

"If we never heard from them or any other treating provider, such as an occupational therapist, GP, or physio, we'd likely assume nothing was needed."

Because the accident happened during the Easter holiday break, the boy did not return to school for two weeks. Dr McGinn said an adult who suffered the same injuries would not return to work for two years and then only on a part-time basis.

Children who suffer traumatic brain injury symptoms feel "dreadful", suffer blinding headaches and cannot handle any stimulation or noise. "They need a really quiet peaceful time and if they don't get that, what happens is the brain becomes overloaded and basically shuts itself down and this is seen and experienced as what we call cognitive fatigue . . . glassy-eyed and sleepy," Dr McGinn told the jury.

"From my experience, they become extremely irritable . . . if you didn't know they had brain damage, you'd think they were being very naughty but they're not being naughty, they're just — their brain can't regulate and it really needs a rest."

Before being hit by the car, he had no learning or behaviour problems recorded on his file. Six months later, his school principal referred him to the youth mental health clinic, the Kari Centre, with "serious concerns".

"[He] teases others. If he feels he has been slighted in any way he will attack them without remorse. Recently he has been demonstrating self-harm behaviour," the principal wrote. "Last week he locked himself in the toilet, smashed the toilet seat and then began to bang his head on the toilet cubicle wall. He often gives up on his school work or says he can't do it."

The boy was recorded as banging his head against the classroom wall and his teacher asked him why. The boy replied: "Because I just don't want to feel any more." On another occasion, he told a teacher he wanted to kill himself. He was reported to become easily frustrated and then verbally intimidating and physically aggressive towards other children.

"So this was about six months after his traumatic brain injury," said Dr McGinn. "This is what happens if a child has a traumatic brain injury and they get put back into an environment . . . nobody could cope with."

Despite this, the Kari Centre declined the referral and did not pick up on the fact he had suffered a head injury. "That was despite the fact they would have access to all his medical records where it's clearly documented that he had a severe traumatic brain injury, so I don't know what went wrong there."

The Kari Centre noted they were also unable to find his social worker at CYF, or her supervisor. A spokesman for the Auckland DHB declined to comment because of an "ethical and legal duty" to protect his privacy.

By the time the boy started high school in West Auckland last year, he had been enrolled in eight schools in as many years. Dr McGinn said each school might not have been aware of his brain injury. "It may have been that by the time they realised, he was on to the next school."

He was truanting regularly in his first year of college. By June 2014, the month he killed Mr Kumar, he had attended just 52 half days out of 148 and the school social worker referred him to the truancy arm of the Waipareira Trust.

Chief executive John Tamihere said Waipareira had 10 weeks with the teen until he was stood down by the school on May 28, for "unsafe behaviour", so they could no longer be involved. Of the 40 days he was supposed to be at Waipareira, he missed 16. Mr Tamihere said the help the 13-year-old needed was beyond what Waipareira could provide.

"Some interventions are quite easy, some interventions — like this kid — are very difficult. A normal person looking at this would scratch their head and say 'Jesus, there's no hope for this kid'. A kid like this needed resources we didn't have."

Before the suspension from school ended the boy's contact with Waipareira, a referral was made to RockOn — Reduce Our Community Kids Offending Now — an inter-agency group with representatives from local schools, police, the Ministry of Education and CYF, among others.

It's not known what the outcome was. The last note on Waipareira's file shows the boy was referred to a counsellor for anger issues after being suspended from school in May.

Around the same time, CYF didn't remove him from his mother's care so he continued to live in squalor and addiction at her doss house on Great North Rd. The boy got stoned on synthetics with some other teenagers at the house, into the early hours of June 14, 2013, before he was woken by another boy who wanted to steal shoes from a store in Henderson. They were egged on by an older boy and left the house carrying a metal pole and a bag, with a knife inside.

The pair didn't break into West City Shoes but crossed the road to the Railside Dairy. The older boy went inside twice to "scope out the lie of the land", according to Justice Lang, then approached the shopkeeper, Arun Kumar. The other boy stood at the doorway holding the pole. One of the boys called out, "Give us the money," although the would-be killer did not present the knife or make overtly threatening gestures at first.

There was no suggestion that Mr Kumar thought he was under severe threat, said Justice Lang, and Mr Kumar did not use the panic button. Instead he adopted the ploy he and his wife had devised to deal with troublemakers, which was to bring out a phone to show them the police were about to be called.

By this stage, the teen was leaning against the counter and had yet to pull out the knife. Mrs Kumar then emerged from the back of the shop holding the phone.

"At that point, things changed dramatically," said Justice Lang. He brandished the knife at Mrs Kumar and knocked the phone out of her hands.

Mr Kumar began walking out from behind the counter, but the teen turned his attention to him and drove him back into a corner with the knife. The shopkeeper picked up a silver pole on the ground and raised it towards him, who responded with three blows of the knife. The third was fatal. The entire episode was caught on camera.

Justice Lang "emphatically" rejected any suggestion of self-defence, but the brain injury the boy suffered when he was 8 became a key part of his legal defence to the murder charge.

Dr McGinn described the lack of rehabilitation following the traumatic brain injury as "medical neglect". Combined with his dysfunctional home life, she said, his recovery was significantly disadvantaged.

"We know [he] . . . had exposure to drug culture, he began to use drugs himself from quite a young age . . . Sometimes young people who have a brain injury may start to use drugs partly because they're impulsive and they don't think through, but also because they don't feel that well and they kind of self medicate.

"He didn't get medical treatment and he did slip into addictions and he is predisposed to addictions because it runs in his family."

Despite this, he had been a "bright boy" with a normal IQ and slightly below average scores in reading, writing, spelling and mathematics. Specialist tests showed the brain injury meant he is now slow to process information, particularly in complex situations when "overloaded" with stimulation. This means he had a limited ability to make appropriate decisions and acted impulsively, said Dr McGinn — like lashing out with a knife at Mr Kumar when the robbery went wrong. It seems the jury agreed and the teenager was convicted of manslaughter, not murder.

Now 14, he walked out of court carrying a Harry Potter book after being sentenced to six years in prison. Having served some time in a youth justice facility awaiting trial, he is eligible for parole by the time he is 16 years and 9 months.

Speaking to media outside the High Court, his lawyer, Ms Pecotic, said her client's family "certainly did play a big part in where he is now".

"It's a family life that none of us would want a young person to live through. It's an absolute tragedy."

An experienced advocate in the Youth Court, Ms Pecotic told the *Weekend Herald* he was not a hardened criminal, that he lacked the "toughness" of many of her other clients.

She agreed with the principle of the CYF Act — to try to keep a family unit together as much as possible — but in this case believed he should have been taken from his mother's care. "These were children that CYF knew were at risk. They should have been removed."

Drugs and alcohol, violence, criminal influences, unemployment, little food and clothing in the house, no medical treatment, moving schools, moving houses, truancy — all the warning signs were there, said Ms Pecotic.

"There are a lot of things about him I find incredibly sad. He was only 9 and making suicidal comments. Most normal people would hear that and say: 'This is not how a 9-year-old behaves. What is going on in this child's life?' And look into it," said Ms Pecotic.

"This case is the epitome of neglect and the failure of the welfare state. And at what cost? Two lives."

And at the beginning of it all, Ms Pecotic said there was a "mother who's broken", born into the dysfunction of her own criminal parents and who fled the violence of her son's father when he was a toddler.

The *Weekend Herald* has obtained the mother's criminal history of 50 convictions dating back to 1991 — as well as nine aliases — including a five-month stint in prison when her son was 5.

Her rap sheet includes shoplifting, stealing cars, receiving stolen property, false cheques, burglary, common assault, wilful damage, possession of methamphetamine utensils, resisting police, cultivating cannabis, wilful trespass, drink driving, stealing bank cards, and breach of bail.

Shortly after her son was charged with the murder of Mr Kumar, the police again raided her home, which was known as a place to hang out and consume drugs. They found pipes, home-made and commercial, as well as bongs made from plastic bottles used to smoke cannabis, in nearly every room of the house.

Cellphone records revealed text messages in which she offered to supply methamphetamine to another person.

By way of explanation, the 42-year-old told police she let people smoke drugs at the address "as it keeps them off the street". She also denied offering or supplying drugs and, incredibly, blamed the 13-year-old as being responsible. At her son's trial at the High Court, she was supposed to give evidence about his life on his behalf. She never turned up.

She has since pleaded guilty to offering to supply a Class A drug and was sentenced to 300 hours' community work and intensive supervision when she appeared in the Auckland District Court this month.

According to Radio New Zealand, the mother wiped away tears as Judge Evangelos Thomas spoke of how her "appalling" background had flowed on to those in her care, including her son and those who suffered at his hands.

Drug addiction had fuelled her behaviour but Judge Thomas said the focus of sentencing was the methamphetamine charge — not any of her other mistakes.

"You will live with those for the rest of your days, as will plenty of others to their great sadness — and, to no doubt, yours."

Mr Tamihere said the wider family was well-known to social agencies in

West Auckland. "The problem with this kid is he's born into a family that is already a vortex. His grandparents were in gangs and marginally employed, at best. So [his] parents were born into dysfunction, which they'd say is normal," said Mr Tamihere.

"Piss and dope is on the table, everyone is going to have a good time, therefore it's a good thing. 'We're eating well today, we've done a burglary', therefore stealing other people's stuff is a good thing. When you're into the third generation of that, you're in a very tough spiral.

"Unless interventions have occurred earlier in life, when they first come to the attention of officialdom, those ingrained behaviours — even without a brain injury — are tough to break."

His solution? "There are 350 families in West Auckland that I'd ringfence. I'd take the kids out, pretty quickly, and micro-manage the so-called adults in the family," said Mr Tamihere.

And removing the child most at risk is not just for their benefit. "The likes of [him] in this world, they are kids that can disaffect and lead. They create knock-on impacts on siblings, cousins, nieces and nephews in the house, other kids at school . . . so there can be a high cost of fixing that one bad apple."

Information-sharing and data matching between government agencies was also crucial. "There's police intelligence, Winz data, Housing New Zealand data, CYF, schools, Waipareira in and out of their lives . . . but you know what? There's no one standing over everyone who says 'no no, you're not pulling your weight, you can do more'," said Mr Tamihere.

"Nothing's going to change because the systems that we've got won't talk and act together. There will be another case around the corner."

Dr Russell Wills, the Children's Commissioner, listened intently as the *Weekend Herald* recited the teen's childhood. "The first thing I would say, is the family have failed this child. And it's not at all surprising that a boy born and raised into a household with drugs and domestic violence would have this ending. It's tragic, but not at all surprising."

These are the families that "the system" has the worst success rate with, said Dr Wills. "There won't be any one culpable agency: everybody let this boy down. This is the repeated story in every death review I've ever seen dating back to James Whakaruru," he said, referring to the 4-year-old murdered by his mother's partner in 1999.

"All those reviews find the same thing. No one takes responsibility. Information is not shared. When families fail to engage, they aren't followed up. This is not surprising. In fact, it's heartbreakingly typical."

There was no silver bullet, as the repeated problem showed how difficult it was to change, but Dr Wills said sharing information about the child and their parents was at the heart of the solution. "The reviews find that everybody has a piece of the information but we don't sit down and share. No one puts the whole story together."

CHAPTER THIRTY-TWO

On the trail of tax avoiders

2016, *The New Zealand Herald*: Matt Nippert names the global companies that pay little tax in New Zealand.

Late in 2016, New Zealand Prime Minister John Key was in Peru for a summit of world leaders. At the meeting, he spotted Mark Zuckerberg, the founder and owner of Facebook — probably the world's most powerful media company. Instead of the usual banalities and mutual backscratching, Key did something unusual — he took Zuckerberg to task. The issue? Tax. Or rather, the lack of it. Facebook, despite global revenues of around $US18 billion a year, pays, in many countries, little or no tax. While this might look clever to the corporate accountants, Key told Zuckerberg it was hurting the company, and he needed to fix it.

'I was reasonably blunt. I said I thought Facebook did have an issue in terms of global tax, with the perception of its tax policy, and I thought he needed to change that,' Key said. 'You've now got the OECD asking all these countries to hold hands together at major tax reforms when it comes to global multinationals, and at the forefront of that, one of those . . . is Facebook.' One day the users would wake up and ask 'why they had to pay tax if this company is not going to,' Key said.

Key admitted that Zuckerberg 'was a bit surprised' by the conversation (Small, 2016).

While many New Zealand Facebook users would probably have applauded Key for taking Zuckerberg on, few would have known that he probably would not have done so without the help of a New Zealand journalist.

At the beginning of 2016, Matt Nippert, of *The New Zealand Herald*, began an inquiry into how much tax is paid by global companies in New Zealand. The results were startling. Nippert found that 20 global companies that reported revenues in New Zealand of $NZ10 billion paid only $NZ1.8 million in tax. Facebook, with more than $NZ100 million in New Zealand revenue, paid tax of only $NZ43,261 — less than many individual salary earners (Nippert, 2016a).

Not all investigative journalism has a big public impact. But sometimes it has a significant impact on government, when it highlights a problem that needs to be fixed and helps to mobilise support within bureaucratic and political circles. That is why investigative journalism has been called the 'first draft of legislation'. Nippert's tax investigation is a good example. It did not prompt an immediate response, but change did come. The first sign that the story had been noticed came when it won Nippert the EY Business Journalism Award in June 2016. Later, a *Herald* 'Mood of the Boardroom' survey found that two-thirds of business leaders thought the issue was a problem for New Zealand, while less than a fifth (16 per cent) thought the government was doing enough about it (Nippert, 2016b).

In November, the head of the Inland Revenue Department, Naomi Ferguson, took corporates to task, urging them to 'rebuild the trust of the New Zealand public' about tax (Nippert, 2016c). Finally, in December, the government acted, with Revenue Minister Michael Woodhouse announcing new powers for the Inland Revenue Department to crack down on global tax avoiders. These included granting broader information-gathering powers to Inland Revenue investigators, shifting the burden of proof to multinational companies in disputes over transfer pricing, and tightening loopholes that allowed companies to claim that they had no taxable presence in New Zealand. As Nippert pointed out in a later story, the initiatives are less than those taken by Australia, and the United Kingdom's diverted profits tax, but they are a start (Nippert, 2016d).

Like Brian Rudman, Nippert tends to let himself be drawn into an issue that is of interest rather than setting out to 'do an investigation'. Something of a lone wolf, he is motivated by 'discovering new things, and finding out the way the world works'. He likes defining his own issues, and exploring them, rather than hanging around with a pack of other journalists. 'It's more asking questions independently. It doesn't have to take a lot of time. You can run up a big story or you can, over the course of a year, slog away at something. It's more a state of mind' (Nippert, 2016e).

The tax story is a product of that way of thinking. Nippert had been thinking about the tax issue for about a year, after noticing that it was gaining traction offshore. However, he wasn't sure how to attack it, as much of the information he thought he'd need appeared to be hidden behind commercial walls. After talking to New Zealand's 'Mr Accounting', Victoria University's Emeritus Professor of Accountancy and Law, Don Trow, he found a way.

Trow suggested that he attack the story by comparing profits declared locally and internationally. After pitching it, Nippert had to convince news executives that there was a story there; and after doing the initial run of a couple of companies, he realised that Trow's idea would work. But there was still a lot of work to do — weeks of going through company statements, and slowly building up data sheets that enabled robust comparisons that couldn't be picked apart. The story is a credit not only to his ability to stand back and ask the right questions, but also to his appetite for serious-minded journalism about policy.

While many New Zealand journalists would hate to be described as policy nerds, Nippert embraces the term. After growing up in the Hutt Valley he took an Honours in Public Policy at Victoria University, and got a taste for journalism on the student magazine, *Salient*. He only got into journalism because his application to become a diplomat was rejected. 'So I have a reasonable idea of what it takes to get these things through. Public policy needs motivation to move it through. If you stick on issues long enough, the government needs to be seen to be doing something. I view the stuff I'm doing as oil to grease the public policy machinery' (Nippert, 2016e).

Nippert has never been afraid to set his own course: he abandoned a journalism course at AUT, opting instead to study for a Master's degree in New York's prestigious Columbia Journalism Programme. Coming back to New Zealand, he's steadily worked his way up, to become Business Investigations Reporter at *The New Zealand Herald*. After years grafting at smaller publications, he's enjoying the kind of traction that the front page of the *Herald* can give to the issues he's interested in. 'It's as good as it gets. If you view your role as helping to diagnose problems in society and the economy, and the steps [needed] to remedy those, it's extremely satisfying' (Nippert, 2016e).

With the confidence to set his own agenda, the intellectual capacity to engage with complex policy issues and the skill to be able to set them before the public in simple, accessible form, Nippert is helping cement the role of investigative journalism as a core part of New Zealand public life.

Nippert, M. (2016a, March 18). The tax gap — where do their profits go? How Apple, Facebook and Google move their earnings overseas. *New Zealand Herald*. Retrieved from http://www.nzherald.co.nz/business/news/article.cfm?c_id=3&objectid=11607279

Nippert, M. (2016b, September 27). Mood of the boardroom: Foreign firms not paying fair share. *New Zealand Herald*. Retrieved from http://www.nzherald.co.nz/business/news/article.cfm?c_id=3&objectid=11716162

Nippert, M. (2016c, November 18). Inland Revenue throws down gauntlet. *New Zealand Herald*. Retrieved from http://www.nzherald.co.nz/business/news/article.cfm?c_id=3&objectid=11750677

Nippert, M. (2016d, December 14). Government planning action to target multinationals over tax. *New Zealand Herald*. Retrieved from http://www.nzherald.co.nz/business/news/article.cfm?c_id=3&objectid=11766215

Nippert, M. (2016e, December 14). Interview with author, J. Hollings.

Small, V. (2016, November 20). John Key to Mark Zuckerberg: Facebook's tax not a good look. *Stuff*. Retrieved from http://www.stuff.co.nz/business/86659350/John-Key-to-Mark-Zuckerberg-Facebooks-tax-not-a-good-look

The Tax Gap – Where do their profits go? How Apple, Facebook and Google move their earnings overseas

New Zealand Herald, 18 March 2016

In high-rise offices around the world, small armies of tax accountants and lawyers are playing their own, insanely high-stakes version of *The Biggest Loser*. As business has become detached from bricks and mortar and national ties, companies are now free to shed profits in one country and send them to another — out of New Zealand, to low-tax territories or no-tax havens.

This reality production occasionally descends into comedy, when participants argue self-interest plays no role in their shifting of profits.

Last year, oil giant Chevron was hauled before an Australian Senate inquiry and questioned about 200 companies it had registered in Bermuda, insisting this location was chosen entirely because of its superlative record in "maritime safety", and had nothing to do with the haven's zero per cent corporate tax rate.

New Zealand is not just a spectator to all this profit-shuffling. A *Herald* analysis of financial data from more than 100 multinational companies with operations in this country reveals how the game is played: most report much lower levels of profit in this country than their parent companies do in other, lower-tax jurisdictions.

For example, the 20 companies listed [at the end of this article] made an average profit of only 1.3 per cent on their reported NZ revenue. Their parent companies, however, reported an average profit margin of more than 20 per cent on their revenue.

Victoria University Emeritus Professor of accounting Don Trow, who suggested comparing the profit margins on pre-tax income as a simple measure of profit-shifting, says the big difference between subsidiaries and their parents raises worthwhile questions.

"It's reasonable speculation that they're shoving costs to those countries where there's more tax to be paid and transferring revenue to those areas where the tax is lower," he says.

The motivation to save money shouldn't surprise anyone, says Trow, even though New Zealand's 28 per cent corporate tax rate is hardly punitive and sits in the middle of the OECD pack. "It's just human nature, isn't it?" he says.

Out of the sea of numbers thrown up by the analysis, some striking trends and observations emerge.

For example, it's not a stretch to say New Zealand's oft-maligned banking sector more than pulls its weight in contributions to Inland Revenue. The sector has revenue of $19 billion, which accounts for less than 30 per cent of the data set, but its income tax contribution of $1.8 billion makes up 80 per cent of all taxes paid by the companies analysed.

(Calls to the Bankers Association to congratulate the sector on its sterling contribution to government coffers were not returned. Taxation may still be a tender subject: in 2009, a settlement with Inland Revenue saw the four

Australian-owned banks pay $2.2 billion in taxes after allegations they had been using structured finance arrangements to artificially suppress taxable profits.)

The 20 companies whose subsidiary profit margins varied most from those of their parents — a cluster of technology, energy and drug companies — collectively booked $10 billion in revenue in New Zealand, but only $133 million in profit and, after a range of deductions, paid only $1.8 million in income tax.

The 1.3 per cent average local profit margin reported by those 20 companies stood in stark contrast to the rude health of their parents, which profited at a rate of 20.6 per cent on their revenue.

Former senior Inland Revenue manager Adam Hunt says that while the *Herald*'s analysis is simple, it measures discrepancies that should interest authorities and at least spark a once-over.

"It's not rocket science," he says. "What we did was exactly what you've done: go through the database looking at profit and tax paid."

Hunt cautions against thinking there's any definitive way to count missed income taxes, but suggests ballpark estimates thrown up by the *Herald* analysis of $500 million annually — calculated by the overall gap between local and overseas profitability rates — are likely to be on the low side. "It's probably about half of what's at stake," he says, noting that, while it is a lot of money, it represents only 5 per cent of the corporate income tax take.

Speaking generally, Hunt says there are two main ways to play *The Biggest Loser* and massage profits downwards and back to a lower-tax jurisdiction. The first — what he characterises as "hardcore transfer pricing" — involves internal charges between different branches of a company, allowing money to be moved from one country to another.

The second approach is more involved, but relies on either loading a subsidiary in a higher-tax jurisdiction with debt — the interest payments count against profit — or charges for things such as royalties, licences, marketing or management.

Hunt says the principal question is "how do you capture a tax and where does it arise?" While consumer goods are generally counted at the point of consumption, he says the field is shrouded in mist when it comes to services and intellectual property, and it becomes less clear where these should be counted.

The problems with capturing income tax have become so tricky, Hunt argues, that the only way forward may be to rely more on indirect taxes like GST. "It's the only way you can really assure yourself you'll capture this stuff, because income floats around," he says.

It's worth noting here that this is not a story about criminality, and is instead about the messy world of accounting and tax law that is evolving and strewn with intangibles.

All companies approached by the *Herald* were keen to stress their compliance with local laws. ("It is always the priority for Roche to follow local laws and regulation," says drug company Roche, for example.) Many stressed they had arrangements with Inland Revenue on agreed levels of income, or noted substantive differences in the nature of their New Zealand business to explain the difference in margins.

Other companies, notably from the alcohol industry, stress that their total tax payments — including PAYE for local employees, GST and excise taxes on the sale of alcohol — are a better measure of their contribution to New Zealand than income taxes alone.

However, Labour Party finance spokesman Grant Robertson and Green Party co-leader James Shaw are both calling for Revenue Minister Michael Woodhouse to ensure everyone operating in the economy is paying their fair share.

Robertson wants Inland Revenue to get a shot in the arm to allow it to more closely scrutinise the torrent of money leaving the country. "We already know from IRD that every dollar we give them in enforcement we make back manifold," he says.

Shaw argues that without government action, the economy will tilt further out of balance. "This is a government problem, where we've created a legal scenario where large multinational companies don't have to pay tax in New Zealand, but New Zealand companies do," he says.

Woodhouse, despite repeated requests, declined to comment.

The issue exercises more than just Opposition MPs. Rumbles are also beginning to be heard at the highest levels of the New Zealand business community, as concerns mount about competitors capitalising on their tax advantage and the potential consequences of hollowed-out national economies.

Simon Moutter, chief executive of telecommunications giant Spark, says profit-shifting undercuts domestic businesses competing in the same industry and threatens the ability of governments to provide essential services.

"It is a material advantage to pay no tax in a country," he says.

"What we're seeing is the emergence, particularly with these digital businesses, which are very lightweight and don't have much economic footprint on the ground of New Zealand. They are profit-shifting and stripping a lot of value out of the country and not leaving much behind."

Moutter — like Robertson and Shaw — points to Australia as an example of how governments can respond. Last year the Australian Tax Office announced a crackdown on profit-shifting by the pharmaceutical and technology industries, helping secure A$1 billion in additional tax payments.

Moutter says such a dragnet would help share the tax load presently borne mostly by New Zealand individual taxpayers and companies. "A few hundred million dollars is a prize worth having: that would make a material difference in New Zealand today if we had that tax being paid in," he says.

International debate about the issue has been bubbling under the auspices of the OECD's Base Erosion and Profit-Shifting (BEPS) talks. There, officials have been locked in discussions since 2012, looking for ways to co-ordinate tax policy in order to present a wide-ranging response to the problem and minimise the risk of regulation pushing economic activity further offshore.

Moutter agrees with the thrust of a multilateral approach but argues that specific action could complement and reinforce moves taken internationally. "In the short term, let's put some interim measures in place which ensure that these large corporations who're paying no tax anyway, effectively, make a fair contribution to the countries from which they take that value," he says.

Inland Revenue's head of international audits, John Nash, calls the *Herald* from Paris, where, as it turns out, he's been sitting through more talks on [BEPS].

Nash says he is unsurprised by the numbers thrown up by the *Herald* analysis, but says the issue is more complex than a mere comparison of profitability ratios.

"Take the pharmaceuticals sector. It's amongst the most profitable corporate sectors in the world, absolutely no question about that," he says. But the local pharma industry is effectively just a distribution agent.

"In terms of the way we tax — you tax the value-add. I wish it wasn't like this. But you can only tax what gets added in New Zealand and we're right at the end of the value chain. Unfortunately, that's the state of the industry in New Zealand; it's not necessarily a reflection of profit-shifting," he says.

Nash, perhaps unsurprisingly for a public servant, isn't lobbying for a radical change in policy or a fresh crusade against specific industries as suggested by Opposition MPs. He says the struggle to define profits and keep them in New Zealand is a "continuous battle" — one that he is not willing to say we are winning.

"I'd never say winning; we're trying to hold our own. I don't think there's a country out there saying they're winning that battle. It is becoming progressively difficult to maintain levels of tax, there's no doubt about that. That's why we really have been so involved in the global debate."

And beyond the faceless boilerplate responses from the multinational corporations topping the Herald's list, there is also debate and opinions being expressed. One representative who spoke only on the condition that neither they nor their globe-spanning employer would be identified, says they sympathise with those crying foul but are concerned about the solutions being touted.

"We totally agree with the sentiment, but some people don't understand that it's complex when they say 'why can't corporations pay more tax?' It's not as simple as that," the corporate spokesperson says.

The prospect of new laws or regulations sprouting in countries where the issue of profit-shifting is a hot-button political issue is the worst-case outcome, the spokesperson says, and would crimp a country's export earnings. "It cuts both ways and you only end up with increased red tape. We don't think unilateral action makes the most sense."

That argument has attracted some sympathy from within Inland Revenue, with tax policy director Emma Grigg agreeing that authorities have to simultaneously play good cop and bad cop in a bid to achieve compliance, while also trying to attract new businesses. "We try to walk with that balance. A lot of the concern is that you end up with a huge amount of complex legislation that could put people off investing in New Zealand," she says. "But at the same time, you want people to pay their fair share of tax."

But it's this quest for fairness that drives Spark's Moutter, and others, to make the debate more public, in a bid for change sooner rather than later.

"It's complex, I get that, and the sort of the thrust of the logic here is that we need New Zealand to be one of the dozens of countries in some large consensus solution," he says. "That's probably the right answer in the long term, but that's my fear: it's the long term and we'll be waiting for too long for that to result in anything."

So far, he says, in New Zealand *The Biggest Loser* has been only of niche interest.

"Anything about tax," he says, laughing at his own intense interest in the subject, "is probably considered relatively uninteresting and complicated."

Getting to the numbers

The *Herald*'s analysis compared tax paid and profitability margins (the ratio of pre-tax profit to revenue) of multinational corporations with their New Zealand subsidiaries.

Using Deloitte's top-200 list of New Zealand's biggest firms as a starting point, then adding subsidiaries of the world's largest listed companies, and high-profile companies involved in overseas debates on the tax issue, the *Herald* identified 103 local companies whose performance could be directly compared with the audited accounts of their listed parent.

The process was laborious, involving collecting more than 500 annual and financial reports — many comprising hundreds of pages — with each having to be read in order to pluck out the required numbers from statements of consolidated income.

Companies were excluded if they reported particularly unusual results, typically from business sales or write-downs, and multinationals whose New Zealand operations were split across several subsidiaries [that] had their domestic results combined.

The data fails to capture income from New Zealand which is directly booked by offshore firms. For example, Facebook New Zealand's reported revenue of $1.2 million is clearly only a fraction of the sum Kiwi businesses spent advertising on the world's largest online platform.

The data also omits the New Zealand operations of firms which are owned offshore, but not by listed companies, as audited information about their profitability is not readily available. This means outfits such as salmon and forestry conglomerate Oregon Group, owned privately by Malaysia's billionaire Tiong family, escapes measure.

Despite these caveats, and the group being non-comprehensive, the *Herald* data nevertheless captures a surprisingly large chunk of the economy. The 103 companies recorded $67 billion in annual revenue, accounting for 30 per cent of New Zealand's gross domestic product, and the data set appears to be one of the most comprehensive of its kind.

Parliamentary written questions to Inland Revenue, asking whether authorities had an estimate of the scale of multinational companies in New Zealand, or the tax they paid, were answered by Revenue Minister Michael Woodhouse.

"I am advised that Inland Revenue does not hold information in a way that enables it to readily identify multinational companies. I am therefore unable to provide the figures requested."

The 20 companies that make overall $10 billion but pay no tax

Company	Annual NZ revenues	NZ income tax provision	Profit margin in NZ
Goldman Sachs	$23,390,000	$1,726,000	-4.9%
Facebook	$1,196,979	$43,261	1.0%
Merck, Sharp & Dohme	$46,923,000	$127,000	5.1%
Independent Liquor	$378,324,000	-$29,444,000	-21.7%
Apple	$732,011,253	$8,879,373	3.6%
Constellation	$214,232,000	$8,584,000	14.2%
Roche	$111,868,000	$1,314,000	1.8%
Pfizer	$91,273,000	$771,000	2.8%
Johnson & Johnson	$133,448,000	$2,188,000	6.3%
Novartis	$47,952,000	$632,000	4.8%
Google	$14,925,180	$361,542	3.5%
Holcim	$211,440,000	-$7,264,000	-5.7%
Pepsi	$128,072,000	-$60,000	-3.4%
Harvey Norman	$734,611,779	$6,803,777	3.5%
Exxonmobil	$2,783,901,000	-$14,364,000	-1.7%
Methanex	$1,501,246,000	$1,071,000	7.0%
Procter and Gamble	$86,092,290	$746,850	3.1%
Unilever	$262,121,000	$4,030,000	3.6%
Pernod Ricard	$227,590,000	-$2,056,000	0.7%
Chevron	$2,237,256,000	$17,763,000	2.7%
TOTAL	$9,966,427,481	$1,852,803	1.3%

Parent profit margin	Company response
35.8%	Did not reply.
39.4%	"Facebook complies with New Zealand tax law, as we do in all countries where we operate. We take tax obligations seriously and work closely with national tax authorities to comply with local law."
40.9%	Did not reply.
7.2%	Did not reply.
31.0%	Acknowledged receipt of questions, said "We are unlikely to comment."
40.7%	"We are strongly committed to complying with all applicable laws and regulations, including tax and accounting laws, in New Zealand and wherever we do business.
26.4%	"It is always the priority for Roche to follow local laws and regulation."
24.7%	"We are strongly committed to complying with all applicable laws and regulations, including tax and accounting laws, in New Zealand and wherever we do business."
27.7%	"The Johnson & Johnson Family of Companies in New Zealand complies with both the letter and the spirit of New Zealand tax law and pays its fair share of taxes."
23.5%	"Novartis Group is fully compliant with all New Zealand tax laws and pays tax on taxable income earned in New Zealand."
21.9%	"Google complies with the law in every country where we operate."
11.6%	"Holcim New Zealand today confirmed that it complies with all New Zealand tax laws and is committed to paying tax locally as it has done since beginning operations there in 1888."
13.1%	Did not reply.
19.9%	Said parent company did not operate as a retailer and just licensed brand to New Zealand stores.
13.1%	Acknowledged receipt of questions. Did not reply.
20.5%	"We can assure you that Methanex complies fully with all tax legislation and requirements in the countries it operates in, including New Zealand."
15.5%	"P&G pays all the taxes we owe, worldwide. All of our business activities are fully compliant with the law and longstanding international standards, including the OECD Guidelines."
15.8%	Did not reply.
12.9%	"The figures analysed are based on an incomparable combination of profit margins for two very different entities . . . Pernod Ricard Winemakers New Zealand fulfills its tax obligations."
14.7%	"Chevron NZ operations cannot be compared to its MNC Parent in the manner that you are currently undertaking . . . we meet all local tax obligations."
20.6%	Source: Most recent financial reports filed with Companies Office; audited Annual Reports published by parent companies for corresponding period; profit-margin calculated as pre-tax earnings to revenue; weighted mean for average margins; list represents top 20 from list of 103 major firms owned by public-listed foreign owners and ranked by difference between New Zealand and parent margins.

CHAPTER THIRTY-THREE

Victims of the child-killers

2016, *Stuff*: Blair Ensor tells the story of one boy's death at the hands of his stepfather.

Campaigns aren't unheard of in New Zealand's mainstream media, but they are rare, because of a generally conservative editorial culture that tends to see them as antipathetic to journalistic values such as balance and neutrality. Most 'campaigns' I have seen seem to be driven more by an attempt to woo middle-class readers than by any moral concern.

But in 2015, Fairfax Media began a campaign that seemed quite different. First, the *Faces of Innocents* series focused on a very difficult topic, with no clear villain. Second, it had little appeal to the pockets or daily lives of the majority of middle-class readers. Third, it generated stories that were very disturbing, and difficult to read. Fourth, it was time-consuming, with no clear end-point, and vastly more thorough and resource-intensive than almost anything seen before.

For all of these reasons, and more, *Stuff*'s campaign to record the names and stories of the victims of child-killers — which sprang from the same impulse Lesley Max felt to write about Delcelia Witika in 1992 — was unexpected. What's more remarkable is that it took so long for a news organisation to do it. If there's one social issue in New Zealand that is a national shame, that should have been the subject of scores of investigations, it is violence against children. In 2007 UNICEF found that New Zealand teens were more likely to die before they turned 19 than in any other developed country.

A significant part of the reason for that is the terrifying numbers of violent attacks on children. In 2015 alone, 15 children were killed. Several government inquiries had attempted to reduce this toll, yet each year it seemed to be getting worse. Astonishingly, until the *Stuff* team began their investigation, no one had actually counted how many children had died.

When the figures were added up, they were horrifying: since 1992, the year of Max's story, more than 200 children have been beaten, kicked, burned, strangled, stabbed, drowned or otherwise killed in New Zealand by adults who should have protected them.

The *Stuff* investigation began around 2013, when the idea of a database of child deaths was floated. Fairfax reporter Clio Francis did a lot of work on it, then when she left Fairfax she passed her work on to another Fairfax reporter, Katie Kenny. When Kenny and fellow Fairfax reporter Blair Ensor attended an Investigative Reporters and Editors conference in Philadelphia, they saw a project by the *Miami Herald*, called Innocents Lost. 'It was at that point we decided to get what Clio had been doing off the ground,' says Ensor (Ensor, 2016).

An experienced crime reporter, Ensor had seen his share of stories about child homicides, and felt strongly about the topic. Together with *Stuff's* projects editor, John Hartevelt, and political reporter Stacey Kirk, they started to gather the stories and data needed to give the project momentum.

At first, they weren't sure how the public would react. It wasn't seen as a sexy topic, or one that would necessarily concern *Stuff's* predominantly middle-class audience. Many of the victims and perpetrators were from lower socioeconomic groups. But, over time, the project has steadily built momentum, and has won plaudits for its moral courage and reporting excellence, including a 2016 Canon Media award for best investigation.

It is a series that has what scholars would call 'integrity of social judgement' or a 'central moral value'; something we can all agree is important. Thus it should, in hindsight, really have been no surprise that it has resonated deeply with the New Zealand public. As the great former *Sunday Times* editor Harold Evans pointed out, campaigns take time, and about the time journalists are getting bored is about the time the public is starting to take notice.

There are many stories in this series that could have been reprinted here, but this account of the life of Glen Bo Duggan was, for me, the most moving. Ensor came across it while reporting on Duggan's killer, Peter Ryder. He says he had a sense that there was more to Glen's story, but until the *Faces of Innocents* project was floated, he was unable to justify the kind of time needed to take it further. Because Glen had left little digital trace, Ensor knew that the story was not going to be easy (Ensor, 2016). 'I got someone to go through the microfiche and pull some articles,' says Ensor. 'There was just this mystery, about who was Glen? And how did he die?'

Luckily, a source helped him track down Glen's sister. She was looking for answers as well. Ensor says she was trying to get hold of Glen's official files, to try to understand how he had ended up back with his mother, and the man that eventually killed him. 'She didn't know how that final step had occurred. So that was something that I set out to do. To give her the answers.'

After a lot of digging, he eventually found all the people who had interacted with Glen over the years. Some fell into place, almost while he wasn't looking.

One crucial interview came while he was on holiday in Motueka; another, the discovery of the school memorial, came about when he was sitting at home on a day off and decided to wander down to Glen's old school.

Ensor grew up on a horticultural block in Marlborough, where his parents grew cherries. After studying journalism at the University of Canterbury, he initially planned to become a sports reporter. His first job was back in Marlborough, at the *Express*, as a rural reporter. But that didn't last long, as he found himself drawn to the police desk. 'The then police reporter got pretty sick of me wanting to dash out to every crash/fire. When she moved into another role I put my hand up for that round pretty quickly.'

At the *Express*, then *The Dominion Post*, and now *The Press*, he's built a reputation as one of the country's best crime reporters. Working on the *Faces of Innocents* series has helped him develop a long-standing interest in investigative work. But even for a seasoned veteran of the crime round, working on this series has taken a toll. 'I have done so many death knocks [interviewing relatives of victims], and managed to keep myself reasonably removed from the situation. But by the time you have read 200 coroner's reports [about child violence] you reach saturation point, and it's more difficult to stay detached' (Ensor, 2016).

Despite that, he has found it deeply satisfying to be able to go beyond the gruelling details documented in the court records, and tell a fuller story of who Glen was. Unlike much crime reporting, which inevitably often dehumanises crime victims by presenting only the most gruesome moments of their lives, this story rehumanises a boy who had touched many people. 'Rather than just gory court reporting, you can [honour] the memory of a troubled boy. That was kind of what we were trying to do. There's a great deal of satisfaction in being able to do that. People feel that it really captured who Glen was. They were quite intrigued by this kid and they didn't know the background. Lots of people had little interactions with Glen and none of them knew the full story.'

He says it's hard to quantify the impact the *Faces of Innocents* series may have had, but says it has at least started a conversation around child abuse in New Zealand. He takes some satisfaction from the fact that only two to three children died from domestic abuse in 2016, compared with 15 the previous year. 'I do wonder what Glen would have grown up to be like. Being able to tell a lad's life, all that hasn't been told before, is it an honour? You feel a great sense of ownership . . . being able to tell it. At the end [Glen's sister] was hugely grateful for what we had done. If the series saved one child, then it's done its job.'

Ensor, B. (2016, December 1). Interview with author, J. Hollings.

Faces of Innocents: Glen Bo Duggan was a neat kid with a troubled upbringing

Stuff, 25 July 2016

In a shaded corner between empty classrooms, where weeds grow next to an upturned desk, a tree stands in memory of a little boy.

Richmond School in Christchurch has largely been deserted since it was closed by the Ministry of Education in 2013. There used to be a small plaque under the tall silk tree telling visitors it was planted as a memorial to 10-year-old Glen Bo Duggan. That plaque is gone.

"It's like he's been forgotten," former student and friend Julian Phillips says.

Glen is among scores of New Zealand children who have been murdered in the past two decades. His case did not capture big headlines, despite the horrific abuse he endured at the hands of his mother's boyfriend, Peter Wayne Ryder.

The Faces of Innocents project, a *Stuff* investigation into child homicide, is telling the stories of victims so they are not forgotten.

Glen died on April 18, 1994 — four days after he was admitted to Christchurch Hospital with serious brain damage. A court would later hear Ryder kicked, punched and hit the child with a hearth brush during a two-day beating at an inner city home. The assault started after $5 went missing from his wallet.

Those who knew Glen say he was a neat kid with a troubled upbringing. There were no outward signs he was being abused before his death, they say. However, an aunt, Maureen Wixon, is haunted by a decision she made that allowed Glen to stay with his mother after he was removed from her care by social welfare several years earlier.

"I should not have sent him to his death," Wixon says. "I have never forgiven myself for that."

. . .

Glen was born in Nelson on September 14, 1983. His father, Terry, was a fisherman and a member of the now defunct Lost Breed motorcycle gang. His mother, Annette, was a housewife on the unemployment benefit. The pair were heavy drug users, often shooting up heroin or something similar.

"There was obviously a lot of chaos in our household — quite a lot of neglect, dangerous situations and pretty seedy individuals coming and going," Glen's older half-sister, who wants to remain anonymous, says.

"Often, we were left at home on our own. Quite often, I didn't go to school. Mum would just be out of it and we'd be left to our own devices."

Glen's sister recalls taking needles to a neighbour to keep them out of his way, and an incident where their mother fell asleep at night after taking drugs and her mattress caught fire, filling the house with smoke.

"I woke up and basically got Glen out . . . and then went and tried to rouse her. It took a long time, but eventually I managed to wake her up. If I hadn't been there, they could have died."

Glen's sister says her grandparents on her father's side were her saving grace. She spent most weekends with them and they successfully fought for custody. Glen wasn't so lucky.

"I was able to look out for him and once I'd gone from the home, there was obviously more concerns about him," Glen's sister says, adding that there was nobody to take him.

Social welfare eventually intervened and Glen, aged 4, was placed into foster care at the Riverside Community, 8 kilometres from Motueka.

. . .

Glen's foster mother, a 67-year-old woman who does not want to be identified, knew nothing about his background when she took him in. She remembers being drawn to his big brown eyes when they first met. He was a cute kid who would do anything to please, she says.

"He was lovely, a wee sweetie."

It didn't take long for her to realise Glen's upbringing was rough. His rotten teeth were a giveaway. Several of them had to be removed. He was also socially inept and sometimes quite inappropriate in public, she says, unable to elaborate other than that he had no idea of right and wrong. "There was bad language if he couldn't get his own way."

That was one of the reasons he continued at kindergarten rather than going to school when he turned five, she says.

Social welfare removed Glen from the woman's care and placed him with another family in Nelson after a year. She's not sure why. However, after about four months, they asked if she would have him back, because he wasn't fitting in with the family's other children. She welcomed him with open arms. "I wasn't keen on him going in the first place. I'd got quite attached."

While living in Nelson, Glen was enrolled at St Joseph's School. When he returned to Riverside he attended Lower Moutere School, which had a roll of about 100 and was walking distance from the community. It was there he learned to read and write.

"Things went well . . . for quite a while," she says. "He absolutely loved his mum and I'm absolutely sure she did the best she could, but she didn't always turn up for visits, which made him angry with me. It's easy to hurt the one nearest to you at the time."

Terry visited less often. According to a coroner's report, he died in a car outside his home on July 31, 1991. Causes of death included respiratory failure consistent with narcotic or sedative drug overdose.

Glen was fiercely loyal to both his parents. After Terry's death, Glen put him on a pedestal, his foster mother says. "He wanted to grow up to be his father. He was very, very angry that he had died."

Glen became more of a handful and began to withdraw co-operation, she says.

"He really, really wanted to be with his mother. That's all he wanted."

Glen attended counselling sessions with his foster mother, but the tension between the pair became unmanageable and she asked social welfare to intervene.

"I took him in because I wanted to make a difference to a child's life. When things fell apart . . . I felt like I hadn't achieved much of anything."

Members of Glen's extended family sought guardianship through the Family Court. A custody order was made in favour of his aunt and uncle, Maureen and Larry Wixon, and his mother was granted access. Glen's foster mother says she sent him presents for his birthday and Christmas after he left, but never heard from him again.

. . .

Maureen and Larry, a fisherman, lived on a 1.2 hectare property in Waimangaroa, a small rural town 16km north of Westport on the South Island's West Coast. The couple had two children together, Becky and Kodie, who were the same age as Glen, and it was thought he would "fit in perfectly", Maureen, 62, says. And he did.

Each morning, Glen, who by that stage had "beautiful bucked teeth" because he sucked his thumb, would catch the bus with Becky and Kodie to Waimangaroa School. He became involved in judo and Scouts, and narrated a play, Maureen says.

At night, the children played spotlight together at home, where there were plenty of places to hide. Glen's favourite food was mayonnaise mashed into potatoes. He would go to sleep with his favourite soft toy, Jaffa.

"He was absolutely gorgeous. I adored him," Maureen says. "He was a very happy boy. He could connect with young people as well as old people. I can't say enough about him."

Glen and the family lived together happily for many months. It was only really after his mother, Annette, and her boyfriend, Peter Ryder, visited and took him out for dinner that he began asking if he could go and stay with them.

"It sort of came out of nowhere," Maureen says. "It doesn't matter what a mother does they are still their mum and I couldn't take her place."

It is unclear when, but after several holidays, it was agreed Glen would move to Christchurch to live with Annette, who seemed to have straightened herself out. Maureen says she told Annette to call if she couldn't cope and arrangements would be made to pick him up. Social welfare was never alerted.

"He [Glen] was really excited about the situation. She'd made up the room [at her home] really nice for him," Maureen says.

It was the last time she would see him alive.

. . .

In Christchurch, Glen was enrolled at Richmond School where he was taught by Cleve Shearer in Room 7. Shearer says Glen was a "bright kid" who would read books including Tolkien's *Lord of the Rings*, a novel usually assigned to older students. He was well-liked by his classmates.

One of those children was Julian Phillips, now 32, who has fond memories of Glen. "He had a real gift for art . . . and he was really generous with that gift," Phillips says. "He'd always take requests to draw muscle men or monsters or motorcycles."

The pair would share lunch together, sitting on the concrete next to the playing field. "I could always tell that whoever prepared his lunch, and I'm assuming it was his mother, really loved him. The sandwiches were always nice and tidy and he always had variety."

It was Glen who introduced Julian to roasted peanuts, something he still eats every day. "I've never, ever forgotten."

. . .

Glen would walk out the gates at Richmond School for the last time on Wednesday, April 13, 1994.

He was taken unconscious to Christchurch Hospital by Ryder about 1pm the next day, and underwent emergency surgery for a severe brain injury. Glen died four days later when life support was removed.

An autopsy revealed more than 50 bruises, mostly on his torso and limbs. A head injury was blamed for his death. Ryder initially told hospital staff he was teaching Glen kickboxing when the child fell and hit his head. Some of Glen's extended family were told he'd fallen out of a tree.

At trial, Crown prosecutor Jane Farish, today a district court judge, said Ryder was caring for Glen while his mother attended a week-long drug rehabilitation programme at Sunnyside Hospital.

During the afternoon of April 13, Ryder questioned Glen over $5 that was taken from his wallet and then beat him over five hours — punching, kicking and hitting the child with a hearth brush. The assault continued the next morning, apparently because Glen wouldn't give a straight answer about what he had done with the money.

Later, when Ryder went to a pharmacy to get his methadone, he asked for some smelling salts to bring around a person he had knocked unconscious. Ryder then tried to contact Annette at Sunnyside to tell her Glen was in a bad way. He was told by a nurse to take him to hospital, which he did.

In a statement to police, Ryder said he did not believe the blows to Glen were serious and that he did not remember hitting the back of his head. He believed Glen's head hit a wall when he fell.

The Crown successfully argued the fatal head injury could not have resulted from an accidental blow, which forced Glen's head onto a hard surface. Stomping on the child's head while he lay on the ground was the most likely cause.

Ryder was found guilty of murder and received the mandatory sentence of life in jail. He has been released on parole twice, but recalled to prison on both occasions, most recently in 2013, after he attacked an ex-partner and threatened to kill her.

. . .

Glen's death devastated the Richmond School community.

"His classmates were traumatised for the rest of the year," Cheryl Doig, the school's principal from 1993 to 2000, says.

His funeral service was held in the chapel at Shone & Shirley Funeral Directors in Nelson on April 23. Hundreds attended a memorial service at the Richmond School hall several days later.

Phillips says at the time he struggled to comprehend what had happened to his friend. "After [a while] it hit me. I started picturing him getting beaten. I couldn't picture a circumstance that would have required that sort of discipline."

As he grew older, Phillips says he realised Ryder's actions could never be justified and he was a "scum bag".

Glen's death scarred Shearer's career in the education sector, where he worked as a teacher and principal for 42 years until his retirement last year. "When I spoke at my farewell last December, I touched on it briefly. It's not something you forget, that's for sure."

Shearer says the school had no idea about Glen's background, including the fact he'd previously been removed from his mother. "We didn't realise he was that at-risk," Shearer says, adding that sort of information should be made available. "It would have informed how we interpreted things that we came across."

. . .

Maureen Wixon often kisses a photo of Glen, her nephew, which sits at her home in Nelson. "He's not forgotten. He's in my heart every day."

She sometimes wonders what might have become of her nephew and blames herself for what happened.

"Glen was an innocent wee boy that shouldn't have been sent down to them by me. It's something I live with every day of my life — a young boy like that, wanting to stay with his mum. I shouldn't have allowed the child to make that decision — I was the adult. I should have questioned him more. "I just wish she [Annette] had rung me and said, 'Hi Maureen, we're not handling this, could you please come and pick him up?'. That's why I'm angry with her."

Glen's mother declined to be interviewed.

"It's something that she's never really gotten over," her daughter says. "She just has huge regrets about leaving him there [with Ryder]."

Maureen Wixon's niece Kellie Warren says: "I know my aunty blames herself for what happened to Glen Bo. As a family we do not in any way think she should feel this way. His death remains the sole responsibility of Peter Ryder."

. . .

There are concerns about what will happen to the memorial for Glen Bo Duggan when landscaping begins at Richmond School in August. The Ministry of Education had earmarked two trees as protected on the proposed plans for the site, but not the silk tree planted in his memory. *Stuff* identified the discrepancy and raised it with the ministry.

"We are grateful to have been alerted and have now marked that tree on the plans too and made it clear to our on-site contractors that this tree should be protected," the ministry's head of sector enablement and support, Katrina Casey, says.

As for the plaque that's disappeared? Casey says that was removed for protection and will be placed at another site.

Editor's note

The following piece describes the long and dismal history of government attempts to quell attacks on children. It was written by Stacey Kirk and Katie Kenny, who are part of the *Faces of Innocents* team. Since the publication of this series, the government has announced yet another reorganisation of child protection services. CYFS has been replaced by a new ministry dedicated to child welfare, the Ministry for Vulnerable Children Oranga Tamariki.

A trail of broken promises: 1992–2015

Stuff, 24 November 2015

Every time a child is killed it generates countless reports, reviews and reforms from those with the power to make change. High-profile deaths are often followed by a guilt phase, and successive Governments have tried and failed to make any decent inroads into the number of children being killed. While the state cannot be in every home, there must be an expectation services will fulfil their roles as well as they can.

Stuff's database begins at 1992, the year District Court Judge Ken Mason released a report saying the Children and Young Persons Service (CYPS) was "dizzied and demoralised".

It found widespread incompetence with staff lacking adequate training. CYPS general manager Robin Wilson said Mason "got it badly wrong", but no one from the department contacted Mason to discuss the report's contents.

In 1993, Children's Commissioner Dr Ian Hassall's review of 11-year-old Craig Manukau's death found the boy's death the previous year was "foreseeable and preventable". In 1994, police were informed Auckland's Wayne Marshall Kairau-Sandhu, 11, was missing. He had been beaten to death by his stepfather the previous year. A review into that case in 1995 found CYPS should have acted sooner and "more authoritatively" to try to help the boy.

In March 1999, four-year-old James Whakaruru from Hawke's Bay was beaten to death by his stepfather. Coroner Peter John Dennehy found there were "innumerable instances of abuse of the body of James". James had been abused for years, but no one helped him. A damning report by Children's Commissioner Roger McClay, published in 2000, said lack of communication between health and welfare agencies contributed to the death, and he called for sharing of health information.

In response to the death of Hinewaioriki Karaitiana-Matiaha (Lillybing) that year, Prime Minister Helen Clark said New Zealand's horrific level of child abuse was unacceptable and the Government could consider a review of the effectiveness of community health services. The Carterton toddler was beaten, shaken and scalded at the hands of her aunts then left to to die from internal bleeding.

The Government never formally called for such a review.

However, there was action elsewhere. ACC launched a scheme to notify the organisation now-known as CYFS if a child was recorded as having more than 10 accidents before their fifth birthday. McClay also asked for a free 24-hour emergency phone line to combat child abuse. The result was the 0508 FAMILY direct line.

Principal Youth Court Judge Mick Brown's report found CYFS was under "extreme pressure" and change was urgently needed. Things would be different, Social Welfare Minister Steve Maharey promised in December 2000.

In 2001, CYFS launched New Directions, a strategy to implement most of Brown's 57 recommendations. Maharey estimated it would take two years to complete them all. Three years later, in March 2004, documents showed just 34 had been completed, 19 partially completed, and four considered no longer relevant.

In response to the deaths of Masterton sisters Saliel Aplin and Olympia Jetson in 2001, who were murdered after years of violence, CYFS in 2002 set up a strategy for abused Maori children.

Wairarapa school girl Coral Ellen Burrows, 6, was murdered by her stepfather in September 2003. Just months before she died, her father contacted CYFS with concerns about her wellbeing. The call was not recorded, and there was no investigation.

As a result, Children's Commissioner Cindy Kiro suggested all CYFS phone calls should be taped and the policy was changed.

The 2003 First Principles Baseline Review of CYFS — by the Treasury, the Ministry for Social Development, and CYFS — found "deep and systemic problems" which were "about much more than just levels of resourcing". Chief Executive Jackie Pivac resigned as a result.

In 2004, the Families Commission was launched, advocating for the interests of families in general. The Government established the Taskforce for Action on Violence within Families in 2005. The Taskforce for Action was to advise the Family Violence Ministerial Team, set up by Maharey four years earlier. With members including Kiro, family court judge Peter Boshier and Families Commissioner at the time Rajen Prasad, it was to be the "workhorse" for child abuse issues. In reality, it fell far short of expectations.

A State Services Commission review and restructure in 2006 found that in seven years as a separate financial body, CYF made the headlines hundreds of times, seldom in a good way. The public read of botched decisions which left children vulnerable to fatal attacks by their state-appointed caregivers, thousands of unallocated cases that languished as over-worked social workers battled to keep up, and a parade of CEOs who struggled to turn the organisation around. Staff morale sank lower with every public relations disaster. It has arguably never fully recovered.

The Government also introduced its Vulnerable Families programme in 2006, which was built on coordination between government department staff focusing on welfare cluster families. Despite early success with the programme and its rapid expansion, the Rotorua household where Nia Glassie was abused — containing a solo mother with three children and four adult beneficiaries — remained under the radar.

The following year, 2007, heralded significant legislative change and a famous anti-violence campaign. It was also the year Unicef found New Zealand teens were more likely to die before they turned 19 than in any other developed country.

Championed by Green MP Sue Bradford, anti-smacking legislation removed the legal defence of "reasonable force" for parents prosecuted for assault on their children. But it allowed police the discretion not to prosecute complaints against a parent when the offence was considered "inconsequential".

By the middle of 2007, the Ministry of Social Development's "It's Not OK" campaign was established to alter attitudes toward family violence. In 2009, the death of 22-month-old Hail-Sage McClutchie outraged the nation. No arrest was ever made over the death of the Hamilton toddler, as police were unable to gather sufficient evidence over how she gained massive brain injuries.

But her death prompted a review from the Families Commission, commissioned by then Social Development Minister Paula Bennett, which found inadequate information sharing and systems between agencies were putting children at risk. Bennett also launched a second public awareness campaign; "Never ever shake a baby".

Throughout 2010 and 2011, the Government sought to tighten laws around dangerous and violent offenders. Parole eligibility was removed for repeat serious violent offenders and offenders who commit the worst murders. Police Safety Orders were introduced, allowing police to issue on-the-spot restraining orders for up to five days if they had reasonable grounds to believe violence had, or would, occur. It also became illegal, with penalties of up to 10 years' imprisonment, for an adult to stay silent if they knew a child was in danger, or being hurt.

In 2012, the Government sought to undertake a major project to protect vulnerable children. It began with the Children's Green Paper, for which more than 10,000 submissions across New Zealand were received. That fed into the Children's White Paper — the final copy of a report to outline a programme of change, shining a light on abuse, neglect, and harm. The Children's Action Plan was the final stage, providing the legislative and regulatory framework for making the fundamental changes outlined in the white paper.

It has been largely out of the Children's Action Plan — a "living document" — that most change has stemmed since. That includes Children's Teams of social workers, designed to be a single point of contact for an entire family to access support, a national phoneline to triage and refer calls from the public and 24-hour GPS tracking for high-risk child sex offenders. The controversial trialling of a predictive modelling tool also attempts to predict abuse, welfare dependency and the likelihood of a child's downward spiral into crime on the path to adulthood, as well as the chances they will make it to adulthood.

One of the most pleasurable parts of writing a book is thanking all those who helped make it possible. Like the stories herein, this book is a team work. Julia Hollingsworth spent many hours in the archives finding the originals of these stories, and made many insightful suggestions about which to include. Emily Menkes also contributed much in the archives, in editing and on the introductions. My colleagues at Massey University, including Grant Hannis, Jim Tully, Alan Samson, Fran Tyler, Catherine Strong and Sean Phelan, provided many useful suggestions, while Shiv Ganesh and Elizabeth Gray were unstinting in their financial support. I would especially like to thank my publisher, Nicola Legat, for her enthusiasm, encouragement and wise and tactful counsel; she is an under-sung champion of New Zealand journalism. Massey University Press's managing editor, Anna Bowbyes, provided a professional and engaged supervision of the publishing process together with copyeditor Teresa McIntyre and proofreader Mike Wagg.

My partner, Kate Duignan, and my family, especially my late mother, Lesley Hollings, were also unstinting in their encouragement and support. Going further back, my own fortunate road in journalism has been made possible by the encouragement of many wonderful journalists and editors: Brian Priestley, Peter Burke, Kevin Ikin, Peter Kitchin, Alastair Morrison, Tim Pankhurst, Rick Neville, Paul Kavanagh, Suzanne Carty, Paul Elenio, Ian Spicer, Tony Wilton, Don and Ian Carson, Penny Harding; thank you.

Thanks to the following organisations for permission to reproduce the extracts in this collection: Awa Press, Bauer (*Metro, New Zealand Listener, North & South*), Fairfax (*The Auckland Star, The Dominion Post, The Evening Post, The Press, Stuff, Sunday Star-Times, Taranaki Herald*), NZME (*The New Zealand Herald*), Oxford University Press, *Pacific Journalism Review*, Penguin New Zealand and Potton & Burton.

Lastly, and above all, I would like to thank all the journalists who generously allowed me to include their work, and were so encouraging about this collection. Interviewing these men and women has been one of the great unexpected joys of writing this book. Encountering their commitment to excellence in their craft, their compassion for the less fortunate, their intellectual rigour and their often droll humour was both humbling and inspiring. In the end, though, what has left the most lasting impression is their ethical core; their usually quietly voiced but always fiercely held determination to help people through good journalism. Some remarkable people are featured in this book. I hope it does them justice.

James Hollings
July 2017

For more information about our books, go to
www.masseypress.ac.nz